The Essential

MBA

SAGE has been part of the global academic community since 1965, supporting high quality research and learning that transforms society and our understanding of individuals, groups, and cultures. SAGE is the independent, innovative, natural home for authors, editors and societies who share our commitment and passion for the social sciences.

Find out more at: **www.sagepublications.com**

The Essential

MBA

Edited by **SUSAN MILLER**

Los Angeles | London | New Delhi
Singapore | Washington DC

SAGE Publications Ltd
1 Oliver's Yard
55 City Road
London EC1Y 1SP

SAGE Publications Inc.
2455 Teller Road
Thousand Oaks, California 91320

SAGE Publications India Pvt Ltd
B 1/I 1 Mohan Cooperative Industrial Area
Mathura Road
New Delhi 110 044

SAGE Publications Asia-Pacific Pte Ltd
33 Pekin Street #02-01
Far East Square
Singapore 048763

Library of Congress Control Number: 2010943243

British Library Cataloguing in Publication data

A catalogue record for this book is available from the British Library

ISBN 978-1-84787-060-5
ISBN 978-1-84787-061-2 (pbk)

Typeset by C&M Digitals (P) Ltd, Chennai, India
Printed by MPG Books Group, Bodmin, Cornwall
Printed on paper from sustainable resources

Dedication

This book is dedicated to the memory of my parents, and to John whose constant love and support have meant more than words can say.

Summary of Contents

Contents

About the Author

Susan Miller is Professor of Organizational Behaviour at Hull University Business School in the UK where she is also Academic Director of the MBA programmes. Prior to this she worked at Durham University where she was Director of the Part-time MBA programme. She has wide experience of designing MBA programmes and teaching MBA students both in the UK and internationally, including Bahrain, Hong Kong, Singapore, Oman, Barbados and the Netherlands. She is involved in the Association of MBAs which accredits MBA programmes worldwide.

Besides a long-standing interest in issues associated with management learning and education, her other research focus has centred on strategic decision making in organizations. This research has examined how major decisions are taken and implemented in organizational settings and she has published widely in this area.

She held a position of non-executive Director of a large public health organization for four years and, prior to becoming an academic, she worked in both manufacturing and service organizations in the private and public sectors for nine years.

Notes on Contributors

Emmanuel D. Adamides is Associate Professor of Operations and Technology Management at the University of Patras, Greece. His research interests are in the areas of operations strategy, and innovation and sustainable technology management. He is particularly interested in the application of systems approaches to analyze and support managerial activity in these areas.

Tony Boczko is a Lecturer at the Hull University Business School. He has held senior positions in Local Government and the UK Health Service, undertaken business consultancies for a range of UK organizations and presented academic papers at national and international conferences. Tony has also co-authored a number of texts on accounting, finance, and information systems.

Timothy Campbell is currently the Director of the MBA programme at the University of Dubai. Tim has extensive industry, academic and management training experience. He is the co-author of *Organizational Behaviour*, with Stephen Robbins and Tim Judge, and his research has appeared in international publications such as the *Journal of Business Ethics; Business Ethics: A European Review;* and *Systems Research and Behavioral Science*.

Tony Cockerill is the Leverhulme Emeritus Fellow at the Faculty of Economics, University of Cambridge. He has wide experience of executive education, having designed, directed and contributed to an extensive range of tailored and open programmes. His principal clients include Halifax Bank of Scotland, HM Customs and Revenue, HSBC, Kodak, and the former UK Department for Education and Skills. He was Director of Executive Education at Manchester Business School from 1987 to 1994.

Dianne Dean is a Lecturer at the University of Hull Business School. Her current research interests are in the area of consumer behaviour and social and political marketing and communications. She has published a number of papers in political marketing including the application of consumer behaviour concepts to political marketing. Previously she worked as a client-side market researcher, before joining the University of Lincoln in the early 1990s. She moved to Hull University in 2002. Dianne has a degree in politics from Hull University and a doctorate from Stirling.

Peter M. Hamilton is a Senior Lecturer in human resource management at Durham Business School, University of Durham. He has previously worked at Imperial College and the University of Central Lancashire. Before that he worked in the National Health Service. He is currently researching in the areas of dirty work and service work.

Christos-Dimitris Tsinopoulos is a Lecturer in Operations and Project Management at Durham Business School, University of Durham. Christos has a PhD from the University of Warwick as well as Bachelor and Master degrees in Mechanical Engineering from the University of Sheffield. Christos is an assessor of the Institution of Mechanical Engineers' Manufacturing Excellence awards. He has been a research fellow in new product development at the Warwick Manufacturing Group as well as a quality and maintenance engineer for copper and aluminum industries in Greece.

Acknowledgements

I would like to acknowledge the help and contribution of my fellow authors and the publishing team at SAGE who have been unfailingly supportive of this endeavour.

Guided Tour

Welcome to the guided tour of *The Essential MBA*. This tour will take you through the main sections and special features in the text.

Purpose of *The Essential MBA*

Embarking on a Master of Business Administration (MBA) degree is a challenging prospect. Whether you are doing so to help further your current career, to change careers, or to gain specific knowledge and skills – or a mixture of these – there is little doubt that an MBA will introduce you to a wide range of theories, ideas, concepts and debates, many of which may be new to you and some controversial and contested. Few Masters degrees require a learner to have quite such a wide-ranging command of so many, often fairly disparate, areas of enquiry. The knowledge needed to succeed on an MBA is drawn from a variety of academic disciplines, each with their own set of concepts and theoretical perspectives and each necessitating some familiarity with the 'language' being employed. Many students can find the diversity of subject-matter daunting, and to make matters worse (or better, if you like the rough and tumble of debate) the ideas and theories will often be contested, or will contradict each other, or will prove inconclusive – or all three.

Chapter overview and Key concepts: A brief chapter overview and list of key concepts will help you to navigate your way through each chapter.

Case illustration

The British born editor of this book found her Malaysian PhD students expressed great reluctance to call her by her first name, even when asked to do so. The much higher power distance in Malaysia made it seem disrespectful to be on first-name terms with someone who was ostensibly in a superior position, even though the 'students' were themselves senior professionals. Thus those from a lower power-distance culture may make others uncomfortable by attempting to play down perceived status differences.

These dimensions have been utilized and modified by many other researchers, perhaps most notably in the GLOBE (Global Leadership and Organizational Behaviour Effectiveness) project, a longitudinal study of leadership and organizational culture in 62 countries (House et al., 2004) which identified some additional dimensions including *assertiveness* (the degree to which individuals are encouraged to be tough, aggressive and confrontational), *performance orientation* (the degree to which members of a society are rewarded for performance improvement and excellence), and *humane orientation* (the degree to which society encourages people to be fair, altruistic, generous, caring and kind to others). These researchers also used two collectivism dimensions: *institutional collectivism*, referring to how far the society encourages the collective distribution of resources and collective action and believes that individuals have collective duties and obligations that outweigh personal concerns (Waldman et al., 2006), and *in-group collectivism*, referring to the degree to which individuals express pride and loyalty in their membership of organizations and families or particular groups in society.

Finally the work of Trompenaars and Hampden-Turner (2006) will be mentioned briefly. Their research and consultancy with managers and companies on cross-cultural issues has led them to distinguish seven features of cross-cultural differences, summarized in Table 2.4.

These studies on cross-cultural differences have ramifications for many other areas of OB, most obviously leadership and organizational (rather than national) culture, and we will return to some of these themes again. However, this kind of work is not without controversy. It could be argued that it simply replaces some well-worn stereotypical characterizations that different societies have about each other with some rather more sophisticated, but nonetheless caricature portraits, where the methodology employed means that while the findings may indicate some general features of a society as a whole, they do not necessarily pertain to any one individual in that society.

Organizational structure

Turning to the organization itself, early research soon established a link between the environment in which a firm operated and the firm's structural arrangements. It

Case illustration: Case illustrations reinforce your understanding of the key concepts.

Business Process Reengineering: a radical redesign of the core organizational processes by focusing on activities that add value to the customer and removing duplication and non value-adding activities in order to speed up cycle times and improve efficiency.

Era 3: Networking, hollow, modular and virtual organizations

BPR develops the idea of networking individuals within an organization in order to share knowledge and resources. This is at the heart of **network organizations**, that is, groups of organizations which are linked together in order to manage co-production and create new capabilities. While there have always been linkages between organizations in the form of strategic alliances and joint ventures, some have argued that in order to cope with increasingly uncertain and complex environments and the challenges of globalization, we are now witnessing a new form of organization. This is the 'network form', where parts of many different organizations and institutions – such as other competitors, customers, research and development organizations and government departments – all work closely together to deliver joint goals. This enhances flexibility and learning and can be highly advantageous, especially in fast moving, unpredictable environments, but it also requires trust, reciprocity, and a clear understanding of, and commitment to, joint goals. It is argued that network organizations bring challenges in terms of their management, as traditional hierarchical arrangements are replaced by looser structures where power and authority are less clearly demarcated and organizational allegiances can become blurred.

Network organization: a group of organizations, or specific parts of autonomous organizations, that behave as a single entity in order to achieve collective goals.

At a societal level it should be noted that the idea of networks can also be linked to other co-dependent systems that have arisen within particular national cultures, such as the Korean *chaebols*, Japanese *keiretsu*, and overseas Chinese businesses. These forms develop interlocking business arrangements on the basis of trust, shared ethnicity or kinship patterns.

Alongside networking, many organizations are seeking to outsource aspects of their operation, which may itself be a reason for networking. 'Hollow' companies such as Nike and Reebok spearheaded the relocation of production to Southeast Asia some 20 years ago but many others have followed since. Thus hollow organizations will outsource non-core business *processes* to other firms. However 'modular' companies will go further and outsource pieces of the *product* to other organizations (Anand and Daft, 2007). Airbus provides an example of this. It sources parts of the A380 from countries such as Germany, Spain and the UK and assembles them in

Definitions: Key terms are clearly defined for quick reference.

Summary

This chapter has covered the key topics usually discussed on MBA organizational behaviour/management courses. Moving from macro to micro perspectives it has reviewed theory that focuses on the organization in its environment, through an understanding of organizational processes, to a focus on groups and individuals. Generally speaking, orthodox approaches to each topic concentrate on developing understanding to improve managerial practice and organizational functioning. Critical approaches seek to understand what happens in organizations, to explore why things happen in the way that they do, and to identify how different interests are affected by what goes on. This may also improve organizational effectiveness and it should not be construed that critical perspectives are always negatively intransigent in the face of modern capitalism and automatically set against managerial initiatives. However, they do cause us to reflect on the assumptions underlying the way we organize and manage and also force us to ask challenging questions about the wider interests being served by contemporary organizations.

Questions for reflection

1. What are the implications of research on organizational structure for designing contemporary organizations?
2. What kinds of leadership might be appropriate in multicultural firms?
3. How useful is the concept of corporate culture to the practising manager?
4. What part does rationality play in organizational decision making?
5. How do firms make use of 'emotional labour'?
6. How might issues of gender and diversity impact on organizational functions and processes?
7. What are the functional and dysfunctional aspects of groups and teams in the workplace?
8. Is the motivation of employees a legitimate management task?
9. How useful are insights about personality and perception for understanding organizations?
10. What do critical perspectives bring to an understanding of organizational behaviour?

Summary and Questions for reflection: We review the main concepts and issues to be sure that you are clear on what was covered, and why. Questions are provided at the end of each chapter to encourage you to explore what you have learnt.

Further reading

Organizational structure and design

Anand, N. and Daft, R.L. (2007) 'What is the right organization design?' *Organizational Dynamics*, 36 (4): 329–344.
Harris, I.C. and Ruefli, T.W. (2000) 'The strategy/structure debate: an examination of the performance implications.' *Journal of Management Studies*, 37 (4): 587–603.
Olson, E.M., Slater, S.F., Tomas, G. and Hult, M. (2005) 'The performance implications of fit among business strategy, marketing organization structure, and strategic behaviour.' *Journal of Marketing*, 69 (July): 49–65.
Wrege, C.D. and Hodgetts, R.M. (2000) 'Frederick W. Taylor's 1899 pig iron observations: examining fact, fiction and lessons for the new millennium.' *Academy of Management Journal*, 43 (6): 1283–1291.

National cultures

Fok, L.Y., Hartman, S.J. and Kwong, K. (2005) 'Differences in business ethical values: a study of differences in business ethical values in mainland China, the US and Jamaica.' *Review of Business*, 26 (1): 21–26.
Hickson, D.J. and Pugh, D.S. (2003) *Management Worldwide: Distinctive Styles amid Globalization*. London: Penguin.
Hofstede, G. (2003) *Culture's consequences: Comparing Values, Behaviours, Institutions and Organizations across Nations*. Thousand Oaks, CA: Sage.
House, R., Hanges, P.J., Javidan, M., Dorfman, P.W. and Gupta, V. (2004) *Culture, Leadership and Organizations: The GLOBE Study of 62 Societies*. Thousand Oaks, CA: Sage.
Minkov, M. and Hofstede, G. (2011) 'The evolution of Hofstede's doctrine.' *Crosscultural Management: an international journal*, 18(1): 10–20.

Management and leadership

Special Issue on Leadership (includes work on Emotions) (2004) *Harvard Business Review*, 82 (1).
Bartlett, C.A. and Ghoshal, S. (2003) 'What is a global manager?' *Harvard Business Review*, 81 (8): 101–109.
Goleman, D. (2000) 'Leadership that gets results.' *Harvard Business Review*, 78 (2): 78–90.
Carey, C. (1999) '"We are all managers now, we always were": on the development and demise of management.' *Journal of Management Studies*, 36 (5): 561.
Watson, T.J. (1994) *In Search of Management, Culture, Chaos and Control in Managerial Work*. London: Routledge.

Organizational culture and change

Jones, O. (2000) 'Scientific management, culture and control: a first-hand account of Taylorism in practice.' *Human Relations*, 53 (5): 631–653.
Marshall, J. and Adamic, M. (2010) 'The story is the message: shaping corporate culture.' *Journal of Business Strategy*, 31 (2): 18–23.
Ogbonna, E. and Harris, L.C. (2002) 'Organizational culture: a ten year, two-phase study of change in the UK food retailing sector.' *Journal of Management Studies*, 39 (5): 673–707.
Van de Ven, A. and Scott Poole, M. (2005) 'Alternative approaches for studying organizational change.' *Organization Studies*, 26 (9): 1377–1404.

(Continued)

Further reading: Relevant articles and book chapters will enhance your understanding of each chapter.

1 Introduction and Overview

Key concepts

Critical approaches; Critical Management Studies (CMS); Functionalism; Postmodernism; Reflexivity; Self-reflection

Purpose of *The Essential MBA*

Embarking on a Master of Business Administration (MBA) degree is a challenging prospect. Whether you are doing so to help further your current career, to change careers, or to gain specific knowledge and skills – or a mixture of these – there is little doubt that an MBA will introduce you to a wide range of theories, ideas, concepts and debates, many of which may be new to you and some controversial and contested. Few Masters degrees require a learner to have quite such a wide-ranging command of so many, often fairly disparate, areas of enquiry. The knowledge needed to succeed on an MBA is drawn from a variety of academic disciplines, each with their own set of concepts and theoretical perspectives and each necessitating some familiarity with the 'language' being employed. Many students can find the diversity of subject-matter daunting, and to make matters worse (or better, if you like the rough and tumble of debate) the ideas and theories will often be contested, or will contradict each other, or will prove inconclusive – or all three.

This book is intended to provide a route map for the MBA. Its aim is to offer a guide to the key subjects, topics and debates that make up the general area of business and management, and from where much of the material that you will study will be drawn – all in one clear, readable text. It takes you through the 'essential' elements of your MBA, provides an overview of the core areas you will be studying, indicates the main theories and ideas in each, and provides a short and speedy way of getting to the essence of each subject. Indeed, while it is intended primarily for MBA students, because of the content and approach the book should also be of help to other Masters students and undergraduates studying business and management degrees.

One distinctive feature of the book is that it covers so many areas of the MBA in one text; another is that we take a critical approach to the study of each subject. More will be said about this below but, at its simplest, what this means is that each author not only presents the main theories and concepts, but also gives you a critique of these. A critical perspective incorporates an analysis of the underlying assumptions together with a review of alternative perspectives which may run counter to more traditional, orthodox views. This should be invaluable since most MBA programmes require students to take a critical stance towards the subject matter and provide critical reflections in their assessed work.

The main objective of the MBA is to provide students with an understanding of the key areas of management and business. To that end programmes will need to ensure students have a developed understanding of how macro factors at global and national levels, firm-level operating practices and processes, and more micro human processes interact to influence the management and performance of firms, as well as an appreciation of the wider implications for individual workers and society as a whole. Hence, while the following list is by no means exhaustive, an MBA usually encompasses subjects such as Organizational Behaviour (OB); Human Resource Management (HRM); Marketing; Accounting and Finance; Economics; Operations Management; and Strategic Management. This book therefore contains a chapter on each of these, written by a subject expert. However, recognizing the changing imperatives of the business world, many MBA programmes are now incorporating discussions on ethical and moral dimensions of management such as corporate social responsibility and environmental concerns. The chapter on Corporate Social Responsibility (CSR) addresses this area. In addition, a large number of programmes require students to carry out a significant piece of research, often in the form of a dissertation or a project, and the chapter on Research Approaches will guide you through this. Finally, there is a chapter on Study Skills, to help you get the most from your programme of learning.

How To Use This Book

This book provides a comprehensive summary of the central academic contributions to the MBA curriculum. It contains a separate chapter on the core areas covered in most MBA programmes as follows:

- Organizational Behaviour
- Human Resource Management

- Marketing
- Accounting and Finance
- Economics
- Operations Management
- Corporate Social Responsibility
- Strategic Management
- Research Approaches
- Study Skills

The aim is to give the reader a clear overview of each subject so that they gain a picture of the overall terrain. However, a word of caution is necessary here. While the subjects are presented separately this should not be taken to mean that they are segregated in real life. The troubling fact is that many business problems are complex, multi-faceted and interrelated. They impact on both people and systems and can have financial, operational and strategic implications, both at firm-level and beyond. Many MBA programmes attempt to recognize this by designing courses around multi-dimensional themes. This is sensible, given the nature of the business world. But is also helpful to be able to understand the particular concepts and ideas that emanate from, say, Marketing, and to distinguish those that are more readily associated with, say, Organizational Behaviour. This way, an understanding of particular domains of knowledge can be built up. So, while it would be possible to write a book which attempts to bring together different subjects, this would be a different book with a different purpose. The aim of this text is to clarify an already complex area, and for that reason it is felt that maintaining the integrity of the subjects for explanatory purposes is sensible.

Even so areas of knowledge cannot always be circumscribed within tightly defined and impermeable boundaries. Different subjects will sometimes draw from each other. One example would be in the area of Strategic Management where many of the ideas about strategy implementation can also be found in the area of Organizational Behaviour because implementing strategy is usually about getting people in the firm to do something different and managing the process of change. Where these overlaps occur they are discussed in the text. So while academic boundaries are somewhat artificial, they do serve a purpose – however the fact that they are artificial should not be forgotten.

So, how should you make use of this book? It can be utilized in a number of ways and at various points during the programme. One way would be to dip into it before you even start your degree to get an idea of the kind of subjects you will be tackling. Another would be to read the appropriate chapter before embarking on the teaching sessions for that subject so you have some familiarity with the subject matter beforehand. Finally, the book should provide a useful way of highlighting the key points after teaching sessions as well as offering a source of information for assignments and serving as an *aide-mémoire* for exam preparation. Each chapter includes a 'further reading' list to guide further study.

It should also be noted that there may be subjects on your MBA that are not covered here. Some MBA programmes may also include law, information systems, quantitative methods and so on, as well as a host of more specialist electives in addition to the core subjects. We have chosen to concentrate on the elements most commonly taught in most MBA programmes for this text, which is already quite lengthy.

We have tried to ensure some overall consistency in style and presentation throughout the book, even though the subjects are very different. In terms of format, we have incorporated some features that will make the text easier to navigate. Each chapter is organized as follows:

- Chapter overview
- Discussion of main ideas and theories
- Definitions of key concepts (in bold in the text and defined in boxes)
- Summary
- Questions for reflection
- References and further reading

What is 'A Critical Approach'?

We said earlier that this book would take a **critical approach** to the subject matter – but what does this mean? At one level 'to be critical' in academic terms means not simply accepting received ideas and assertions, but instead questioning the underlying assumptions that have been made, interrogating them to carefully examine their evidential base, and evaluating their strengths and weaknesses. In many ways this amounts to adopting a questioning approach. For example, what assumptions has the author of a theory/idea made about the nature of the matter under study (are these assumptions explicit, justified and reasonable), how strong is the evidence used to arrive at the conclusions (is it relevant, sufficient and robust), what are the strengths of the theory/idea and where does it fall short (for instance, does it apply only in highly specific situations or contexts)? Thus 'being critical' means retaining a little scepticism. It means not accepting opinions as fact, and also not accepting 'facts' until they have been subjected to careful scrutiny. It does not mean just being negative about everything. It is not about rejecting a theory or research merely because it runs counter to one's own experience or prejudices. It is about coming to your own conclusions after a careful and systematic examination of the evidence and arguments.

Critical approaches: encourage a reflexive and questioning approach in examining the underlying assumptions and evidential basis of ideas and theories.

This links up with ideas of **self-reflection** and **reflexivity**, both of which you will need to consider in order to hone your critical skills. Let's take reflectivity first. Being reflective means being self-aware; having some insights about your own behaviour and ways of seeing the world and therefore conscious of your own potential biases and value-judgements. You will be utilizing your own experience on the MBA, but you will also be asked to be self-reflective about this experience, and to attempt to arrive at a deeper understanding of both your own and others' behaviour. These processes of introspection will help to promote new insights. MBA students are sometimes encouraged to be 'reflective practitioners'; being reflective is there-fore about being critically self-aware.

> **Self-reflection**: the process of introspection which focuses on a conscious awareness of the human condition and the individual's fundamental nature, essence and purpose.

Next we have reflexivity. This is a complex term that is not always used in the same way by authors. 'Reflex' means 'bent' or 'turned back', so being reflexive is about understanding how one's actions can be influenced by the fact that we are consciously aware of them and their effects. Put another way, reflexivity is about the dynamic relationship between how we act in the world and how we understand and make sense of our actions. Because we are consciously aware of our behaviour, this knowledge may affect our actions in the first place or lead us to reinterpret what these actions actually mean. When applied to the process of learning and the MBA, being reflexive is about being aware of how knowledge is created and being sensitive to our own and others' role in making sense of the world. Knowledge is created through a complex process of social construction in which you are engaged along with others (fellow students, tutors, textbook authors, and so on). Knowledge is not 'given', nor is it independent of the process of construction. These ideas connect to the discussion about 'Learning Independently' in Chapter 11 on Study Skills. In summary, it could be said that a critically aware learner is reflexively self-reflective.

> **Reflexivity**: a self-referential relationship in which the actor's thinking or action refers back to, and affects, their thoughts and actions.

The skills required for critical analysis are central to many areas of academic endeavour as well as being essential to the practising world of management. They are used when making sense of ideas and perspectives presented by tutors and oth-ers, when reviewing texts, articles in journals and other documents, and will also apply when marshalling your own arguments, writing assignments and business reports. Writing or presenting arguments is an exercise in persuasion. You will need to convince others, and others will need to convince you, that the analysis is well founded, makes sense, and is ultimately justifiable.

However, within the domain of business and management 'a critical approach' can also have another meaning – one which refers to a particular stream of work that is concerned with critically evaluating the nature and function of business and management in contemporary society. This perspective, often given the appellation **Critical Management Studies (CMS)**, has had a long genesis but gathered momen-tum, especially within European academia in the 1980s and 1990s. Drawing on sociological and political science traditions, scholars in this field have contributed to a vigorous and wide-ranging debate about management in general, which has led to discussions about the role and purpose of management education, particularly in business schools and specifically at MBA level. It is important for MBA students to be aware of the broad parameters of this exchange because the arguments it encompasses focus on fundamental questions that are at the heart of MBA education. The next section will therefore address these.

Critical Perspectives in Management

It must be said at the outset that there is a wide variety of contributors to debates within Critical Management Studies and a diverse range of concerns. It is not a coherent movement or a unified body of thought and, as with many emerging intellectual traditions, some internal contradictions remain. To properly analyze the origins of the debate and encompass all its different facets would take a book in its own right, so what follows is a much abbreviated and simplified outline of a few general themes.

The overarching concern of CMS has to do with the role and purpose of business and management, but this covers a range of elements including, for example, power relations in the workplace and beyond, questions of gender and diversity, and the nature of managerial knowledge. It follows that critiques emanate from a variety of standpoints, including political theory, labour (employee) relations, feminism and philosophy, to name but a few.

Perhaps what binds together proponents of this broad perspective is a desire to question the view that sees management as a neutral activity that is employed for the public good, and to explore the possibility that it is primarily concerned with the advancement of some sectional interests (typically those of corporations and business institutions) to the neglect of other stakeholders. In this view the interests of some sections of society are privileged over others, resulting in inequality and discrimination. Going further, if managers are not neutral technicians then it follows that initiatives to improve managerial practice will require careful scrutiny, since the anticipated benefits may not accrue equally to all interests and indeed may augment the potential for marginalization and the exploitation of one group by another. Since MBA programmes are perceived to be concerned with enhancing managerial skills and knowledge, they have also become subject to critical inspection, and their function and educational responsibilities interrogated.

Critical management scholars take the view that most traditional business theory is firmly rooted in a managerialist agenda, is uncritical in nature, and ignores wider business and societal concerns. This orthodox theory emanates from a functionalist form of sociology, **functionalism** being based on the assumption that individuals and social practices have a purpose in maintaining the equilibrium necessary for society as a whole to survive. The work of the scholar therefore is to understand the way in which particular activities and processes contribute to this functioning.

Functionalism: a sociological perspective that views society as having particular needs in order to survive and seeks to understand how various parts of society contribute to achieving these.

However, what is deemed to be functional very much depends on whose aims are being served. What is functional for some may be deleterious to others. As a result Critical Management Studies (CMS) hold that an examination of business and management ideas means being aware of the implicit values that underpin, inform, and shape these. Such ideas are not 'value-free' – they are imbued with particular ways of seeing the world, specific sets of beliefs, and particular positions on ethical questions. While these beliefs and values are often unstated they can often be inferred by an attentive reader who is alert to such matters. A critical approach therefore requires taking a moral position on taken-for-granted assumptions, for example that increased efficiency is always a legitimate goal and extracting the maximum productivity from labour is always desirable. It also means being self-reflexive about one's own beliefs and attitudes.

Some of the areas mentioned above (power, gender and the nature of management knowledge) will now be examined. The implications for management education will then be explored.

Critical Management Studies: a range of perspectives that seek to offer a critique of contemporary business and management ideas and practices.

Power

CMS has deep-rooted concerns about the supposition that objectives are shared by all the parties engaged in a business enterprise, and instead emphasizes the plurality of goals that can exist within the firm. In taking this position CMS highlights notions of power, seeing organizations as locations where the consequences of fundamentally unequal power distributions in society are played out. In other words, the differential allocations of power at a macro level are mirrored in the hierarchical and occupationally segregated arrangements found in most organizations. This is more than a simple pragmatic division of labour introduced to achieve order and efficiency; it is a deliberately engineered feature of stratified societies whereby particular groups try to achieve domination by reproducing the structures, ideologies and value-systems that maintain their power within organizational and institutional frameworks. Hence organizational discord and conflict are symptoms of opposing goals and values and cannot be simply 'managed away'.

Issues of conflict are often discussed within the domain of management-labour relations, and are sometimes seen as an inevitable outcome of the inherently oppositional aims of owners or their agents (managers) and alienated workers (see Chapter 3 on employee relations within HRM). In this view managers are focussed primarily on maximizing productivity and employees concerned with minimizing exploitation. The prevailing managerial preoccupation is therefore with control and surveillance. However, this explication reveals essentially modernist and neo-Marxist interpretations of power, owing much to the debates which centre on the work of the Frankfurt School and writers such as Habermas, Marcuse, Adorno and Horkheimer, among others. At the same time Critical Management is not confined to this intellectual base, and many streams of discussion demonstrate a sympathy with poststructuralist and/or **postmodernist** debates. Care is needed here because neither poststructuralism nor postmodernism lends itself to straightforward definition. The terms sometimes appear to be used inter-changeably in the literature and yet, while the approaches do share some common ground, they can be traced to different origins. Having said this it is difficult to definitively locate particular authors within particular approaches, as many of the writers often cited as being connected with either poststructuralism or postmodernism have been at pains to deny any affiliation, resisting any attempt to pin down their philosophical positions.

There is not the space here for a lengthy exposition of these philosophical movements and simplifying such complex and intellectually demanding ideas is fraught with problems, but it can be argued that poststructuralism questions the assumptions of structuralism that there are relatively stable underlying structures, particularly in cultural products such as texts and symbols, through which meaning is produced and reproduced. Poststructuralism would take the view that books, for example, are open to multiple interpretations as the reader will 'translate' and give meaning to what is written. In many ways the reader's interpretation takes primacy over the author's intended meaning. Yet these interpretations are fluid and transient, and are shaped by historical, cultural and societal influences, so that meaning itself is in a state of flux.

Many writers within CMS make reference to postmodernist themes. These are also concerned with meaning, emphasizing the active role of 'deconstruction' in surfacing the frames of reference and assumptions of the author. Deconstruction involves challenging arguments and statements by questioning the premises and foundations of the logic on which they are built. Thus, for example, even reasoning which purports to be objective (and therefore is presumed to be unbiased; generally taken as being a hallmark of good science) is open to questions about the ways in which it has been labelled 'objective' and thus accorded such legitimacy. Postmodernists are deeply sceptical about the modernist search for 'truth' based on a shared notion of some objective reality, instead arguing that humans impose their own logic on events and actions, continually constructing and reconstructing their own worlds which are sustained and renegotiated in the process of 'making sense' of what is experienced. Fundamentally meaning and understanding are not given – they are created. Language plays a central part in helping to create this understanding. We know the world through our creation of the language and discourses (ways of communicating) used to describe it but this knowledge is both indeterminate and provisional. Therefore postmodernists reject the notion of 'meta narratives' such as Marxism which purport to offer grand explanatory schemas. Instead, given the simultaneous availability of many theoretical positions, the emphasis is placed on shifting explanations for phenomena which will be subject to on-going revision.

Thus humans construct versions of reality but these have no universal or absolute status. Indeed, no single voice has automatic priority over others, a suggestion which has interesting implications for academia and the status of books such as this one. The key thinkers frequently referenced by writers in the CMS tradition would include Foucault, Derrida, Bourdieu, Lyotard and Baudrillard, but would also encompass a host of other authors. Foucault's concept of power is relevant here, and is markedly different from the views outlined at the beginning of this section. In his analysis power is not a property of structural arrangements such as those that give rise to the hierarchical distinctions between management and labour, but is embedded in social relationships. While this may be most evident in institutions such as the military and penal system (the subject of one of Foucault's seminal analyses), it is an inescapable feature of all aspects of life, operating through the routine activities of everyday existence. Individuals create their own networks of power through their ongoing interactions and relationships, and their acceptance of the prevailing codes of behaviour which shape these relations. Power is diffused through society, and all individuals possess some countervailing power, hence the modernist portrayal of a clear-cut demarcation between a minority elite who possess power and a disenfranchised powerless majority, is replaced by a more complex version in which power fluctuates within and between different groups and individuals.

This perspective on power is one that emphasizes its potentially shifting and transitory nature as well as its location within heterogeneous and only loosely bounded groupings. This serves as a reminder that the terms 'management' and 'worker' give a misplaced sense of the uniformity within groups and mask the significant differences that may exist within collections of individuals. So 'managers' are differentiated along many dimensions, including age, profession, status, religion and gender. Indeed, any individual may have multiple identities – for example, an executive who is simultaneously a member of the accounting profession may also belong to the senior management team, be a husband and father, and hold membership of a local trade organization. One of these dimensions, gender, has been the subject of much debate within CMS and will be discussed further in the next section.

Postmodernism: philosophical perspectives that emphasize the social construction of texts and discourses, the multiple ways of interpreting them, and hence call into question universalistic notions of reality and truth.

Postmodernism in turn has been criticized from a number of viewpoints. Foucault's conception of power is seen as underplaying the role of ideology and wrongly decoupling it from state and institutional influences. The notion that cultural artefacts can be 'read' in multiple ways appears to suggest a relativist position where all interpretations are of equal worth and are given equal consideration. The postmodernism stance seems antithetical to ideas of advancement, especially in science where the assumption is that progress is founded on the accumulation of an established body of knowledge. Many commentators have criticized postmodernists' reluctance to make their principles and premises clear, instead seeming to prefer the safety of ambiguous indeterminacy and rhetorical verbal game-playing. Finally, it is argued that postmodernism does not represent a break with modernism – which in any case was not a static, unchanging, unified theoretical position – but is merely an evolution of it.

Some key elements of postmodernist approaches are summarized below.

- An emphasis on the deconstruction of texts and symbols to reveal underlying meanings
- A consequent 'de-centring' of the author's voice since the reader plays an active part in constructing meaning
- The belief that there are shifting, often conflicting, multiple interpretations and realities
- A focus on the centrality of power within social relationships
- A stress on the fragmented, indeterminate, and fluid nature of things rather than seeing them as fixed, stable and final
- A suspicion of meta theories that offer universalistic propositions and explanations
- A depiction of the individual as having multiple, shifting identities

Power is at the heart of CMS preoccupations. How power is manifested and deployed in organizational settings, and to what effect, is central to understanding modern business and society. The unmasking of hidden relations of power is an important task. At its roots, many of the proponents of a critical perspective have a liberalizing and emancipatory agenda and this is where the study of business and management takes on an explicitly political mantle.

Gender and diversity

Questions of gender are another central ingredient of the CMS debate, acknowledging wider reflections in management and organization studies where there has long been an interest in the under-representation of women in managerial positions, particularly at more senior levels, and a recognition of occupational segregation, both vertically (where women, though well represented in occupations such as teaching, are confined to more junior positions) and horizontally (where women are under-represented in particular occupations, such as surgery).

But beyond this some CMS scholars suggest that studies of management are characterized by an overly masculine orientation. This is manifested in a number of ways. Firstly it is argued that much of the research in business and management focusses predominantly on male subjects but also assumes that findings apply to both men and women. Secondly the position of women in business tends to be ignored giving the impression that organizations are gender-neutral. So gender-specific findings about men are extrapolated to apply universally, and women in organizations are ignored as a specific research category.

To take some examples, much of the work looking at effective managers has been carried out by observing men. It is therefore unsurprising that many of the traits associated with successful leaders, such as assertiveness, are ones more typically associated with men. Many writers have highlighted the way in which the implications of gender have historically tended to be ignored. Well-known examples include the female workers overseen by male supervisors in the Hawthorne experiments (where the findings concentrate on factors affecting productivity in the Western Electric Company's Hawthorne Works, but do not explore the gendered nature of authority relationships in the firm), and the male maintenance workers in Crozier's tobacco firm who accrued power by controlling one of the residual sources of uncertainty – fixing the machines when they broke down – in an otherwise routinized, bureaucratic assembly plant, ignoring the fact that the female operatives on the production line were strongly discouraged from interfering with the machinery, this being seen as a male province.

Another way in which business practice is argued to embody a masculine perspective is in the language and metaphors of management and business which tend to be stereotypically masculinist in nature. Business is presented as being war-like, any competition has to be beaten, tactics are deployed as in a military operation and leaders have to be strong and good at commanding. The more cooperative, emotional and relationship-oriented aspects of business, seen by some as more feminine qualities, are consequently downplayed or downgraded. This discourse of management is inextricably linked with relations of power, since the way that power may be realized is in the shaping and legitimizing of a discourse, which sets the boundaries for talking, thinking and enacting management. If the discourse of management is essentially masculine then it frames how individuals think and act as managers and is ultimately linked to how we construct our sense of self and identity. It is argued that female managers – especially senior executives who are very much a minority in most firms and are more visible as a consequence – may have particular difficulties in enacting managerial roles since the prevailing role-models are overwhelmingly male. Women may not feel comfortable with these and there is some evidence (see for example Cassell, 1997) that behaviours associated with men, such as assertiveness, may be less acceptable when coming from a woman.

However, postmodernist perspectives would urge caution here. Much of the debate surrounding issues of gender takes the view that gender categories are fixed and stable. An alternative view would be that there are multiple ways of 'being female', or male, and that individuals will choose from a broad repertoire of traits, behaviours and attitudes that have been socially sanctioned as either feminine or masculine. Thus we learn to become female or male in a process that is transformative, fluid and on-going, and since we are capable of inhabiting multiple identities this occurs repeatedly as we act out our notions of 'self' in different circumstances.

This alerts us to an important point that femininity and masculinity are to a large degree culturally determined, so that prescribed male and female behaviour may differ according to what is thought acceptable in a particular cultural context. Critical Management Studies is therefore concerned with developing awareness not just of gender, but also of wider aspects of diversity, acknowledging that management ideas are located within specific contexts. The degree to which such ideas are universally relevant or culture-bound must be carefully considered in any serious evaluation of their utility. This is a point we will take forward in the next section.

The nature of managerial knowledge

The vast majority of research and writing about business and management has historically come from the West. This should give us cause for reflection, and underscores the need to critically examine ideas for cultural bias and cross-cultural relevance. Underpinned by Western notions of logic and reason management 'science' has tended to try and emulate the natural sciences by emphasizing the canons of the 'scientific method' (see Chapter 10 on Research Approaches), even though the subject matter in the social sciences is markedly different. Orthodox approaches stress the rationality of management. This invites contrasts with non-rational or emotional processes (often imputed to women, thus making them less suitable for managerial positions) and marginalizes the role of intuition and instinct.

Yet the body of knowledge that informs the study of management is neither coherent, nor agreed. Indeed, following Foucault, a postmodernist interpretation is that knowledge is a label applied to the practices and discourses embedded in networks of power rather an objective version of the 'truth'. In the realm of business much of what passes for knowledge is mere anecdote, supposition and conjecture, a canon of 'best practice' and 'how to do' books which are rather frequently based on narrow experience in limited contexts. The ever-increasing numbers of books about management (see the expanding shelves in airport bookshops for examples), the rise of the management 'guru' (often either former CEOs or management consultants), together with the plethora of short-lived fads and fashions (many not new but simply recycled), support the view that the market is hungry for ideas but is not much bothered about provenance or evidential rigour. At the same time, there is a mounting array of 'academic' research papers and journals, which purport to give a scientific basis to the subject, but which are couched in esoteric language and seldom actually used. One proficiency that a good MBA education should provide is the ability to make judgements about the evidence on offer, to discriminate between different opinions and to recognize old ideas in new guises – invaluable skills in the current climate where management ideas are themselves a highly marketable commodity.

Thus the foundations of management knowledge are both precarious and contested. Practitioners and academics are sometimes suspicious of each other, with practitioners finding much academic work arcane, abstract and of questionable relevance, and academics finding much practitioner-based work superficial, unreliable and a-theoretical. While there is an array of techniques to aid with the technical aspects of, say, operational or financial decision making in organizations, it is less clear what methods exist as a basis for the study of management itself. Unlike well-established professional groups such as doctors or engineers there is not the same kind of agreed corpus of knowledge, attainment of which acts as a gateway to the profession for qualified members. One can argue that the MBA is a constituent of the drive to professionalize management, but the qualification does not regulate entry into management by licensing or excluding members in the same way as a medical degree does for doctors.

Thus an MBA programme should recognize the contested nature of the terrain of management and the MBA student must become accustomed to contradictory assessments and debates. CMS emphasizes the need to understand differing positions and views in management rather than gloss over them. An appreciation of the deep-seated divisions that exist within the domain of management theory marks the beginning of a meaningful educational experience for a student undertaking an MBA.

The status and nature of management knowledge has implications for how management is taught, and the issue of management education, particularly as it relates to the MBA, is addressed in the next section.

Management Education

The discussions about 'critical approaches' to management and the debates within CMS have a number of repercussions for the realm of management education. Firstly they suggest forms of curricula and pedagogy that encourage a questioning approach to subject matter. Ideas, concepts and theories require critical scrutiny and open discussion rather than didactic teaching and an unquestioning regurgitation by students. The subjects comprising business and management studies need to be taught in ways that explicitly acknowledge their political, ethical, and philosophical nature (Grey, 2004: 180). Since the topic of management is not 'value-free' there should be space in the curriculum to allow the implicit values informing managerial practice to be debated and not merely accepted. This should also allow for any partiality in theories – for example in terms of cultural or gender bias – to surface and be examined.

Given the somewhat indeterminate and provisional nature of much of the knowledge in this area, ideas need to be carefully examined for continued currency and the possibility of revision entertained. As many participants on MBA programmes have managerial experience this provides a way in which new ideas can be tested out and is one reason why assessments that require the application of theories to the workplace are frequently used. However, the previous discussion about the potentially sectional nature of interests within business calls into question the view that the sole purpose of managerial education is to advance managerial practice. Hence relevance or importance to practice is only one criterion that might be applied; relevance or benefit to the local community or wider society might be another.

It is not the purpose of this book to prescribe how the MBA should be taught. Different programmes, and different teachers, will have their own preferred methods, styles and pedagogic rationales, and it is likely you will encounter a variety of approaches including case studies, lectures, small group work and so on. However, issues of power and control are also relevant to the classroom setting, especially if the learner is simply relegated to being a passive recipient of knowledge.

Having said this it is possible to create opportunities for active learning where learners can frame their own questions, test out their own assumptions and form their own conclusions. In the final analysis an MBA is not about equipping the individual with a box of tools to solve organizational problems, it is about that person having the skills to better understand complex issues and the ability to continue to learn in new environments as unfamiliar situations arise. Given the plethora of new ideas in management and the continued recycling of old ones, this is becoming an increasingly indispensable skill for students and practising managers. An MBA marks the beginning of learning, not the end.

In conclusion, it can be argued that Critical Management Studies takes a critical approach (see above) in that it questions the assumptions underpinning theories and debates but does so with a particular emphasis on issues of power and control, gender and diversity and so on. This book will take a critical approach by interrogating the issues and ideas presented in each domain. Since there is overlap between a critical approach and CMS the generic terms 'critical perspective' or 'critical approach' will be used to denote a range of viewpoints that seek to offer a reflexive critique of particular topics. It should be noted that not all MBA subjects have developed critiques in the same way or to the same degree. Many of the debates referred to in this chapter have emerged from, and feature most prominently in, organizational theory (organizational behaviour) and human resource management. Particular aspects of these debates have permeated other subjects to a greater or lesser extent; therefore each author will present the key critiques and alternatives that have emerged in their own domain. In areas where some of these debates are less developed, students should find that the ideas presented in this chapter offer useful starting points for further reflection.

Outline of The Book

While there is no model for an MBA in that different programmes will organize subjects differently, many will study the core 'building blocks' such as Organizational Behaviour, Human Resource Management, Marketing, Accounting, Economics and Operations at the first stage, before moving on to look at subjects such as Strategy and Corporate Social Responsibility (CSR) which will overlay and connect the core elements. Students can then either deepen their existing knowledge or extend their breadth of knowledge through elective choices, before finally moving on to a dissertation which is intended to bring together learning gained on the rest of the programme in a major, usually research-based, project.

The chapters have been organized with this implicit model in mind, as depicted in Figure 1.1, beginning with Organizational Behaviour, Human Resource Management, Marketing, Accounting and Finance, Economics and Operations, and then reviewing Corporate Social Responsibility and Strategy before examining the area of Research Approaches. A final chapter looks at those Study Skills that can help with the generic skills involved in successfully undertaking an MBA.

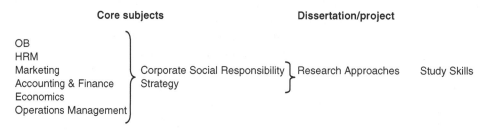

Figure 1.1 Organization of *The Essential MBA*

Summary

This chapter has attempted to do a number of things. It has offered some hints about how to make use of this text and given an overview of what it will cover. It has also tried to put the MBA in some kind of context. The MBA is a challenging degree but it is also a very rewarding one. In part the challenge comes from the sheer diversity of topics studied, but it also emanates from the type of intellectual terrain that will be covered. Students who can appreciate some of the debates outlined here should be in a good position to develop their knowledge and understanding, thereby lessening the danger of them becoming confused and overwhelmed.

This chapter has spent some time examining the debates within critical perspectives. It is recognized that it is not necessarily the case that your MBA will deal with CMS in any depth, if at all. At least, not in terms of requiring you to read about it directly, but studying for an MBA cannot, and should not, avoid some of the key questions raised here. As indicated earlier, you are likely to be required to take a critical approach to your work and that of others, and while this may not necessitate a direct familiarity with the contributors to CMS, a critically aware and questioning approach is common to critical perspectives more generally and increasingly features in a wide range of MBA subjects as the chapters here will demonstrate. This makes this book both timely and essential reading.

Critical perspectives direct our attention to the relations of power that often lie hidden, reminding us that there are different versions of reality and truth statements and that outward manifestations often belie underlying conditions. Management education is about engaging with politics and – while it is not always a comforting prospect – good education will sometimes rouse us from our comfort zones. There are fundamental links between the kinds of issues raised in this chapter and the perceived nature and purpose of management education. It is hoped that having some idea of these should help you to be better equipped to get the most from your MBA studies and organizational role – not in providing a tool kit, but in offering a way of thinking and learning that will retain its currency, even if the theories and ideas taught on your MBA eventually go out of fashion.

Good luck!

Further reading

Rousseau, D.M. and McCarthy, S. (2007) 'Educating managers from an evidence-based perspective.' *Academy of Management Learning and Education*, 6 (1): 84–101.
Thomas, A. B. (2003) *Controversies in Management*. London: Routledge.
Voronov, M. (2008) 'Towards engaged critical management studies.' *Organization*, 15 (6): 939–945.
Wallace, M. and Wray, A. (2006) *Critical Reading and Writing for Postgraduates*. London: SAGE.

References

Cassell, J. (1997) 'Doing gender, doing surgery: women surgeons in a man's profession.' *Human Organization*, 56 (1): 47–52.
Grey, C. (2004) 'Reinventing business schools: the contribution of Critical Management Education.' *Academy of Management Learning and Education*, 3 (2): 178–186.

2 Organizational Behaviour

Key concepts

Business Process Reengineering (BPR); Contingency approach to organizational structure; Emotional intelligence; Emotional labour; Group; High performance work systems; Lean manufacturing; Motivation; Network organizations; Nomothetic and idiographic approaches to personality; Organizational culture; Perception

Introduction

The study of organizations is known by various titles including Organization Theory, Organization Studies and Organizational Behaviour. While some writers may seek to differentiate between them, in practice textbooks with these different titles tend to cover similar intellectual terrain, as do many textbooks about Management. This chapter will use the term Organizational Behaviour (OB) to refer to the broad area of knowledge that encompasses the study of organizations, their environments, and the behaviour of people within them.

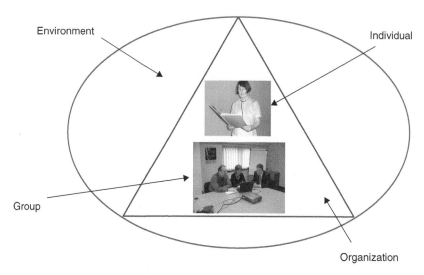

Figure 2.1   The study of organizations: four levels of analysis

Table 2.1   The domain of Organizational Behaviour

Environment	Organization	Group	Individual
National culture	Management and leadership	Group formation and development	Motivation
Organizational structure	Organizational culture, innovation and change	Group dynamics	Perception
	Decision making and power	Work teams, technology and work design	Personality
	Emotions and humour	Knowledge management and learning	

The Domain of OB

OB is informed by a number of academic disciplines, including history, economics, politics, sociology, psychology and anthropology. It is multi-disciplinary rather than interdisciplinary in nature and covers a potentially vast field. This is depicted in Figure 2.1 which gives some indication of the terrain, arranged in four levels of analysis from macro to micro. Table 2.1 gives a more comprehensive though not exhaustive list of the different topics included in OB, arranged across the four levels of analysis. These areas are not discrete, they interrelate and often overlap; the separation into different levels is for analytical purposes only and the implications of key interrelationships will be addressed as we go through the chapter. It is not the intention to cover all these topics in depth. The focus will be on identifying the central themes in each of these areas, starting with the environmental level and moving through to the individual level, and illustrating how critical approaches can open up novel perspectives and raise important questions.

It should be said that the study of OB is relevant for all kinds of organizations and therefore pertains to voluntary and charitable bodies as well as business firms. However much of the research covered in business and management courses tends to focus on the private sector. There is interest in public sector organizations and their management and OB is certainly relevant here, but this has tended to develop into a somewhat separate and distinct area of study.

Work Organizations and OB: a condensed history

Organizations in the form of military and religious institutions have long been with us and rulers and monarchs worldwide have long been concerned with matters of organization and governance. However the study of organizations was given impetus in Western Europe by the Industrial Revolution – a period of rapid growth in technological and productive techniques in the late eighteenth and early nineteenth centuries – which spurred the development and spread of work organizations. Increased mechanization contributed to a re-thinking of the ways of organizing work and workers. But while the centralization of work within the factory system undoubtedly offered opportunities for innovation, efficiencies and quality improvements, it also permitted a much closer scrutiny of the employee and opportunities for the surveillance, control and direction of work practices. Hence there are those who argue that the rise of the work organization was primarily motivated by a quest for efficiency, while others suggest that of equal importance was the need to exercise control over labour and its product. As a result while many would concede that both control and efficiency are important in that some control is needed to ensure effective working practices, the vexed question has always been how much of the former is required to achieve the latter. Indeed many of the ideas about how best to design company structures and individual jobs have their basis in this recurrent tension, often manifested as a choice between centralization and decentralization or control and autonomy (Chapter 5 on Accounting and Finance covers how accounting systems link with managerial control).

Certainly early 'classical' management thinkers – often practising managers themselves such as Henry Ford and Frederick Winslow Taylor – were preoccupied with attempts to define best practice in organizational structures and patterns of work. Fordist principles based around the division of labour and specialization utilizing Tayloristic practices of job design held sway, particularly in manufacturing industries, for much of the twentieth century, even though the Human Relations movement, which gathered pace from the 1930s, highlighted the need to attend to the human element in the workplace. While classical approaches can be argued to be still evident today and, some would say, infiltrating ever greater spheres of economic and social activity, the 1970s saw some revised thinking as post-Fordism appeared as a response to the new competitive conditions in world markets. With increasing turbulence from the oil shocks that occurred in the early part of the decade, together with the rise of Asia as a strong competitive force on the world stage, the emphasis began to centre on flexible specialization, just-in-time techniques

Table 2.2   Features of Industrialization and Post-industrialization

Industrialization	Post-industrialization
Division of labour	Flexible specialization
Mass production	Mass customization
Fordism/Taylorism	Lean manufacturing
Hierarchical structures	Decentralized structures
Standardized work practices/routines	Fragmentation and diversity
Top management leadership	Distributed leadership
Emphasis on control and efficiency	Emphasis on culture-building, visioning
Unitary organizations	Partnering and networked organizations

and TQM, all designed to deliver 'mass customization' in contrast to the mass pro-duction of the previous era. The service sector increased significantly over this period, as did the part played by information technologies in enabling firms to work across geographical boundaries – utilizing international workforces, and allowing customers to gain greater knowledge about products, services and prices, wherever companies were located. Thus the conditions of a global marketplace were laid down, and more recent theories of organizations have been framed within the imperatives of globalized economies where product life cycles are short, markets are fragmented, and suppliers and customers span the globe.

Most theories (and theorists!) tend to be products of their time. It is important to recognize the way in which theories are embedded within specific social contexts and historical conditions, since this serves both to shape potential interpretations and to provide a starting point for their critique. So changing global and economic conditions have shaped ideas about how organizations should be structured and managed. With Fordism and post-Fordism we have moved through industrialization to arrive at what many argue is now the 'post-industrial' period, and which to some degree resonates with the shift from modernism to postmodernism outlined in Chapter 1. Table 2.2 attempts to distil the essential distinctions between these phases which have given rise to different preoccupations and priorities in the field of OB.

Critical Approaches to OB

Mainstream approaches to the study of OB are predominantly concerned with understanding and improving the functioning of organizations and the people work-ing in them. In other words, the emphasis is on effectiveness and efficiency – doing the right things and doing them well. The vast majority of research has, and contin-ues to be, about improving practice. However, as we have seen in Chapter 1, critical approaches direct our attention toward the underlying structures and power rela-tionships that give rise to and shape outward manifestations of organizational life, and also prompt us to query the assumptions that underlie notions such as efficiency and effectiveness, for example by asking questions about the hidden costs of effi-ciency gains. The main thrust of critical approaches is therefore to explore organizing and the process of being organized, in order to situate the study of organizations and management in a broader historical, political and social context. This should be borne in mind as we now turn to look at specific topics in each of the levels of analysis outlined above, beginning at the macro level.

Organizations and their Environments: National Culture and Organizational Structure

National culture

Organizations are influenced by the societies in which they are embedded. Global organizations particularly must take account of local sensitivities and ways of doing business. We therefore begin by examining the influence that national cultures – and particularly their societal norms and values – can have upon organizations.

The pioneering study that explored cultural differences and paved the way for what has now become an extensive arena of research was undertaken by a Dutch researcher, Geert Hofstede, in the 1970s and 80s. Hofstede carried out a large-scale examination of how cultures differ by analyzing data gathered from employees in subsidiaries of IBM across 64 countries, identifying four dimensions of culture. His subsequent projects, including one with Michael Bond, distinguished a fifth dimension. These are set out in Table 2.3.

Different countries in the study were rated from high to low, relative to the rest, and placed along each dimension or continuum. The findings have important implications for companies working across cultural boundaries or operating with a multinational workforce. To give an example, a firm operating in a low power-distance culture (where the differences between supervisors and subordinates are down-played) might find its attempts to involve employees in decision making are met with hostility and suspicion by non-native workers who, coming from a high power-distance culture where 'what the boss says goes', do not expect to be involved.

Table 2.3 Hofstede's dimensions of cross-cultural difference (adapted from Hofstede, 1991, 2003; Hofstede and Bond, 1988)

Power distance:	the extent to which less powerful members of a society accept that power is distributed unequally
Individualism-collectivism:	the extent to which individuals are integrated into groups
Masculinity-femininity:	the extent to which roles are differentiated between genders
Uncertainty-avoidance:	the extent to which ambiguity and uncertainty are tolerated in society
Long-term/short-term orientation (Confucian Dynamism):	the extent to which the society pursues long-term or short-term goals

Case illustration

The British born editor of this book found her Malaysian PhD students expressed great reluctance to call her by her first name, even when asked to do so. The much higher power distance in Malaysia made it seem disrespectful to be on first-name terms with someone who was ostensibly in a superior position, even though the 'students' were themselves senior professionals. Thus those from a lower power-distance culture may make others uncomfortable by attempting to play down perceived status differences.

These dimensions have been utilized and modified by many other researchers, perhaps most notably in the GLOBE (Global Leadership and Organizational Behaviour Effectiveness) project, a longitudinal study of leadership and organizational culture in 62 countries (House et al., 2004) which identified some additional dimensions including *assertiveness* (the degree to which individuals are encouraged to be tough, aggressive and confrontational), *performance orientation* (the degree to which members of a society are rewarded for performance improvement and excellence), and *humane orientation* (the degree to which society encourages people to be fair, altruistic, generous, caring and kind to others). These researchers also used two collectivism dimensions: *institutional collectivism*, referring to how far the society encourages the collective distribution of resources and collective action and believes that individuals have collective duties and obligations that outweigh personal concerns (Waldman et al., 2006), and *in-group collectivism*, referring to the degree to which individuals express pride and loyalty in their membership of organizations and families or particular groups in society.

Finally the work of Trompenaars and Hampden-Turner (2006) will be mentioned briefly. Their research and consultancy with managers and companies on cross-cultural issues has led them to distinguish seven features of cross-cultural differences, summarized in Table 2.4.

These studies on cross-cultural differences have ramifications for many other areas of OB, most obviously leadership and organizational (rather than national) culture, and we will return to some of these themes again. However, this kind of work is not without controversy. It could be argued that it simply replaces some well-worn stereotypical characterizations that different societies have about each other with some rather more sophisticated, but nonetheless caricature portraits, where the methodology employed means that while the findings may indicate some general features of a society as a whole, they do not necessarily pertain to any one individual in that society.

Organizational structure

Turning to the organization itself, early research soon established a link between the environment in which a firm operated and the firm's structural arrangements. It

Table 2.4 Trompenaars and Hampden-Turner's elements of cross-cultural difference (adapted from Trompenaars and Hampden-Turner, 2006)

Universalism-particularism	the extent to which society expects adherence to general rules (contracts, for example) or expects rules to be adapted to particular circumstances or for particular relationships
Individualism-communitarianism	the extent to which the rights of the individual or the group prevail
Neutral-affective relationships	the extent to which it is acceptable to be guided by emotions or express them openly
Specific-diffuse relationships	the extent to which individuals operate within a large public arena and have a small (closely guarded) private one (a specific culture), or a small public arena (closely guarded) but a large private one (a diffuse culture)
Achievement-ascription	the extent to which the society accords status to role or to individual characteristics such as age or gender
Relationship to time	the extent to which the society has a long- or short-term time horizon, and engages in sequential (linear) or synchronic (parallel) thinking
Relationship to nature	the extent to which the society seeks to control or adapt to nature

appeared there needed to be some kind of fit between the specific environmental conditions faced by the firm and the way the firm was organized. With reference to the internal arrangements the challenge then was to find a way of reconciling the need for specialization with the resultant need for coordination. Following Anand and Daft (2007) we will divide this section into three, corresponding to three eras in the study of organization design. The first, from the mid 1800s to the late 1970s, saw the organization as a unitary entity with an identifiable boundary. Attention was focussed on the contingent factors which influenced design, such as the environment and technology, and the ways in which activities could be divided up while remaining synchronized. The second era began in the 1980s where increasingly competitive environments demanded a new responsiveness, leading to the move away from functional silos and the reengineering of workflow processes along horizontal lines both within the organization and between it and its customers and suppliers. Global challenges saw the mid 1990s heralding a third era, one that was centred on breaking down organizational boundaries, outsourcing and networking. Specialist capabilities were dispersed within the network and coordination was now required throughout the value chain, not just in one firm. We examine the dominant characteristics of each of these eras below.

Era 1: Contingency approaches

Developed through empirical studies published in the 1960s and 1970s by researchers such as Lawrence and Lorsch, Burns and Stalker, Woodward, Chandler and the Aston group (researchers based at Aston University in Birmingham, England), **contingency** approaches represent a move away from the 'one best way to organize' approach favoured by Ford and Taylor, instead examining a number of factors that appear to influence organizational design. The work of Lawrence and Lorsch and Burns and Stalker drew attention to the need for congruence with the environment.

The former stressed the need to match environmental unpredictability and complexity by appropriate *differentiation* within the structure (for example, creating more departments or sub-groups to aid environmental scanning and information gathering) together with commensurate *integration* to allow for coordination within the differentiated elements of the structure. Burns and Stalker also made a connection between the organization's environment and its structure. Their research in the fast-moving Scottish electronics industry showed that firms which operated with more *mechanistic* (bureaucratic) structures found it more difficult to change to cope with environmental turbulence. The rigidity of inflexible routines and responsibilities, together with centralized decision making in which information flows were filtered through hierarchical levels and where decision makers were distanced from day-to-day activities, all combined to slow down or stifle responsiveness. In contrast, *organic* structures with fewer hierarchical levels, devolved decision making, more lateral communication, and better information sharing and learning helped such firms to cope with change. In reality many firms today will have elements of both structures (stereotypically, more mechanistic arrangements for functions such as auditing or accounting and more organic forms for functions such as research and development), and the mechanistic/organic distinction should be thought of as a continuum rather than as discrete typologies.

Alongside the environment, 'contingency theorists' have identified other factors that appear to influence the structure of the firm. Joan Woodward highlighted the impact of technology in manufacturing firms, noting that the more *complex* the technology the greater the proportion of managers to total employees and of direct to indirect labour, and the greater the supervisor's span of control. Charles Perrow refined this by considering the *predictability* of the technology involved. Generally speaking, the more predictable the technological process the more bureaucratic routines can be used, but when the technology is less predictable then flatter hierarchies and more cross-functional working will be needed. Alfred Chandler pointed out that environmental demands often mean changes to a firm's strategy and these in turn would necessitate changes to existing structural arrangements. For example, the huge expansion of the railways in the USA during the nineteenth century opened up vast new markets, so that over time many small-scale, family-owned businesses developed into larger firms incorporating activities such as marketing, purchasing and financing that had previously been contracted out. This ties in with the work produced from the Aston studies which found that the increasing size of firms tended to lead to increased bureaucratization in terms of the specialization of job descriptions and design, the standardization of operating procedures, and the formalization of formal policies and agreements.

Contingency approach to organizational structure: a perspective that views effective organizational structures as being contingent on factors such as the environment in which a firm operates, the technology it uses, its strategy and size.

Contingency approaches have been criticized for being too deterministic (for example, seeming to suggest that a given environment *determines* the kind of structure that will be effective) and thus not permitting managers to have 'strategic choice'; for imprecisely specifying variables such as 'environmental uncertainty'; for underplaying the subjectivity inherent in making judgements about the degree of fit between the structure and these variables; and for failing to offer a coherent model of change in order to achieve congruence. Furthermore, the challenges of fast-moving global environments suggest a need for more flexible forms of organization both within and across firms.

In more recent times Mintzberg (1983) has gone some way towards refining contingent forms of organizational design, though his work does not allay all the criticisms voiced above. He put forward five types of structure: simple, machine bureaucracy, professional bureaucracy, divisional form and adhocracy (and a possible sixth, the missionary configuration) each of which uses particular forms of coordination. In the simple structure (for example a small, owner-managed garage) coordination is achieved by direct supervision; the machine bureaucracy (for example a large mass producer) coordinates through standardized work processes; the professional bureaucracy (for example a hospital) coordinates through the standardized input of people in that the professionals have to be highly skilled before they can practise; the divisional form (a collection of relatively autonomous units within a larger organization) coordinates through standardizing the outputs, and the adhocracy (a highly organic structure) is coordinated by mutual adjustment. The missionary structure achieves coordination through shared norms, generated through indoctrination and ideology. Mintzberg recognizes that different situational factors such as the environment, the age and size of the firm, the technology and power will influence the design, but also stresses the dynamic interplay between these factors so that everything depends on something else.

Contingency approaches continue to have currency and the link between types of structure and organizational performance is a key debate in the field of strategic management (see Chapter 9).

Case illustration

In June 2009, *Coca-Cola* announced a reorganization of three of its core functions into a new organization to be called Global Business and Technology Services. This is the latest in a long series of restructurings. *Coca-Cola*, the biggest brand in the world (Interbrand, 2011), has had its fair share of problems over the years with falling share prices and sales. As with many companies with problems one response has been to reorganize its internal operations and *Coca-Cola* has done this a number of times, though many commentators have seen these reorganizations as disruptive and not likely to help performance. However, the chal-

(Continued)

(Continued)

lenge for large companies like *Coca-Cola* is to be as agile and responsive to changing customer demands as a small firm. As Tom Long, Head of Operations for the UK and Ireland, once commented, 'The way to be big is by being small'. However big companies don't usually find it easy to develop structural solutions that match size and flexibility. There is a need to try to incorporate organic and mechanistic elements but this isn't always easy in practice.

(Sources: *Coca-Cola* website, accessed 4 August 2010; *Guardian* newspaper, 2 October 2000)

Era 2: Thinking horizontally – reengineering business processes

Business Process Reengineering (BPR), now often simplified to 'reengineering', was put forward by two consultants, Michael Hammer and James Champy, in their book *Reengineering the Corporation* in 1993. They argued that most organizational structures were products of history; these develop in a piecemeal fashion over time until there is a danger that they bear no relation to what is actually required to organize the tasks of the firm. They therefore advocate taking a 'blue skies' approach, starting with a clean sheet of paper, to think through how an organization can best deliver value to the customer. In this approach, the customer's needs are paramount. Organizations should begin by identifying the key processes that add value to the customer and then work backwards through the organization, bringing people and resources together to deliver what the customer needs. In theory this breaks down the functional silos which have been created by traditional structures, flattens hierarchies, and concentrates on outputs not inputs. In this radical re-think the aim is to strip out those activities which do not add value or indeed duplicate other activities. Devolving discretion and autonomy to the lowest level is meant to empower employees, and networking everyone in the organization through IT and knowledge-sharing systems is intended to enhance individual- and firm-level learning.

The danger is that this approach is revolutionary rather than evolutionary and not all organizations require such drastic revision. It also appears to underplay the problems that can come with change. While it may well speed up activities this has led to 'downsizing' and 'delayering' in many organizations and thus has been viewed as an attempt to get rid of staff and cut costs. Finally, some have argued that these attempts to reengineer processes appear to echo some aspects of Taylorism (Taylor reengineered jobs; see the discussion in the section on Management and Leadership in this chapter) and are in fact not so new after all.

Overall, BPR has had a mixed reception, but the term has passed into the lexicon of organization theory and many firms have attempted this on a smaller scale, in one or two areas of their operation. The difficulty with this scaled-down approach is that key processes, by their very nature, often cross departmental boundaries and different sub-systems are interlinked, which tends to undermine the fundamental principles of BPR which is intended to be organization-wide.

Business Process Reengineering: a radical redesign of the core organizational processes by focusing on activities that add value to the customer and removing duplication and non value-adding activities in order to speed up cycle times and improve efficiency.

Era 3: Networking, hollow, modular and virtual organizations

BPR develops the idea of networking individuals within an organization in order to share knowledge and resources. This is at the heart of **network organizations**, that is, groups of organizations which are linked together in order to manage co-production and create new capabilities. While there have always been linkages between organizations in the form of strategic alliances and joint ventures, some have argued that in order to cope with increasingly uncertain and complex environments and the challenges of globalization, we are now witnessing a new form of organization. This is the 'network form', where parts of many different organizations and institutions – such as other competitors, customers, research and development organizations and government departments – all work closely together to deliver joint goals. This enhances flexibility and learning and can be highly advantageous, especially in fast moving, unpredictable environments, but it also requires trust, reciprocity, and a clear understanding of, and commitment to, joint goals. It is argued that network organizations bring challenges in terms of their management, as traditional hierarchical arrangements are replaced by looser structures where power and authority are less clearly demarcated and organizational allegiances can become blurred.

Network organization: a group of organizations, or specific parts of autonomous organizations, that behave as a single entity in order to achieve collective goals.

At a societal level it should be noted that the idea of networks can also be linked to other co-dependent systems that have arisen within particular national cultures, such as the Korean *chaebols*, Japanese *keiretsu*, and overseas Chinese businesses. These forms develop interlocking business arrangements on the basis of trust, shared ethnicity or kinship patterns.

Alongside networking, many organizations are seeking to outsource aspects of their operation, which may itself be a reason for networking. 'Hollow' companies such as Nike and Reebok spearheaded the relocation of production to Southeast Asia some 20 years ago but many others have followed since. Thus hollow organizations will outsource non-core business *processes* to other firms. However 'modular' companies will go further and outsource pieces of the *product* to other organizations (Anand and Daft, 2007). Airbus provides an example of this. It sources parts of the A380 from countries such as Germany, Spain and the UK and assembles them in

Toulouse, France. The difficulties that Airbus initially faced in bringing together different sections of the jet serve as a warning of the kind of challenges sometimes raised by this kind of organizational form.

Finally, companies may collaborate to set up another, virtual, organization to respond to particular market needs. Anand and Daft (2007) give the example of Symbian, a software developer for mobile phones set up by a consortium of players including Nokia and Sony Ericsson to look at exploiting the links between PDAs and mobile phones. These collaborations are often temporary and Symbian was eventually bought out by Nokia in 2008. The rapid advance of information and communication technologies (ICT) means that employees can be geographically dispersed but still work together and this has facilitated the growth of virtual organizations and virtual teams within organizations. However these structural forms share many of the problems inherent in network organizations, including potential confusion about the location and exercise of power and authority; the building of commitment, motivation and trust; and the adherence to common goals within a dispersed group of employees. A critical perspective would highlight the rise in sophisticated software for electronic control and surveillance (for example, monitoring the log-in and email response times of employees) which has been introduced in parallel with the rise of virtual teams and organizations. Historical concerns with direction and supervision still lie at the heart of twenty-first century organizations.

Case illustration: Linux – networking virtually

The operating system Linux was developed through a loose confederation of volunteer programmers working independently on pieces of code, refining the software and working on bugs. Given direction by Linus Torvalds, the Helsinki student who spearheaded the operation, this virtual, networked group of individuals is argued to be an example of a 'self-organizing' entity. Self-organizing 'organizations' present a marked contrast to traditional, centrally orchestrated and hierarchically controlled operations such as Microsoft, and also pose interesting questions about control, authority and management. This form of organizing offers a different view of what an organization is, or might be.

Critiquing work on organizational structure

Designing organizational structures can appear to be very much a technical matter whereby managers carry out the required analyses and effect a transition to a new structural form. But some writers have argued that managers actually have little control over organizations. Work arising from research in the area of chaos and complexity sees organizations as complex systems which are much less amenable to managerial control. There are numerous dynamic factors both within and outside organizations, many actions can lead to unexpected consequences, and small events can become amplified and lead to more consequential and unpredicted outcomes. All these characteristics are suggestive of 'chaotic' systems. So – as with attempts to predict weather systems and the stock market – the idea that we can manage (that is, control) organizations is simply misplaced. Our best strategy is to adapt flexibly to whatever the weather and the environment throw at us. This view is also addressed in the section on decision making below, and has profound implications for the field of strategic management which are explored further in Chapter 9.

Another difficulty with traditional stances is that the willingness of managers and employees to reconfigure their ways of working is treated unproblematically. The potential effects of internal politics and wider power relationships in society are given scant attention. More critical perspectives (see Chapter 1) would argue that structural forms are less about organizing for efficiency and more about reproducing the hierarchical power relationships which exist in the wider society. The structure mirrors and replicates the divisions between groups and individuals that occur outside of the organization. Hence if particular social entities (say ethnic or religious groups) are marginalized in society they may be under-represented in organizations too, especially in the upper echelons.

Much of this work on structure is not sensitive to cultural differences and while research discussed in the first part of this section may provide a glimpse of how cultures vary, more fine-grained studies are needed if we are to go beyond broad dimensions of culture to better understand how culture and structure are intertwined.

Organizational Processes: Managing and Being Managed

The way in which an organization is structured has profound repercussions for ways of managing and being managed in organizational settings. The structure influences many factors, including how people communicate with each other and how work is designed. Indeed, beliefs about the best way to organize these may well influence the structure of the organization in the first place. This is an extensive area and we will concentrate on particular aspects. We need to start with the topic of management itself. This ties in with leadership which we will also cover in passing before looking at some of the activities that managers are meant to be involved with, such as managing change and organizational culture.

Management and leadership

Classical approaches to the study of management – such as those propounded by writers such as Fayol, Taylor, Gilbreth, Gantt, Gulick and Urwick – were concerned to improve organizational processes and productivity. In doing so an articulation of the management role began to emerge. Gulick's functions of the executive are captured in the well-known acronym of POSDCORB: planning, organizing, staffing, directing, coordinating, reporting and budgeting, which echo Fayol's main functions of forecasting and planning, organizing, commanding, coordinating and controlling. While Mary Parker Follett's writing expressed concerns for the human side of the firm and more democratic forms of governance her work was some way ahead of its time (and still lacks wider recognition), and it was Taylor's notion of scientific management that most clearly expressed the division between mental and manual labour that was to allocate the design and supervision of work to managers and the execution of tasks to lower level employees, something which still has resonance today. The idea that people choose jobs for which they have the mental capacity (and thus manual labourers would be simply incapable of devising the most efficient working methods) has an insidious and persuasive logic. Taylor's 'Theory X' view of the worker as lacking responsibility and needing close supervision seems as omnipresent today as it ever did, and can be argued to have now spread to all kinds of work, service and manufacturing, white collar and professional, as well as manual labour.

Henry Mintzberg's empirical research in the 1970s began to flesh out what managers did, identifying ten areas: interpersonal roles such as figurehead, leader and liaison; informational roles such as monitor, disseminator and spokesperson; and decisional roles such as entrepreneur, disturbance handler, resource allocator and negotiator. He also found managerial life was characterized by *brevity* (short spans of time devoted to any one task), *variety* (undertaking many diverse tasks), and *fragmentation* (tasks continually being broken off and re-started) – all some way removed from the prescriptive formulations of the classical writers.

While other writers such as Rosemary Stewart and John Kotter have also described the work of the manager, Tony Watson's (1994) long-term study of managers within one company, ZTC Ryland, begins to move away from a somewhat de-contextualized study of managerial jobs and tries to offer a reflexive understanding of the nature of management and the people who occupy managerial positions. By paying close attention to the language and frameworks managers utilize to make sense of their experiences, Watson demonstrates how they construct their own interpretations of their situation and their identities as managers. This presents a view of management as being indeterminate, fluid and malleable, shaped by changing interpretations which are constantly re-worked, and echoes postmodernist stances, in contrast with more traditional perspectives that seek to offer stable role categorizations. This line of research has generated increasing interest, moving away from depictions of what effective management ought to be towards an understanding of how management is enacted in the daily on-going routines of organizations. A focus on identity also sensitizes us to the diversity rather than the homogeneity of 'management' and reinforces the need to understand how gender, ethnicity, and individual value systems shape interpretations and expectations about management and how managers ought to operate. Hence the picture of management that begins to emerge is less concerned with normative prescription, and more with the process of identity construction in situations of flux and ambiguity.

This move away from traditionalist concerns about managerial effectiveness is to some extent mirrored in work on *leadership*. There has been a long and inconclusive debate about the degree to which managers are leaders (and vice versa). Given contemporary views about the need for devolved decision making and empowerment, the notion that leadership should be distributed more widely throughout the organization rather than being the sole province of senior figures has become popular. Leadership theories abound; the study of leaders and what they do having long been a source of fascination for management theorists as well as popular commentators. One difficulty is that there are just so many types of leaders – from Ghandi to Ghengis Khan, from Joan of Arc to Margaret Thatcher – and the situation is complicated by having to consider the myriad factors that potentially influence leadership, including the leader's personality and the nature of the task, situation and followers.

Early writers simplified this by concentrating on leaders' *traits*, looking at their physical attributes, abilities and personality characteristics. However, a plethora of studies has revealed an ever-multiplying list of traits while the variability between studies has made it problematic to reach any consensus about a parsimonious list of quintessential leadership characteristics. In any case, as subsequent theorists pointed out, the way leaders behave is as important as their personality, and behaviour can be modified whereas key traits are assumed to be innate. Moving away from the assumption that leaders are born rather than 'made' also paved the way for a market in leadership development programmes. Hence from the late 1940s onwards behaviour or *style* theories came to prominence, with analyses identifying two broad styles of leading, often termed 'consideration' and 'initiating structure'. These are more prosaically defined as a concern for people (the leader is concerned for subordinates and promotes good working relationships) and a concern for task (the leader focusses on defining the task and scheduling activities).

While some findings seemed to point to the optimum leadership style as displaying high levels of concern for both people and task it was soon clear that other factors influenced when each style might be appropriate. Thus the situational or *contingency* approach to leadership was born. Mirroring contingency approaches to organizational structure, the implications are that no one style of leadership (in this case) is thought to be optimum, but what works depends on various contingencies – including the nature of the task, the power of the leader and the relationship with, and needs of, subordinates. In the case illustration below, the UK Prime Minister Clement Attlee eloquently expresses how his predecessor, Winston Churchill, was the right leader for the particular exigencies of war-time. This view of 'the right man (or woman) for the job' suggests there needs to be a match between leadership style and task. The work of Fielder (1967, 1993) and Hersey and Blanchard (1988) is associated with this school of thought since it emphasizes that the choice of effective leadership style depends on the context, but questions about the assumptions and validity of the models and inconsistent findings have tended to undermine support for this view.

Case illustration: Leadership as a mixture of traits and circumstance?

Winston Churchill, the UK war-time Prime Minister was described by his successor Clement Attlee as '... one of the greatest men that history records ... He was brave, gifted, inexhaustible and indomitable ... Energy rather than wisdom, practical judgement or vision, was his supreme qualification ... However ... it is not the full story of what he did to win the war. It was the poetry of Churchill, as well, that did the trick. Energy and poetry, in my view, really sums him up ... He was, of course, above all, a supremely fortunate mortal. Whether he deserved his great fate or not, whether he won it or had it dropped in his lap, history set him the job that he was the ideal man to do.'

(Attlee, C. (1965) 'The Churchill I Knew', *Observer* newspaper, p.35, abridged from Holmes, R. (2006) *In the Footsteps of Churchill*, London, BBC Books)

Modern leadership theorists have labelled the leaders depicted in these traditional approaches 'transactional' leaders because their relationships with subordinates are based on an exchange of rewards and privileges in return for compliance. Transactional leaders are then contrasted with current depictions of leaders as being 'transformational' – individuals whose visionary powers and personal charisma inspire followers to higher levels of performance by developing and empowering employees. While some have argued that gender may be of relevance here in that women leaders may more readily exhibit transformational qualities such as being open to ideas and mentoring colleagues, generally this 'new' leader seems to align with contemporary notions of the 'superleader'; the business 'guru' whose extraordinary capabilities set them apart from ordinary employees. This perspective seems to fit well with the huge growth in popular business books that chart the meteoric rise of some CEOs of large corporates, however it could also be argued that transformational leadership represents a return to earlier trait approaches with its stress on the personal qualities and characteristics of the leader.

Critical management approaches draw attention to the way in which leaders (and managers) are the embodiment of a socially sanctioned stratification of power, whereby leaders legitimately have more power than subordinates. Even transformational leaders, while ostensibly tasked with empowering employees, remain embedded in existing power relations, with the notion that a leader can empower others depending on subordinates believing others have power over them in the first place. Furthermore, transformational leaders may have the capacity to utilize more subtle, and perhaps more insidious mechanisms to influence others, such as shaping the overall vision of the organization and the language and emotional responses of employees (we shall return to the subject of emotions later in this chapter).

Another central criticism of leadership theory is that the bulk of the research emanates from the West and consequently displays a Western preoccupation with the ambitions and achievements of individuals rather than the wider group. There is an obsessive interest in people at the top of organizations and a ready willingness to ascribe organizational success (and failure) to the decisions and actions of a few senior employees. Thus while leadership may not be a central leitmotif in non-Western cultures, non-Western students will still find MBA programmes devote considerable time to this subject.

This acts as a timely reminder that the concept of leadership is socially constructed and that individuals and groups are active in shaping understandings and interpretations of what leadership is and what leaders do. Postmodernist perspectives tend to turn the study of leadership on its head by stressing the role of followers in creating discourses about leadership. In this vein Boje and Dennehey (2008) outline their version of the SERVANT model of leadership (a term first coined by Greenleaf, 1977), where the leader is in fact the Servant of the network he/she is part of, Empowers participation, Recounts stories about the values and vision of the firm, is Visionary, Androgynous (speaking in both male and female voices), is a Networker and Team builder – mobilizing autonomous work teams. While there is a danger that this too will become yet another modernist ideal, locked into a view of leadership as a stable set of transformative behaviours, postmodernist reconceptualizations of leadership are centred on de-differentiating the roles of leader and follower (stressing their interconnectedness and mutual co-creation), while exploring how less well researched elements such as story-telling can shape and transmit versions of organizational realities.

This discussion begins to link with debates about the creation and transmission of 'corporate culture', where once again we will find polarized arguments about whether or not leaders (and managers) can control and change it. It is to this that we now turn.

Organizational culture and managing change

Managers continue to be tantalized by the prospect of increasing organizational success through changes to **organizational culture**. It has become something of a Holy Grail yet remains an often poorly defined concept, and is often a residual explanation when others have been exhausted.

So what is it? Many facets of culture are not outwardly observable but are manifested through, for example, the norms and values prevalent in an organization, the power structures and routines, the codes of behaviour and dress, the stories and myths that circulate, and the language and symbols used and displayed. 'The way we do things round here' is the phrase often used to encapsulate all this. It is often said that culture is more easily recognized by people outside an organization than by people within it because what makes a firm distinct is so familiar to insiders that it no longer registers.

Organizational culture: sets of belief systems, values and norms commonly held by organizational members that shape perceptions, attitudes and patterns of behaviour.

Culture is therefore multi-faceted and complex, and while some aspects such as dress and behaviour may be observable, the underlying value systems and assumptions that give rise to these will be much less obvious. Therefore, as with an iceberg (to use a much quoted metaphor), many aspects of culture will be hidden and will have to be inferred from their outward manifestations. But even tangible elements still have to be interpreted to make sense of them. What does it signify if all staff wear casual clothes rather than suits, if they work in open plan rooms rather than individual offices, or if the reception area is well decorated or shabby? There may be multiple interpretations of these signs and symbols which will mean that different views of an organization's culture could co-exist.

The main thrust of debates in this area centres on whether culture is something an organization 'has', or something that it 'is'. The former is a more instrumental, functionalist perspective that sees culture as being something that managers can manipulate. Thus it can be changed through actions such as re-branding, altering a company's policies and practices, and training staff. A more critical approach would argue that culture is something an organization 'is', in that while social practices shape cultures, the organization itself is also the embodiment of such practices and shapes them in turn. This suggests that cultural transformations are much more difficult to effect. This is because culture is continually being created and re-created through the dynamic daily routines of organizational life, because it is shaped by numerous factors that are both internal and external to the firm – many of which are not under managerial control – and because it is a product of history, taking time to root and therefore time to disestablish. Writers who take this latter view often point to the well-documented failure of many mergers and acquisitions as being due, in large part, to cultural incompatibility.

There is also the possibility that firms do not have a single, monolithic culture, but a number of sub-cultures flourishing in different parts. So, conceivably, a research and development laboratory might operate with rather different sets of values, norms and ways of working than, say, an auditing department. This calls into question the concept of a 'corporate' culture and begins to explain why culture change programmes that do not appreciate the subtleties of culture and recognize its potential heterogeneity may not realize expectations.

Case illustration

Operating in 65 countries around the world, Mars has grown from being a small, home-based business selling candies in 1911 to become established as one of the largest privately owned US corporations. The firm is proud of its

(Continued)

(Continued)

'family values' which are based on five principles: quality, responsibility, mutuality, efficiency and freedom. Mars claims that these are at the heart of everything it does and contribute to its success with such well known brands as Mars bars, Snickers confectionery, and Whiskas cat food. The company is notoriously secretive and shuns publicity but business commentators have argued that its culture has contributed to its long-run success.

(Source: Mars website at http://www.mars.com/global/home.htm)

Culture change and change management are clearly linked; the whole domain of change management being another somewhat vexed area of enquiry which has spawned a range of prescriptive models about how to effect change successfully as well as a series of critiques which pour cold water on such ideas.

The literature on change management covers a number of issues including types of change, models of change, and resistance to change. To take the first, *types* of change, it is usually pointed out that not all change is the same. Strategic change is usually organization-wide and involves a fundamental re-definition of what the organization does and/or how it does it. The terms 'frame-breaking', 'transformational' and 'revolutionary' are often applied to this kind of change. Operational change is at the other end of the continuum, and usually refers to less significant change which involves fine-tuning existing strategies, processes or routines. Of course what is strategic in one firm may be operational for another and vice versa, and even small changes can have significant, unforeseen repercussions.

Another way of thinking about types of change is to distinguish between those that are deliberate (that is, planned) and those that emerge over time without any clear steering by management. Indeed, there are also changes that are imposed on management so again they are not deliberately 'chosen' by the organization, but rather the environment (for example government, consumers or competitors) forces changes on the organization. Be aware that this overlaps with the field of strategy where the discussion about types of strategies that firms pursue covers much of the same ground (see Chapter 9).

There are numerous models that offer advice about how to manage change. Kurt Lewin's (1951) 'force-field' model is particularly well known. He argued that the driving and restraining forces need to be identified and unbalanced (since if they are in equilibrium the status quo will prevail) and then change occurs in three stages: unfreezing (building the commitment for change and unfreezing existing attitudes), changing (mobilizing the resources to carry it out), and refreezing (reinforcing new ways of working to ensure the change sticks). Whilst still widely used the model is rather simplistic, but there are many others to choose from. Kotter's (1995) model offers eight steps as follows and epitomizes the kind of recipe-driven advice that is often given:

- Establish a sense of urgency
- Form a powerful, guiding coalition
- Create a vision

- Communicate the vision
- Empower others to act on the vision
- Plan and create short-term wins
- Consolidate improvements and produce still more change
- Institutionalize new approaches

One immediate criticism that comes to mind is the assumption that change can be planned and implemented in a series of linear steps and that people will react in a logical manner to proposals.

There has been some movement away from prescriptive 'how to' models of change towards an attempt to gain a better understanding of the processes of change in organizations. This is driven by a belief that change is often messy and confused as well as iterative rather than linear, with strategies and their implementation woven together rather than the latter following the former in a neat and tidy manner. In this view some elements are planned but others simply happen, and since the process cannot be completely controlled the outcomes are often unexpected. Pettigrew and his colleagues have mapped this out by depicting change episodes as comprising a number of elements: the content of change (which is influenced by factors such as assumptions, objectives and the methods by which change will be evaluated); the context of change (both internal and external factors); and the process of change (including time horizons and the models of change being employed). From empirical research they identified five interrelated factors which appear to be linked to successful change (Pettigrew and Whipp, 1993). These are:

- Environmental assessment – effective learning about the environment
- Leading change – linking actions together
- Human resources – developing the human capabilities of the organization
- Linking strategic and operational change – because intentions are implemented over time and the cumulative effect of separate strategies will provide a context for future action
- Coherence – taking account of the overall consistency of the strategy, its consonance with the environment, its feasible and ability to maintain competitive advantage

These factors may provide a receptive context for change, but the authors stress that change is an uncertain and iterative process and these factors do not guarantee success. This notion of a receptive context echoes the work of Hickson and his colleagues who looked at strategic decision making: this is discussed in the next section.

While some factors may facilitate change, it is often resisted. Common causes include fear and a low tolerance of change, misunderstandings about what change will mean, and a lack of trust that any assurances will be upheld. It follows that managing resistance will entail good communication, lobbying and negotiating, compromise, and perhaps coercion.

Criticisms of the culture and change management literature can be made on a number of grounds. Much of the work takes a rather simplistic, recipe-driven approach that assumes change is legitimate and amenable to managerial imperative. The assumption is that managerial prerogative should prevail and any resistance should be managed away rather than recognizing there may be a legitimate basis for dissent. Ethical and moral issues associated with control and domination are seldom addressed directly.

It is also possible to take two contradictory positions on the seemingly ubiquitous nature of change. Whereas the popular view is that the rate and intensity of change is increasing faster than ever before and that the only constant thing today is change, others have observed that there are strong inertial pressures, both inside the organization in the form of existing structural arrangements, and outside of it, in the form of environmental pressures. However, from a postmodernist perspective the emphasis on change is misleading because it relies on a false interpretation which sees the world as stable and fixed and where change is an interruption to the natural state of equilibrium. An alternative vision is one where transience and impermanence are the norm and stability is an aberration (for an elaboration of this argument see Chia, 1999; Tsoukas and Chia, 2002). In this view change is ever-present and attempts to move in particular directions require managers to operate flexibly within a forever shifting set of circumstances. Change is an on-going process rather than a discrete episode.

Postmodernist approaches also foreground issues of context, criticizing change recipes for their insensitivity to local conditions. The diversity of local situations needs to be recognized and taken into account. From a feminist perspective the question of diversity is also important. As was pointed out in Chapter 1, it can be argued that the usual portrayal of organizational activities is an overwhelmingly masculine one which applauds strong-minded and decisive action. Yet in the field of organization change it is suggested that women may be sensitive to contextual matters, have skills in building relationships and alliances, and be comfortable with handling issues of diversity and ambiguity – all aspects that many have argued contribute to successful change. While research findings are not conclusive, it should be recognized that gender issues may influence how change is dealt with. Finally the issue of diversity in terms of cross cultural distinctions should also be noted. As we saw in the discussions above, there may well be differences in the way that societies perceive change in the first place, with lower uncertainty-avoidance cultures having a greater tolerance of change. Discussions of diversity highlight the fact that change is a contested concept where individual and cultural perceptions play an important part in shaping how change is conceived and reacted to.

Decision making and power

The literature on decision making has developed somewhat separately from that on change, yet there are overlaps as well as distinctions. Decisions often mean doing something differently and implementing decisions means managing processes of change.

Discussions of decision making often begin with rational choice models. These offer a predominantly economic view, portraying the decision maker as a rational profit-maximizing entrepreneur who will arrive at optimum choices after a logical and linear process of problem identification and diagnosis, searching and evaluating alternative solutions, before their final selection and implementation. However, it was soon apparent that the making of strategic (novel and consequential) or 'non-programmed' (Simon, 1960) decisions within organizational settings would often not fall into this pattern. The reasons for this included problems of information availability and accuracy, individual cognitive limitations and the political machinations of competing, shifting coalitions in the firm. Thus while some fields of business (the areas of finance and economics for example) retain assumptions of rational choice behaviour as the basis for their theoretical propositions, much work in organizational theory now recognizes that rationality is 'bounded' and may even seem irrational by objective criteria. Overall, decision makers 'satisfice' (Simon, 1960) in that the decision satisfies and suffices rather than optimizes outcomes.

Empirical research has illuminated a number of other differences between classical, rational models of decision making and the reality of what goes on in organizations. Firstly, as problems are examined they are often reconceived, so interpretations of what the issues are about change. There are also periods of recycling as new information and thinking trigger a reappraisal of what the problem really is and what is required to solve it. The search for alternatives is often limited to those that are similar to what is already being done and 'local' rationalities are employed which means that decisions taken separately may contradict each other. Overall the process may be iterative and incremental rather than linear and the course of events and the results some way from being objectively rational.

A large UK study of decision making conducted by David Hickson and colleagues (Hickson et al., 2000; see also Cray et al., 1988) identified that the *politicality* and *complexity* of what was being decided shaped the process of deciding. Politicality refers to the degree of influence brought to bear on the decision – some issues attract more attention than others and they bring different people into the process of whom some have more influence than others. Complexity refers to the nature of the problems encompassed by the decision – some problems are more unusual, require more information from different sources or have more serious or widespread consequences, and this all adds to the complexity. This study provides an explanation for why decision processes differ; it is due to variations in the political and complex nature of what is being decided.

However making a decision is not the same as carrying it out. Developing this earlier work Hickson (Hickson et al., 2003; see also Miller et al., 2004) found that two approaches – the Experience-based and the Readiness-based – when used either singly or, preferably, together, appeared to give the best chances of a successful implementation. The Experience-based approach depends on there being appropriate familiarity with what has to be implemented; this is gained either through prior experience internally or through bought-in expertise (for example through new personnel or consultants). This facilitates the assessment of objectives, specification of tasks and allocation of resources. This approach, the more planned of the two, does not of itself lead directly to success, but instead to an acceptance within the organization so that those involved will go along with what is being done, thereby giving a greater chance of a successful outcome. The Readiness-based approach relies on there being a receptive context in which to launch implementation which, as we have seen, echoes some findings on change. Here receptivity facilitates the allocation of appropriate responsibilities and roles and ensures implementation is made a priority, which also enhances the possibility of success.

In contrast to the above, the evocatively named 'garbage can' model (Cohen et al., 1972) depicts the seemingly disorganized processes that take place in what the authors call 'organized anarchies' – organizations characterized by ambiguity and uncertainty where even organizational members do not fully understand what is going on. In organized anarchies, the four components of decision making (problems, solutions, decision makers, and decision opportunities) mill about in the garbage can. Every so often they coincide, that is, a group of decision makers will come together where a decision can be made (for example at a meeting) and attach a solution to a problem – and thus a choice is arrived at. They may not be the most appropriate people to make the decision and could have attached the wrong solution to the problem, so in fact little will have been resolved but at least a decision will have been made. The garbage can model presents an imaginative and arresting idea of how organizational processes actually occur. In questioning the assumptions of organizational rationality, it encouraged greater interest in work on complexity and chaos which led to some developments in both organizational theory and in strategy (see the section on structure above, and Chapter 9). The garbage can model is a reminder that organizations are complex entities where processes are rarely fully understood and seldom under the complete control of organizational actors.

Decision making can provide a window for examining power in organizations. Hickson et al.'s (1986) concept of politicality is a reminder of the scope for power play in making decisions. While rational models suggest a *unitary* perspective, where all the participants share common interests and goals, empirical studies have tended to illustrate a *pluralist* view, where a variety of changing interest groups vie with each other to secure their own ends. However these studies look at decisions that have actually been taken. What about the ones that are not? It is possible that some areas for discussion are silenced by powerful interests who exert their influence to ensure certain matters do not make it onto the agenda. This is the dark and epistemologically challenging area of 'non decisions'. Non decisions are those issues or problems that never arise as matters requiring a decision. This is not because they are unimportant, but because they are suppressed, sometimes so successfully that it is not even realized that there might be alternatives to what is already being done. But finding out about these presents a methodological challenge of some magnitude. How is it possible to track something that has no trace because nothing happens? One way is to examine instances where something should have happened, but has failed to. Matthew Crenson's seminal (1971) study of air pollution in two US cities argued that the industrial concern responsible for the pollution (the United States

Steel Company) had managed to shape the inhabitants' preferences to such an extent that the citizens (many of whom worked for the company) saw their key interest as being in employment and enjoying the economic growth which the firm provided, rather than in concerns for public health. This *radical* view of power shows that power does not have to reside in action. Insidious but highly effective it is not evidenced by conflict, since it prevents any conflict from arising in the first place. The outcome is not action, but inaction – a non decision. More recently, one could argue that the former US president, George Bush, adopted a similar position by refusing for some time to acknowledge scientific data on global warming and climate change, thus long delaying the need for discussions or decisions about US policies to reduce carbon emissions and save energy.

The radical view of power is further developed by postmodernist interpretations which explore how power defines what statements are allowable in particular contexts and circumstances. Foucault's notion of the episteme is the 'apparatus' that permits the separating out of some statements as being more acceptable than others; in practical terms this covers those statements which are more likely to be considered 'true' or 'false'. Put more simply, this suggests that at different times there will be differing sets of (implicit) assumptions about what is, and what is not, acceptable or legitimate and these beliefs will then shape an individual's sense of self, and how they observe and make sense of what they see. This is not simply about the possibilities of repressive power, but also about how power can influence the possibility that particular statements and views are produced in the first place. Flyvbjerg's (1998) study of power within communities in Denmark illustrated how power was diffused within different networks in the community and how it was exercised through every-day interactions and routines. In this view power does not reside within a central dominant elite but is manifested through a dispersed and fragmented network of social relationships.

Emotions and humour

By raising questions about how far behaviour is rational the work on decision making also draws attention to the role of emotions in organizational settings. Rational choice models of decision making tend to exorcise emotions from the analysis of how decisions are made, since optimizing choices depend upon a strictly objective treatment of the facts rather than capricious subjective judgements. Except, of course, that as humans we are subject to all manner of emotions, and anger, fear, happiness and frustration are but a few of the varied range of feelings each one of us is likely to experience at work. It is therefore more than likely that our decisions are shaped not just by rational analysis but by individual and collective emotions.

The study of emotions has been somewhat neglected, not only in decision making but also in organization theory as a whole. What literature there is has tended to take two contrasting paths, one concerned with understanding emotions in order to improve managerial effectiveness, the other with taking a more critical stance in showing how the manipulation of emotions is yet another form of managerial control.

The first is epitomised by the work on **emotional intelligence** (EQ), popularized by Daniel Goleman (1996), which seeks to persuade that EQ is at least as important as mental capabilities (IQ) in career development. The emotionally intelligent manager will be self-aware and self-motivated, be able to regulate feelings, display empathy and will have effective social skills.

Emotional intelligence: the ability to perceive, analyze and manage one's own emotions and those of others.

The second path has been developed by writers who have drawn attention to the increasing tendency for managers to seek to prescribe the emotional repertoire which employees are permitted to display. Naturally, permitted emotions are usually positive ones such as enthusiasm and satisfaction. Employees are required to project a warm and friendly disposition, especially in customer-facing roles and in service organizations, while simultaneously repressing negative feelings associated with frustration, anger or boredom. Gender issues come into play here as it is often documented that emotions are subject to segregation according to gender. Women are often expected to display stereotypical emotions associated with nurturing and caring, whilst emotions associated with more aggressive and assertive behaviour are deemed more appropriate for men.

Emotional labour: the regulation of the employee's emotions to contribute to the achievement of organizational goals.

The term **emotional labour** has been used to depict the way in which emotions are another element of labour that has been annexed, exploited and managed. Emotional labour is not unlike manual labour in that it is hard work, and needs particular skills and practice. But there is also work that illustrates how employees may resist such pressures and subvert managerial intentions by engaging in covert unsanctioned activities. Such 'organizational *mis*behaviour' ranges from milder forms of resistance – such as the use of humour to communicate less acceptable feelings – to more radical measures – such as inciting industrial unrest or forms of sabotage.

It should be noted that the role of humour in the workplace has spurred much interest in its own right and it has been shown that it can be deployed in a variety of ways for a range of purposes. From a sociological perspective humour can be utilized by employees to either uphold, or subvert, organizational dogmas. 'Poking fun' at something can be a good way to vent frustrations, challenge authority and get serious messages across in a less confrontational manner. Humour can also be used to demarcate and maintain group boundaries (for example employees making fun of management, or making jokes about other employees, or the use of racist or sexist 'banter'). Indeed, in terms of gender, it appears there may be marked differences in the ways that women can use humour. In particular it may be the case that the telling of 'risqué' jokes by women is more likely to be negatively received by subordinates than similar jokes told by men.

Humour can also be used by management as a way of breaking down hierarchical divisions, motivating or building a rapport or commitment, softening criticism, and defusing tension. It is interesting to note that, historically, management has had an ambivalent attitude towards humour. In Ford's factory laughing was viewed as a disciplinary offence, yet contemporary managers are often urged to use humour to improve workplace relationships.

The ways in which humour, and other emotions, are used by both management and labour are varied and complex, and are influenced by societal expectations about what is permissible or reprehensible. From a critical perspective, the use of humour and other emotions is simply an additional weapon in the management arsenal used to get more work from employees with the aim of improving productivity. However a postmodernist perspective would urge caution in taking the view that emotions, particularly humour, can be so readily deployed with such predictable results. Instead, we need to take account of the variety of ways that humour may be both used in organizations, and 'read' or understood by those exposed to it. Finally, as we have seen earlier in this chapter, there are cultural differences in the degree to which societies find the open display of emotions acceptable. Any attempts to manipulate emotions are clearly not straightforward.

Groups and Teams in Organizations

As we noted above, at one level organizations are simply collections of **groups** of people, whether they are organized into business units, departments or functions, work teams, or some other sub unit. In addition, since organizations are social places, both formal and informal groups are likely to exist – the former being set up by the organization, the latter arising spontaneously as individuals interact.

Group: a collection of people who think of themselves as 'us'.

The study of work groups owes much to research carried out in social psychology, beginning in the first half of the twentieth century. Increasing recognition of the limitations of Tayloristic principles – which narrowly viewed efficiency gains as only being possible through rigid constraints on how the individual worker did their job – spurred interest in the relationship between the social side of work and productivity. Taylor saw groups as a potential threat to productivity. Their capacity for 'soldiering' (clandestinely setting their own unofficial targets for output and ensuring no individual in the group exceeded them) reduced efficiency. The so-called Human

Relations School of management which followed Scientific Management saw the understanding of groups and social relationships at work as a way of increasing this. While the second perspective intuitively sounds more liberating, it could be argued that both are concerned with the manipulation of workers in order to achieve organizational aims, a point we will return to later.

The kinds of issues usually examined in this area include how groups form and develop and how dynamics within a group will impact on performance. It should be noted that much modern management theory proposes that organizations are (or should be) increasingly characterized by teams and the terms 'group' and 'team' are often used interchangeably. Teams are synonymous with task-based structures where the emphasis is on devolved decision making and delegated authority, where power is based on expertise and knowledge rather than hierarchy, and where functional barriers are broken down as empowered employees work collaboratively and interdependently on cross-cutting tasks or projects. Critical perspectives question this somewhat rosy picture and offer a rather different analysis as we shall see. This section will therefore discuss the concept of work groups and teams and critically evaluate the roles these might play in organizations.

Group formation and group dynamics

Most studies argue that work groups go through various stages in their development. These stages encompass a beginning, where individuals consider their own role and that of others within the group and test out ideas and assumptions; a middle stage where conflicts surface and members vie for power and status; and a final stage where the group begins to agree on norms and codes of behaviour and work collectively towards objectives. These stages may overlap and repeat – for example, if underlying conflicts are left unresolved during the middle phase they may resurface later on.

What goes on when individual activity becomes coordinated through a group has long been of interest to psychologists and social psychologists. To do this area justice would require much more space than we have here so this section will concentrate on some key concepts and ideas. Taylor's notion of soldiering captures the power of the group in exerting peer pressure on individuals. The 'norming' phase of group development is also about setting rules and standards with which members of the group will comply. *Conformity* occurs when individuals change their behaviour in response to these pressures (either real or imagined). When individuals conform in response to people perceived to have more authority, or power, this is termed *obedience*, and many studies have shown the extreme lengths people will go to in order to obey those whom they believe have authority.

Belonging to a group may give feelings of security and confidence, but these can go too far. The *risky shift phenomenon* suggests that groups may sometimes make riskier decisions than they would have done as individuals – especially if there are potentially high pay-offs. This is because responsibility is diffused so no-one bears sole responsibility if things go wrong. Having said this other research suggests the reverse, finding that sometimes groups can be more risk-averse; even so the idea that groups may act differently, and sometimes with very negative consequences, is given credence by the work of Irving Janis who developed the concept of *groupthink*. This is a complex phenomenon, paradoxically occurring when it appears the group is working well, with little conflict or dissension. In fact this is the root of the problem, for a group that is too coherent may begin to ignore those facts and perspectives that do not accord with its own view of reality, may start to hold stereotyped views of others outside of the group and may also brush aside ethical or moral questions. In conforming to the group's expectations individual group members can feel unable to speak out and there is thus the illusion of unanimity leading to poor quality decision making.

A measure of conflict may therefore be beneficial in ensuring a heterogeneity of views, challenging assumptions and testing out ideas and evidence, though personal conflict, either within the group or between different groups, is usually seen to be unhelpful.

Work groups and organizational performance: Japanization, knowledge management and learning

The rise of Japan as a major global player in the 1970s and 80s spawned interest from Western researchers in trying to discover how Japanese work and human resource practices contributed to such marked economic and competitive success. Commentators identified a number of factors but the essence of these appeared to revolve around team working. As well as encouraging team working within the organization, Japanese workers were urged to think of the firm as a whole as a team so that everyone played a part in contributing to organizational performance and the demarcations between individual groups of workers, and workers and managers, were consequently played down.

Building on methods first developed by the US statistician William Deming and also those of Joseph Juran, a Romanian who emigrated to the USA, as well as those put forward by the Japanese quality management academic Kaoru Ishikawa, Japanese companies focussed on quality and continuous improvement. Quality circles are based on groups of workers who meet regularly to discuss potential production improvements. Kaizen develops this, the idea here being to utilize the knowledge and skills of the worker through a process of dialogue and discussion, centring on the identification of numerous, small, incremental changes which, over time, can lead to significant efficiencies and productivity gains.

Japanese work practices are encapsulated in the concept of **lean manufacturing** – an approach honed at Toyota which stresses a minimization of resources, striving to produce the same output with fewer inputs, reduced costs, less time and least effort. 'Just-in-time' techniques such as the 'kanban' flow production system help to achieve this. The kanban is a system to trigger action. Items are 'pulled' through the production process as and when required. This contrasts with traditional 'push' methods which rely on the forecasting of demand and result, if forecasts are inaccurate, in large stocks of inventory sitting idle in the factory (see Chapter 7, Operations Management).

Lean manufacturing: a focus on waste elimination and the improvement of process flows to continuously improve quality and efficiency in the production process.

At the heart of such systems is the notion of teamwork, but whether this is about the empowerment of workers or simply another way to take advantage of them is still much debated. Some of these ideas have fed through into more recent ideas about **High performance work systems** which also stress empowerment, engagement and flexibility and which link with developments in human resource management.

High performance work systems: organizations that emphasize empowerment, engagement and flexible working practices to improve organizational performance.

A critical view would point out the difficulties for workers to opt out of such systems, so that engagement is compulsory and not voluntary. While they might have some autonomy workers must be controlled to ensure their efforts are firmly fixed on managerial objectives and encouraging them to share in these simply masks the true relations that exist.

Hence it has been argued that the notion of teamwork masks the true nature of authority relations in the workplace, encouraging workers to actively engage in perpetuating inequalities by engaging in the surveillance of other workers and self-discipline. Self-discipline rather than managerial coercion is a much less conflictual way of exerting control – though the ends may be the same. Many writers have noted that not all workers will willingly assume such roles and have drawn attention to the forms of resistance that can be employed (see for example Sewell, 1998). Such critical perspectives build on a long tradition of critique in this area that comes under the label of *labour process theories*: these were given prominence through the work of Harry Braverman in his book *Labour and Monopoly Capital: The Degradation of Work in the Twentieth Century* (1974) which offered a fairly explosive commentary on the way in which capitalist systems and new technologies exploited labour by de-skilling and intensifying work and passing control and discretion from workers to management. Braverman's work was a major contribution to the still-continuing debate about how far technology empowers or exploits, enhancing or reducing employees' skills and expertise.

Such debates still rumble on and the rhetoric around 'knowledge management' and the 'learning organization' can be seen as an extension of this in that the imperative is for the organization to exercise proprietorial rights over personal knowledge and learning, thereby codifying tacit knowledge so that it becomes communal (this is developed further in Chapter 9 on Strategy). From a postmodernist stance, Foucault's attention to the relationship between knowledge and power is very relevant in discussions of learning and knowledge. Power is seen to have a foundation in knowledge, but what is construed as knowledge is shaped through relations of power which are ubiquitous and dynamic. Thus the labelling of some areas of discourse as 'knowledge' is a political act, but since power is unstable what constitutes knowledge – and thus what should be learned – is not fixed but shifting. These views emphasize the need to recognize the social and political context in which knowledge formation and learning imperatives arise.

Modern technologies and work practices have moved on considerably since the 1970s and methods of surveillance and control have become more sophisticated. However, there now appears to be increasing recognition that power without conflict is much the best way, hence the attempt to 'normalize' behaviour through workplace ideologies that promote and legitimize certain behaviours. This includes the shaping of subjective identities so that seeing oneself as a team member, rather than as an individual, has a powerful influence on the self-identify and behaviours of organizational members. This is returned to in the discussion of motivation below.

The Individual in the Organization

At the most micro level of analysis organizations are made up of individuals. We will look at three commonly discussed aspects here: motivation, perception and personality.

Motivation at work

The idea of being part of a group links with notions of social identity. Group membership gives us a place and position in an organization and may contribute to our feelings of belonging, esteem and self-worth. It could be argued that most changes to work design are based on the view that efficiency will be increased, at least in part, by improving the individual's satisfaction and enjoyment of work – in other words their **motivation**. This topic has a long history, with the challenge of finding out what makes people work better and harder being of great interest to both theorists and practitioners. Motivation also has clear links with the structuring of organizations (some structures, for example organic ones, are argued to be more motivating to work in) and with the organization of production discussed in earlier sections, and work in human resource management (particularly performance management and reward systems); see Chapter 3.

Motivation: the reasons that induce individuals to engage in particular behaviours.

The first thing to note about much of the work in this area is that it is overwhelmingly North American and masculine in origin, having been conducted by white US male researchers, and that many of the research subjects would also fall into this category. Immediately, then, there are concerns about the degree to which findings relate to other racial and cultural groupings as well as to women.

Theories of motivation can be organized into two broad groupings: those that are concerned with *what* motivates the individual (the so-called 'content' theories) and those that are concerned with *how* individuals are motivated (the process theories). Following on from these is a range of models and theories that propose how jobs should be enriched in order to provide appropriate motivational conditions. These groupings will now be summarized.

Content theories include the well-known models created by Maslow, McClelland, Alderfer, and Herzberg. Maslow's hierarchy of needs is usually expressed in the form of five levels of need. It begins with basic physiological needs such as the need for food, water, and sexual expression, and then moves to the need to feel safe and secure, the need to feel socially accepted ('belongingness' needs), the need for self-esteem and, finally, to the need to self-actualize (to reach one's full potential). The idea is that, once satisfied, a need no longer motivates and so the individual moves up the hierarchy to the next level, though Maslow did not believe all individuals would be capable of achieving self-actualization. Note that this model was not developed with the workplace in mind, has little predictive value, and seems to equate with middle-class Western aspirations, though to be fair, Maslow did not intend it to be universally applied. Even so, it is still much quoted, and writers such as McClelland and Alderfer have further developed this kind of thinking. McClelland dispensed with the notion of a hierarchy, suggesting instead that individuals differed in their need for achievement, for power, and for affiliation. Alderfer also proposed three categories (existence, relatedness, and growth), maintaining that all of these could be present at any one time.

It is Herzberg's work that most directly relates to ideas of job enrichment. In research into job satisfaction based on a sample of 200 US accountants and engineers Herzberg distinguished two sets of factors. *Hygiene* factors seemed to cause dissatisfaction at work, and included things like pay, security, supervision, company policy, working conditions and interpersonal relations. However if these were satisfactory this did not lead to motivation. The *motivators* were a different set of factors, including achievement, recognition, the work itself, responsibility and advancement. Hygiene factors were extrinsic to the job; motivators were intrinsically about the job itself. Hence attempts at job enrichment (increasing the motivational potential of a job) were thought to be achieved by widening the skill base and by *vertical loading*, which would increase autonomy and discretion, although Herzberg did not believe that all jobs, or all workers, needed to be or were capable of being enriched. Hackman and Oldham's Job Characteristics Model is a more developed version of this thinking and links together the core dimensions of a job with the individual's experience, motivation and performance.

Individual experience is at the heart of process theories. The view that we are motivated by perceptions of fairness has given rise to equity theories, most notably that of Adams, who argued that we compare the amount of effort and reward that we receive with that received by others. Interestingly, we tend to tolerate a modest over-reward, but we tend to be motivated to redress an imbalance which is not in our favour. Also in the category of process theories is that of expectancy theory. Tolman proposed that behaviour is influenced by expectations about what our behaviour will lead to. Victor Vroom developed this in the work setting by suggesting that our expectations about the outcomes of our behaviour may lead us to be motivated – if we value the outcomes. For example, if we believe that hard work will lead to promotion we may be motivated to work hard if we want to get promoted. The strength of motivation is thus dependent on whether or not we believe there is a relationship between effort and reward and whether or not we value that reward.

Goal setting theories such as that proposed by Edwin Locke relate to process theories as they suggest that setting challenging (but feasible) goals, being able to participate in goal-setting, and being given timely feedback also help to motivate employees.

In general content theories can be criticized because in their efforts to define a universal sets of needs they underplay or ignore the complex and changing set of needs of different individuals. Since motivation is, at least in part, socially constructed, it follows that what individuals find motivating will depend to some extent on the norms and values of particular cultures and societies. It is perhaps unsurprising therefore that individualistic cultures such as the United States have spawned theories that stress individual achievement and personal self-actualization rather than collective attainment (for the organization, or one's family) and growth. Process theories allow for individual variation, but they are inevitably less simple and thus harder to apply in practice. Indeed this poses the question of how far managers can (and should) motivate others. It could be argued that we can only motivate ourselves, and all the best managers can do is to create an environment where we can choose to be motivated or not. And when does motivation become manipulation? Overall, motivation theories are clearly concerned with improving the productivity of employees and – while many theorists were genuinely concerned with finding ways of improving the experience of people at work – are clearly functionalist in nature, as well as rooted in the belief that shaping environments and expectations to achieve organizational goals is justified.

Newer thinking on motivation stresses the importance of understanding the meaning of work and relating this to identity (for example, see Linstead et al., 2004). Work means different things to different people and the importance of work to any one individual may change over time as their personal and environmental conditions change. While achievement and advancement may be important early on in one's career, fulfilling work may be more significant as one gets older and more immediate financial concerns become less pressing; similarly job security may become more of a priority in times of high unemployment and redundancies. Therefore one's working persona becomes an important part of our notion of 'self'. We may become identified by our occupation, for example as a doctor, electrician, teacher, shop assistant, or housewife. In a world where global pressures and fierce competition have contributed to an increase in part-time, casualized work and a rise in short-term contracts, many people now have a precarious relationship with the world of work and this has an effect on their own identity as a worker. Consequently the things that motivate us may be associated with how we see ourselves, with who we perceive our peer group to be, and with the sorts of aspirations that then seem socially acceptable or desirable in order to fit with this self-image. Since our self-image is neither stable nor unified (how we perceive ourself changes, and we can be many things to many people), what motivates us at any one time may be transient.

The conclusion here is that motivation is a complex and still not well understood concept. Much traditional theory does not fully appreciate how gender, culture and other societal factors can influence individual motivation, and the links between employee motivation and performance are also poorly understood. The main thrust of this literature is to find better ways of using motivational techniques to enhance productivity. Although critical thinkers may take comfort from the fact that there is still a question mark over whether anyone can indeed motivate anyone else, the ability of corporations to adopt increasingly sophisticated ways of controlling both employees (by shaping working practices and environments) and customers (by shaping how they are represented in the media and by directing customer/corporate interactions) means that the ability of both producer and consumer to be self-determining is ever-more called into question.

Case illustration

Siemens is in the business of innovation. It concentrates on training and motivation in order to give its staff the up-to-date skills needed to retain a competitive advantage in the electronics and electrical industries in which it operates. Already offering induction and apprenticeship schemes, in 2005 the company set up the Siemens Commercial Academy to offer a four-year programme to develop financial and commercial expertise: this was seen as an alternative to university. As with many organizations employee motivation is viewed as being the way to enhance company performance.

Perception

Identity and **perception** are closely related. The way we construct our identity depends on our perception of ourselves and others. Here, and in the next section on personality, we move more into the realms of psychology. Perception is about how we collect data about the world, interpret and make sense of it in order to act in the world. We act according to our perceptions of reality, not necessarily to reality itself. Obviously this is central to all aspects of our being, not just to working and managing in organizations, but understanding processes of perception helps to explain what goes on in organizations and certainly affects aspects such as communication that we have already touched on.

Perception: the process of collecting, organizing and interpreting sensory data.

Psychologists tend to explore perception by addressing the ways in which perceptions are distorted. We often tend to see what we want to see, not what is there. Since we perceive by gathering data about the world through our senses there is first the problem of *selective attention*. The world is too full of data for us to comprehend it all. We are constantly bombarded with information, noise and visual stimuli, much of it irrelevant or of low priority for us. We therefore have to select the data we will pay attention to – a process that is often done unconsciously as we screen out unwanted or unimportant stimuli and 'notice' others. What does get noticed is what we are interested in, what we are alerted to, and what our background, upbringing and experience prepare us to be 'interested' in. The rest is unnoticed or ignored. Over time we get used to some stimuli and become unaware of it through a process known as *habituation*. The road noise outside your office, background 'music' in shops and restaurants, or birdsong may all be heard if you consciously listen, but will soon blend into the background as you concentrate on other things.

We do not capture everything around us and even then, *perceptual filters* will influence how we interpret this data. For example, in making judgements about people we may *stereotype* them, making generalizations about them on the basis that they belong to a group or category with which we are already familiar. So, for example, our beliefs about accountants being boring or computer technicians being geeks may well predispose us to make assumptions about the next accountant or computer technician we meet. Stereotypes may be helpful, in that they can assist us in quickly sorting out new data into existing categories, but they may also lead to overgeneralizations. Other ways that perceptual filters may shape our understanding is through the *halo/horns* effect. This is where we will latch onto one characteristic of an individual, either good (halo) or bad (horn), and then ascribe other characteristics on the basis of this. This often happens in selection interviews, where interviewers will note one feature (often something to which the interviewer relates, like sharing a similar interest or hobby) and then proceed to use the rest of the interview to build a confirmatory picture of the individual, filtering out any information that appears to contradict this early judgement.

Once we have our data we need to organize it in order to make sense of it. Karl Weick (1995) calls this 'sensemaking' and argues that we literally 'make sense' of what we see. We *enact* our reality, that is, we are active in creating our own experience, rather than passively receiving stimuli – we actively attend to, collect, sort, and synthesize data to try and understand the world around us. We also do this retrospectively, because what we see, hear, taste, smell or touch is always in the past, even if only by a few micro-seconds; it has already happened by the time we apprehend it and so we must process the data after the event has occurred. According to Weick, sensemaking is driven by plausibility rather than accuracy. It may make sense but not be sensible, because we distort and filter information and reason on the basis of incomplete data. The implication for working and managing in organizations is that we all create our own realities to some extent, and do so retrospectively, based on distorted and incomplete data – hardly a basis for rational decision making!

In some ways an understanding that our perception is shaped by individual and social constructions aligns with some of the critical and postmodern concerns. The view that meaning is given to objects and situations rather than being something which is an intrinsic part of an object or situation echoes this thinking. There are multiple realities, not just one. Postmodernism stresses the role of language in shaping our understanding of what we perceive and thus the importance of deconstructing the 'text' to perceive better the underlying meanings. We, the reader, will provide our own meanings for what we observe, hear or read. However, some critical perspectives are less sanguine about our ability as readers to impart subjective meaning and point to the persuasive abilities of those in power to shape individual perceptions of reality. Hence the language of managerialism sets the context for our perceptions of how we act as managers, or perceive ourselves as employees. In this way perceptual distortions are not simply due to selective attention and individual perceptual bias, they are also orchestrated attempts by powerful groups to form collective perceptions in a way that masks the true relations of power.

Personality

Finally, we turn to the question of who we are. It is a truism to say that, as individuals, we are all different, but it is this diversity that leads to both creativity and conflict in organizations and we both benefit from differences in others and become confused or irritated by them.

Someone's personality is generally considered to consist of relatively stable characteristics, behaviour patterns or traits. These characteristics can be viewed as being innate or learned, or a mixture of both, and different psychological traditions lean towards explanations that stress either nature (innate) or nurture (learned). **Nomethetic approaches** tend to view personality as a collection of traits (such as assertiveness or self-confidence) which are largely innate, observable, and therefore amenable to identification through questionnaires and measurement techniques. These perspectives have tended to dominate much of US and UK research. These contrast with **idiographic approaches** that take the view that the way traits manifest themselves can vary with the individual, that personality can develop over time, and that it can only be understood in the context of the complex web of social relationships in which it is embedded. Research here tends to result from case studies, personal diaries and biographies.

Nomethetic approaches: view personality as being manifested through observable characteristics that can be objectively identified and measured.

Examples of nomothetic approaches include the work of Hans Eysenck who argued that personality was genetic and thus largely inherited. He identified two dimensions of personality: extroversion and introversion (the 'E' dimension – to do with levels of social ability and propensity to take risks) and neuroticism and stability (the 'N' dimension – neurotics tend to be emotional and unstable and stable people tend to be more easy going and realistic). Together these give rise to four personality types: high N and high E – unstable extroverts; high N and low E – unstable introverts; low N and high E – stable extroverts; low N and low E – stable introverts.

Generally, trait research has tended to coalesce around what have become known as the Big Five traits. These broad dimensions of personality are:

- **O**penness: responsive to aesthetics, unusual ideas, a variety of experiences
- **C**onscientiousness: to do with self-discipline, achievement, planned rather than spontaneous behaviour
- **E**xtraversion: stimulation-seeking, gregarious
- **A**greeableness: compassionate and cooperative
- **N**euroticism: anxious, angry, vulnerable

Together these give rise to the acronym OCEAN.

Goleman's work mentioned above would also fit into the nomothetic category. In general nomothetic approaches have tended to underpin many organizational training and development activities, as well as personality assessment, psychometric tests and so on.

While not necessarily fitting neatly with the nomothetic paradigm Carl Jung's work is probably some of the best known in the area of personality assessment, having provided the foundations for the work of mother and daughter Katherine Briggs and Isobel Myers who developed the Myers-Briggs Type Indicator (MBTI) that is often used in management development. This is based on Jung's notion of *preferences*, the idea that we are born with a preference for operating in particular ways across four dimensions. These are extraversion – introversion; sensing – intuition;

thinking – feeling; and a fourth which was added by Myers and Briggs, judging – perceiving. These dimensions are described below.

- *Extraversion* – gaining one's energy primarily from external sources and other people
- *Introversion* – gaining one's energy primarily from the inner world of thoughts, reflection and ideas
- *Sensing* – gathering data primarily through the five senses
- *Intuition* – gathering data through intuition, 'flashes of insight'
- *Thinking* – making decisions through detached, objective reasoning, according to rules
- *Feeling* – making decisions through empathizing with the situation, considering the needs of people involved
- *Judging* – preferring a more planned approach when dealing with the outside world
- *Perceiving* – preferring to stay open to new information and ideas when dealing with the outside world

Idiographic approaches question the nomothetic search for universalistic, law-like traits or personality dimensions and instead emphasize the unique, complex, and contextualized nature of our personalities. Carl Rogers' 'person-centred' approach to therapy takes a more idiographic approach, as does Erik Erikson's work which looks at how our personality develops through different life stages and experiences. Such approaches are not concerned with the categorization of individuals but with understanding people's uniqueness.

Idiographic approaches: view personality as an interrelated and dynamic set of characteristics that need to be understood in the context of each individual.

In summary, it can be seen that nomothetic theories tend to take a positivistic stance, whereas idiographic theories tend towards a phenomenological one. Nomothetic approaches have tended to be used in organizations for selecting, training and developing those individuals according to organizational aims and purposes. Idiographic approaches are also used in areas such as counselling, stress management, and understanding diversity. Indeed the topic of diversity has come to the fore in recent years and now features in many training programmes. However, while it can be claimed that understanding diversity may counter negative stereotypes, it can also be argued that the focus tends to be overwhelmingly placed on the business benefits rather than on moral or ethical issues (except for avoiding costly discrimination cases).

Summary

This chapter has covered the key topics usually discussed on MBA organizational behaviour/management courses. Moving from macro to micro perspectives it has reviewed research that focusses on the organization in its environment, through an understanding of organizational processes, to a focus on groups and individuals. Generally speaking, orthodox approaches to each topic concentrate on developing understanding to improve managerial practice and organizational functioning. Critical approaches seek to understand what happens in organizations, to explore why things happen in the way that they do, and to identify how different interests are affected by what goes on. This may also improve organizational effectiveness and it should not be construed that critical perspectives are always negatively intransigent in the face of modern capitalism and automatically set against managerial initiatives. However, they do cause us to reflect on the assumptions underlying the way we organize and manage and also force us to ask challenging questions about the wider interests being served by contemporary organizations.

Questions for reflection

1 What are the implications of research on organizational structure for designing contemporary organizations?
2 What kinds of leadership might be appropriate in multicultural firms?
3 How useful is the concept of corporate culture to the practising manager?
4 What part does rationality play in organizational decision making?
5 How do firms make use of 'emotional labour'?
6 How might issues of gender and diversity impact on organizational functions and processes?
7 What are the functional and dysfunctional aspects of groups and teams in the workplace?
8 Is the motivation of employees a legitimate management task?
9 How useful are insights about personality and perception for understanding organizations?
10 What do critical perspectives bring to an understanding of organizational behaviour?

Further reading

Organizational structure and design

Anand, N. and Daft, R.L. (2007) 'What is the right organization design?' *Organizational Dynamics*, 36 (4): 329–344.

Harris, I.C. and Ruefli, T.W. (2000) 'The strategy/structure debate: an examination of the performance implications.' *Journal of Management Studies*, 37 (4): 587–603.

Olson, E.M., Slater, S.F., Tomas, G. and Hult, M. (2005) 'The performance implications of fit among business strategy, marketing organization structure, and strategic behaviour.' *Journal of Marketing*, 69 (July): 49–65.

Wrege, C.D. and Hodgetts, R.M. (2000) 'Frederick W. Taylor's 1899 pig iron observations: examining fact, fiction and lessons for the new millennium.' *Academy of Management Journal*, 43 (6): 1283–1291.

National cultures

Fok, L.Y., Hartman, S.J. and Kwong, K. (2005) 'Differences in business ethical values: a study of differences in business ethical values in mainland China, the US and Jamaica.' *Review of Business*, 26 (1): 21–26.

Hickson, D.J. and Pugh, D.S. (2003) *Management Worldwide: Distinctive Styles amid Globalization.* London: Penguin.

Hofstede, G. (2003) *Culture's consequences: Companing Values, Behaviours, Institutions and Organizations across Nations.* Thousand Oaks, CA: Sage.

House, R., Hanges, P.J., Javidan, M., Dorfman, P.W. and Gupta, V. (2004) *Culture, Leadership and Organizations: The GLOBE Study of 62 Societies.* Thousand Oaks, CA: Sage.

Minkov, M. and Hofstede, G. (2011) 'The evolution of Hofstede's doctrine'. *Crosscultural Management: an international journal*, 18(1): 10–20.

Management and leadership

Special Issue on Leadership (includes work on Emotions) (2004) *Harvard Business Review*, 82 (1).

Bartlett, C.A. and Ghoshal, S. (2003) 'What is a global manager?' *Harvard Business Review*, 81 (8): 101–109.

Goleman, D. (2000) 'Leadership that gets results.' *Harvard Business Review*, 78 (2): 78–90.

Grey, C. (1999) '"We are all managers now; we always were": on the development and demise of management.' *Journal of Management Studies*, 36 (5): 561.

Watson, T.J. (1994) *In Search of Management, Culture, Chaos and Control in Managerial Work.* London: Routledge.

Organizational culture and change

Jones, O. (2000) 'Scientific management, culture and control: a first-hand account of Taylorism in practice.' *Human Relations*, 53 (5): 631–653.

Marshall, J. and Adamic, M. (2010) 'The story is the message: shaping corporate culture.' *Journal of Business Strategy*, 31 (2): 18–23.

Ogbonna, E. and Harris, L.C. (2002) 'Organizational culture: a ten year, two-phase study of change in the UK food retailing sector.' *Journal of Management Studies*, 39 (5): 673–707.

Van de Ven, A. and Scott Poole, M. (2005) 'Alternative approaches for studying organizational change.' *Organization Studies*, 26 (9): 1377–1404.

(Continued)

(Continued)

Decision making and power

Linstead, S., Fulop, L. and Lilley, S. (2004) 'Power and politics in organizations.' In *Management and Organization: A Critical Text.* Hampshire: Palgrave Macmillan. pp. 182–209.

Miller, S. and Wilson, D.C. (2006) 'Perspectives on organizational decision making.' In S. Clegg, C. Hardy, T.B. Lawrence and W. Nord (eds), *Handbook of Organization Studies.* London: Sage. pp. 467–484.

Miller S., Wilson, D.C. and Hickson, D.J. (2004) 'Beyond planning: strategies for successfully implementing strategic decisions.' *Long Range Planning,* 37: 201–218.

Emotions and humour

Ashforth, B.E. and Humphrey, R.E. (1993) 'Emotion in the workplace: a reappraisal.' *Human Relations,* 48: 97–125.

Collinson, D.L. (2002) 'Managing humour.' *Journal of Management Studies,* 39 (3): 269–288.

Griffin, R.W. and Lopez, Y.P. (2005) '"Bad behaviour" in organizations: a review and typology for future research.' *Journal of Management,* 31 (6): 988–1005.

Huy, Q.N. (1999) 'Emotional capability, emotional intelligence, and radical change.' *Academy of Management Review,* 24 (2): 325–345.

Romero, E.J. and Cruthirds, K.W. (2006) 'The use of humor in the workplace.' *Academy of Management Perspectives,* 20 (2): 58–69.

Groups and teams

Druskat, V.U. and Wolff, S.B. (2001) 'Building the emotional intelligence of groups.' *Harvard Business Review,* 79 (3): 80–90.

Organizational Dynamics (2009) Special Issue: 'The ins and outs of leading teams', 38 (3).

Sewell, G. (1998) 'The discipline of team: the control of team-based industrial work through electronic and peer surveillance.' *Administrative Science Quarterly,* 43 (2): 397–429.

Thompson, L. (2003) 'Improving the creativity of organizational work groups.' *Academy of Management Executive,* 17 (1): 96–111.

Motivation at work

Academy of Management Review (2004) Special Topic Forum, section on 'The Future of Work Motivation Theory', 29 (3).

Ambrose, M.L. and Kulik, C.T. (1999) 'Old friends, new faces: motivation research in the 1990s.' *Journal of Management,* 25 (3): 231–292.

Pearson, C.A.L. and Tang Yin Hui, L. (2001) 'A cross-cultural test of Vroom's expectancy motivation framework: an Australian and a Malaysian company in the beauty care industry.' *International Journal of Organization Theory and Behavior,* 4: 307–327.

Perception

Fletcher, W. (2000) 'Let your body do the talking.' *Management Today,* March: 30.

Mullins, L.J. (2007) *Management and Organizational Behaviour.* Essex: Pearson. pp. 208–248.

Weick, K. (1995) *Sensemaking in Organizations.* Thousand Oaks, CA: Sage.

(Continued)

(Continued)

Personality

Buchanan, D. and Huczynski, A. (2010) *Organizational Behaviour*. Essex: Pearson. pp. 167–200.

Knights, D. and Willmott, H. (2007) *Introducing Organizational Behaviour and Management*. London: Thomson. pp. 74–117.

References

Anand, N. and Daft, R.L. (2007) 'What is the right organization design?' *Organizational Dynamics*, 36 (4): 329–344.

Boje, D.M. and Dennehy, R.F. (2008) *Managing in the Postmodern World: America's Revolution against Exploitation*. Charlotte, NC: Information Age.

Braverman, H. (1974) *Labour and Monopoly Capital: The Degradation of Work in the Twentieth Century*. New York & London: Monthly Review Press.

Chia, R. (1999) 'A "rhizomic" model of organizational change and transformation: perspective from a metaphysics of change.' *British Journal of Management*, 10 (3): 209–227.

Cohen, M.D., March, J.G. and Olsen, J.P. (1972) 'The garbage can model of organizational choice.' *Administrative Science Quarterly*, 17 (March): 1–25.

Cray, D., Mallory, G.R., Butler, R.J., Hickson, D.J. and Wilson, D.C. (1988) 'Sporadic, fluid and constricted processes: three types of strategic decision making in organizations.' *Journal of Management Studies*, 25 (1): 13–39.

Crenson, M.A. (1971) *The Un-politics of Air Pollution: A Study of Non-Decision Making in the Cities*. Balitmore, MD: Johns Hopkins.

Fiedler, F.E. (1967) *A Theory of Leadership Effectiveness*. New York: McGraw-Hill.

Fielder, F.E. (1993) 'The leadership situation and the black box in contingency theories.' In M.M. Chemers and R. Ayman (eds), *Leadership Theory and Research: Perspectives and Directions*. New York: Academic.

Flyvbjerg, B. (1998) *Rationality and Power: Democracy in Practice*. Chicago: University of Chicago Press.

Goleman, D. (1996) *Emotional Intelligence*. London: Bloomsbury.

Greenleaf, R. (1977) *Servant Leadership: A Journey into the Nature of Legitimate Power and Greatness*. New Jersey: Paulist.

Hammer, M. and Champy, J. (1993) *Reengineering the Corporation: A Manifesto for Business Revolution*. New York: Harper Business.

Hersey, P. and Blanchard, K.H. (1988) *Management of Organizational Behaviour: Utilizing Human Resources*. Englewood Cliffs, NJ: Prentice-Hall.

Hickson, D.J., Butler, R.J., Cray, D., Mallory, G.R. and Wilson, D.C. (1986) *Top Decisions: Strategic Decision-making in Organizations*. Oxford: Blackwell.

Hickson, D.J., Butler, R.J., Cray, D., Mallory, G.R. and Wilson, D.C. (2000) *The Bradford Studies of Strategic Decision-making*. San Francisco: Jossey-Bass.

(Continued)

(Continued)

Hickson, D.J., Miller, S.J. and Wilson, D.C. (2003) 'Planned or prioritized? Two options in managing the implementation of strategic decisions.' *Journal of Management Studies*, 40 (7): 1803–1836.

Hofstede, G. (1991) *Cultures and Organizations*. London: McGraw-Hill.

Hofstede, G. (2003) *Culture's Consequences: Comparing Values, Behaviours, Institutions and Organizations across Nations*. Thousand Oaks, CA: Sage.

Hofstede, G. and Bond, M. (1988) 'The Confucian connection: from cultural roots to economic growth.' *Organizational Dynamics*, 16 (4): 4–21.

House, R., Hanges, P.J., Javidan, M., Dorfman, P.W. and Gupta, V. (2004) *Culture, Leadership and Organizations: The GLOBE Study of 62 Societies*. Thousand Oaks, CA: Sage.

Interbrand [online] (2011) www.interbrand.com/en/best-global-brands/Best-Global-Brands-2010.aspx. Accessed 07 March 2011.

Kotter, J. (1995) 'Leading change: why transformation efforts fail.' *Harvard Business Review*, 73 (2): 59–67.

Lewin, K. (1951) *Field Theory in Social Science, Selected Theoretical Papers*. Edited by Cartwright, D. New York: Harper and Row.

Linstead, S., Fulop, L. and Lilley, S. (2004) *Management and Organization: A Critical Text*. Hampshire: Palgrave Macmillan.

Miller, S., Wilson, D. and Hickson, C. (2004) 'Beyond planning: strategies for successfully implementing strategic decisions.' *Long Range Planning*, 37 (3): 201–218.

Mintzberg, H. (1983) *Structure in Fives: Designing Effective Organizations*. Englewood Cliffs, NJ: Prentice-Hall.

Pettigrew, A. and Whipp, R. (1993) *Managing Change for Competitive Success*. Oxford: Blackwell.

Sewell, G. (1998) 'The discipline of team: the control of team-based industrial work through electronic and peer surveillance.' *Administrative Science Quarterly*, 43 (2): 397–429.

Simon, H.A. (1960) *The New Science of Management Decision*. New York: Harper and Row.

Trompenaars, F. and Hampden-Turner, C. (2006) *Riding the Waves of Culture*. London: Nicholas Brealey.

Tsoukas, H. and Chia, R. (2002) 'On organizational becoming: rethinking organizational change.' *Organization Science*, 13 (5): 567–582.

Waldman, D.A., Sully de Luque, M., Washburn, N. and House, R.J. (2006) 'Cultural and leadership predictors of corporate social responsibility values of top management: a GLOBE study of 15 countries.' *Journal of International Business Studies*, 37 (6): 823–837.

Watson, T.J. (1994) *In Search of Management, Culture, Chaos and Control in Managerial Work*. London: Routledge.

Weick, K. (1995) *Sensemaking in Organizations*. Thousand Oaks, CA: Sage.

3 Human Resource Management

Key concepts

Human Resource Management (HRM); Labour power; Performance; Personnel management; The employment relationship

The chapter offers an introduction to key issues relating to the theory and practice of HRM. All organizations are typically involved in employment management, employing individuals to carry our designated tasks. This is not however always a straightforward managerial activity and needs to be understood as a socio-economic and political process. The chapter will therefore discuss some of the key issues involved in understanding this process.

By the end of this chapter the reader should be able to:

- Define HRM
- Appreciate the difference between personnel management and HRM
- Understand some of the debates relating to HRM and strategy

- Understand the perspectives on the employment relationship
- Appreciate the multi-dimensional character of the employment relationship
- Appreciate some of the critical commentaries on HRM

The chapter is structured as follows. The following section highlights the on-going importance of HRM as an organizational activity. The chapter then provides a discussion around what HRM is, together with some of the key associated practices. There is then a short discussion which traces the historical development of personnel management and HRM within the UK. Following this the debate around the difference between personnel management and HRM is described. The chapter then proceeds to identify some of the approaches that have been advanced which link HRM and organizational performance and to analyze the nature of the employment relationship. The latter includes a short discussion of the main perspectives on the employment relationship. This is followed by an overview focussed on the character of the employment relationship. Finally, there is a short discussion of some critical commentaries on HRM.

The Importance of Human Resource Management

Human Resource Management (HRM) as an area of managerial practice continues to evolve and change. This is, in part, due to its situated nature within an external context comprising those economic, political, technological, social and environmental influences which affect organizations and the people who work within them. This has of course been particularly pronounced over the last few years as the global financial crisis has had a profound effect – for example, on the numbers of people employed in organizations, on the regulatory responses by government which can impact on how people are managed, on the pay and rewards which individuals receive and on individuals' feelings of job security. More broadly the last couple of decades have been characterized as a period of globalization in which we have seen changes in terms of scale and interdependency (Morgan, 2010). This has impacted on business in a number of ways. For example, Brawley (2003) claims that economic globalization has resulted in a number of significant changes. These include international markets and products becoming more interdependent; a change in the nature of goods traded; the movement of factors of production from one country to another; the integration of financial markets; more fluid international capital flows; the creation of a global market; and changes in work and employment matters.

It is predominantly the last of these which has the greatest resonance within HRM and it is certainly the case that the last couple of decades have resulted in a variety of changes to employment processes and practices. For example, there has been a significant increase in the levels of global outsourcing (Contractor et al., 2010) and advances in information technologies which have enabled the globalization of service work (Batt et al., 2009). It has also been claimed that organizational hierarchies have reduced, that there is a greater emphasis on flexible working, and that many organizations have implemented numerous change programmes, including quality initiatives, new **performance** management systems, culture change initiatives and new reward management systems. These changes are both a private and public sector phenomenon. Each of these as well as other such pressures prompt an on-going requirement to reflect on and consider the nature of HRM.

What is HRM?

HRM, in the vast majority of organizations – whether private or public sector, manufacturing or service based, small or large, Chinese or American – would include some or all of the following: the recruitment and selection of staff; training and development; performance management; reward management; career management; employee relations; health and safety; equal opportunities and diversity management; and strategic planning. For example, recruitment and selection might be concerned with ensuring high quality employees join an organization, but at a minimum cost. It might also involve the preparation of job descriptions, the use of recruitment methods such as advertisements which seek to attract appropriate candidates, and the implementation of a variety of selection methods to choose between those people attracted by the advert. Selection methods could include using interviews, assessment centres, personality tests and references. Performance management processes might be adopted to ensure an integrated approach to how employee performance is managed. These will typically involve some form of assessment which will determine whether, for example, any agreed objectives have been met. This might be conducted through an annual appraisal interview, in which a manager and employee will engage in a dialogue with the purpose of both evaluating an individual's performance and attempting to aid their future development. Finally, reward management is concerned with both financial and non-financial rewards and benefits. It is of course one of the most controversial aspects of HRM as many individuals might be extrinsically motivated to work on the basis of how much reward they will receive.

   In terms of all these different HR practices, we could analyze organizations to see whether, how and why they might undertake some or all of these activities. For example, one organization may pay above a specific hourly wage rate simply because there is minimum wage legislation in existence, while another might pay above what they apparently need to, but will do so as part of a broader strategy to enhance organizational commitment. However, as with any organizational phenomenon there is a lexicon or language which we first need to appreciate in order to understand how the thing in question has developed. Indeed where HRM is concerned discussion of the language of HRM has been an on-going issue, as over the years many writers have noted that the term 'HRM' is often confusing and ambiguous. One reason for this (as noted by Karen Legge some time ago) is that 'In the last ten years, in both the UK and USA, the vocabulary for managing the employment relationship has undergone a change' (1995: 62). Thus, over the decades we have witnessed the use of such terms as 'personnel administration', '**personnel management**', 'human resource management' and, more recently, 'strategic human resource management'. Alongside this, and related to HRM, we have also seen use of the terms 'industrial relations', 'employee relations' and 'employment management'. In a similar vein Watson has written that, 'we have to come to terms with the rather messy situation that currently exists whereby the term "human resource management" is used in a confusing variety of ways' (2006: 404). Watson contends that such ambiguity and confusion are a result of the different ways in which the term 'HRM' is used. These include the following: as a catch-all phrase which brings together personnel management, industrial relations and aspects of organization behaviour; as a reference to any managerial work which concerns employees; as a re-labelling of what was more commonly referred to as personnel management. Much of this is encapsulated in discussions around the historical development of personnel management and in the debate relating to whether and if so how HRM differed from personnel management.

The Development of HRM in the UK

In relation to the historical development of personnel management and HRM in the UK, Torrington et al. (2005) contend that personnel management and HRM have historically developed through five related themes: social justice; human bureaucracy; negotiated consent; organization; and human resource management (a more detailed description and discussion of the management of human resources can be found in Gospel, 2010). The social justice theme emanated from the activities of such nineteenth-century social reformers as Robert Owen and Lord Shaftesbury who were concerned with reforming and improving factory working conditions. This led to some factory owners appointing the first personnel managers who were focussed on improving workers' conditions of employment. Welfare officers then followed in some of the larger employers such as Cadbury, Rowntree and Lever Brothers. It would be wrong however to view such action only from an ethical perspective.

We need also to appreciate that these appointments, and any improvements which followed, had a business-case rationale as well: treat your staff decently and they will be more committed, more productive, and less likely to engage in acts of misbehaviour. The second theme of humane bureaucracy involved a shift towards organizational concerns that went beyond welfare matters. As organizations grew personnel management was re-focused on the administration of the employment relationship – changing the paternalistic emphasis into an organizational one. Personnel management became focussed on recruitment and selection, training and organizational design, with all of this designed to match workers' needs with the organization's objectives. Efficiency became a hallmark of personnel management and the influence of F.W. Taylor (1856–1915) was pronounced (see Chapter 2), although eventually the human relations school's approach to fostering social relationships through the work of Elton Mayo (1880–1949) would also prove to be influential. The post-Second World War period was characterized by the third theme of negotiated consent. This involved a context of full employment resulting in a scarcity of labour and growth in trade union membership.

Personnel management therefore became involved in the new collective institutions which many organizations had established. These included collective bargaining machinery between management and trade unions, and joint consultative committees. From the late 1960s onwards, the organization theme was to become established as personnel management became more integrated with managerial activities such as workforce planning. Other emerging issues at this point included equal pay.

In arguing that the next theme was HRM, Torrington et al. (2005) are not claiming that each theme superseded the other completely. Instead elements of all the themes are still evident in contemporary employment management. However, when taken together the first four themes seemed to result in a stereotype which projected personnel management as operational, conflict-oriented, specialist, compliance-driven, bureaucratic, and reactive. HRM, on the other hand, seemed to offer a discourse which reflected a proactive, strategic, integrative, and managerialist activity that was aimed at enhancing organizational performance. Initially this was associated with the work of such US academics as Fombrun et al. (1984) and Beer et al. (1984). Such work recast the employment management, the nature of work, and how to maximize employee potential. Throughout the 1980s, as the label 'HRM' began to replace 'personnel management' and 'industrial relations', there emerged something of an HRM bandwagon; new academic journals were introduced; professorial chairs in HRM (where there had never been a professorial chair in personnel management in the UK) became commonplace in many UK universities; and many organizations renamed their departments and practitioners as HR departments and HR managers/officers. These changes also ran in tandem with debates about whether or not and if so to what extent HRM was different to personnel management.

Personnel Management and HRM

According to Legge (1995), HRM was different to personnel management since it was focussed on the development of the organization's management, emphasized line management, and was concerned with the management of organization culture. As Legge wrote, 'These three differences in emphasis all point to HRM, in theory, being essentially a more central strategic management task than personnel management in that it is experienced by managers, as the most valued company resource to be managed, it concerns them in the achievement of business goals and expresses senior management's preferred organizational values' (1995: 75). While not suggesting that there was consensus, in the late 1980s and early 1990s the difference between PM and HRM seemed to relate to the following:

- HRM was more employer-centred than **personnel management**
- There was a strategic, integrative dimension to HRM
- HRM was more individualistic than collectivist
- HRM viewed core employees as social capital whose value could enhance the organization
- HRM was concerned with the development of strong corporate values and culture

A further important point concerning the rise of HRM was that it was typically situated within the context of the rise of the 'New Right' in countries such as the UK and the USA, and associated with the governments of Margaret Thatcher and Ronald Reagan. Amongst other things this 'New Right' was associated with neo-liberal economic policies and social conservatism (Gamble, 1994). Related to• this was the rise of a managerialist discourse which it has been argued mutually interacted with the radical political agenda of the New Right (Clarke and Newman, 1997).

The academic debate concerning the differences between personnel management and HRM can certainly be seen as a distraction. As Storey (2007) implies it is possible to get overly fixated with some kind of essential definition. Instead, as he points out, the term 'HRM' has since its earliest appearance always been used in two different ways: as a generic term to denote any approach to the management of labour; and as a more specific term denoting a particular form of employment management. Gospel (2010) makes a similar point in his historical perspective on HRM when he distinguishes between human resources management (in lower case) and Human Resources Management (in upper case). The former, he contends, 'has been an eternal phenomenon in all organizations over time' (2010: 12); the latter he views as a term which has a shorter time span, having developed over the last few decades. This capitalized, more recent use of the term is viewed by Storey as distinctive and is defined by him as, 'a distinctive approach to employment management which seeks to achieve competitive advantage through the strategic development of a highly committed and capable workforce, using an array of cultural, structural and personnel techniques' (2007: 7). In earlier work Storey (1992) drew this distinction principally around four general dimensions: beliefs and assumptions; strategic aspects; line management; and key levers. For example, the beliefs and assumptions of HRM de-emphasized conflict, were unitarist, valued flexibility and commitment, and aimed for workers to go 'beyond contract'. The strategic aspects meant that initiatives were integrated, the corporate plan was central to the development of HR policies, and the key relations were not between workers and management, but between the organization and its customers. While line management would have a greater role in HR matters, the key levers for managing the employment relationship would include the following: a wide-range of cultural and personnel strategies; performance-related payment systems; individually based employment contracts; teamworking; and a marginalization of trade unions.

Whether we favour referring to HRM as a generic or a specific approach to employment management, as Storey writes, 'Both forms are defensible and both are in current use. Each form of use has its merits and each has its limitations' (2007: 6). However, for the purposes of an introductory chapter such as this the following definition is put forward as offering a clear sense of what the label 'HRM' signifies. As Watson stated it is:

> **HRM** is that part of managerial work which is concerned with acquiring, developing and dispensing with the efforts, skills and capabilities of an organization's workforce and maintaining organizational relationships within which these human resources can be utilised to enable the organization to continue into the future. (Watson 2006: 453)

This definition allows us to appreciate HRM in either a generic or a specific sense of the term. It also seems to acknowledge implicitly Schiappa's (2003) point that definitions may report either a real definition or a fact of usage. The one above from Watson can also be adopted in relation to understanding the employment management practices of organizations, whether these encompass a small newsagent's shop or a large global retail organization such as WalMart or Tesco. The small newsagent may have relatively unsophisticated human resource practices, which might have begun with staff recruitment through word-of-mouth, training being limited to on-the-job instructions, and payment set at the minimum wage rate. The likes of Tesco, on the other hand, might have adopted a sophisticated array of human resource policies, procedures and practices. These could vary depending on the individual being hired, trained and performance managed, but ultimately – as with the newsagent – they will be utilized to ensure the organization continues in the future. Thus to subsume a small newsagent and a retail giant within the parameters of a common definition is not to imply that there is not huge variation in their approach to HRM. It only contends that the definition above can help us move beyond the miasma of definitional disputes, allowing us in the process to acknowledge a generality to employment management, but at the same time being able to see the possibility of particularity whether at a geographical, sectoral, industrial or organizational level.

HRM and Organizational Performance

While Torrington et al.'s (2005) thematic imaging of UK personnel management contended that HRM was the most recent such image, the notion of strategic HRM (SHRM) has now also become a common label. In this regard, many areas of managerial activity have been accorded the designation 'strategic'. Today we seem to have a plethora of specifically designated strategic activities, including strategic marketing, strategic management accounting, strategic information systems, strategic innovation, and global strategic management. The breadth and ubiquity of the use of the term 'strategic' supports Carter et al.'s (2010) argument that strategy has indeed become the master discourse of the last 30 years. In the context of HRM, the main impetus for importing the master discourse of strategy is in order to stress that the employment relationship should (and can) be managed in a manner which optimally contributes to the achievement of an organization's goals and objectives. Strategic

HRM therefore links to the growing interest in business strategy that has been instigated in part by changes to the environment in which organizations are located.

The best-practice approach

In examining links between HRM, strategy and organization performance, Boxall and Purcell (2003) identified two main approaches: best practice and best fit. These two approaches differ in terms of their broad approach, with the former being universalistic and the latter contingent. In saying that the best-practice model is universalistic, the claim is that a series of HR practices are appropriate for all organizations, irrespective of their sector or geographical location. Employees, it is contended, are a key source of competitive advantage since they can enable an organization to innovate and adapt to changed environmental conditions. While there is no agreement over which HR practices should be adopted to allow this to happen, there is some agreement around having policies promoting autonomy, commitment and participation. A number of writers have therefore advocated a 'bundle' of HR practices which when combined will have a significant impact on performance (Huselid, 1995; MacDuffie, 1995). Clearly such bundles should be complementary otherwise they will risk producing what Delery (1998) has referred to as a 'deadly combination'. For example, combining a production system based around teams and an individual performance pay system may, as Delery (1998) suggests, undermine the team concept on the basis that such practices might not fit coherently since an individual performance pay system may undermine the cohesion of a team by generating negative intra-team competition. In Delery's terms these practices would not support and enhance each other.

One well-known example of the best practice approach can be seen in work by Pfeffer (1998) who provides a list of seven HR practices which he contends all successful organizations should have. In exhorting employers to adopt high-cost, high-skill employment policies he suggests they utilize: employment security, selective hiring, self managed teams, high pay based on organizational performance, extensive training, a reduction of status differences, and extensive information sharing. While research in this area has claimed to show an association between HR practices and organizational performance (Huselid, 1995; Huselid and Becker, 1996), there have been major criticisms levelled at such research. For example, Kinnie and Swart (2009) outlined a number of methodological and theoretical problems associated with such types of research. In relation to methodological problems they asked about the line or direction of causality, i.e. is it the HR practices which cause successful organizations or is it that already successful organizations can afford to have advanced HR practices? Likewise they asked whether performance measures which were typically based on financial criteria, excluding employee attitudes and wellbeing, were appropriate. As such research is typically based around self-completed surveys, Kinnie and Swart also highlighted the potential problem of mis-reporting by single respondents who completed the survey for their organization but who may also not have possessed an adequate awareness of the extent and use of their organization's HR practices.

In terms of theoretical problems, Kinnie and Swart identified a number of potential problems, including a very basic question – who is the best practice for? For example, Marchington and Grugelis in their critique of 'best practice' HRM argued that, 'In all of the persuasive rhetoric on "best practice" HRM, one element is noticeable by its absence – independent employee voice' (2000: 1119). Thus in their critique of Pfeffer (1998) they argue, *inter alia*, that his work does not acknowledge that within the employment relationship the interests of employees might diverge from those of their managers. They also highlight the 'potential contradiction between [the] nice words and harsh realities' (Marchington and Grugelis, 2000: 1109) within each of Pfeffer's list of HR practices, arguing that these are not necessarily as positive as best practice advocates imply. For example, team working might enhance managerial control rather than extend any power to employees (Chapter 2 also discusses this point), while information sharing might simply be top-down management communication with little meaningful employee involvement.

Kinnie and Swart (2009) then note further theoretical problems including the fact that different writers have included other practices in their lists, thereby begging the question as to which are best at inducing improved performance. It can also be argued that since many of the studies which exhort a 'best-practice' approach are US-based then we can question the degree to which their claims around universality are appropriate. For example, many US studies ignore the significance of trade unions which still feature as a central aspect within many Western European approaches to employment management. However, amongst the various criticisms made of the best-practice approach, perhaps the most telling is that whatever the flaws within it, 'A key question, especially for policy makers and practitioners, however, remains the need to understand why relatively few firms adopt such measures rather than become mired in a debate about the precise HR practices which constitute best practice' (Bach, 2005: 9).

The best-fit approach

The second approach which Boxall and Purcell (2003) identified was best-fit. As a contingent approach, the focus here is on environmental 'fit'. The context in which an organization is situated is therefore the significant feature in terms of how HR practices link to strategy. The best-fit approach is concerned with ensuring that the organization's array of HR practices 'fit' with the environment. Unlike best practice it is therefore a contingency approach in which the underpinning viewpoint is that an organization's HR practices are contingent on the kind of business conditions which the organization faces. As with best practice there is an assertion that HR practices and competitive advantage are linked – however, the nature of these HR practices is here contingent upon what circumstances an individual organization faces. A number of factors will therefore influence choosing those HR practices which will best 'fit' with the organization's environment. These could encompass the organization's product market, size and technology, as well as the employees' characteristics in terms of skills and knowledge. Referred to as 'matching models', two approaches can be identified.

The first – the business life-cycle approach – as suggested by its name, links HR practices to an organization's stage of development (Kochan and Barocci, 1985). In this approach an organization in its earliest phase of development would be seen to require different HR practices from those an organization in a decline phase of development would need. During the earliest phase HR practices might have to be flexible enough to encourage enterprise and creativity. When in decline redundancy and reducing the headcount may be the major HRM challenge. The second best-fit approach links HR practices within the organization to how the organization achieves its competitive advantage. One such example of this can be seen in work by Schuler and Jackson (1987) that was based around Porter's (1985) three strategic options for gaining competitive advantage – innovation, quality enhancement, and cost reduction. When linked to the HR strategy each has a set of employee role behaviours and HR policies. For example, a strategy of quality enhancement may have expected employee role behaviours which show a high concern for quality. In order to ensure such behaviours there would be a need for such HR practices as extensive and continuous training and development. The central claim here would then be that the business performance would improve due to the HR practices mutually reinforcing the quality enhancement strategy.

A number of criticisms have been levelled against contingency approaches. Gilmore (2009) summarizes a number of these, including the point that there is a tendency towards over-simplifying the manner in which a competitive strategy is defined. Here it might be argued that firms do not fit neatly into one of Porter's three strategic choices. Hence HR practices cannot be simply related to one of these. Companies might pursue a number of different strategies that would then lead to some confusion as to which HR practices would be most appropriate. The environmental uncertainty in which many organizations operate might also entail needing to ensure that they have suitable employees whose knowledge and skills can meet what might be unknown business challenges. Finally, and in a similar vein to the criticisms made against the best-practice approach, the best-fit approach it is argued also overlooks employee interests and does not give consideration to how an organization can align itself with the employee whose knowledge and skills are central to its survivability. As Gilmore writes, 'this does not undermine the idea of a fit existing between business strategy and HRM, but it does reassert the claim that, whilst HRM supports the attainment of the company's competitive goals, it also has to meet employee needs and comply with social and legal requirements for the management of staff' (2009: 36). Such a point suggests that there is a need to locate our understanding of HRM much more within the context of the employment relationship.

The Employment Relationship

While the best-practice and best-fit approaches continue to attract much research and there have been attempts to reconcile them (Legge, 2005), we can see both have been criticized in relation to the **employment relationship**. To remind ourselves of this, both Marchington and Grugelis (2000) and Gilmore (2009) have highlighted how best practice and best fit ignore or diminish the role of employees within the employment relationship. However, this is not an entirely uncommon phenomenon within the mainstream HRM literature. For example, Keenoy (2009) is strongly critical of the manner in which the academic analysis associated with HRM has tended to progressively marginalize theories which emphasize the conflict-based nature of the employment relationship. More broadly we can also say the employment relationship does not feature significantly as a central topic for discussion within the mainstream HRM literature. This is evident after even the most cursory of glances through the main UK and US textbooks, which while they may debate the psychological contract, often at best relegate any discussion of the employment relationship to a single chapter on employee relations. More typical, any study of the employment relationship is left to texts on industrial or employment relations, as though the employment relationship is not central to the academic analysis of HRM. Such a closure of this subject matter, it can be argued, is suggestive of HRM having only a managerialist orientation as opposed to reflecting a broader sense of the employment relationship as an exchange relationship between owners/managers and employees. In this section it is therefore argued that for HRM to avoid the charge of only having a narrow sectional managerialist orientation, discussion of the employment relationship should be a central topic. After all, as Legge puts it, HRM 'is about the management of the employment relationship and the indeterminacies in the employment contract' (2005: 220).

Perspectives on the Employment Relationship

As was noted, one of the criticisms which Marchington and Grugelis (2000) made of Pfeffer's (1998) work was that it was unitarist. They also approvingly cited Boxall (1996), who argued that 'existing notions of internal and external fit in the strategic HRM literature do not amount to a theorization of the employment relationship because they merely prescribe an elegant alignment of managerial practices in a unitary conception of the firm. Much more difficult, and more apposite, is the question of how to achieve at least a minimal alignment of interests in a pluralistic conception of the firm' (1996: 68, quoted in Marchington and Grugelis, 2000: 1119). Amongst other things, such criticism points to an overly narrow conceptualization of the employment relationship through viewing it only through the lens of a unitarist perspective. This is an important point because while the employment relationship is an exchange relationship between employers/managers and employees, how this relationship is perceived can vary. Thus it is possible to adopt a different frame of reference or set of beliefs as to how the employment relationship should be managed (Fox, 1974).

As discussed by Fox, the three perspectives are the unitary, the pluralist, and the radical. The unitary viewpoint sees no distinction or difference between the interests of management and employees. It does not consider conflict to be a natural phenomenon in relations between these two parties. Where there is conflict it considers this to be pathological or a result of poor management communication. Trade unions are treated or viewed as an intrusion into employer/employee relations. It is also contended that the authority of management should not be questioned and opposition to it is deemed as deviant or irrational. In contending that the unitarist perspective is ideological in character, Fox notes that it serves three purposes: 'it is at once a method of self-assurance, an instrument of persuasion, and a technique of seeking legitimation of authority' (1966, quoted in Flanders, 1969: 395). The main criticism of unitarism is that it is ideological and does not represent reality. However, as has been made evident in numerous surveys many managers hold unitary views in relation to how they would prefer to manage and regulate employment relationships (Blyton and Turnbull, 2004). As a result many managers will stress common objectives and shared goals and interests between employers and employees. A unitarist perspective is also held to underpin many of the developments associated with change in the workplace over the last couple of decades, including the rise of individualized forms of employee involvement and individual performance-related payment systems. Returning to the criticism that Pfeffer's best-practice HRM is unitarist, the point of such criticism is that such conceptions of HRM assume an homogeneity of interests between management and employees. So whatever is best for managers must also be best for the employees since there is no inherent antagonism within employment relationships.

Contrary to unitarism, a pluralist frame of reference does not view conflict as pathological or deviant. This is predicated on the basis that since we live in a society of plural and competing interests and outlooks, then this will be reflected in the workplace (Clegg, 1975). Consequently within employment relationships there will be a basic antagonism between employers and employees. However, while conflict will therefore be a distinct possibility, a central concern of those holding a pluralist viewpoint is to ensure the management of conflict in order to avoid too much disruption. From the pluralist perspective, trade unions are therefore viewed as a legitimate representative of employee interests and the anticipated outcome from the legitimate expression of organized interests is a 'negotiated order' (Blyton and Turnbull, 2004). Therefore to an extent the emphasis is on the development and utilization of procedures as mechanisms for conflict resolution. These would include collective bargaining machinery or other joint management–employee processes which would be premised on the understanding that the interests of the two sides are not the same, hence they need to be resolved through the establishment of appropriate joint arrangements.

Finally, the radical perspective was developed as a critique to pluralism's reformism and apparent unjustified optimism in improving employees' conditions. That is, there was an assumption that joint mechanisms of conflict resolution could and would resolve the antagonisms between the parties to the employment relationship. While this perspective shares with pluralism a view of the employment relationship as conflictual, the radical analysis is much more fundamentally rooted within the economic and political structure of society (Hyman, 1975). The employment relationship will therefore be reflective of exploitative and asymmetrical social relations. The radical perspective would contend that in relation to unitarism and pluralism, the power disparities between management and employees will not be addressed or changed. The other perspectives would also be labelled as ideologically conservative, that is, their intent is to uphold or retain the status quo. Even pluralism's acknowledgement of the inevitability of conflict through the establishment of jointly agreed conflict resolution mechanisms does not really challenge the balance of power.

Understanding the Employment Relationship

The existence of different perspectives to understanding the employment relationship is important for appreciating that there are a variety of ways in which we can grasp the nature of the relationship between the buyers and sellers of labour. However, whatever our perspective, at its core the employment relationship is an exchange relationship between these buyers and sellers of labour (Coyle-Shapiro and Conway, 2004). The employment relationship is therefore the relationship which such HR practices as recruitment and selection, training and development, performance appraisal, reward management, and employee involvement are all directed towards modifying, improving or maintaining. The use and configuration of such HR practices may well be oriented towards heightening employee commitment and improving organizational performance. However, particular HR practices may exist or be introduced simply to ensure that an organization meets the legal obligations which organizations in many countries are expected to comply with. Particular HR practices, while locally mediated by managers and employees, may therefore exist because they have to according to the grounds of external imposition. While this external imposition could include trade unions being able to challenge management to introduce or extend forms of employee participation and involvement in order to change the balance of power within a workplace, statutory obligation is obviously a major external pressure which will shape what occurs within an employment relationship.

This point is significant since at the heart of the employment relationship is a contract of employment which establishes a variety of rights and responsibilities on the part of both buyer and seller. Such rights and responsibilities are central to employment management irrespective as to whether we label it HRM, SHRM, high commitment management, human capital management or whatever. Although different legal systems may extend different employment rights to different categories such that employees might have more extensive rights than contractors, many countries have a range of individual and collective employment laws relating to, for example, pay, maternity and paternity rights, hours of work, holiday, non-discriminatory treatment, trade union recognition, notice periods and employment protection. Among these are the laws protecting employees from discriminatory practices, including *The Labor Contract Law of the People's Republic of China* (2008), the USA's *Civil Rights Act* (1964), and the UK's *Disability Discrimination Act* (1995). For the member countries of the European Union there is also legislation which covers equal treatment, health and safety, and working time (see for example Taylor and Emir, 2009). A legal understanding of the employment relationship can therefore help us appreciate the terms on which exchange is founded. However, while statutory rights and duties do play an important role in understanding the employment relationship, we also need to appreciate that they do not encompass every aspect of the employment relationship. Thus while they have been argued to be the 'cornerstone' (Kahn-Freund, 1954) of this relationship this is still much more multi-dimensional and we should avoid conflating the legal with the whole of the employment relationship.

The notion that this is more than simply a legal relationship is evident when, for example, it is referred to as a 'wage-effort bargain' (Baldamus, 1961). While such a term might be labelled today as a 'reward-effort bargain', it can help us appreciate that the employment relationship is wide-ranging and dynamic. Because of this, the distribution of economic resources, the various power resources at people's disposal, and the structures in which the employment relationship operates, can all be influential in helping us understand, for example, why a group of workers might decide to engage in industrial action or why a manager may find it difficult to gain worker cooperation towards some new initiative. As a purely legal explanation would be insufficient we therefore need to appreciate that while the employment relationship is legally constituted it is also an economic relationship, one involving power and authority, and there is a psychological dimension to it as well.

In acknowledging that the employment relationship has an economic dimension and exists within the context of a 'wage-effort bargain', the point is made that employees must sell their labour for some reward. This could be monetary, social or psychological. The employer, on the other hand, is in the position of buying labour in order to transform it so that it produces value in the form of goods or services which can then be sold, usually to make a profit. As Blyton and Turnbull put it, 'At its most basic level, every employment relationship is an *economic exchange*, an agreement between employer and employee over the sale of the latter's capacity to work' (2004: 38). As these writers put it, this is commonly referred to as **labour power** (i.e. an individual's capacity to work) and it is this which the employer purchases, even though the employer's main interest is in the performance of work, for example, physical and mental labour. Although the state of a labour market will influence the price paid for labour power, other factors such as statutory obligations, the existence of trade unions, company profitability and technology, are also significant influences. For example, if there is minimum wage legislation, then irrespective of the state of the labour market employers will still have to meet their legal obligations. We also need to be clear that within the context of this economic exchange the two parties will not necessarily be looking for the same things and as a result their objectives can vary. Employee objectives may include job security, purchasing power, responsibility, autonomy and feelings of fairness. Employer objectives on the other hand could be lower costs, control, increasing productivity, obtaining adequate performance and employee commitment. Given that the objectives of each party can differ then there is clearly the potential here for tensions and antagonism as these give rise to conflict. Thus an employee objective of job security may conflict with an employer objective of lower costs as redundancy might always be a potential response to achieving this. Likewise the employee objective of autonomy could conflict with the employer objective of control. That conflict is an inherent dimension to the employment relationship is something which most academic writers on the subject would consider to be the case and runs contrary to a unitary perspective (Edwards, 2003).

The translation of labour power into work performance is therefore a crucial factor in terms of the success of any organization. This could be exemplified through the two ideal types of high and low commitment HR strategies (Watson, 2009). The former would involve highly engaged employees being given opportunities for long-term development with the organization, together with discretion and autonomy in relation to how tasks are carried out. A low commitment strategy would involve the utilization of employees as and when they were required; the relationship would be highly instrumental and employees would experience close monitoring and supervision. The choice of strategy here might be dependent on the degree of complexity and uncertainty within an organization. The particular employment strategy from an employee perspective might also be significant in relation to the degree to which the employee experiences dignity at work (Hodson, 2001).

While the economic aspect will often dominate, we also need to appreciate that the employment relationship involves power as well. Certainly if we acknowledge that conflict is at least a possibility within employment relationships then power is potentially ever present. Power is not an easy concept to define and has been debated for millennia. While Lukes' (1974) three-dimensional view of power is one of the most widely cited approaches to understanding power, specifically within the organizational literature, Clegg (1989) has conceptualized it in terms of circuits, while Townley (1994) has more narrowly explained power through the work of the French social theorist Michel Foucault. While we could endlessly discuss and critique the various concepts put forward, perhaps for our current purposes a more straightforward question would be this: where, in the context of employment relationships, does power emanate? And further, why would a manager have more power than an employee for example? Why would a trade union official be able to garner the loyal support of a majority of the workforce? While Kelly (1998) is right to highlight that power is often underplayed or ignored in writings on management, it is clearly a factor in the employment relationship since management often involves getting people to do things that they otherwise might choose not to do.

Similarly management often involves modifying or altering the behaviour and attitudes of others, again potentially requiring power. In terms of HRM, power seems central to such practices as performance management, the allocation of rewards, the handling of disciplinary situations, and decisions relating to the forms of employee involvement within an organization. Related to this also is authority, usually defined as legitimate power. In the context of the employment relationship, we can say that employees accept they are under some control, although that degree of control is uncertain and part of an on-going debate (Thompson and van Broek, 2010). The question of managerial authority is therefore an important one.

Finally, the employment relationship also has a psychological dimension to it. In recent years there has therefore been a burgeoning interest in what has come to be referred to as the psychological contract (Rousseau, 2004). The psychological contract is defined by Herriot as 'the perception of the two parties, employee and employer, of what their mutual obligations are towards each other. The term "psychological" distinguishes the contract from the legal contract of employment, and puts it firmly into the perceptual and social spheres of activity' (2001: 38). The nature of the psychological contract is that it is subjective, unique and idiosyncratic, and central to it are the expectations which employees have in relation to their role and what the employer will give them in return (Grant, 1999). In terms of employees, such expectations could include potentially safe and pleasant working conditions; interesting and satisfying jobs; attempts at ensuring job security, involvement or consultation; equality of opportunity; opportunities for personal development and progression; being treated with consideration and respect; and fair and equitable remuneration. Employer expectations could include a desire that employees accept the organization's main values; employee diligence and conscientiousness in pursuing objectives; employees avoiding abusing the trust and goodwill of supervisors; employee concern with the organization's reputation; loyalty and a willingness to tolerate some inconvenience for the good of the organization; trustworthiness and honesty; conformity to accepted behaviour norms; and a consideration for others (Dundon and Rollinson, 2004). Unsurprisingly, in light of the changed environment in which organizations are now situated, it is often commented upon that there have been changes to the psychological contract (Torrington et al., 2005).

Research into the psychological contract has also included work into how this is shaped by past and current employment experiences, as well as by the nature of managerial rhetoric (Grant, 1999). The key point about rhetoric is that it is concerned with the process of persuasion and the generation of identification (Hamilton, 2001). In the context of establishing a positive psychological contract it is therefore crucial that management should try to match their rhetoric with the experience which employees perceive. Management must therefore strive to ensure that across their HR processes and practices they take care in relation to how they construct their talk about the experiences employees will face. The key issue here could be avoiding heightening those expectations which are unlikely to be met or are simply unattainable. The benefits that are considered to flow from a managerial consideration of employees' psychological contracting with the organization include the following: it generates a sense of agency; it develops a degree of confidence and trust; it can ensure that employees will be personally motivated as their personal needs are met; and the employer benefits from having responsible and committed employees.

Amongst other things this section of the chapter has attempted to convey is a sense of the employment relationship as not simply a formal, legal relationship. Instead it is multi-dimensional. It is composed of a number of different dimensions which need to be appreciated and understood before we can really comprehend the dilemmas, tensions, contradictions and difficulties that may arise in the context of employment management.

Critical Perspectives on HRM

The most obvious point to make in the context of discussing a critical perspective on HRM or employment management is that we should avoid attempting to justify a perspective which tries to acknowledge and/or marginalize employee interests. Whether the interests of managers and employees are the same might be an empirical question which robust research can address. However, it is not something that should simply be assumed into existence. There are instead powerful arguments which point to employment management and therefore HRM being required to be understood in light of an unevenly balanced economic exchange, asymmetrical power relations, and complex psychological processes. There are also important broader points raised, for example, by Bolton and Houlihan (2007) that whatever the rhetorical thrust of HRM, claims to be an employee champion have simply not materialized. Instead employees are treated as part of the balance sheet. In their search for the missing human side to HRM they write that, 'the rich, warm and unpredictable faces of humanity are all too clearly absent' (2007: 1). Their discussion, amongst other things, raises important questions around the way in which economic and financial imperatives can diminish the sense and possibility of attaining an employee beneficial employment relationship and an enlightened form of HRM. Any critical perspective on HRM and employment management therefore needs to be attuned to the socio-political aspects of what is only partly an economic exchange.

Karen Legge (2005), one of the leading critical HRM scholars, provides us here with a critical analysis that is beyond the economic. In examining critical perspectives on HRM practices she has produced a review which examines, at a micro level, the experience of those who work under new work regimes. Specifically the focus rests on employees' experiences of lean production and teamworking, and their impact on identity. The context for Legge's discussion is the influence of Japanese production methods in light of the country's economic success in the 1980s. One effect of this was a celebratory rhetoric around Japanese production systems and especially in the form of lean production. Such celebratory rhetoric had clear unitarist assumptions, falling into the trap of yet again ignoring or downplaying employees' interests in the employment relationship. And here again were instances of claims that production techniques and HR practices inducing commitment would be associated with improved organizational performance. Legge summarizes a number of studies which examine workers' experiences in such systems. Such studies – which also tended to adopt a qualitative rather than quantitative approach – painted a picture of workers experiencing high management control, high stress, and considerable work intensification. For example, Garrahan and Stewart's (1992) study of lean production at Nissan's UK plant in Sunderland portrayed a contrasting story to that of Wickens (1987). Wickens – who had been the Personnel Director at the Nissan plant – applauded their 'tripod of success' based around flexibility, quality and team-working. Garrahan and Stewart (1992) controversially re-labelled this as a 'tripod of subjugation', equating Wickens' tripod to work intensification and stress, control and management-through-blame, and peer surveillance and compliance.

While many will simply refer to the contrast between managerial intent/promises or words as a rhetoric which contrasts with the reality as discovered by the shrewd researcher (Bach, 2005), Keenoy (2009) goes beyond such simplicities. As a result he offers us a critical account of the mainstream HRM literature through a discourse analytical focus. Such an analysis, entailing an interest in how language resources construct and re-constitute social reality, can draw out the apparent underlying assumptions within such constructions. These might include how a particular HRM discourse could exclude or marginalize. The discourse of best-practice HRM might therefore be argued to exclude employees from how it constructs an organizational reality. Amongst Keenoy's critique of mainstream HRM is the view that this is uti-lized as 'an unproblematic conceptual metaphor' (2009: 455) in relation to the range of policies and practices used to manage human resources. To Keenoy there is a danger that HRM is assumed to be about managing the human resource in a changed environmental context. Instead, drawing on the work of Jacques (1996) he argues it has much earlier origins which go back to the early part of the twentieth century. Keenoy's concern seems to be that the mainstream narrative around HRM tends to underplay or even ignore its much longer historical antecedents, as well as its destructive power in reshaping the language of employment management, but also longstanding socio-economic traditions for managing employment relation-ships. Keenoy places the discourse of HRM very much in the sort of neo-liberal context which was earlier noted as being a feature of the 'New Right'.

In advancing a discursive analysis of HRM, Keenoy (2009) also considers a search for an essential definition of HRM as unwarranted. Instead, since discourses are both historically situated and culturally conditioned, then a term such as HRM is best viewed as, 'a generic term with a range of possible culturally situated meanings' (2009: 457). Marchington and Grugelis (2000) earlier noted concern that Pfeffer's (1998) advocacy of teamwork might instead involve work intensification highlights this. Here there might be what Keenoy would consider to be a tension in the framing of HR practices and the enactment of these HR practices. Keenoy is also critical of the manner in which the academic construction of HRM took a distinctively mana-gerialist turn in prioritizing employee performativity. Specifically referencing the work of Guest (1987) and Storey (1992) he contends that their work resonates with neoliberalism and frames HRM as a prescriptive unitarist endeavour. Work by those trying to establish a link between HRM and performance, whether in the form of best practice or best fit, Keenoy views as a project with 'obvious normative appeal' (2009: 461). This we might consider paradoxical since those engaging in such research would typically view themselves and what they do as rigorous social science based on robust empirical evidence and largely devoid of a normative dimension. This becomes another criticism which Keenoy lays at the door of mainstream writings on HRM as he forwards a trenchant critique of the methodological flaws of such writings.

Summary

This chapter has introduced some of the key issues which relate to HRM. It has discussed what HRM is, as well its historical development in the UK. The chapter then examined work which links strategy, HRM and organizational performance. A number of criticisms of such work were also identified. On the basis that this work has been criticized in relation to a conceptually limited view of the employment relationship, the chapter went on to argue that HRM needs to place the employment relationship at the centre of its analysis. This is contrary to some criticism which argues that it is too narrowly focussed around managerial concerns alone, in the process ignoring or downplaying employees' role and need to be part of any analysis relating to employment management. In discussing the employment relationship the chapter focussed on the different perspectives which can help us see that the employment relationship has been argued to be a relationship in which there are tensions, contradictions and different interests on the part of employers and employees. Finally, an overview was presented which highlighted the need to understand the employment relationship as a multi-dimensional concept. It was argued that while economics matter we must also take account of power in order to understand what can and does occur within employment management.

Questions for reflection

1 Is HRM better conceptualized as a generic approach to employment management or as a distinctive approach?
2 What is the most appropriate way in which to conceptualize the link between strategy, HRM, and organizational performance?
3 Can the employment relationship ever be understood on the basis of shared interests between managers and employees or should we always assume potential conflict?
4 How can organizations reconcile the different interests between managers and employees?

Further reading

Boxall, P., Purcell, J. and Wright, P. (eds) (2008) *The Oxford Handbook of Human Resource Management*. Oxford: Oxford University Press.

Edwards, P. and Wajcman, J. (2005) *The Politics of Working Life*. Oxford: Oxford University Press.

Fleetwood, S. and Hesketh, A. (2010) *Explaining the Performance of Human Resource Management*. Cambridge: Cambridge University Press.

Martin, J. (2010) *Key Concepts in Human Resource Management*. London: Sage.

Noon, M. and Blyton, P. (2007) *The Realities of Work* (3rd edn). London: Palgrave.

Rowley, C. and Jackson, K. (2010) *Human Resource Management: The Key Concepts*. London: Routledge.

Strangleman, T. and Warren, T. (2008) *Work and Society*. London: Routledge.

References

Bach, S. (2005) 'Personnel management in transition.' In S. Bach (ed.), *Managing Human Resources* (4th edn). Oxford: Blackwell.

Baldamus, W. (1961) *Efficiency and Effort*. London: Tavistock.

Batt, R., Holman, D. and Holtgrewe, U. (2009) 'The globalization of service: comparative institutional perspectives on call centres.' *Industrial and Labor Relations Review*, 62 (4): 453–488.

Beer, M., Spector, B., Lawrence, P., Quinn Mills, D. and Walton, R. (1984) *Managing Human Assets*. New York: Free.

Blyton, P. and Turnbull, P. (2004) *The Dynamics of Employee Relations* (3rd edn). London: Macmillan.

Bolton, S. and Houlihan, M. (2007) 'Beginning the search for the H in HRM.' In S. Bolton and M. Houlihan (eds), *Searching for the Human in Human Resource Management*. London: Palgrave.

Boxall, P. (1996) 'The strategic HRM debate and the resource-based view of the firm.' *Human Resource Management Journal*, 6 (3): 59–75.

Boxall, P. and Purcell, J. (2003) *Strategy and Human Resource Management*. London: Palgrave.

Brawley, M.R. (2003) *The Politics of Globalisation*. Ontario: Broadview.

Carter, C., Clegg, S. and Kornberger, M. (2010) 'Re-framing strategy: power, politics and accounting.' *Accounting, Auditing and Accountability Journal*, 23 (5): 573–594.

Clarke, J. and Newman, J. (1997) *The Managerial State*. London: Sage.

Clegg, H. (1975) 'Pluralism in industrial relations.' *British Journal of Industrial Relations*, 13: 309–316.

Clegg, S. (1989) *Frameworks of Power*. London: Sage.

Contractor, F.J., Kumar, V., Kundu, S.K. and Pedersen, T. (2010) 'Reconceptualising the firm in a world of outsourcing and offshoring.' *Journal of Management Studies*, 47 (8): 1417–1433.

Coyle-Shapiro, J. and Conway, N. (2004) 'The employment relationship through the lens of social exchange.' In J. Coyle-Shapiro, L.M. Shore, S.M. Taylor and L. Tetrick

(Continued)

(Continued)

(eds), *The Employment Relationship: Examining Psychological and Contextual Perspectives*. Oxford: Oxford University Press.

Delery, J.E. (1998) 'Issues of fit in strategic human resource management: implications for research.' *Human Resource Management Review*, 8 (3): 289–309.

Dundon, T. and Rollinson, D. (2004) *Employment Relations in Non-Union Firms*. London: Routledge.

Edwards, P. (2003) 'The employment relationship.' In P. Edwards (ed.), *Industrial Relations: Theory and Practice* (2nd edn). Oxford: Blackwell.

Flanders, A. (ed.) (1969) *Collective Bargaining*. London: Penguin.

Fombrun, C., Tichy, N. and Devanna, M. (eds) (1984) *Strategic Human Resource Management*. New York: Wiley.

Fox, A. (1966) 'Industrial Sociology and Industrial Relations.' (Royal Commission Research Paper No. 3). London: Her Majesty's Stationary Office.

Fox, A. (1974) *Beyond Contract*. London: Faber.

Gamble, A. (1994) *The Free Economy and the Strong State*. London: Macmillan.

Garrahan, P. and Stewart, P. (1992) *The Nissan Enigma: Flexibility at Work in a Local Labour Economy*. London: Mansell.

Gilmore, S. (2009) 'The strategic dimensions of HRM.' In S. Gilmore and S. Williams (eds), *Human Resource Management*. Oxford: Oxford University Press.

Gospel, H. (2010) 'HRM: A historical perspective.' In A. Wilkinson, N. Bacon, T. Redman and S. Snell (eds), *The Sage Handbook of Human Resource Management*. London: Sage.

Grant, D. (1999) 'HRM, rhetoric and the psychological contract: a case of "easier" said than "done"'. *International Journal of Human Resource Management*, 10 (2): 327–350.

Guest, D. (1987) 'Human Resource Management and industrial relations.' *Journal of Management Studies*, 24 (5): 503–521.

Hamilton, P.M. (2001) 'Rhetoric and employment relations.' *British Journal of Industrial Relations*, 39 (3): 433–449.

Herriot, P. (2001) *The Employment Relationship: A Psychological Contract*. London: Routledge.

Hodson, R. (2001) *Dignity at Work*. Cambridge: Cambridge University Press.

Huselid, M. (1995) 'The impact of human resource management practices on turnover, productivity and corporate financial performance.' *Academy of Management Journal*, 38 (3): 635–672.

Huselid, M. and Becker, B. (1996) 'Methodological issues in cross-sectional and panel estimates of the human resource-firm performance link.' *Industrial Relations*, 35 (3): 400–422.

Hyman, R. (1975) *Industrial Relations: A Marxist Introduction*. London: Macmillan.

Jacques, R. (1996) *Manufacturing the Employee: Management Knowledge from the 19th to 21st Centuries*. London: Sage.

Kahn-Freund, O. (1954) 'Legal framework.' In A. Flanders and H. Clegg (eds), *The System of Industrial Relations in Britain*. Oxford: Blackwell.

Keenoy, T. (2009) 'Human resource management.' In M. Alvesson, T. Bridgeman and H. Willmott (eds), *The Oxford Handbook of Critical Management Studies*. Oxford: Oxford University Press.

Kelly, J. (1998) *Rethinking Industrial Relations*. London: Routledge.

(Continued)

(Continued)

Kinnie, N. and Swart, J. (2009) 'HRM and organizational performance: in search of the HR advantage.' In T. Redman and A. Wilkinson (eds), *Contemporary Human Resource Management* (3rd edn). London: Pearson.

Kochan, T. and Barocci, T. (1985) *Human Resource Management and Industrial Relations.* Boston, MA: Little, Brown.

Legge, K. (1995) *Human Resource Management: Rhetorics and Realities.* London: Macmillan.

Legge, K. (2005) 'Human resource management.' In S. Ackroyd, R. Batt, P. Thompson and P.S. Tolbert (eds), *The Oxford Handbook of Work and Organization.* Oxford: Oxford University Press.

Lukes, S. (1974) *Power: A Radical View.* London: Macmillan.

MacDuffie, J.P. (1995) 'Human resource bundles and manufacturing performance: organizational logic and flexible production systems in the world auto industry.' *Industrial and Labor Relations Review,* 48 (2): 197–221.

Marchington, M. and Grugelis, I. (2000) 'Best practice human resource management: perfect opportunity or dangerous illusion?' *International Journal of Human Resource Management,* 11 (6): 1104–1124.

Morgan, G. (2010) 'Globalization.' In P. Hancock and A. Spicer (eds), *Understanding Corporate Life.* London: Sage.

Pfeffer, J. (1998) *The Human Equation: Building Profits Through People.* Boston, MA: Harvard Business School Press.

Porter, M. (1985) *Competitive Advantage: Creating and Sustaining Superior Performance.* New York: Free.

Rousseau, D. (2004) 'Psychological contracts in the workplace.' *Academy of Management Executive,* 18 (1): 120–127.

Schiappa, E. (2003) *Defining Reality: Definitions and the Politics of Meaning.* Southern Illinois University Press.

Schuler, R. and Jackson, S. (1987) 'Linking competitive strategies and human resource management practices.' *Academy of Management Executive,* 1 (3): 207–219.

Storey, J. (1992) *Developments in the Management of Human Resources.* Oxford: Blackwell.

Storey, J. (2007) 'Human resource management today: an assessment.' In J. Storey (ed.), *Human Resource Management: A Critical Text.* London: Thompson.

Taylor, S. and Emir, A. (2009) *Employment Law* (2nd edn). Oxford: Oxford University Press.

Thompson, P. and van den Broek, D. (2010) 'Managerial control and workplace regimes.' *Work, Employment and Society,* 24 (3): 1–12.

Torrington, D., Hall, L. and Taylor, S. (2005) *Human Resource Management.* London: Prentice-Hall.

Townley, B. (1994) *Reframing Human Resource Management.* London: Sage.

Watson, T.J. (2006) *Organizing and Managing Work.* London: Prentice-Hall.

Watson, T.J. (2009) *Sociology, Work and Industry* (5th edn). London: Routledge.

Wickens, P. (1987) *The Road to Nissan.* London: Macmillan.

4 Marketing

Key concepts

Distribution; Grey marketing; Marketing; Marketing communications; Positioning

This chapter aims to provide students with an introduction to the concepts and tools of marketing. It will commence with the definitions that illustrate marketing's contribution to the organization, then move on to discuss the strategic and tactical imperative of marketing and describe the interaction between organizations, suppliers, customers and consumers. It should be noted that there are many linkages between this area and that of strategic management. It would therefore be useful to read this chapter in conjunction with Chapter 9 on Strategy which covers related material such as environmental analysis, strategic groups and portfolio planning.

This chapter will give a critical evaluation of the development of marketing with a particular focus on the relationship between the organization and the customer. Although the difficulties of defining critical theory have been articulated by a number of scholars (see for instance Burton, 2001; Scott, 2007), for the purpose of this chapter I will use critical theory as a mechanism to deconstruct marketing theory, evaluate the historical context (Alveson and Sköldberg, 2000: 111), analyze from a variety of alternative perspectives (usually interpretivist), and explore how marketing theorists attempt to build (in marketing terms) a 'new and improved' marketing theory. Hence this chapter will firstly deconstruct the principal concept of exchange, the antecedents, and debates around its applicability to marketing and then illustrate how this subsequently led to other ways of using marketing, for instance in the development of relationship marketing.

Marketing Concept

> **Marketing**: The Chartered Institute of Marketing defines marketing as: 'The management process responsible for identifying, anticipating and satisfying customer requirements profitably'.

This definition of the **marketing** concept implies an implicit relationship between the organization and the customer; through research the organization can identify consumer needs and then provide the product or brand to the customer that meets those needs, with the price set accordingly to ensure profitability for the organization. Marketing is a management tool – it can be used to inform, remind, educate and reinforce behaviour, but for some areas of marketing it is seen as one of the 'Dark Arts', one that can manipulate and mislead. This can lead in turn to associations with propaganda.

Marketing Philosophy

Through the employment of a marketing philosophy, the organization will direct all its activities and focus its attention on customers. Customers are sovereign and fulfilling customer needs and wants is paramount to every department in an organization, including finance, purchasing and production, as well as the more obvious sales and marketing. Hence the organization must be structured in such a way as to maximize customer satisfaction; it has to hear and act upon customer concerns; identify supplier markets that will produce customer value; and build strategies to encourage long-term consumer loyalty.

Customer needs

So what are these customer needs? Kotler and Keller (2009) described people's *needs* as biological or functional, for instance, those for food, water, warmth and shelter; they also included a sense of belonging and esteem. However, these can be distinguished from *wants* which are determined by social influences and the environment, including marketing activity. Maslow (1999) categorized needs in his

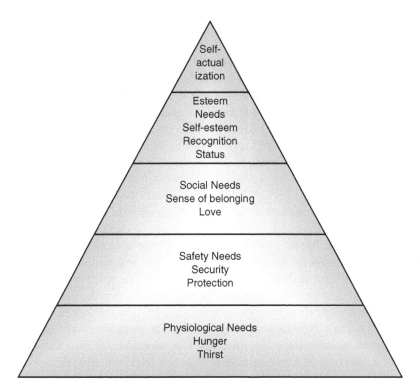

Figure 4.1 Maslow's hierarchy of needs

widely cited *hierarchy of needs* where there is a progression from food and shelter to self-actualization (see Figure 4.1 and Chapter 2 on Organizational Behaviour).

Maslow's model suggests that there is a progression from our most basic biological or physiological needs (such as satisfying hunger and thirst) to finding shelter and ensuring our safety and protection. The later stages are not essential for survival but are essential for the nature of being human, because as social beings we need to belong to our social group, our families and friends, and we also need love.

In addition we need to be recognized as being worthy members of our group so our needs relate to our reputation, our status, and our self-esteem. The final stage here is self-actualization where we move on from needs to desires; this is where the individual has the choice to be whatever they want to be according to their abilities.

However, this gradual evolution is not quite as simple as it first appears: Firat and Dholakia (1998), for instance, discuss the blurred distinction between needs and wants – and of course desires – and this then begs the question '*what do we actually need?*' The distinction between needs and wants is hazy for a number of reasons, for instance because of personal priorities, situational factors and also marketing activities. There is also the assumption that we are rational when making decisions about what it is we require to fulfil our needs.

Marketing as Exchange

The definition articulated by the Chartered Institute of Marketing is restricted to the market exchange between buyer and seller and it does not take into consideration competition and other extraneous factors in the market environment. Moreover, it focusses on the customer rather than the consumer and doesn't take into consideration aspects such as customer loyalty. It also presents each actor as autonomous and working independently, with the freedom to pick and choose from the marketplace (Willmott, 1999). According to Berlin this is a myth and his critique rests on the exchange process as a free and independent catalyst for choice focussed on the notion of liberty, namely positive and negative liberty (Galbraith, 2002; 2004). He has argued that in the market economy the possession of capital creates positive liberty which is enabling, whilst in contrast the lack of capital creates negative liberty and leads to exclusion and alienation. This aspect of power relations in the exchange process has been articulated by a number of authors (see Galbraith, 2002; also Perrow, 1988; Firat and Dholakia, 1998). This led Wilmott (1999: 215) to argue that what marketing 'fails to acknowledge and address are the social relations of inequality that either privilege or exclude participation in marketized transactions'.

Hence this narrow definition of market exchange between buyer and seller was developed from neoclassical economics and the parsimony of the model limits the efficacy of marketing as a managerial application. Nevertheless, as Brown (1995: 107) suggests, 'marketing ... reflects developments in the social, economic and cultural spheres' – which indicates that marketing is far more entrenched in consumer society, absorbing *cultural norms and values* and re-interpreting them through product offerings and communicational tools. In line with the acceptance of a broader application of marketing there has been a gradual evolution in marketing philosophy which has taken it, as Brown et al. (1998) and Hunt (1994) have suggested, from being a 'science to an art'. This debate explored the reliance upon the *positivist paradigm* and the inability to adequately explain consumer choices and behaviour. It appeared that marketing seemed to be succumbing to a 'crisis of confidence', a 'marketing crisis', and (some would imply) even a 'demise' or the 'end of marketing' (Brady and Davis, 1993; Hunt, 1994; Thomas, 1994; Brown, 1999). Araujo (1999) pointed out that this crisis seemed to be due to the over reliance on the neoclassical concept of exchange (see Chapter 10 on Research Approaches for a discussion of positivism and ontological debates in business and management). Hence the marketing concept has been adapted and extended to include wider social variables and also to broaden the process of exchange to encompass customers, consumers, and supplier markets.

Exchange and the Consumer

Transactional marketing theory has drawn from the same research pool of economics, psychology and sociology, but critical marketing has been significantly less loyal to the notion of *homo economicus*. Why – if these concepts developed from the same foundation – did marketing remain constrained within the hypothetical construct of exchange and the notion of the rational consumer when it did not reflect reality? Many scholars in the critical marketing discipline have explored other ways to understand some of the theoretical concepts of postmodernism (Thomas, 1994; Brown, 1995; Brownlie, 1997; Firat and Shultz, 1997). According to Maffesoli (1997, cited in Desmond, 2003) people who live in an advanced consumer society are not rational, isolated and self-disciplined folk. Rather they are bound together with

> powerful emotional bonds and are connected through a variety of diffuse and fleeting encounters, from those which bind together people who live in neighbourhoods ... to those swarms of consumers who populate city-centre high streets and shopping malls. (Desmond, 2003: 19)

Consumer behaviour theory reflects a shift in this thinking towards the experiential, affective, 'symbolic' consumer. Traditionally, consumer behaviour theory has focussed on two key paradigms: the consumer as a rational information-processing person, moving later to the consumer whose decisions are shaped by socio-psychological factors (Markin, 1979). Later studies point to these models' inability to build an understanding of consumer behaviour, so they sought to explore other factors of influence, principally emotion (Markin, 1979; Shiv and Fedorikhin, 1999; Loewenstein, 2001). Williamson (2002) examines the power of emotion as a 'behavioural driver' and suggests that in a complex environment everyday decisions will be undertaken with no cognitive processing or 'involvement of our conscious minds'. If we recognize that in such complex environments even simple decisions 'rapidly overwhelm human cognitive capacities' (Loewenstein, 2001) so other factors must be at work. Bakamitsos and Siomokos (2004) identify that mood has a significant impact upon decision making, which is interesting when we consider how many governments try to embody feel-good factors that will arise from events such as royal weddings, jubilee celebrations and international football competitions. Nelson (2002) highlights the idea that in marketing there is an acknowledgement of an increasing complex environment where the enthusiasm for choice and the capacity for decision making are determined by our ability to evaluate the diversity of choices. However, Klein and Yadav (1989) suggest that even amongst those respondents with strong cognitive capabilities there is evidence that relatively few decisions are made using analytical processes, such as generating a variety of options and contrasting their strengths and weaknesses.

Clearly situational factors are at work here, and the higher the risk or uncertainty the more complex the decision making process. The argument follows that risk can both complicate the exchange process and extend the decision making process by increasing the level of motivation in that process. This in turn increases the level of involvement, leading to an advancement in marketing theory that discusses the complexity of the decision making process. It is argued that this process consists of five stages and depending upon the level of risk or uncertainty involved in the decision behaviour at each stage will vary: thus marketers will use different marketing

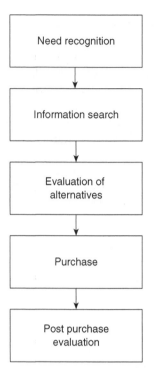

Figure 4.2 Decision making process

strategies and tactics to encourage consumer advancement through the decision-making process.

The consumer decision making process extends the boundaries of the exchange process and defines the stages consumers may go through as they search for the right product, or service, to satisfy their needs. The model suggests a logical, deliberative progression through the cognition stages as early marketing theory assumed the same economic rationality. Figure 4.2 outlines the key stages from a decision-making perspective (Kotler, 1991: 182). However, Foxall et al. (1998) argue from a behavioural standpoint that the model is a simplified abstract version of reality but also useful for identifying those factors that do shape consumer decision making. Work in this area might usefully be compared with the discussion of decision-making in Chapter 2 on Organizational Behaviour.

Subsequent thinking in marketing outlines a greater understanding of the complexity of the decision making process and this then highlights that, at each stage, there are a number of factors that can influence or prevent consumers from making a purchase. For instance, the time spent on each stage is determined by the product type; the level of involvement; situational factors or the degree of risk involved in making a decision.

There is an assumption throughout much of the literature that there is some sort of goal pursuit inherent in the activity (Markin, 1979; Bagozzi and Dholakia, 1999).

It is recognized that problem identification is usually consumer driven but could be stimulated by marketing communication activity, which arouses a latent need. According to Blackwell et al. (2001), need recognition occurs if there is a difference between the actual situation and the desired situation. If it is a matter of product replacement there are two options – either to replace or to trade up and improve, for instance with a television. Bagozzi and Dholakia (1999) distinguish between three goal-directed needs. Firstly, habitual goal-directed consumer behaviour where there is a measure of deliberative processing or learning or a combination of both of these. Secondly, impulsive behaviour which involves the awakening of a latent need but no prior deliberation; and finally, goal pursuit activities which concurs with Engel et al. (1995). In addition to all this, rather than follow the deliberative, information-processing model, there is evidence to suggest little cognitive thinking occurs (Loewenstein, 2001; Bargh, 2002). With this in mind, the consumer can – at times and at each stage in the model – demonstrate levels of irrationality, apathy, enthusiasm and rationality (Reid and Brown, 1996).

There are many factors that can impact upon the decision making process, both internal and external, and Figure 4.3 highlights these. Within the extant marketing literature there is a debate over the assumed rationality of the consumer: sometimes they will behave rationally and at other times aspects of irrationally can be identified (Holbrook, 1986; Reid and Brown, 1996). Figure 4.3 identifies the determinants of problem solving and each of these fits together differently depending on the context of the decision. This indicates that there are many outcomes and different consumer groups will also make decisions differently. There are also numerous studies identifying a myriad of consumer typologies (see for instance Stone, 1954; Westbrook and Black, 1985).

This combines deliberative decision making with social cognition models but adds on experiential and affective components and the notion of risk. If we commence

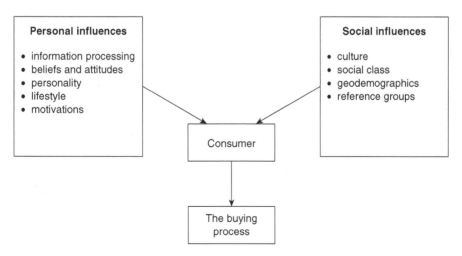

Figure 4.3 Influences on decision making

with an exploration of the decision making process and the problems inherent within it, consumption begins with the identification of a need. The information searching stage and the degree to which this occurs will depend upon the product type, the consumer (Alba and Hutchinson, 2000; Ariely, 2000; Campbell and Kirmani, 2000), the consumer's existing knowledge of the product (Kivetz and Simonson, 2000), and the environment (Pratkanis and Greenwald, 1993). In marketing theory this could generate high or low involvement decisions, but even for a highly priced product for some consumers there will be little involvement again, depending upon the degree of risk. Involvement is an important component when looking at consumers' reasoning processes. However, it is a crucial element in any decision making process.

Involvement as defined by Antil, and cited in Engel et al. (1995: 161), is 'the level of perceived personal importance and/or interest evoked by a stimulus (or stimuli) within a specific situation'. Thus involvement is determined by the consumer's motivation after they have evaluated how relevant the product or service is to them. A consumer can be highly involved in the decision making process or exhibit low involvement characteristics.

Simplistically, the level of searching will be much greater for a high involvement product such as a washing machine than will be for toothpaste, generally described as a low involvement decision. The determinants of involvement are complex and varied, depending upon the product type and the consumer's situation (Laurent and Kapferer, 1985; Williams, 2002). For Foxall et al. (1998) involvement is not a single construct to be taken in isolation; rather, it is an integrated framework that may be used to build an understanding of the determinants of decision making. However, to a great extent all these notions of involvement involve a certain level of deliberation and this deliberation is determined by the level of risk. Moreover, in marketing there are a number of risk factors (Antonides and van Raaij, 1998: 257) that have been identified as influential in the decision making process and which could also be applied to political decision making.

These are:

- Financial risk
- Functional risk
- Physical risk
- Social risk
- Psychological risk

These aspects determine the level of involvement in the product or service and this could be viewed as either actual risk or perceived risk. For instance, Volvo claim their cars have a number of safety features that reduce the risk of driving. But it is *how* risk is conceptualized that is important here, and levels of risk will increase during times of uncertainty.

In consumer theory an elaboration of the results of the information search with existing knowledge is determined by the type of product or existing data relating to that product. This elaboration is also dependent upon the ability and motivation of the consumer (Petty and Cacioppo, 1986). It is these two stages that consumer behaviour theorists have focussed upon most closely, judging whether the consumer behaves rationally or not.

The consumer stage of product purchase can be equated with casting a vote. Product purchase is relatively straightforward but behaviour is different for certain product sectors, so the marketing communications strategy needs to be adapted. For instance, with a high involvement product there is usually a high level of elaboration and an extensive information search.

The final stage is post purchase evaluation; this is where the product must perform as promised. If there is any mismatch between the performance of the product and the expected benefits from its purchase, then cognitive dissonance arises and the risk associated with the purchase of the product is increased. Possibly the product will not be purchased again.

Consumers had been identified as 'problem solvers', searching out information and consciously seeking solutions to their consumer needs. Conversely, researchers had also identified the 'cognitive miser' (Hoyer, 1984; Taylor, 1986; Zaichkowsky, 1991), someone who will not take time to search for information either because they were unwilling or unable to do so, and who will rely instead on their existing knowledge base. These studies had some consistency with the notion of the rational consumer, who will make conscious decisions based on evaluating alternatives and considering issues such as price, quality, etc. However, they still could not provide an adequate explanation of consumer decision making, as it had become increasingly evident to marketers that rationality was not applicable for many products, including for example, cosmetics for women and cars for men.

Marketing theorists were beginning to define the characteristics of an irrational consumer (Zaichkowsky, 1991). Ernest Dichter (1964), building on work done by Bernays, drew on Freudian and Pavlovian theories and introduced the notion of the 'irrational consumer' (Zaichkowsky, 1991). Using motivational research methods, he argued that he could uncover consumers' unconscious needs and wants, and ultimately their latent desires, which could then be used to influence decision making.

This is where the concept of risk becomes so important. If a researcher could determine what insecurities affected the consumer, this could be capitalized upon and utilized to influence consumer behaviour. This is linked to the notion of emotion and during the 1990s research had been focussed upon symbolism, experiences, semiotics through postmodernism (Hirschman and Holbrook, 1992; Holbrook, 1994; Brown, 1995), and the hedonistic consumer who builds an emotional connection with a brand. In conclusion, there is now a growing acceptance that the consumer can behave in different ways depending upon their situation, their emotional state, and the time pressure they face. These behavioural patterns are difficult to predict but once recognized can provide a greater understanding of consumers, rather than the more unsatisfactory notion of economic rationality which fails to acknowledge any decisions based on irrationality. It should be noted that critical perspectives might highlight the ethical questions raised here.

This leads us on to how difficult it becomes to segment the market: there is a diversity of consumers with different needs and wants, but they will also have different backgrounds and situations and these situations will change over time.

Segmentation, Targeting and Positioning

Maurice Holbrook (1995: 49) joked that someone once said: 'there are two kinds of people in the world (a) those who divide everything into two groups and (b) those that don't'.

This section will discuss accepted theories regarding segmentation, targeting and positioning but also illustrate how the positivist undercurrent within marketing has an impact upon how the market is divided. For instance, in economic terms in times of scarce resources it is sensible to maximize utilities and focus on key customers rather than compete in an undifferentiated market. This means that the market is segmented into different groups; these groups will share certain characteristics such as being members of the same socio-economic group, or being within the same age range, or sharing similar lifestyles. The traditional segmentation variables include:

- Geographic: regional
- Demographic: age, gender, life cycle
- Psychographic: lifestyle, personality
- Behavioural: benefits, purchase situation, usage

There are a number of criteria that can be adopted in order to identify the most appropriate segment. Firstly, the segment has to be *measured*, in terms of *volume or value*, and the availability of information to measure this has to be ascertained – is there information available to measure this? Secondly, how *accessible* is the segment, can it be reached? Thirdly, is the segment *substantial enough*? Is the market attractive in terms of size, market potential, competitor power? Finally, there is *congruity* – how closely does the market opportunity match the capabilities of the organization?

The market is then segmented and the choice for the organization is whether to opt for an *undifferentiated* strategy, a single segment or *concentrated* strategy, or a multi-segment or *differentiated* strategy. However, Holbrook (1995) points to another 'proliferation strategy' that has also been adopted when products or brands are being marketed to a largely homogeneous market – detergents and breakfast cereals are examples here. In this strategy there is little distinction between consumers and as the products are largely similar the distinction will often come in the packaging and marketing communications strategies that create the difference. In contrast, as markets become more competitive organizations will look to create a competitive advantage by targeting ever smaller groups, providing specialist products for their chosen niche markets (Brown, 1995).

I am not a target market (Coupland, 1996).

This positivist notion of categorizing people into boxes is becoming more complex; consider the '**grey market**' – a group of people aged over 55. Marketers are beginning to recognize that they are not just one homogeneous group; with increased longevity due to better healthcare, combined with opportunities for early retirement, the age range is much broader. Hence there are key distinctions within this group. Moreover, there are different levels of wealth and disposable income, and some people will have more time for leisure activities such as holidays. Lifestyle and psychographic segmentation may allow for a more accurate drilling-down into more profitable groups.

Grey market:

- Not one homogeneous group
- Increased longevity
- More disposable income
- More time
- Feel younger than actual age
- Growing old disgracefully?
- The older one gets the younger it seems!

As identifying customer needs is paramount in marketing, customers are kings (or queens) according to the prevailing marketing literature. However, the dilemma marketers face here is how closely must they match customer needs, as the closer they go the fewer customers there are which could lead to less profit. Therefore they need to consider how their product offering is presented and how they can provide value to the customer whilst still making a profit.

Positioning

Positioning: the act of designing the company's offering and image to occupy a distinct place in the minds of the target market (Kotler and Keller, 2009: 308).

Once the target segments have been selected the product is then '**positioned**' in the minds of consumers, and although the marketing concept discusses how the product should meet customers' needs marketing decisions can help to present the product in a way the consumer expects to see it. Thus the *marketing mix* is a complex series of decisions that all need to fit together in order to provide a complete product offering with a clearly defined image, identity, and set of benefits to the target group.

Case Study: Star Ferries Hong Kong

Imagine you work for an international marketing consultancy in the Southeast Asia region. You have been approached by Star Ferries to reposition their ferry service. The Star Ferry is an iconic symbol for Hong Kong, providing one of the most memorable boat rides in the world. (For further information see http://www.starferry.com.hk/.)

However, since the development of the MTR and also the renovation and relocation of the Central Pier there has been a decline in passenger numbers. The increased distance from the pier to the Central and Admiralty business districts has added to these declining numbers as it is generally believed to be quicker to use the MTR. But while that journey is speedy it is also hectic and extremely busy, particularly during the rush hour period.

Consider how a marketing consultant would identify those key segments that may be keen to rediscover the pleasure of travelling on the Star Ferry. What segmentation strategy might be appropriate here? And also what barriers to usage might there be and what could be done to overcome these?

The Marketing Mix

The marketing mix or the 4Ps can be defined as a series of variables that are integrated to provide a coherent marketing strategy. These are:

- Product
- Price
- Place
- Promotion

The marketing mix includes decisions on the level of quality of the product offering. The decision on quality should reflect what the consumer expects to receive from the price paid and where they will be able to purchase the product. Furthermore promotion decisions will also mirror the perceived quality of the product. Hence all four variables should be designed to reinforce the image of the product offering and provide a distinct benefit for the consumer.

Product

The product variable includes a series of decisions that relate to the level of quality of the product, from the packaging to the variety, sizes, and particular features. Again these are all designed to provide the benefit the segment requires from purchasing this product. Kotler and Keller (2009: 358) identified five levels in the product hierarchy, the model commences with the core *benefit* that the consumer requires, the iPhone is a classic example where they don't discuss features but emphasize the benefits the user will receive; tyre manufacturers provide safety whilst anti-wrinkle creams provide youth (or the promise of youth!). At the next level is the basic product, this is the basic features the user expects, so for an iPhone user it is a communication device. The *expected product* is a set of attributes that the user would expect to receive, again using the iPhone example, one would expect to have a sound connection to a network, phone and messaging services. The *augmented product* level is where the product exceeds expectations, and in developed markets with intense competition, this is where the product is differentiated. This is why brand management is so important – brands are ubiquitous, they are all around us: in supermarkets, fashion retail, services, business to business, and charities. We know them, we recognize them, they communicate certain values to us, and they can, of course, be an effective heuristic device. Knox suggests that a brand is

> an entity that offers customers (and other relevant parties) added value based on factors over and above its functional performance. These added values ... differentiate the offer and provide the basis for customer preference and loyalty. (2004: 106)

The study of branding has become increasingly complex (Jevons, 2005) as the concept has been stretched across sectors that are far removed from FMCG products. Moreover, it is the augmented product level where brands and image are so important and, continuing with the iPhone example, it is at this level where they identify the cult brand of Apple which emphasizes their mythical anti-corporate image (Belk and Tumbat, 2005). The final level is the potential product, this is where the product can evolve again in order to maintain or create a competitive advantage.

In a competitive market system products need to be differentiated in order to identify the specific needs of their chosen segment or segments. However, in saturated markets there is little distinction – think of the differences between Pepsi Cola and Coca-Cola – so the imagery created through *marketing communications* must maintain any distinctiveness even when there is little to be found. Naomi Klein's (2000) critique of consumerism in her classic text *No Logo* discusses the way in which brands have been developed to differentiate the product. She argues one sneaker is much the same as another, it is only the brand that provides the distinguishing feature. Moreover, the cultural expansion of the brand into our everyday life provides an anchor which protects against the uncertainty of the world and creates a sense of belonging to a community based on the brand. This sense of belonging or association with a brand then generates brand loyalty. However, Klein also argues that realistically a brand cannot recreate an idealistic notion of community so we have to buy yet more product in order to fulfil that need.

According to Kotler and Keller (2009) there are different product types that may be classified according to *durability* and *tangibility*. *Non-durable* goods are frequent purchases that require regular replacement so they are inexpensive and widely distributed. *Durable* goods are white goods such as electrical equipment; as these are more expensive they require more intensive promotional activities and specialist distribution. *Services* are intangible but have other characteristics such as *inseparability, heterogeneity* and *perishability*. In services it is argued that the product is 'intangible' – as a service it cannot be felt or touched, for instance a banking service or a visit to the cinema.

Therefore marketers will spend significant resources enhancing the service delivery through personal service and creating an environment that reflects the projected brand values. This emphasizes the feel of the service, effectively 'tangiblizing' the service offering. This is achieved within the expected and augmented product level of the customer value hierarchy. So for instance, in a *pure service* such as banking where you cannot feel the 'product', attempts to tangiblize this by offering personal bank tellers, or extra facilities such as internet banking, etc., will be made.

Inseparability suggests that a service is produced and consumed simultaneously. For instance, education is a service and students will embark upon their programme of study for a period of time. Furthermore, through their relationship with the teaching staff and the educational materials they will become integral to the success of the service. As Kotler and Armstrong (2010) argue the service outcome is affected by both the provider and the customer.

Perishability means that a service cannot be stored for later use. If an aeroplane takes off and it is only half full then those seats cannot be sold at a later stage. *Heterogeneity* relates to the idea of variability in service delivery and this is dependent upon staff, environment, and where the service is delivered. This is crucial for franchise organizations who need to maintain a regular service wherever they are delivered. For hairdressers consistency of service is problematic to maintain, so the hiring and training of staff is fundamental to reduce any variability in service provision.

For services the product offering is much more complex and consists of a number of added value aspects that attempt to mitigate the characteristics of services.

Price

Pricing performs a number of roles. At the most basic level it is the cost of production plus profit and identifies the cost of the product to the customer. It is however complex because while pricing can indicate value to the customer it is axiomatic to suggest that the higher the price the greater the perception of quality: yet at the same time the relationship between price, quality and value is crucial for marketing strategy. Zeithaml's (1998: 11) means ends model which examined the relationship between price, quality and value suggested that there was 'a gap between actual and perceived price', making it important to understand how consumers encode the prices of products. A pricing strategy can also include providing discounts to larger customers and price reductions to move end of season or out of date stock. It can also encourage purchase by supplying easy payment mechanisms such as credit cards and instalments, although this has been shown to disadvantage poorer sections of society (Caplovitz, 1963). There are a number of different options when selecting the price of a product or brand (Kotler and Keller, 2009) and this action depends upon strategic management decisions and the market environment. For instance, if the market is competitive then *survival pricing* covers the costs, enabling the company to continue its operations. *Maximum current profit* is a risky strategy and focusses on current performance; it does not take into consideration competitor activity, any long-term strategy, nor other aspects of the marketing mix (Kotler and Keller, 2009). If an organization wants to *maximize the market share* which could stimulate market growth it can only do so if the market is price sensitive, but this would discourage other market entrants who would find it difficult to compete. *Market skimming* is used when there is little competition in the marketplace: for instance, new technology products can afford to maximize profit until other 'me too' products enter the market. *Product-quality leaders* are strong brands that can charge premium prices as they are perceived to be premium quality, for example luxury brands such as Mulberry; brands that are perceived to be technically superior to other competitors in the marketplace, such as Audi; and brands like Starbucks who provide a perceived added value over and above a standard cup of coffee.

These pricing strategies must be aligned with the rest of the marketing mix so the price must reflect the perceived product quality.

Promotion

Marketing communications: ' … the means by which firms attempt to inform, persuade, and remind consumers – directly or indirectly – about the products or brands that they sell' (Kotler and Keller, 2009: 510).

There are a variety of **marketing communications** tools, from advertising and sales to direct marketing and public relations. There are also a number of different promotional tools that can be used in a promotional strategy. These range from the more familiar advertising and sales to public relations, exhibitions and sponsorship. All are used to remind, reinforce and persuade at different stages of the decision-making process and each has a specific function. *Advertising* can create awareness within mass audiences using broadcast media whilst *direct marketing* can engage with a specifically targeted segment. *Personal selling* is adopted to provide detailed guidance on a product or brand where there is little knowledge or some uncertainty, such as when buying computers or cars. It is also extensively used in the business to business sector where long-term relationships are built up.

Example of Business to business manufacturing

Boiler manufacturer, Product domestic boiler
Target segments: building contractors, plumbers; councils.
Promotional mix

- Exhibitions
- Trade magazine advertising
- Brochures/leaflets
- Personal selling

Sales promotion can remind and persuade at the point of purchase and is often used for habitual purchases such as shampoo. Sales promotion can also be used tactically to reduce the impact of seasonality (for instance, ice-cream) and it can also move end of season stock. *Public relations* is used to deal with a variety of publics, sending promotional messages through mediated sources who will interpret the message according to their own perspective. Hence, in public relations it is not so easy to control the message content. The key issue for marketing communications is that it has to be integrated into the promotional mix; all the promotional tools must be communicating the same message but in their own particular way. For each different promotional activity there will be a different mix depending on the marketing objectives, the promotional objectives, and the target segment. Marketing communication activities enable information to reach the consumer in the communication codes they are familiar with and these bring in sales personnel with specific expertise who can also provide further information. Consumers will collect the amount of information they believe they will need in order to reduce the element of risk associated with the purchase of a high risk product. Conversely, for a low involvement decision such as an habitual purchase there is little risk, so little cognitive elaboration. In this situation marketing communication tools such as sales promotion and point of sale activities are utilized to remind consumers of and reinforce brand values at the point of purchase.

Place

Distribution: getting the product to the customer in the right place at the right time.

Distribution decisions support the strategic decisions determined by the marketing mix; just as the pricing strategy reflects the product strategy, so too does distribution. The distribution channels employed can also be used to indicate product quality; *exclusive distribution* means that the supply is restricted to an elite group of intermediaries who are bound by strict agreements to provide a quality sales provision and an environment that reflects the brand positioning; *selective distribution* is used when a broader market coverage is needed but control is still required over the presentation and sales of the product; *intensive distribution* is where the product is widely distributed through a variety of outlets in order to enable maximum market coverage.

The strategic decisions that determine which mode of distribution is adopted are closely aligned to the overall marketing strategy. Over recent years, distribution channels have been reprioritized as a crucial element in the marketing mix as the integration of channel management with the promotional activities and pricing strategies works to present a coherent brand to the customer.

Marketing activities continue to rely on the 4Ps, whilst for *services marketing* the 4Ps are extended to become the 7Ps with *people, process* and *physical evidence*. People are the employees of the organization; the process is the procedures that are designed and followed to reduce variability in the product offering; physical evidence provides additional features and benefits that *tangiblize* the product offering.

Consider an airline company as an example. Tickets are first booked either via the website or by phone. The website is designed in the corporate colours with the logo and brand name clearly identified. The transaction process should run smoothly and be simple to use enhancing the service provision. Arriving at the airport there is once again the brand name and the corporate colours. The check-in process is dealt with by airline staff dressed in uniform.

For a detailed discussion of the 7Ps see Kotler and Keller (2009). Note, however, that the concept has come in for some criticism for some time. Brownlie and Saren (1992) suggest that some of the problems here stem from an ideological rather than a conceptual adoption of marketing, thus leading to problems of applicability. Others believe that some of the perceived shortcomings of the 4Ps arise not only from the philosopical foundations of marketing but also from its reducibility. The marketing mix, or more specifically the 4Ps in transactional marketing, has been criticized for the parsimony of the concept (Gummesson, 2002), reducing it to a process driven model that does not suggest an integrative framework (Kent, 1986). The key aspect of the marketing philosophy is that it is more complex than the parsimony of the neoclassical exchange process:

> The concept of exchange also becomes more important where the content and context of exchange is rich and multi-dimensional and episodes of exchange are embedded into an institutionalized pattern of interorganizational relationships. (Araujo, 1999: 86)

So as Araujo suggests the exchange extends along supply chains and to other stakeholders, while for Baker (2003) the problem with the marketing concept has been that it was too focussed on the consumer needs. Marketers should instead look to develop a 'mutually satisfying exchange' amongst all stakeholders. Others (Payne, 1995; Thompson, 1990) believe that there should also be a stronger emphasis on the internal market. The organizational structure and principles should be directed towards the consumer but from an internal perspective. This debate has led the American Marketing Association (2004) to revise the concept of marketing as 'an organizational function and a set of processes for creating, communicating, and delivering value to customers and for managing customer relationships in ways that benefit the organization and its stakeholders'.

Case study: Lotus Evora 'Faceless People'

When Lotus launched its first new car in over ten years the company looked to CMW to create a buzz worthy of the supercar.

Background

At the start of 2008, communications agency CMW was appointed to launch the Evora, the first vehicle from supercar brand Lotus in more than a decade. Lotus had always been positioned as an exciting high-end brand for car lovers and so CMW needed to build that same sense of buzz and anticipation for the launch of the company's newest model.

The car was due out in July at the 2008 Motor Show in London and before that both the design and the name of the car had to be kept top secret. Until that time, the vehicle was simply known as 'Project Eagle'.

Strategy

With budgets tight, CMW needed to generate a disproportionate amount of publicity around the Evora's launch. A traditional advertising approach was dismissed in favour of a 'buzz' campaign that would provide better value for money by generating free publicity through PR and editorial coverage.

CMW's research found that the key target consumer for the Lotus Evora valued their individuality and would express this through their lifestyle choices, opting for brands which reflected these values and might sit outside the mainstream. The launch creative work would therefore focus on the idea that the Evora offered a more individual and unusual automotive experience for a special type of consumer.

Implementation

Lotus played on this concept of 'individuality versus the mass market' by developing a campaign built around the tagline 'True character in a faceless world'. CMW came up with an idea based around 'faceless' people; models

(Continued)

(Continued)

(photograph by Paul Hennessy, commissioned by Focus PR for Lotus)

wearing specially designed latex masks and black suits designed to highlight the contrasting individuality and character of the Evora.

The agency worked with consumer lifestyle and experiential specialists Focus PR to source and place these unsettling faceless people at high profile events around the UK, including Wimbledon, Henley Royal Regatta, Elton John's White Tie & Tiara Ball and *Sex and the City* star Kim Cattrall's visit to London to open Harrods' Summer Sale.

This experiential work was backed up by a microsite and search campaign, meaning that when 'faceless people' and other similar terms were searched for on Google, the top result directed users to www.faceless-people.com, where a countdown timer ticked backwards towards the unveiling at the Motor Show. At the bottom of the page was a discreet Lotus logo.

On 22 July, visitors to the site could watch the live unveiling of the new car through the facelesspeople.com microsite. The stream showed the faceless people surrounding the as yet still-covered car, only for them to disperse as it was revealed. Once the launch had been completed, the microsite turned into a fully functional website for the Evora, featuring video footage, specification details, and downloadable and streamed content, including video footage of the car, images and wallpapers. Visitors to the site both pre- and post-launch could also sign up to receive more information by email, and post-launch they could also use the site to register their interest in buying an Evora (www.lotusevora.com).

(Continued)

(Continued)

Questions

- How would you segment the market for this car?
- Who would you target?
- Critically evaluate the strategic approach Lotus took.
- Critically evaluate the public relations exercise of 'Faceless' people.
- Given the changes to electronic media would you use networking sites to reach your target audience?

Source: utalkmarketing.com

Relationship marketing

The development of relationship marketing was largely influenced by business to business marketing. However, due to the technological advances in communications this led to an opportunity to build databases where key segments could be identified and their needs met with much greater clarity than had been the case with mass communication methods. This was also fortuitous as it could save money on the advertising budgets. Relationship marketing was derided by some as merely a management fad (for a discussion see Palmer, 1996, or Gummesson, 1997). However, relationship marketing recognizes that there is a network of exchange relationships that can have positive influences on the decision making process and also customer satisfaction (Gummesson, 1999).

Whilst the customer decision making model looked at the micro aspects of the process, since the 1990s (and responding to the 'crisis in marketing') there has been a paradigmatic shift in marketing towards 'relationship marketing' (Sheth and Parvatiyar, 2000). Although relationship marketing continued to focus upon the exchange process between the consumer and the seller, it also recognized the importance of the nano and macro associations. Christopher et al.'s (1994) six market model outlined an environment of extended relationships, including internal, customer, referral, supplier, influencer and employee recruitment markets. Nano relationships (Gummesson, 2002) are what Christopher et al. (1994) defined as the internal market. In relationship marketing, it is the employee who holds a pivotal relationship with the customer (Varey and Lewis, 2000). The organization is structured in such a way that all employees, whatever their role or position, work towards customer satisfaction. Customer satisfaction is not only the domain of the sales and marketing departments but also of research and development, human resources, purchasing and also of course production and quality control. In line with this practice the customer is placed at the centre of the model (Peck et al., 1999). All the stakeholder markets (including referral, supplier, influencer and employee recruitment) focus on the customer and along with the internal market work towards customer satisfaction, creating and adding value. Hence the exchange process is broadened both internally to include employees and externally to include stakeholders such as suppliers, recruitment markets and the community.

Summary

As Moufahim and Lim (2009: 767) have reflected 'critical marketing does not draw attention to "new" marketing phenomena, but to the conditions of possibility of the "new": how we might render different images of what we have already decided is knowable'. Given the provenance of marketing theory and its development through the paradigms of neoclassical economics and positivism, it has been useful to see the development of new views of marketing through a relational and interpretivist perspective.

The evolution of marketing theory, and particularly the development of relationship marketing, has been a dialectic process that has drawn on the limitations of transactional marketing. Firstly, there has been focus on the perception of value rather than the production of value (Veloutsou et al., 2002); secondly, this narrow focus on the economic isolates the historical nature of relationships; finally, transactional marketing pays scant attention to the notion that relationships occur within a community (Araujo, 1999; Cova, 1999; Desmond, 2003). The transformation from transactional marketing to relationship marketing has been an extension of the one dimensional economic perspective to include the historical and the social.

This leads us to the problem of the operationalization of relationship marketing (Gummesson, 1994, Fournier et al. 1998); the complexity of the networks of relationships, the articulation of value within each network and relationship, and also the power of supply and demand, market size, and players within the relationships and networks.

The evolution of marketing theory from production through sales to transactional marketing and the ascendancy of relationship marketing is a response to the aforementioned environmental factors. Marketing will continue to adapt to the continuing changes in the marketplace but the primary focus will always be on the organization and its ability to create value for the customer so they can remain competitive and profitable.

The impetus for critical marketing theory draws upon 'substantive critical traditions' (Saren and Brownlie, cited in Bradshaw and Fuat Firat, 1999). The continuous examination and evaluation of marketing and consumption practices from, for instance, critical theory, feminism or postmodernism can only help to provide a stronger understanding of *'knowing'* marketing and *'imagining'* how it can be conceptualized and practised in today's competitive and dynamic environment.

Oman Air – Looking for growth (adapted from *Times of Oman*, 3 July 2010)

The CEO of Oman Air has discussed the market opportunities for the airline: 'The National carrier Oman Air believes the sultanate's route towards aviation success lies in being a niche player in a globally and regionally competitive market. 'Oman Air has been a regional carrier for 15 years, but now we are reaching for the world'.

(Continued)

(Continued)

Oman Air's aim is to be a niche player offering point-to-point services and developing high-frequency operations that will in turn generate high-yield traffic. The new A330–300 aircraft featuring straight out flat seats, direct aisle access, à la carte meals in business and first class and roomy economy seats are some of the features of the airline.

'Our point-to-point service has delivered relatively high yields and historically we have relied on it to get good returns as we chase down every last customer. That has enabled us to get good yields and with the coming month of Ramadan, more people will want to travel home. During the out-of-season periods, we will look at network routes not operated by other carriers to see if we can operate a non-stop service'.

'Oman Air has great products which other airlines are also talking about and we are developing even as many rival carriers are downsizing. Not many people realise that when an airline goes to fresh airports, the potential passengers can actually get great deals and when the market rebounds they would have locked in the great deals. So don't think just for today, instead be a partner with Oman Air for life'.

Questions for reflection

- To what extent do you believe the service has been differentiated in the marketplace?
- Which segments would you target? How would your strategy differ between the segments?
- How would you build the brand loyalty the CEO is envisioning?

Further reading

Blackwell, R.D., Miniard, P.W. and Engel, J.F. (2001) *Consumer Behaviour* (9th edn). Mason, OH: Thompson.

Brown, S. (1995) *Postmodern Marketing*. London: Routledge.

Gummesson, E. (2002) *Total Relationship Marketing* (2nd edn). London: Butterworth-Heinemann.

Hirschman, E.C. and Holbrook, M.B. (1992) *Postmodern Consumer Research*. London: Sage.

Holbrook, M. (1995) *Consumer Research: Introspective Essays on Consumption*. London: Sage.

Klein, N. (2000) *No Logo*. London: HarperCollins/Flamingo.

Kotler, P. and Keller, K.L. (2009) *Marketing Management* (13th edn). London: Pearson.

Saren, M., Maclaran, P., Goulding, C., Elliot, R., Shankar, A. and Catterall, A. (eds) (2007) *Critical Marketing: Defining the Field*. London: Butterworth-Heinemann.

Sheth, J.N. and Parvatiyar, A. (eds) (2000) *Handbook of Relationship Marketing*. London: Sage.

References

Alba, J.W. and Hutchinson, W. (2000) 'Knowledge calibration: what consumer's know and what they think they know'. Journal of Consumer Research, 27: 123–156.

Alvesson, M. and Sköldberg, K. (2000) *Reflexive Methodology: New Vistas for Qualitative Research*. London: Sage.

American Marketing Association (2004) definition cited in P. Kotler and K.L. Keller (2006) *Marketing Management*, 12th edn. London: Prentice Hall.

Antonides, G. and van Raaij, W.F. (1998) *Consumer Behaviour: A European Perspective*. Chicester: Wiley.

Araujo, L.M. (1999) 'Exchange, institutions and time'. In D. Brownlie, M. Saren, R. Wensley and R. Whittington (eds), *Rethinking Marketing*. London: Sage. pp. 84–105.

Ariely, D. (2000) 'Controlling information flow: effects on consumers' decision making and preference.' *Journal of Consumer Research*, 27 (2): 233–248.

Bagozzi, R.P. and Dholakia, U.M. (1999) 'Goal-setting and goal-striving in consumer behaviour.' *Journal of Marketing*, 63: 19–32.

Bakamitsos, G.A. and Siomokos, G.J. (2004) 'Context effects in marketing practice: The case of mood.' *Journal of Consumer Behaviour*, 3 (4): 304–314.

Baker, M. (2003) *The Marketing Book*, 5th edn. Oxford: Butterworth-Heinemann.

Bargh, J.A. (2002) 'Losing consciousness: automatic influences on consumer judgement, behaviour, and motivation.' *Journal of Consumer Research*, 29 (2): 280–285.

Belk, R. and Tumbat, G. (2005) 'The cult of Macintosh.' *Consumption Markets & Culture*, 8 (3): 205–217.

Blackwell, R.D., Miniard, P.W. and Engel, J.F. (2001) *Consumer Behaviour* (9th edn). Mason, OH: Thompson.

Bradshaw, A. and Fuat Firat, A. (1999) 'Rethinking critical marketing.' In *Critical Marketing: Defining the Field*. London: Butterworth-Heinemann.

(Continued)

(Continued)

Brady, J. and Davis, J. (1993) 'Marketing's mid-life crisis.' *McKinsey Quarterly*, 2: 17–28.
Brown, S. (1995) *Postmodern Marketing*. London: Routledge.
Brown, S. (1999) *Postmodern Marketing 2*. London: Routledge.
Brown, S., Doherty, A.M. and Clarke, B. (1998) 'Stoning the romance: on marketing's mind-forg'd manacles.' In S. Brown, A.M. Doherty and B. Clarke (eds), *Romancing the Market*. London: Routledge. pp. 1–21.
Brownlie, D. (1997) 'Beyond ethnography: towards writerly accounts of organizing in marketing.' *European Journal of Marketing*, 31 (3/4): 263–282.
Brownlie, D. and Saren, M. (1992) The four Ps of the marketing concept: prescriptive, polemical, permanent and problematical, *European Journal of Marketing*, 26 (4): 34–47.
Burton, D. (2001) 'Critical marketing theory: The blueprint?' *European Journal of Marketing*, 35 (5/6): 722–743.
Campbell, M. and Kirmani, A. (2000) 'Consumers' use of persuasion knowledge: the effects of accessibility and cognitive capacity on perceptions of an influence agent.' *Journal of Consumer Research*, 27 (1): 69–83.
Caplovitz, D. (1963) *The Poor Pay More, Consumer Practices of Low-income Families, The Costs of Paying Later, The Installment Plan and the Poor Consumer*. New York: Glencow Press Macmillan.
Christopher, R.E., Payne, A. and Ballantyne, D. (1994) *Relationship Marketing*. London: Butterworth-Heinemann.
Coupland, D. (1996) *Generation X: Tales for an Accelerated Culture*. London: Abacus.
Cova, B. (1999) From Marketing to Societing: When the Link is More Important than the Thing, in D. Brownlie, M. Saren, R. Wensley and R. Whittington (eds) *Rethinking Marketing, Towards Critical Marketing Accountings*, pp.65–83. Sage: London.
Desmond, J. (2003) *Consuming Behaviour*. Basingstoke: Palgrave.
Dichter, E. (1964) *The Handbook of Consumer Motivations: The Psychology of Consumption*. New York: McGraw Hill.
Engel, J.F., Kollat, D. T. and Blackwell, R. D. (1995) *Consumer Behaviour*. Hisdale, IL: Dryden.
Firat, A.F. and Shultz, C.Z. (1997) 'From segmentation to fragmentation: markets and marketing strategy in the postmodern era.' *European Journal of Marketing*, 31 (3/4): 182–206.
Fournier, S., Dobscha, S. and Mick, D. G. (1998) Preventing the Premature Death of Relationship Marketing, *Harvard Business Review*, 75: 43–51.
Foxall, G.R., Goldsmith, R.E. and Brown, S. (1998) *Consumer Psychology for Marketing* (2nd edn). London: Thompson.
Galbraith, J.K. (2002) in H. Hardy (ed.) (2002) *Liberty*. Oxford: Oxford University Press.
Galbraith, J.K. (2004) in H. Hardy (ed.) (2002) *Liberty*. Oxford: Oxford University Press.
Gummesson, E. (1994) 'Making relationship marketing operational.' *International Journal of Service Industry Management*, 5 (5): 5–20.
Gummesson, E. (1997) 'Relationship marketing – the emperor's new clothes or a paradigm shift.' *Marketing and Research Today*, 25(1): 53–60.
Gummesson, E. (1999) *Total Relationship Marketing*. Oxford: Butterworth-Heinemann.

(Continued)

(Continued)

Gummesson, E. (2002) *Total Relationship Marketing* (2nd edn). London: Butterworth-Heinemann.

Hirschman, E.C. and Holbrook, M.B. (1992) *Postmodern Consumer Research*. London: Sage.

Holbrook, M.B. (1986) '"I'm hip": an autobiographical account of some consumption experiences.' In R. Lutz (ed.), *Advances in Consumer Research*, 13. Provo, UT: Association for Consumer Research. pp. 614–618.

Holbrook, M.B. (1994) 'Postmodernism and social theory.' *Journal of Macromarketing*, 13 (Fall): 69–75.

Holbrook, M.B. (1995) *Consumer Research: Introspective Essays on Consumption*. London: Sage.

Hoyer, W.D. (1984) 'An examination of consumer decision making for a common repeat purchase product.' *Journal of Consumer Research*, 11 (December): 822–828.

Hunt, S. (1994) 'On rethinking marketing: our discipline, our practice, our methods.' *European Journal of Marketing*, 28 (3): 13–25.

Jevons, C. (2005) Name, brands, branding: beyond the signs, symbols, products and services, *Journal of Product and Brand Management*, 14(2/3): 117–118.

Kent, R.A. (1986) 'Faith in the 4P's: an alternative.' *Journal of Marketing Management*, 2 (2): 145–154.

Kivetz, R. and Simonson, I. (2000) The Effects of Incomplete Information on Consumer Choice, *Journal of Marketing Research*, 37(4): 428–448.

Klein, N. (2000) *No Logo*. London: HarperCollins/Flamingo.

Klein, N. and Yadav, M. (1989) 'Context effects on effort and accuracy in choice: an enquiry into adaptive decision making.' *Journal of Consumer Research*, 15 (4): 411–421.

Kotler, P. and Armstrong, G. (2010) *Principles of Marketing*, 13th edn. London: Pearson.

Kotler, P. (1991) *Marketing Management: Analysis, Planning, Implementation and Control* (7th edn). London: Prentice-Hall.

Kotler, P. and Keller, K. (2009) *Marketing Management* (13th edn). London: Pearson.

Knox, S. (2004) 'Positioning and branding your organization.' *Journal of Product & Brand Management*, 13 (2): 105–115.

Laurent, G. and Kapferer, K.N. (1985) 'Measuring consumer involvement profiles.' *Journal of Marketing Research*, 22 (1): 41–53.

Loewenstein, G. (2001) 'The creative destruction of decision research.' *Journal of Consumer Research*, 28 (3): 499–503.

Markin, R. J. (1979) The Role of Rationalization in Consumer Decision Making Processes: A Revisionist Approach to Consumer Behaviour, *Journal of the Academy of Marketing Science*, 7(4): 316–34.

Maslow, A. (1999) *Toward a Psychology of Being* (3rd edn). New York: Wiley.

Moufahim, M. and Lim, M. (2009) Towards a critical political marketing agenda?, *Journal of Marketing Management*, 25 (7/8): 763–776.

Nelson, W. (2002) 'All power to the consumer? Complexity and choice in consumer lives', *Journal of Consumer Behavior*, 2 (2): 185–195.

Palmer, A.J. (1996) 'Relationship Marketing: a universal paradigm or management fad.' *The Learning Organization*, 3 (3): 18–25.

Payne, A. (ed.) (1995) *Advances in Relationship Marketing* (The Cranfield Management Series). London: Kogan Page.

Peck, H., Payne, A., Christopher, M. and Clark, M. (1999) *Relationship Marketing: Strategy and Implementation*. Oxford: Butterworth-Heinemann.

(Continued)

(Continued)

Perrow, C. (1988) *Complex Organizations: a Critical Essay*, 3rd edn. New York: McGraw-Hill.

Petty, R.E. and Cacioppo, J.T. (1986) *Communication and Persuasion: Central and Peripheral Routes to Attitude Change*. New York: Springer-Verlag.

Pratkanis, A. R. and Greenwald, A. G. (1993) Consumer involvement, message attention, and the persistence of persuasive impact in a message-dense environment, *Psychology & Marketing*, 10: 321–332.

Reid, R. and Brown, S. (1996) 'Square pegs, round holes and shopper typologies: an introspective examination.' Working paper presented at the Marketing Educators Conference, Strathclyde.

Scott, L. (2007) 'Critical research in marketing: an armchair report.' In M. Saren, P. Maclaran, C. Goulding, R. Elliot, A. Shankar and A. Catterall (eds), *Critical Marketing: Defining the Field*. London: Butterworth-Heinemann.

Sheth, J.N. and Parvatiyar, A. (eds) (2000) *Handbook of Relationship Marketing*. London: Sage.

Shiv, B. and Fedorikhin, A. (1999) 'Heart and mind in conflict: the interplay of affect and cognition in consumer decision making.' *Journal of Consumer Research*, 26 (3): 278–292.

Stone, G.P. (1954) City and urban identification: observations on the social psychology of city life, *American Journal of Sociology*, 60: 36–45.

Taylor, S.E. (1986) 'The interface of Cognitive and Social Psychology.' In J.H. Harvey (ed.), *Cognition, Social Behaviour and the Environment*. Hillsdale, NJ: Erlbaum (cited in Petty, R.E. and Cacioppo, J.T., *Communication and Persuasion: Central and Peripheral Routes to Attitude Change*, New York: Springer Verlag).

Thomas, M.J. (1994) 'Marketing – in chaos or transition?' *European Journal of Marketing*, 28 (3): 55–62.

Thompson, K. (1990) *The Employee Revolution – the Rise of Corporate Internal Marketing*. London: Pitman.

Varey, R. and Lewis, B. (2000) *Internal Marketing*. London: Routledge.

Veloutsou, C., Saren, M. and Tzokas, N. (2002) Relationship Marketing, What if...? *European Journal Of Marketing*, 36(4): 443–49.

Westbrook, R.A. and Black, W.C. (1985) 'A motivation-based shopper typology.' *Journal of Retailing*, 24: 258–270.

Williams, T.G. (2002) 'Social class influences on purchase evaluation criteria.' *Journal of Consumer Marketing*, 19 (2/3): 249–276.

Williamson, M. (2002) 'Emotions, reason and behaviour: a search for the truth.' *Journal of Consumer Behaviour*, 2 (2): 196–202.

Wilmott, H. (1999) On the Idolization of Markets and the Denegration of Marketers: Some Critical Reflections on a Professional Paradox, in D. Brownlie, M. Saren, R. Wensley and R. Whittington (1999) *Rethinking Marketing: Towards Critical Marketing Accountings*. London: Sage.

Zaichkowsky, J.L. (1991) 'Consumer behaviour: yesterday, today, and tomorrow.' *Business Horizons* (May/June), 34 (3): 51–58.

Zeithaml, V. (1988) 'Consumer perceptions of price, quality, and value: a means-end model and synthesis of evidence.' *Journal of Marketing*, 52: 2–22.

5 Accounting and Finance

Key concepts

Absorption cost model; Activity-based cost model; Balance sheet; Break-even point; CAPM; Constructionism; Cost; Cost-volume-profit analysis; Dividend model; Economic liberalism; Financial accounting; Financial management; Gearing; Income statement; Internal rate of return; Management accounting; Net present value; Portfolio theory; Present value; Profit; Ratio analysis; Standard cost model; Target-based cost model; Variable cost model; Working capital

> Truth isn't outside power ... Truth is a thing of this world; it is produced only by virtue of multiple forms of constraint. And it induces regular effects of power. Each society has its regime of truth, its 'general politics' of truth; that is, the types of discourse which it accepts and makes function as true ... (Foucault, 1980: 49)

Inasmuch as accounting plays a central role in portraying, evaluating and governing the ever expanding domains of economic and social life, it is socially, politically and economically significant. Not only does it enable social and economic activities to be rendered knowable, measurable, accountable and manageable at a distance, it is also frequently mobilized to adjudicate economic claims between competing constituencies (Boczko, 2000). Indeed, accounting is implicated not only in the conditioning of flows of capital but also in determining/measuring the effectiveness of capital's reorientation and re-organization of the social framework through which social, political and economic power is expressed (Tinker, 1985).

But what is accounting?

Accounting is more than just a system of rational calculation (Colignon and Covaleski, 1991) and certainly more than just a series of technical procedures designed to collate, present, analyze, examine and interpret business-related transactions and activities. It is, contrary to the illusions of liberal economics,[1] anything but a neutral and unbiased technical activity (Gray et al., 1996). It is a politically constructed space – a created form of discourse through which selected aspects of a market-based accumulation process are defined, mediated and legitimated (Bryer, 1995), a view which concurs with Foucault's thinking as indicated in the opening quotation. Accounting is in essence a 'created' form of knowledge, or regime of truth. It is a discourse comprised of a series of constructed models or, more appropriately, simplifications of reality, which derive their meaning and truthfulness not from the objects, practices or outcomes they attempt to represent, but rather from the traditions or the 'general politics' that seek to render them meaningful, purposive and valuable as an active social technology,[2] traditions which are increasingly conditioned by the powerful priorities of capital[3] and its continued promotion and indeed legitimization of a global homogeneity which is both ideologically and culturally Anglo-American in character.[4]

Whilst in a contemporary context these simplifications of reality are often divided into three groups – these being financial accounting models, management accounting models and financial management models – it is important to note that this compartmentalization is purely artificial. It is founded solely on the traditionalistic objectivity enshrined within Western (or Anglo-American) **economic liberalism** and its desire to protect the powerful processes of capital accumulation, to sustain a belief in and dependency upon the market mechanism, and to ensure the maintenance and reproduction of existing relations of power (Willmott et al., 1993).

Nevertheless it does – in a limited sense – provide a useful, if perhaps somewhat contrived framework within which to explore the content and inherent limitations of some of the groups of models mentioned above.

For the following discussion we will restrict this to equity-based companies, although much of the information will also apply to non-corporate entities.

Let's start with financial accounting.

Financial Accounting

Financial accounting is generally concerned with external performance reporting. As such, financial accounting statements (or more appropriately financial accounting models) – the Balance Sheet, the Income Statement[5] – are structured historical statements that are retrospective in nature and externally regulated/controlled.[6] Constructed using a recording technique commonly referred to as double entry bookkeeping,[7] such financial accounting models are primarily transaction orientated. They are concerned with the recording, classification, and presentation of financial transactions in accordance with extant accounting standards and national legal requirements.

Founded upon a number of underpinning principles or fundamental concepts and conventions,[8] the primary uses of such financial accounting models are the measurement of wealth and the evaluation of financial performance.

Financial accounting: a series of techniques concerned with the recording, classification and presentation of financial transactions in accordance with externally imposed reporting requirements.

Measurement of wealth

Balance sheet

The balance sheet provides a structured summary of the financial position of a company. It is a financial snapshot at a specific moment in time (usually the company's financial year end), and contains three main elements – assets, liabilities and capital (equity). These are presented as a representation of the following model (commonly referred to as the accounting equation):

$$\text{Assets} = \text{Liabilities} + \text{Capital (or Equity)}$$

Assets can be defined as the right to receive a future economic benefit as a consequence of a past transaction or event (for example, a contract of exchange). For a company, an asset has three essential characteristics:

- There is an underlying economic resource
- The company has rights or other privileged access to the economic resource
- The economic resource and the rights associated with it exist at the balance sheet date

Assets are generally categorized as either non-current assets, for example tangible non-current assets such as land and buildings; intangible non-current assets, such as patents, trade rights and goodwill; financial non-current assets, such as equity investments; and current assets, for example inventories, debtors (or accounts receivable), prepayments and cash and/or a bank deposit.

Liabilities represent claims against the company. These arise from transactions undertaken by the company in the course of its business-related activities and can be defined as an obligation to transfer economic benefits as a result of past transactions or events. For example, the purchase of assets on credit would result in the creation of a debt which would require future satisfaction as per the terms of credit purchase agreement. For a company, a liability has three essential characteristics:

- The obligation is economic – it requires the company to provide its economic resources to others, or to forgo economic resources that it might otherwise be able to obtain
- The company is obligated to others to act or perform in a certain way – or refrain from acting or performing
- The economic obligation and the legal enforceability both exist at the financial statement date

Liabilities are generally categorized as either non-current liabilities – for example long-term financial debt, long-term trade creditors (or accounts payable) and provisions[9] – and current or short-term liabilities – for example short-term financial debt (a temporary loan and/or bank overdraft), trade creditors (or accounts payable) and accruals.

It is noteworthy here that since a liability cannot be recognized unless a quantifiable legally enforceable claim can be established, such a definition negates the possibility of a company acknowledging, for example, socio-environmental claims/obligations which may arise out of business-related activities.

Capital (or shareholders equity) represents a claim by the owners of the company against the company and is usually divided into the following:

- Share capital (or equity), which is required to be valued at the nominal or face value of the shares
- Share premiums, which are the difference between the nominal value of shares and their issue price
- Retained earnings, which are undistributed revenue profits that have accumulated during previous accounting periods

Internationally, there are two allowable alternative presentations of the Balance Sheet, these being:

- The horizontal format (rarely used in practice) which is presented as a representation of the following model:

$$\text{Non-Current Assets} + \text{Current Assets}$$
$$=$$
$$\text{Capital} + \text{Non-Current Liabilities} + \text{Current Liabilities}$$

- The vertical format, which is presented as a representation of the following model:

$$\text{Non-Current Assets} + [\text{Current Assets} - \text{Current Liabilities}] - \text{Non-Current Liabilities}$$
$$=$$
$$\text{Capital}$$

In addition, national legal requirements often specify that comparative figures for both the current year and the previous year must be provided, and where the company is part of a group of companies the ultimate holding company within the group must supply a consolidated balance sheet[10] for the group in addition to an individual company **balance sheet.**

Balance sheet: a summary model – a representation of the accounting equation containing details of a company's assets, liabilities and capital.

Below is an example of a simplified (vertical presentation) balance sheet for a UK-based public limited company.

Balance Sheet as at 31 March

	2010		2011	
	(£000)	(£000)	(£000)	(£000)
Non-Current Assets		4,300		7,200
Current Assets				
Inventories	1,200		2,900	
Trade receivables	800		1,900	
Other receivables	100		200	
Cash	100		-	
	2,200		5,000	
Current Liabilities				
Trade payables	600		1,300	
Other payables	100		200	
Taxation	200		400	
Dividends	200		300	
Bank	-		2,100	
	1,100		4,300	
Net Current Assets		1,100		700
Total net assets		5,400		7,900
Non-Current Liabilities				
Loan		2,200		3,300
		£3,200		£4,600
Capital and Reserves				
Ordinary shares (£1)		1,600		1,600
Retained profit		1,600		3,000
		£3,200		£4,600

Income statement

The **income statement** (formerly known as the profit and loss account) provides a summary presentation of the **profit** (or loss) of a company, with the various categories of income and expenditure within it classified into turnover, **cost** of sales, other operating costs, other operating income, net interest, taxation, and dividends. It provides a numerical explanation of the trading transactions of a company over an accounting period – namely, a summary of the revenue income that has been generated during a specified accounting period and the revenue costs that have been incurred during a specified accounting period in generating the revenue.

The income statement can be considered in two ways:

- As a statement illustrating the change in wealth between the start of the accounting period and the end of the accounting period which would be a representation of the following model:

$$\text{Assets} - \text{Liabilities} = \text{Capital} + \text{Profit}$$

- As a statement illustrating the change in wealth as a product of the total revenues for the accounting period less the total costs for the accounting period which would be a representation of the following model:

$$\text{Profit} = \text{Total Revenue} - \text{Total Costs}$$

There is of course a close connection between the income statement and the balance sheet, for example:

- With the exception of the purchase/sale of non-current assets, the issue/redemption of shares and/or the borrowing/repayment of debt all other business-related transactions would affect both the income statement AND the balance sheet
- All adjusting entries used to prepare the income statement – including accruals and prepayments, depreciation, provision and re-valuations – would affect both the income statement AND the balance sheet
- Any undistributed profits retained at the end of the accounting period would be reflected within the equity (or shareholders' funds) on the balance sheet as retained earnings

---

Income statement: a summary model which provides a measurement (the profit or loss) of the business performance of a company.

Below is an example of a simplified income statement for a UK-based public limited company.

Income Statement for the year ended 31 March

	2010 (£000)	2011 (£000)
Turnover	7,000	11,500
Cost of sales	3,700	5,800
Gross profit	3,300	5,700
Operating expenses	2,200	3,100

(Continued)

(Continued)

Operating profit	1,100	2,600
Interest payable	200	500
Profit before taxation	900	2,100
Taxation	200	400
Profit after taxation	700	1,700
Dividend	200	300
Retained profit for the year	500	1,400
Retained profit brought forward	1,100	1,600
Retained profit carried forward	£1,600	£3,000

So what are the limitations of the balance sheet and the income statement?

Whilst both can provide some useful information concerning a company's financial performance, its levels of income and expenditure, its financial structure, its relative liquidity and the composition (of some) of its assets and liabilities, the balance sheet and income statement are nonetheless both historical in nature. They do not reflect the current 'market' values of a company's transactions, its assets and/or its liabilities, but merely present a confusing and somewhat awkward combination of market values, deprival values,[11] historical values, and adjusted historical values.[12]

In addition, there is an assortment of both presentation options and valuation options now available within various national regulatory requirements: these are in key areas such as:

- The valuation of inventory (for example LIFO,[13] FIFO,[14] AvCo[15])
- The depreciation of non-current assets (for example the straight line method, the reducing balance method, the sum of digits method)
- The creation and maintenance of revenue provisions (for example, provisions for doubtful debts, provisions for contingent liabilities)

These offer increasing opportunities for companies to use a wide range of imaginative and inventive judgement-based estimates in the preparation of the balance sheet and the income statement, resulting in financial statements which not only lack comparability between different companies (national and internationally) but more importantly a lack of consistency between different accounting periods within the same company.

Finally, the increasing failure of both national and international financial reporting standards as an accepted regulatory framework to keep abreast of the evermore creative and risky practices that now populate international financial reporting has, somewhat unsurprisingly, permitted companies to selectively disregard expenditure-based transactions which are of indeterminate value from their income statement and/or to completely omit high value commitments and liabilities from their balance sheet. This is done in order to creatively improve their financial performance and thus they produce a balance sheet and income statement which are more works of fiction rather than true and fair statements of fact.

Indeed, this issue of 'creativity' and the increasingly fictional qualities of financial statements such as the balance sheet and the income statement has perhaps never been better illustrated than during the global financial crisis of the latter part of the first decade of the twenty-first century, which has witnessed the collapse of a number of established and well-respected companies: many of these had produced not only healthy asset-rich balance sheets but also earnings-rich income statements right up to the very year of their demise.[16] This situation has perhaps unsurprisingly elevated discussions on the truthfulness of company financial statements to the front pages of the financial press[17] and prompted many national and international accounting standards bodies – including the Accounting Standards Board in the UK, the Financial Accounting Standards Board in the USA, the International Federation of Accountants (IFAC), and the International Accounting Standards Board (IASB) – to revisit/review the effectiveness of their respective financial reporting regulatory frameworks.

Evaluation of performance

The main aim of a performance evaluation is to provide an understanding of the company and its financial performance. This can be for a number of reasons, for example:

- In order to assist in the evaluation of an investment decision/opportunity
- In order to identify possible take-over targets
- In order to evaluate the financial strength of an existing customer/supplier

There are two categories of business performance analysis – quantitative evaluation (sometimes referred as hard analysis), and qualitative evaluation (sometimes referred to as soft analysis).

Quantitative evaluation

Hard analysis usually involves the use of quantitative univariate ratios related to profitability, efficiency, liquidity, financial structure, and return on investment. Such ratios are widely used to assess the relative efficiency of a company or a constituent part of a company, to provide cross-sectional analysis and inter-firm comparisons, and/or to establish a company valuation, for example in respect to a loan/debt agreement or possible merger/acquisition. They are also increasingly used to assess/predict company failure.

Profitability ratios are utilized to assess the overall performance of a company and measure its ability to generate revenue profits. Commonly used profitability ratios include the following:

Profitability ratios

$$\text{gross margin} = \frac{\text{gross margin}}{\text{sales}}$$

$$\text{profit before interest and tax (PBIT)} = \frac{\text{operating profit}}{\text{sales}}$$

$$\text{return on investment (ROI)} = \frac{\text{operating profit}}{\text{total assets} - \text{current liabilities}}$$

$$\text{return on equity (ROE)} = \frac{\text{profit after tax}}{\text{equity}}$$

Efficiency ratios are used to measure how effectively a company utilizes its current assets and manages its current liabilities. Commonly used efficiency ratios include the following:

Efficiency ratios

$$\text{trade receivable days} = \frac{\text{trade receivables} \times 365}{\text{sales}}$$

$$\text{trade payable days} = \frac{\text{trade payables} \times 365}{\text{cost of sales (or purchases)}}$$

$$\text{inventory days} = \frac{\text{inventory value}}{\text{average daily cost of sales in period}}$$

$$\text{operating cycle (days)} = \text{inventory days} + \text{debtor days} - \text{creditor days}$$

$$\text{operating cycle \%} = \frac{\text{inventories} + \text{trade receivables} - \text{trade payables}}{\text{sales}}$$

Liquidity ratios are used to measure the company's ability to convert short-term assets into cash and as such reflect the health (or otherwise) of the cash position of a company and its ability to meet short-term obligations. Commonly used liquidity ratios include the following:

Liquidity ratios

current ratio (times) = $\dfrac{\text{current assets}}{\text{current liabilities}}$

acid test (times) = $\dfrac{\text{current assets} - \text{inventories}}{\text{current liabilities}}$

defensive interval (days) = $\dfrac{\text{quick assets (current assets} - \text{inventories)}}{\text{average daily cash from operations}}$

Financial ratios are used to measure the relationship between debt and equity capital that is, the financial structure of a company. Commonly used financial ratios include the following:

 Financial ratios

gearing = $\dfrac{\text{long-term debt}}{\text{equity} + \text{long-term debt}}$

debt equity ratio = $\dfrac{\text{long-term debt}}{\text{equity}}$

interest cover (times) = $\dfrac{\text{profit before interest and tax}}{\text{interest payable}}$

Investment ratios are used to indicate the extent to which the business is undertaking capital expenditure to ensure its survival and stability and also its ability to sustain current revenues and generate future increased revenues. Commonly used investment ratios include the following:

 Investment ratios

earnings per share (eps) = $\dfrac{\text{profit after tax} - \text{preference share dividends}}{\text{number of ordinary shares in issue}}$

(Continued)

(Continued)

$$\text{dividend per share} = \frac{\text{total dividends paid to ordinary shareholders}}{\text{number of ordinary shares in issue}}$$

$$\text{dividend cover} = \frac{\text{earnings per share}}{\text{dividend per share}}$$

$$\text{dividend yield \%} = \frac{\text{dividend per share}}{\text{share price}}$$

$$\text{price/earnings ratio (P/E)} = \frac{\text{current share price}}{\text{eps}}$$

In addition to using single univariate ratios to assess corporate performance and future stability, a number of multivariate ratio-based equations have been developed which use a combination of accounting ratios to calculate a z score (using multivariate discriminant analysis) and predict possible corporate financial failure. The most popular of these multivariate-based equations is Altman's Z-Score (1968), although Taffler's Z-Score (1982) also enjoys some, albeit limited, popularity.

Ratio analysis: the study of the financial performance of a company using relationship ratios (both univariate and multivariate ratios) derived from financial and non-financial information included in the company's financial statements.

So how useful are such accounting ratios?

While both univariate and multivariate ratios are widely used in the evaluation of corporate performance, the usefulness of such quantitative evaluation techniques in reviewing business performance (trend analysis), or in comparing corporate performance against other companies (cross sectional analysis), or indeed in assessing the possibility of future corporate failure is of course severely limited.

The reason for this is primarily due to the inconsistent application of accounting definitions, the inconsistent use of alternative accounting techniques, and the numerous presentation options, financing options and valuations allowable by national GAAPs, together with the inability of such ratios to acknowledge the impact of the socio-political factors/qualitative issues that frequently affect corporate financial performance.

To perhaps compensate for this latter shortcoming, a number of qualitative evaluation techniques or soft analysis-based techniques have become increasingly popular. Such soft analysis usually involves a consideration of non-financial factors/models to evaluate corporate stability and these include, for example, PESTEL[18] analysis, SWOT[19] analysis (see Chapter 9 on Strategic Management), the Balanced

Scorecard[20] analysis, and Argenti's (1976) A-Score. Whilst the use of such qualitative evaluation models has become increasingly widespread in recent years, especially in the UK, USA and Australasia, their credibility has been and indeed continues to be called into question – especially by the 'die hard' functionalists who see no place for the 'human factor' in the evaluation of corporate financial performance.

Management Accounting

Management accounting is generally concerned with the formulation of corporate strategies and policies, with the planning and control of business activities, and with decision making and corporate governance. As such management accounting is often predictive in nature, unstructured, and internally controlled. Management accounting models are generally concerned with decision facilitating, surveillance and control – for example, product costing models; cost volume profit analysis and break-even models; financial planning; and budgetary control models (Chapter 2 on Organizational Behaviour discusses issues of control in more detail).

Management accounting: a series of techniques concerned with creating, protecting, preserving, and increasing business value for the economic benefit of company stakeholders.

Before we look at a selection of the more popular product costing models, it would perhaps be useful to consider what, in an accounting context, is meant by the term 'cost'.

A cost can be defined as an amount of expenditure attributable to a specified asset, event, or activity, and/or a resource sacrificed or forgone. As such costs are dependent on, and will generally change with, the level of activity – that is the greater the volume or complexity of an asset, event or activity, then (normally) the greater the cost. There are three main categories of costs:

- A fixed cost – a cost that does not vary with the level of activity
- A variable cost – a cost that does vary with the level of activity
- A semi-variable cost (or semi-fixed, or mixed cost)

Alternatively, a cost may be categorized as a direct cost which is one that can be directly identified with or related to a cost object (for example, a product or service) and an indirect cost which is one that cannot be directly identified with or related to a cost object and has to be allocated or apportioned to a cost object. In management accounting costs and revenues are – perhaps somewhat unrealistically – assumed to exhibit a linear relationship, that is short-term selling prices are assumed to remain constant, fixed costs are assumed to remain constant and unchanged (but only within a specific range of volumes), and short-term unit variable costs are assumed to remain constant. What this assumption of linearity means is that in management accounting there is an assumed truth that as corporate activity increases so profit increases, and perhaps more importantly, that profit is maximized where maximum capacity is reached.

Product costing

Product costing is concerned with the assessment, analysis and evaluation of the costs accrued in, and associated with, the production and sale of a product or service. In general product costing involves two key stages: cost collection and cost assessment.

Cost collection is concerned with the collection or accumulation of production costs with costs collected/accumulated usually in concert with the actual physical production process and on the same basis as the production methodology adopted by the company/organization. For example, costs could be collected/accumulated on:

- A process basis – where continuous manufacturing or flow manufacturing is used (sometimes referred to as process costing)
- A job basis – where batch manufacturing or intermittent manufacturing is used (sometimes referred to as job costing)
- A production order basis where on-demand manufacturing is used (sometimes referred to as contract costing or order costing)

Whichever methodology is adopted, the stages of the cost collection would normally involve the collection and assignment of all direct material costs, all direct labour costs, and all direct expenses – with the amounts charged on the basis of a standard unit cost and the accumulation and assignment of production overheads – together with the amounts charged on the basis of a standard production overhead rate. For cost assessment purposes, the vast majority of companies will use one of the following approaches (or an amended variation) to determine the cost of a product and/or service; an absorption cost-based model, a variable cost-based model, an activity cost-based model, a target cost-based model, or a standard cost-based model.

The **absorption cost** (also referred to as full cost) **model** considers the total cost of manufacturing a product and/or providing a service – that is in addition to all direct costs, a proportion of production overhead costs is also apportioned (or more precisely absorbed), with each product/service therefore charged with both fixed and variable production costs. Using the absorption cost model, the production cost of a product (or the provision cost of a service) would therefore include:

- All direct material costs – that is, those materials that have become a part of a product, or have been used up in providing a service
- All direct labour costs – that is, those labour costs that can be easily traced to the manufacture of a product, or the provision of a service individual product

- All direct expenses – that is, those expenses directly applicable to the manufacture of a product, or the provision of a service
- A proportion of indirect production overheads

The absorption cost model

	£	£	£
Sales			150
Direct costs			
direct materials		50	
direct labour	40		
direct expenses		10	
Prime cost			100
indirect costs			
production overheads			20
Product cost			120
period costs			
non-production overheads		10	
Total product cost			130
net profit		20	

The advantages of the absorption cost model are that it provides a summary total cost for a product and/or service and it can also be used to identify the profitability of a product and/or service. The main disadvantage of the model is that it is a subjective approach inasmuch as the allocation of fixed costs is arbitrary – and this can be politically motivated, leading (potentially) to the calculation of a misleading total cost for a product and/or service.

Absorption cost model: a model of costing in which the full cost of manufacturing a product or providing a service is considered to be comprised of all direct costs and a proportion of the production overheads which are generally allocated using a pre-planned absorption rate.

The variable cost model (also referred to as the marginal cost model), provides an alternative approach to the costing products/services in which only the variable costs of production, or service provision, are charged to the product/service.

Fixed production costs are not considered to be real costs of product production/ service provision, but rather as those which enable product production/service provision to occur: these are therefore treated as period costs and charged to the period in which they are incurred. Stocks are valued on a variable production cost basis that excludes fixed production costs.

Using the **variable cost model**, the production cost of a product/the provision cost of a service would therefore include:

- All variable material costs – that is, those materials that have become a part of a product or have been used up in providing a service
- All variable labour costs – that is, those labour costs that can be easily traced to the manufacture of a product or the provision of a service individual product
- All variable expenses – that is, those expenses directly applicable to the manufacture of a product or the provision of a service

The variable cost model

	£	£
Sales		150
Variable costs		
direct materials		50
direct labour	40	
direct expenses	<u>10</u>	
Total variable cost		<u>100</u>
contribution		50
Fixed costs		
production overheads		20
non-production overheads	<u>10</u>	
Total fixed costs		<u>30</u>
profit		<u>20</u>

The advantage of the variable cost model is that there is no arbitrary allocation of costs. However, the disadvantages of the model are that it can be difficult to determine fixed costs and variable costs and it does not comply with many national/international inventory valuation requirements.

> **Variable cost model**: a model of costing generally used for internal decision making in which only the variable costing of manufacturing a product or providing a service is charged to a product or service – fixed costs are instead considered to be period costs.

The **activity cost-based model** (more commonly referred to as an activity-based costing or ABC) provides yet another alternative approach to the costing of products and services which arose primarily in response to criticisms aimed at the more traditional volume-based models.

The activity cost-based model is founded on the understanding that costs arise because of the activities utilized and not because of the products and/or services produced, with the management and control of costs best achieved through the management of such activities.[22] Rather than levels/volumes of production, activity-based costing considers four different groups of activities giving rise to overheads, such as movement, production demand, quality and design, and requires all cost types to be identified and classified into those costs which are volume based, those costs which are activity based, and those costs which may have some other basis.

The advantages of the activity cost-based model are that it focusses on activities and not production volumes and it can be used to identify loss-making products. The disadvantages of the activity cost-based model are that it is subjective, that it requires an identification of cost drivers (activities), and as such that it can be expensive and time-consuming. Again, as with the variable cost model, it does not comply with many national/international inventory valuation requirements.

Activity-based cost model: a model of costing in which costs are collected on the basis of a function or activity and are then allocated/apportioned to a product or service on the basis of their relative use of the function or activity during the manufacture of the product and/or the provision of a service.

The **target cost-based model** is often considered to be a reversible cost accounting technique. That is, rather than calculating the total cost of a product/service, and then determining the market price of the product/service based on the total cost – for example, total cost plus a pre-determined profit margin – the target cost of a product/service is established by reference to the external marketplace. There are three alternative approaches to target costing, these being:

- A price-based targeting model in which the target cost of a product/service is derived by subtracting the desired profit margin from a competitive market price for a similar and/or equivalent product/service
- A cost-based targeting model in which the target cost of a product/service is derived by establishing a total cost for a product/service – by reference to costs incurred by the company
- A value-based targeting model in which the target cost of a product/service is determined by estimating the 'value' the market will place on the product/service and then subtracting the desired profit margin

The advantages of a target-based cost model are that it encourages the minimization of total cost, and seeks to eliminate possible excess costs. The disadvantages of a target-based cost model are that it can lead to excessive cost cutting and it can also have a destabilizing effect on the operations of a company.

> **Target-based cost model**: a model of costing which focusses on reducing the overall cost of a product or service over the entire life-cycle of the product or service.

The **standard cost model** is based on using pre-determined costs for materials, labour and expenses so that the standard cost of the product and/or service produced and/or provided in a period can be determined. Whilst such a cost model is widely used in the measurement, assessment and control of business-related activities (see the section on budgetary control later in this chapter), it is also adopted in the valuation of work-in-progress and finished goods and in the establishment of product/service selling prices.

The advantages of a standard cost-based model are that it can be used to highlight areas of strength and weakness and to evaluate performance by comparing actual costs with standard costs, thereby assisting in identifying responsibility. The disadvantages of a standard cost model are it can be difficult to establish the standard and also difficult to administer.

> **Standard cost model**: a model of costing in which pre-determined costs for materials, labour and expenses are allocated to a product or service.

Cost-volume-profit-analysis and break-even analysis

Cost-volume-profit (CVP) **analysis** considers the impact on future profit of changes in fixed costs, variable costs, sales volume, sales mix and selling price. One application of cost-volume-profit (CVP) analysis is break-even (B/E) analysis which is increasingly being used for profit planning purposes, especially where sales mix decisions, production capacity decisions and/or pricing decisions have to be made.

> **Cost-volume-profit analysis**: a financial decision making aid used to determine the level of output required to achieve any target profit level or the financial impact of basic business activities like changes in costs or pricing.

There are three fundamental cost and revenue relationships that form the basis of CVP cost-volume-profit analysis, these being:

- Total Costs (TC) = Variable Costs (VC) + Fixed Costs (FC)
- Contribution (C) = Total Revenue (TR) − Variable Costs (VC)
- Profit (or operating income) (P) = Total Revenue (TR) − Total Costs (TC)

The **break-even point** is the level of activity at which neither a profit nor a loss is made, where:

$$\text{Contribution (C)} = \text{Fixed Costs (FC)}$$

Using this relationship it is possible to calculated the approximate profit or loss at different levels of activity within a limited range, that is:

Break-even Point (in units/volume) = Fixed Costs (FC)/Contribution (C) Per Unit

Break-even Point (in value) = Fixed Costs (FC)/Contribution to Sales (CS) Ratio %

Where the anticipated level of activity and/or the existing level of activity are expected to be greater than the break-even point, the term 'margin of safety' is used to define (and quantify) the difference between the break-even point and the anticipated level of activity, or the existing level of activity. That is, the margin of safety measures the extent to which the anticipated level of activity or the existing level of activity could be reduced before a profitable activity becomes a loss-making activity.

Break-even point: the point where total revenue received from the sale of a product or service equals the total costs associated with the sale of the product or service.

Cost-volume-profit analysis or break-even analysis relies on a number of assumptions which can significantly limit its usefulness, for example:

- Revenues are assumed to change in relation to production and sales
- Costs can be divided in variable cost and fixed cost categories
- Revenues and costs behave in a predictable and linear fashion
- Costs and prices are known with certainty
- Where more than one product/service exists, the sales mix is assumed to remain constant
- The time value of money is ignored

However, despite these it is nonetheless widely used and enjoys substantial popularity. For example, cost-volume-profit analysis and break-even analysis are widely used to:

- Calculate the minimum amount of sales required in order to be able to break even
- Evaluate the consequences of changes in output, selling price or costs on profit levels
- Calculate the level of output required to reach a certain level of profit
- Evaluate alternative what-if scenarios, for example:
  - shutdown or continuation decisions
  - make or buy decisions
  - limiting factors or product mix decisions
  - product/service sales pricing decisions

Financial Planning and Control

Inasmuch as a company needs to ensure that sufficient financing is available at the right time to meet the needs of the company, long-term and short-term financial planning and control are critically important to the future survival and success of a company.

A crucial aspect, and increasingly dominant feature of any corporate financial planning and control process, is the preparation of a budget – a quantified statement, for a defined period of time, which is generally used for two purposes. From a planning perspective, budgets are used to identify and indicate priorities; provide direction and co-ordination; assign responsibility; provide motivation; and assist in improving corporate efficiency. They are used to provide a planning focus for the company and as such aid in the 'top-down' co-ordination of company activities. From a control perspective budgets are used to determine, facilitate, and/or constrain activities by enforcing an adherence to, and a compliance with, approved systems, policies and procedures. They are used to impose a control structure within the company to assist in the monitoring, evaluation and assessment of performance.

Clearly, the adopted methodology used to develop/create a company budget and the political process used to impose its requirements can have significant implications on its efficiency as both a planning and controlling tool.

Financial Management

Contemporary **financial management** is primarily concerned with two key issues:

- Maximizing corporate shareholder wealth
- Minimizing shareholder risk associated with longer-term decision making

Based on a market-orientated finance model contemporary financial management is generally associated with issues such as:

- The appraisal of investment opportunities
- The acquisition of appropriate finance
- The efficient management of company resources
- The distribution of an appropriate return to shareholders

It comprises a number of fundamental ideas (some expressed in the form of simple quantitative models) associated with, for example, asset/investment valuation; gearing (leverage) management; resource (or working capital) management; and of course the management of risk and return.

Before we look at some of these ideas/models in a little more detail, it would perhaps be useful to note that whilst it is the competitive ideology and risk-taking philosophy enshrined within the liberal economic market-based finance model that currently dominates corporate financial thinking, it is by no means the only financial model available. An alternative and increasingly popular model is the Islamic finance model[23] (or Shari'a-compliant finance model) – a model which functions on the basis of co-operative mutual risk sharing.

Based on interpretations from the Qur'an, the Islamic finance model has two central tenets:

- Wealth cannot be created from money – that is, 'money cannot be made from money', for example charging interest on a loan is not permitted
- Wealth can only be generated or created through legitimate socially responsible trade and investments[24]

Whilst knowledge of and indeed use of the Islamic finance model has become widespread within Europe, the United Kingdom and the United States, with many financial institutions now offering a small but growing range of Islamic financing facilities to both corporate and non-corporate customers and clients, it nonetheless remains misunderstood, with many market-based institutions openly insecure and deeply suspicious of its underlying ideology[25]

Financial management: the management of company finances in order to achieve key financial objectives of creating wealth and maximizing shareholder returns.

Time-based valuation – present value theory

The concept of **present value** is founded upon the premise that – all things being equal – a rational investor would prefer to receive payment of a fixed amount of money today rather than a payment of an equal amount of money at some time in the future.

Present value can be defined as the current worth of a future sum of money or stream of cash flows given a specified rate of return. Such future cash flows are discounted using an expected rate of return that can be internally determined or externally imposed.

The present value of a future cash flow can be calculated as follows:

$$P_0 = (FV/(1+i)^n$$

Here (P_0) is the value at time 0 (or today); (FV) is the value at time n (or a future point in time); (i) equals the rate at which the amount will be compounded for each time period; and (n) is the number of time periods.

Present value: the estimated current value of future benefits or costs – derived by discounting the future values using a selected rate of return/discount rate.

Whilst present value theory is widely used in a number of areas within financial management – for example, in the evaluation of capital investment opportunities, in the valuation of equities, and in the valuation of debt – inherent assumptions regarding the accepted reliability of future values, the assumed predictability of future cash flows, and the implied certainty of future expected rates of return nonetheless severely limit its frequently questioned utility.

Capital investment opportunities

A capital investment can be defined as an investment which requires expenditure today (or in the immediate future) in anticipation of the receipt of an expected benefit in the future. Because of the substantial nature of such investments, investment decisions are extremely important because they are invariably concerned with the future survival, prosperity and growth of the company, and as such it is important to ensure that only those investments which not only maintain but more importantly also increase shareholder wealth are selected.

Using (i) to represent the cost of capital (the discount rate), and (n) the number of time periods (usually years) which may have a value from 0 to infinity, a present value discount factor can be calculated as follows:

$$1/(1+i)^n$$

If an investment project has an initial investment cost in year 0 of (I), a cost of capital of (i), and net cash flows (CF) from year 1 to year (n), the **net present value** of the cash flows could be expressed as:

$$NPV = (-I) + [(CF/(1+i)] + [(CF/(1+i)^2] \ldots \ldots \ldots \ldots [(CF/(1+i)^n]$$

> **Net Present Value (NPV)**: is the total present value of a time series of future cash flows.

Whereas the NPV model calculates the net difference in present values between cash inflows and cash outflows by discounting anticipated future cash flows using an appropriate discount rate,[26] the **Internal Rate of Return** (IRR) model calculates the rate of return where the difference between the present value cash inflows and cash outflows is zero, that is where:

$$NPV = \sum_{t=0}^{n} FV_t/(1+i)^t = 0$$

There are a number of ways in which the internal rate of return of an investment may be calculated, the most popular being interpolation using the following:

$$A + [(a/(a - b)) * (B - A)]$$

Here (A) is the lowest discount rate, (B) is the highest discount rate, (a) is the npv @ A, and (b) is the npv @ B.

> **Internal Rate of Return**: the annualized return of rate which can be earned on an investment capital, that is the discount rate that makes the net present value of the investment's income stream zero.

There are of course a number of non time-based models used in investment appraisal, the most popular being:

- The accounting rate of return (ARR)[27]
- Payback[28]

The valuation of equities

Equity can be broadly defined as finance 'provided' by the owners of the company for use within that company, usually by means of preference shares, ordinary shares, and redeemable shares. In general, equities are assumed to be perpetuities (or perpetual annuities) in which a stream of payments or receipts (fixed or growing) will be paid or received over an indefinite period of time[29] – that is where $n = \infty$.

Using present value theory there are two key approaches to the valuation of equities: the dividend-based valuation (without growth) model (which is a fixed perpetuity), and the dividend-based valuation with growth model (which is a growing perpetuity).

The no growth **dividend model** assumes the dividend will not increase, and the fundamental value of a share can therefore be calculated as:

$$P_0 = Div_1/r$$

The growth dividend model assumes the dividend will increase at a regular rate of growth, and the fundamental value of a share can therefore be calculated as:

$$P_0 = Div_1/(r - g)$$

Re-arranging the above equation,

- (r) the expected rate of return on a share can be expressed as:

$$r = (Div_1/ P_0) + g$$

and

- (g) can be expressed as expected return * the retention ratio on equity, that is:

$$g = r * Rr$$

Dividend model: a model for valuing a company based on the theory that a share is worth the discounted sum of all future dividend payments – that is, the current 'fundamental' value of a share is the net present value of its future dividends.

Despite its widespread use, there are of course a number of problems with the dividend model; for example, the dividend growth model not only requires a perpetual growth rate (g) which is greater than -1, but more importantly it also requires a perpetual growth rate (g) that is less than the cost of capital (r). In addition the dividend growth model is extremely sensitive where the cost of capital (r) is very close to the rate of growth (g).

The valuation of debt

Debt can be defined as the borrowing from another person, or persons (including another company), of purchasing power from the future.

Where there is no obligation to repay a sum of capital and only an obligation to pay an agreed amount of interest such a debt is commonly called irredeemable debt. In present value terms, such a debt can be regarded as a perpetuity and its present value can be calculated as follows:

$$P_0 = (i / R_d)$$

Here (i) is the annual amount of interest payable on the debt, and (R_d) is the market rate of the return on the debt expected by investors.

Where there is an obligation to pay an agreed amount of interest and repay a sum of capital, such a debt is commonly called redeemable debt. In present value terms, this can be regarded as an annuity. An annuity is a stream of payments or receipts (fixed or growing) which will be paid or received over a fixed and specified period of time – that is, a series of equal payments or receipts that will occur at evenly spaced intervals.[30] The present value of such a debt can be calculated as the PV of the interest payment annuity plus the PV of the single cash flow payable on redemption of the debt.

In addition a debt can be categorized as either a secured debt or non-secured debt. Secured debt can be defined as debt (usually a long-term debt) in which a lender (creditor) is granted a specific legal right over a borrower's property/assets.

The purpose of securing a debt is to allow a lender (creditor) to be able to seize, or more appropriately sequester, property/assets from a borrower in the event that the borrower fails to properly satisfy the repayment requirements of the debt, and/or adequately adhere to specific conditions imposed by the debt instrument. Such secured debt is referred to as a debenture and any conditions attached to the borrowing would normally be identified in a debenture trust deed.

Unsecured debt can be defined as debt – usually a short- to medium-term debt that is not collateralized, or not secured against any property/assets of the borrower. Such a debt would include, for example, borrowing/using either short-term overdraft facilities, short-term loans – (for example a three or six month money market loan), or medium-term loans – for example, a two-year bond.

The valuation of convertible securities

Convertible securities are securities that can be converted into other securities, for example debt to equity or equity to debt. There are many varieties of convertible securities,[31] for example:

- An optional convertible security – in which the holder of the convertible security has the option to convert the debt into shares at a number of agreed future dates
- An exchangeable convertible security – in which the shares underlying the debt are in a company other than the company issuing the convertible security that is different from that of the issuer

However the most common is a debt instrument such as a bond which can, subject to certain terms and conditions, be converted into equity in the issuing company. The conversion value of the convertible bond can be calculated as:

$$V_n = S \times (1 + g)n \times N$$

where:

- g = the expected annual percentage growth rate of the share price
- N = the number of ordinary shares that will be received on conversion
- S = the estimated ordinary share price at the conversion date

with the current market value of the convertible bond (V_o) determined by calculating the present value of future annual interest (I) plus the present value of the securities conversion value after n years (V_n), using the market rate of return on bonds expected by investors (R_d), that is:

$$V_o = I/(1 + R_d) + I/(1 + R_d)2 + I/(1 + R_d)3 \ldots + (I + V_n)/(1 + R_d)^n$$

Derivative instruments

Equity, debt, and convertible securities are often referred to as primary instruments[32] inasmuch as the market value of the instrument (as opposed to the fundamental value) is determined directly by market supply and demand. Derivative instruments[33] are financial instruments that do not derive their value directly from the market but from the value of another financial instrument, underlying asset, commodity index, or interest rate. The most common types of derivatives include, for example, futures, options, swaps, and securitized instruments (often referred to as asset-backed securities).

Futures are exchange-traded contracts that are traded on various currencies, interest bearing securities, and equity or stock indexes. Options are contracts which give the holder of the option the right – but not the obligation – to buy (a call option), or sell (a put option), a specified underlying asset at a pre-agreed price (the strike price), at either a fixed point in time, or at a number of specified times in the future, or at a time chosen by the holder up until maturity. Swaps are contractual agreements entered into between two parties under which each party agrees to make periodic payment to the other for an agreed period of time based on a notional amount of principal/capital.

Asset-backed securities are securities whose value and income payments are derived from and collateralized (or backed) by a specified and identifiable pool of small and sometimes illiquid assets.[34] This pooling or repackaging of cash-flow-producing financial assets into marketable securities is a process which is often referred to as securitization, with the latter part of the twentieth century witnessing a phenomenal growth in the use of asset-backed securities, primarily as an alternative to debt finance and especially by those companies with large amounts of illiquid assets.

It is perhaps worth considering here the extent of the collapse of the US sub-prime mortgage market and its impact on the value of mortgage-backed securities together with the failure of financial institutions worldwide to fully appreciate the risks associated with such asset-backed securities financing, and to fully disclose the extent of their financial commitment/exposure to such asset-backed securities that precipitated the world-wide financial instability and global financial crisis of the latter part of the first decade of the twenty-first century: one which (as suggested earlier) witnessed the demise and ultimate collapse of a number of established and well-respected corporate and non-corporate organizations.[35]

Gearing (or leverage) management

Gearing is a description of the relationship between the levels of debt and equity within a company/organization – a relationship that is often expressed in the form of a gearing ratio, namely:

$$[(\text{market value of debt/market value of equity}) * 100]$$

Inasmuch as the gearing ratio of a company can be used as a measure or indication of financial risk, a company/organization with low levels of debt – that is a low geared company/organization – is generally considered to be a low financial risk, and a company/organization with high levels of debt – that is a highly geared company/organization – is generally considered to be a high financial risk.

Gearing (or leverage): a measure of the extent to which a company is funded by debt.

So if debt increases the financial risk, should companies borrow?

Whilst there are a number of alternative views/theories on the impact of gearing – for example the traditional view of capital structure, the debt irrelevancy view, trade off theory, pecking order theory, agency theory, and corporate life cycle theory – companies borrow because in the short/medium term when compared to equity, debt has a lower direct cost.

Why is this the case?

First, in the event of a company liquidation and distribution of assets, secured lenders such as debenture holders will generally take priority over shareholders. Such security often results in lenders/investors requiring a rate of return which is lower than that normally required by shareholders. Second, all legitimate debt-related interest payments will take priority, they MUST be paid before any dividend payments are made, and these are – in the UK at least – allowable as a tax expense … dividend payments to shareholders are not!

However, borrowing does carry a number of disadvantages.

Growing levels of debt within a company/organization can increase the possibility of financial distress[36] and the risk of corporate/organization failure, inasmuch as when combined with falling revenue incomes and/or high interest rates excessive levels of debt within a company can increase the possibility of debt default – that is, a company being unable to meet its outstanding debt commitments. In addition, and perhaps more importantly, increasing the levels of debt within a company can adversely affect shareholder earnings inasmuch as higher levels of debt will normally require higher levels of interest (although not necessarily higher interest rates – see below). Such increases in interest, where they exceed any increases in earnings generated by the use of the additional debt funds within the company/organization, will of course produce a reduction in the profits available for distribution to shareholders as dividends payments. This, somewhat unsurprisingly, will often result in shareholders demanding a higher rate of return as compensation and will therefore increase the cost of equity.

Risk assessment

Risk is the chance or possibility of loss or bad consequence. It arises from a past, present and/or future hazard or group of hazards of which some uncertainty exists about possible consequences and/or effects. Whilst in a business context there are many varieties of risk – for example social risk, political risk, economic risk, and financial risk – in a financial management context, risk, or more specifically the risk associated with holding an investment or undertaking a project, is often divided into two types:

- Systematic risk, which is an economy-wide macroeconomic risk that affects the whole market. It is sometimes called market risk or non-diversifiable risk. Such risks will affect all companies, industries and/or investments, although sometimes to differing degrees
- Unsystematic risk, which is a business-related microeconomic risk that will only affect one type of company, industry, and/or investment. Unsystematic risk is sometimes called inherent risk, unique risk, or diversifiable risk

In an investment context, risk is related to volatility of return. The risk of an investment can be estimated using the volatility of historical returns – that is, if historical returns can be used to estimate current and future rates of return then shares or securities with wider fluctuations in rates of return (measured using standard deviation (σ)) could be assumed to be more risky.

Portfolio theory assumes that if two investments (or two portfolios) have the same return but different risks a rational investor would normally choose the least risk option, and if two investments (or two portfolios) have the same risk but different returns a rational investor would normally choose the greatest return option. More importantly, where an investor holds a collection of shares or investments portfolio theory suggests that diversification using negatively correlated shares or investments will reduce the overall risk of the portfolio.

It is however important to remember that diversification can only reduce unsystematic risk – systematic risk must be accepted by the investor.

> **Portfolio theory**: a mathematical framework which assumes that risk can be reduced by diversification and that returns are a function of expected risk.

Since unsystematic risk can be eliminated through diversification only systematic risk (or market risk) is relevant. For a diversified investor the relevant measure of risk is no longer σ, it is Beta (β). Beta (β) measures the covariance between the returns of a particular share (or portfolio) with the return on the market as a whole, inasmuch as:

- A share (or portfolio) with a β greater than 1.0 can be termed aggressive – that is, more riskier than the market
- A share (or portfolio) with a β less than 1.0 can be termed defensive – that is, less riskier than the market
- A share (or portfolio) with a β equal to 1.0 can be termed neutral – that is, the same risk as the market

An investor's required rate of return from a share (s) can be expressed as

$$Rs = Rf + \beta(Rm - Rf)$$

The Capital Asset Pricing Model (**CAPM**) is concerned with how systematic risk affects required returns and share prices.

Whilst CAPM is a single factor equilibrium-based model that enjoys widespread use – especially in determining a 'correct' equilibrium market value of a share or a portfolio of shares and/or in establishing the cost of capital in a company's equity – it is nonetheless a simplification of reality which assumes that investors are risk averse, that everyone in the market has the same forecast, that investment opportunities are the same for all investors, and that there are no transaction costs and/or taxation. It also assumes that investors can borrow and lend freely at a risk less than the rate of return, that all investors have a single period planning horizon, that the cost of insolvency is zero, and that investment markets are efficient.

> **CAPM**: a pricing model which takes into account an asset or investment's sensitivity to non-diversifiable risk (also known as systemic risk or market risk), often represented by the quantity beta (β) as well as the expected return of the market and the expected return of a theoretical risk-free asset.

Management of working capital

Working capital (WC) is normally defined as:

current assets – current liabilities[37]

Whilst the working capital policy adopted by a company will be dependent on a range of factors – for example, an aggressive working capital policy would seek to increase profitability through holding low levels of cash and inventories but increase the risk of potential cash shortages and stock-outs, whereas a conservative working capital policy would seek to provide greater flexibility with higher levels of cash and inventories, which would provide lower risk at the expense of reduced profitability – as a general rule, in the longer term working capital should always be positive. Indeed, regardless of the working capital policy adopted, improved management of working capital can have a significant impact on the level of requirement for external financing.

Working capital: the operating liquidity available to a company. Working capital is considered a part of the operating capital of a company and is calculated by deducting current liabilities from current assets.

Working capital management

Working capital management is generally concerned with cash management, inventory management, payables management, and creditor management.

Cash management

Cash management is concerned with the establishment of an adequate cash management model for the efficient matching of organizational funds and operational requirements to ensure adequate cash resources are available within the company/organization as and when these are required. Whilst there are many alternative cash management models available the most popular model is the (1952) Baumol cash management model. The Baumol model is an EOQ-based model (see below) and suggests the cost of meeting a cash demand (that is, the buying and selling of marketable securities to meet a cash demand) is the transaction cost plus the opportunity cost of the interest foregone.[38]

The cash management model generally assumes that a company can forecast its cash requirements with certainty and will then receive a specific amount at regular intervals as well as pay cash payments uniformly. In addition, it also assumes that the cost of holding cash is known with certainty and that this will not change over time, that the same transaction costs will be incurred whenever securities are converted into cash. As a consequence the Baumol cash management model may only be of relevance if the pattern of a company's cash flows/transfers is uniform (the same size), fairly consistent (occurring on a regular basis), and predictable (known with a degree of certainty).

Inventory management

Inventory management is concerned with ensuring that not only are there appropriate levels of stocks available within the company/organization to meet anticipated production requirements, possible legal requirements, and/or predicted customer/client demands, but also and more importantly, that excessive working capital is not tied up in unwarranted/unnecessary stocks – stocks that are surplus to transaction processing requirements. Although the level of inventory would be dependent on a vast range of interrelated company/organization-specific business factors, the selection would most certainly be influenced by the costs associated with holding/storing products – inventory holding costs, and the costs associated with ordering products (inventory ordering costs). There are a number of alternative inventory management models that can be adopted and indeed are used by companies/organizations, not only throughout the UK but also throughout the world: the most common of these is the economic order quantity (EOQ) model.[39] In a broad context, inventory management is concerned with the trade off between the additional income and profit that may be generated as a result of holding stocks and the administrative and financial costs and risks associated with holding such inventories.

Receivables management

Receivables management is concerned with the trade off between the additional income and profit that may be generated by providing and/or extending credit facilities to customers and/or clients and the administrative and financial costs and risks associated with providing and/or extending credit facilities to customers and/or clients. For example, whereas granting trade credit to customers/clients could result in a loss of interest due to the deferred receipt of income, a loss of purchasing power due to the deferred receipt of income, increased costs associated with debtor management-related administration and the risk (or consequential cost) of possible bad debts, denying trade credit to customers/clients could also result in a loss of customer goodwill and a possible loss of sales income.

Payables management

Payables management is concerned with determining an appropriate company-wide credit policy and establishing effective company/organization-wide internal controls in order to ensure the efficient management and administration of all creditor-related purchases. In a broad context, payables management is concerned with obtaining satisfactory credit from suppliers; with extending, where necessary, credit during periods of cash shortage; and with maintaining good relations with regular and important suppliers. The costs/risks associated with taking trade credit from suppliers/service providers could include possible price increases as a result of credit-related costs and potential restrictions to taking credit on other business-related activities. The costs/risks associated with not taking trade credit from suppliers/service providers could include a possible loss of interest and the inconvenience associated with not taking credit.

Summary

This chapter has provided a broad overview of the most popular accounting models used by companies to assist in achieving what is often regarded as their primary objective – the maximization of shareholder wealth – and has explored the use and perhaps more importantly the limitations of such models. It has also emphasized the 'constructed' nature of these accounting models and sought to dispel the notion that accounting (and finance) is concerned with 'truth' and 'fact'. Accounting has been, is, and indeed always will be, an art rather than a science – an art primarily concerned with creating highly elaborate 'models' of a company and its activities and versions of reality which not only *communicate* reality but more importantly also *construct* reality. As eloquently surmised by Hines in his (1988) discussion on the power of such constructed simplifications of reality and those who created them ... the accountants:

> ... We ... (accountants) ... create a picture of an organization or the 'economy', whatever you like, and on the basis of that picture (not some underlying 'real' reality of which no-one is aware), people think and act. And by responding to that picture of reality they make it so: it becomes 'real in its consequences'. And what is more, when people respond to that picture, and the consequences occur, they see it as our proof as having conveyed reality. Clever, isn't it ... (1988: 259)

Indeed it is!

Questions for reflection

1 What are the main limitations of the contemporary financial statements?
2 What accounting models are used in determining the cost of a product and/or service?
3 What is the CVP analysis and for what type of decision is it generally used?
4 What is present value theory and why, in a financial management context, is it considered important?

Further reading

Alexander, D. and Nobes, C. (2010) *Financial Accounting: An International Introduction* (4th edn). London: Pearson.

Alexander, D., Britton, A. and Jorissen, A. (2007) *International Financial Reporting and Analysis* (3rd edn). London: Thompson International.

Arnold, G. (2008) *Corporate Financial Management* (4th edn). London: FT/Prentice-Hall.

Bhimani, A., Horngren, C.T., Datar, S. and Foster, G. (2008) *Management and Cost Accounting* (4th edn). London: Pearson.

Davies, T., Boczko, T. and Chen, J. (2008) *Strategic Corporate Finance*. London: McGraw-Hill Irwin.

Drury, C. (2009) *Management Accounting for Business* (4th edn). London: Cengage Learning.

Elliot, B. and Elliot, J. (2009) *Financial Accounting and Reporting* (9th edn). London: Pearson.

McLaney, E.J. (2009) *Business Finance – Theory and Practice* (8th edn). London: Pearson.

McLaney, E.J. and Atrill, P. (2008) *Accounting: An Introduction* (4th edn). London: Pearson.

Watson, D. and Head, A. (2010) *Corporate Finance – Principles and Practice* (5th edn). London: Pearson.

Weetman, P. (2010) *Financial Accounting: An Introduction* (5th edn). London: Pearson.

Notes

1   In the contemporary context, the tradition of economic liberalism is often utilized as a 'way of thinking' or 'way of knowing' which assumes that knowledge and understanding of economic activity can be separated from the politics of its accomplishment. Such a claim is appealing because it extends the prospect of representing and regulating the world in ways which maintain prevailing structures (Cooper and Puxty, 1996) and therefore sustains the continued dominance of market-based capitalism.

2   Whereas a reflective theory of representation presupposes that a constructed model/discourse can mirror true meaning, the constructionist perspective contends that meanings communicated by/through discourse can neither reflect reality nor simply express the intentions of those involved in the communication process. Meaning is contextual inasmuch as all meaning, all understanding, is dependent on the traditions or practices through which the world is rendered knowable (Hall, 1997).

3   The contention here is that the emergent spatial and temporal consequences of globalization, and thus the increasing amalgamation of local culture(s), the accelerated redistribution of traditional political boundaries, the intensified re-fabrication of social constituencies, and the increasing transferability of commodities and capital between first, second and third world (inter) dependencies, are more or less

(Continued)

(Continued)

products of an increasingly disorganized (re)structuring of the capitalist accumulation process and the ever-changing priorities of the capital accumulation process.

4   Why this is the case is complex – although the history of this influence can be located within the hegemonic power exercised not only by US-based market institutions but also to some extent by European-based market institutions in the nineteenth and twentieth century and in particular the second half of the latter century (Harvey, 1989).

5   In addition, some national regulatory systems require a Cash Flow Statement together with a vast amount of additional financial and non-financial information.

6   A collection of national and international accounting standards, pronouncements, guidelines and legal requirements used to 'regulate' the preparation and content of published financial accounting statements is commonly referred to as a national GAAP, or Generally Accepted Accounting Practice.

7   The first substantial writing on double entry bookkeeping is commonly regarded as being Luca Pacioli's treatise *'Suma de Arithmetica, Geometrica, Proportioni et Proportionaliti'* (A review of arithmetic, geometry and proportions) in 1494, of which part 1, section 9, treatise 11, *'Particulars de Computis et Scriptus'* (Particulars of reckonings and their recordings) contained a brief discourse on double entry bookkeeping which Luca Pacioli acknowledged as being based on the methods originating in Venice more than 100 years earlier. Although extensive documentation exists to indicate double entry bookkeeping was indeed in operation long before the development of the 'Italian method', the weight of evidence suggests that double entry bookkeeping (in its present context and utilization) did indeed develop in Italy.

8   Examples of which would include:

- the prudence concept
- the accruals concept
- the consistency concept
- the going concern concept
- the separate valuation concept
- the business entity concept
- the money measurement concept
- the historical cost concept
- the materiality concept
- the periodicity concept
- the realization concept
- the substance over form concept and,
- the dual aspect concept.

9   It is conventional to show such an asset-related provision as a negative asset – that is, as a deduction from the relevant asset. For example, a provision for depreciation is normally deducted from the relevant group(s) of non-current asset(s).

10   A consolidated Balance Sheet is a Balance Sheet which is prepared by the holding company of a group which incorporates the Balance Sheets of all subsidiary companies using a technique known as acquisition accounting. Where associate companies exist within the group, the Balance Sheets of such companies are incorporated using a technique known as equity accounting.

(Continued)

(Continued)

11   The deprival value of an asset can be defined as the lower of its replacement cost and its recoverable value. The term recoverable value can be defined as the higher of what the company could sell the asset for and the value that the company could create by using the asset within the business.

12   Historical values adjusted depreciation or another provision.

13   Last In First Out.

14   First In First Out.

15   Average Cost.

16   An interesting example is the (2008) Bernard L. Madoff investment securities fraud. See 'Wall Street legend Bernard Madoff arrested over $50 billion Ponzi scheme', at http://www.timesonline.co.uk/tol/news/world/us_and_americas/article5331997.ece.

17   See for example the widely reported collapse of Lehman Brothers. The global financial service company filed for Chapter 11 bankruptcy protection on 15 September 2008, yet in its 2007 annual report Lehman Brothers, which had equity at a reported market value of $39,315 million (March 2007), announced:

- revenues for the year of $46,709 million (an increase of 44% on 2006),
- profits for the year of $4,007 million (an increase of 23% on 2006),
- assets of $503,545 million.

18   Political, Economic, Sociocultural, Technological, Environmental, and Legal.

19   Strengths, Weaknesses, Opportunities, and Threats.

20   The grouping of performance measures in general categories (perspectives). The four general perspectives proposed by the Balanced Scorecard (see Kaplan, R.S. and Norton, D. (1996) *The Balanced Scorecard: Translating Strategy Into Action*, Harvard Business School Press) are:

- the financial perspective
- the customer perspective
- the internal process perspective
- the innovation and learning perspective

21   The absorption rates used to absorb overhead costs would normally be calculated on the basis of expected production output and budgeted overheads. Since actual overheads and levels of production are unlikely to equal such budgeted amounts, an under and/or over absorption of overhead is likely to occur, for which a profit and loss account adjustment would be required.

22   Such activities are often referred to as cost drivers.

23   The main categories within Islamic finance are:

- *Ijara* – a leasing agreement whereby the bank buys an item for a customer and then leases it back over a specific period
- *Ijara-wa-Iqtina* – a similar arrangement, except that the customer is able to buy the item at the end of the contract
- *Mudaraba* – a specialist investment in which the bank and the customer share any profits

(Continued)

(Continued)

- *Murabaha* – a form of credit which enables customers to make a purchase without having to take out an interest bearing loan
- *Musharaka* – an investment partnership in which profit-sharing terms are agreed in advance and losses are pegged to the amount invested

24   However, investments in organizations/companies associated with or involved in:

- the manufacture, distribution and retailing of alcohol and/or tobacco
- the promotion of gambling and/or,
- the production, distribution and/or retail of pornography

are not permitted.

25   For further details on Islamic financing see Davies, T., Boczko, T. and Chen, J. (2008) *Strategic Corporate Finance*, London, McGraw-Hill.

26   Usually a company's weighted average cost of capital.

27   ARR is a profits-based measure and is calculated as follows:

$$\frac{\text{average accounting profit over the project} \times 100\%}{\text{initial investment}}$$

28   Payback, which is a measure of the number of years it will take for the cash inflows from an investment to equal the cash outflows of the investment.

29   The present value of a perpetuity (a perpetual annuity) can be calculated as follows:

$$P_0 \, (P) = (A/i)$$

Where the perpetual annuity payment is growing at a fixed rate (g) the present value can be calculated as follows:

$$P_0 \, (GP) = [A \, /(i–g)]$$

30   The present value of an annuity $P_0 \, (A)$ can be calculated as follows:

$$P_0 \, (A) = A * [(1/i) – (1/i(1 +i)^t)]$$

where:

- $P_0 \, (A)$ is the value of the annuity at time 0 (or today)
- A = the value of the individual payments in each compounding time period
- i = the interest rate that would be compounded for each time period
- n = the number of time periods

Where an annuity is growing – that is where cash flow is increasing by a factor of (1+g) – the present value of a growing annuity $P_0 \, (GA)$ can be calculated as follows:

$$P_0 \, (GA) = [A/(i–g)] * [(1 – [(1+g)/(1+i)]^t)]$$

31   For example:

- an optional convertible security – in which the holder of the convertible security has the option to convert the debt into shares at a number of agreed future dates, and/or,

(Continued)

(Continued)

- an exchangeable convertible security – in which the shares underlying the debt are in a company other than the company issuing the convertible security that is different from that of the issuer.

32 Another example of such an instrument would be the transferrable warrant which is a security that entitles the holder of the warrant to buy or sell a certain additional quantity of an underlying security, at an agreed price, within an agreed period of time. The right to buy an underlying security is referred to as a call warrant, whereas the right to sell an underlying security is known as a put warrant.

33 Derivative instruments can be categorized in a number of ways. For example, they can be categorised as either linear or non-linear derivatives. Alternatively they can be categorized as either plain vanilla or exotic derivatives. There is however no definitive rule for distinguishing between either linear or non-linear, and plain vanilla or exotic. The distinction tends to be a matter of custom and interpretation and as such usage of the terms does vary.

34 Such pools of underlying assets can include for example credit card payments, car loan repayments, mortgage loan repayments, royalty payments, and movie revenues.

35 It is also worth noting that the public sector has not been insulated from the consequences of this world-wide financial crisis. Many local authorities, government agencies and national charities such as Age Concern, Cancer Research and the RNLI suffered substantial losses – in particular from the collapse of the Icelandic financial institution Landsbanki.

36 … and the costs associated with managing such financial distress – that is the costs associated with activities/operations designed to limit the possibility of company/organization failure: for example, restructuring costs and/or re-financing costs.

37 This can also be stated as:

$$(\text{inventories} + \text{receivables} + \text{prepayments}) - (\text{payables} + \text{accruals} + \text{short-term debt}) + \text{cash}$$

38 The Baumol cash management model suggests that the optimal deposit size is given by:

$$c = \sqrt{(2kt/i)}$$

where:

- t = annual transactions volume (assumed to be uniform over time)
- k = fixed cost per transaction
- i = annual interest rate
- c = size of each deposit

39 The economic order quantity model can be expressed as:

$$Q = \sqrt{2cd/h}$$

where:

- Q = the quantity to order
- d = the number of product units required per annum (annual demand)
- c = the cost of placing an order
- h = the holding cost per product unit per annum

References

Altman, E.I. (1968) 'Financial ratios, discriminant analysis and the prediction of corporate bankruptcy.' *Journal of Finance*, 23 (4): 589–609.

Argenti, J. (1976) *Corporate Collapse – the Causes and Symptoms*. London: McGraw-Hill.

Boczko, T. (2000) 'A critique on the classification of contemporary accounting: towards a political economy of classification – the search for ownership.' *Critical Perspectives on Accounting*, 11: 131–153.

Bryer, R.A. (1995) 'A political economy of SSAP 22: Accounting for goodwill.' *British Accounting Review*, 27: 283–310.

Colignon, R. and Covaleski, M. (1991) 'A Weberian framework in the study of accounting.' *Accounting Organizations and Society*, 16 (2): 141–157.

Cooper, C. and Puxty, A. (1996) 'On the proliferation of accounting (his)tories.' *Critical Perspectives on Accountancy*, 7: 285–313.

Davies, T., Boczko, T. and Chen, J. (2008) *Strategic Corporate Finance*. London: McGraw-Hill.

Foucault, M. (1980) *Power/Knowledge*. Brighton: Harvester.

Gray, R., Owen, D. and Adams, C. (1996) *Accounting and Accountability*. London: Prentice-Hall.

Hall, S. (1997) 'Representation, meaning and language.' In S. Hall (ed.), *Representation: Cultural Representations and Signifying Practices*. London: Sage/Open University.

Harvey, D. (1989) *The Condition of Post Modernity*. London: Blackwell.

Hines, R.D. (1988) 'Financial accounting: in communicating reality we construct reality.' *Accounting, Organizations, and Society*, 13 (3): 256–261.

Kaplan, R.S. and Norton, D. (1996) *The Balanced Scorecard: Translating Strategy Into Action*. Harvard Business School Press.

Taffler, R.J. (1982) 'Forecasting company failure in the UK using discriminant analysis and financial ratio data.' *Journal of the Royal Statistical Society*, Series A 145 (Part 3): 342–358.

Tinker, A.M. (1985) *Paper Prophets*. New York: Holt, Rinehart and Winston.

Willmott, H.C., Puxty, T. and Sikka, P. (1993) 'Commentary, losing one's reason: On the integrity of accounting academics.' *Accounting, Auditing and Accountability*, 6 (2): 98–110.

6 Economics[1]

Key concepts

Allocative efficiency; Average total cost; Backward induction; Nash-Bertrand equilibrium; Constant returns to scale; Consumer surplus; Cournot-Nash equilibrium; Creative destruction; Cross-price elasticity of demand; Deadweight loss; Decreasing returns to scale; Diminishing marginal utility; Economic efficiency; Economies of scale; Efficient markets hypothesis; Elasticity of demand; Externalities; Fiscal policy; Fixed costs; Game theory; Gross domestic product (GDP); Income elasticity of demand; Increasing returns to scale; Indifference curve; Isoquant; Long period; Marginal cost; Marginal product; Marginal rate of substitution; Marginal rate of technical substitution; Marginal revenue; Monetary policy; Monopoly; Monopsony; Nash equilibrium; Nash-Bertrand equilibrium; Nash-Cournot equilibrium; Normal profit; Oligopoly; Opportunity cost; Own price elasticity of demand; Pareto optimum; Perfect competition; Producer surplus; Production function; Random walk theory; Short period; Sunk costs; Technical efficiency; Total factor productivity; Utility; Variable costs

The Scope and Purpose of the Chapter

It is just before nine o'clock on a cold winter's morning. The mood of the MBA class, about to begin the Economics module, is one of scepticism if not downright disbelief. Having just left demanding jobs in order to take a year or more to deepen their business knowledge and improve their career profiles, the class members have had first-hand experience of the effects of the turmoil in global financial markets and have increasing doubts about the relevance and robustness of economic theory and analysis which have failed to predict or prevent the deepest worldwide recession since the 1930s. The lecturer, who has yet to appear, runs the risk of being greeted with derisive laughter.

But despite the class's scepticism, Economics offers rich insights into strategic decision making in organizations and into the wider environment in which those organizations operate, flourish, and sometimes decline. The analysis is relevant to: pricing, output, investment, and other production and marketing decisions; performance measurement; financing and the setting of financial objectives; employment decisions; and the development and implementation of strategy.

It therefore links closely with the other main subjects that make up an MBA programme: accounting and finance; human resource development; information systems; international business management; operations management; and strategic management. So, if the imminent session can be related to current issues in industry and commerce, the public realm, and to non profit-driven activity in the social economy, the lecturer might make it through relatively unscathed to the lunch break.

As that lecturer, I have written this chapter against that background of relevance tinged with doubt and uncertainty. The chapter surveys briefly the main theories of Economics and shows how these contribute not only to Economics in the MBA course but also to the other cognate subjects. It is not intended to replace MBA courses in Economics but rather to complement them by critically examining and explaining the theoretical and analytical frameworks on which they draw.

The under-pinning approach for Economics in the MBA continues to be the marginalist-based demand and supply framework developed by Alfred Marshall – the so-called 'neoclassical' approach. Its main characteristics are that decision makers are assumed to be rational and motivated solely by self-interest, and that freely functioning markets will lead inexorably to a stable equilibrium in which economic efficiency and economic welfare are maximized.

But any analysis needs to be set within the wider national, regional, and now global economy in which goods and services are produced and exchanged. Our understanding of that wider (macro-) economy was transformed by John Maynard Keynes (1883–1946), as a direct challenge to the market-clearing, equilibrium-seeking orthodoxy of the neoclassical economists. The Keynesian approach has been extended to include the (post-Keynesian) theory and analysis of persistent disequilibria, and the causes of economic growth and fluctuations.

This in turn is challenged, on the one hand, by those who see scope for the stabilization of economic activity by a more active intervention on the part of government (the neo-Keynesians) and, on the other, by those who favour a general retreat from intervention and a return to unfettered market capitalism (Milton Friedman and the Chicago School). In light of the largely unanticipated financial turbulence that hit the global economy in the opening years of the twenty-first century, it is not hard to think of the weaknesses of each of these frameworks and how they need to be modified to relate realistically to business and management.

The chapter starts by reviewing the economic basis of decision making by individuals. The analysis then moves to the organization and examines revenues, resources and costs. The focus on the organization rather than on the firm, as is conventional, is deliberate. Organizations may be profit- or non profit-directed, and exist in the private, public or social sectors. Economic analysis applies to them all. But in some parts of the text, in the interests of clarity and brevity, it is helpful to refer to 'the firm' as the unit of analysis.

The following section considers organizations in relation to the markets in which they operate and the strategies they develop. They are then set in the context of their wider environment in the section that follows. The concluding section gives a brief summary and suggests directions for future research.

The Individual

Scarcity and choice

Individuals are critical to organizations as customers or clients on the one hand and as suppliers of labour on the other. The concept of the supply of labour goes far beyond the notion of physical efforts to include the services that flow from the stock of human capital that people have amassed through education, training and experience. We can think of the individual as customer *and* supplier.

In both cases, Economics sees the individual facing scarcity. People have many and varied wants, but they are short of both income and time. They therefore have to make choices – between alternative bundles of goods and services and between work and leisure. These choices are guided by rational self-interest: on the basis of the information that is available to them, they will aim to get the maximum net benefit out of the resources they have. This benefit can be assessed in either monetary or psychic terms, or in a combination of both.

In Adam Smith's (1723–1790) initial framework for modern Economics, self-interest leads to an efficient outcome for society: 'It is not from the benevolence of the butcher, the brewer, or the baker that we expect our dinner, but from their regard to their own self-interest. We address ourselves, not to their humanity but to their self-love, and never talk to them of our own necessities but of their advantages' (Smith, 1977).

In many respects, Smith's analysis outlined the whole of neoclassical Economics as it developed subsequently: a commitment to the free operation of markets guided collectively by the decisions and actions of many self-interested individuals and firms (the 'hidden hand'), conditioned by the need for an institutional, legal and moral framework to ensure equity and justice as well as efficiency (see Harcourt, 1995). Moral actions were important for Smith. He held the Chair of Moral Philosophy at Glasgow and his first major work was *The Theory of Moral Sentiments* (1976), which he returned to revise in the last years of his life.

The principal impediments to the efficient and equitable operation of markets are a monopoly on the part of sellers, control of vital inputs (including labour) on the part of suppliers, and differences in the amount of information available to market participants. Market failure – its causes, effects, and policies to correct it – is still a major issue in modern Economics.

Rationality

The economist's systematic analysis of individuals' behaviour can be – and frequently has been – criticized with regard to its assumptions about rationality, self-interest, and the apparently uncaring pursuit of efficiency. These criticisms go back at least to the clash of ideas between David Ricardo (1772–1823) and John Stuart Mill (1806–1873). Ricardo was the architect of the logical-mathematic approach to economic analysis, which starts from *a priori* assumptions that are then subjected to rigorous testing in logic before policy prescriptions are drawn. This approach underpins much of today's theory-based mathematical modelling in economics.

In contrast Mill argued for economic analysis to be set on a broader canvas, where complex economic and social issues could be considered within a framework of philosophical analysis which would take account of empirical evidence. The debate is still raging; at present, the logical mathematicians have the upper hand. The danger is that this approach leads to a framework that is too narrow in construction and in analysis.

From outside Economics, and within business schools, the criticism is that insufficient account is taken of the methods and findings of cognate disciplines that have behaviour as a main focus, in particular psychology, sociology, and biology. Stimulated in part by the failure of elaborate mathematical models to capture accurate actions and outcomes on the part of both individuals and groups, work in behavioural economics is trying to put some of these deficiencies right.

Biology and animal behaviour studies show how members of species both compete and co-operate in order to protect and promote the interests of the groups of which they are part. One interesting study linking the appetite for risk to the physical and personality characteristics of financial market traders is helping to shed light on apparently erratic behaviour and on the factors that give rise to financial bubbles (Coates et al., 2009). But while this richness of knowledge is welcome, the assumptions of rationality and self-interest are useful starting points for analysis against which observed complex behaviour patterns can be assessed and analyzed.

If self-interest can be reconciled with the collective welfare of the group, the issue of morality is largely, although not entirely, resolved. Group norms can be enforced through self-regulation or via administrative or legislative fiat. From the standpoint of the MBA, individual moral concerns that do not bear on the conduct and performance of organizations within a liberal democratic society are not relevant, unless cross-cultural comparisons are being made.

Financial bubbles, business scandals, and modern developments in Economics and other subjects have now thrown the issue of rationality – and hence the rigour and relevance of analysis based on the assumption of self-interested individual actions – into sharp relief. The behavioural sciences have shown that **rational behaviour**, like common sense, is a rare phenomenon. But the enduring merit of the approach is that it gives a firm basis for initial analysis and quantification that may be absent in other disciplines. Once the framework for analysis has been built, the binding assumptions can be relaxed to give a richer, but still controlled, insight into complexity.

Utility: the individual as consumer

The starting point for the analysis of rational behaviour is the notion of **utility**: the expected satisfaction that comes from the consumption of goods (and services) and from wealth. The general principle is 'the satisfaction of more': overall satisfaction increases as more and more goods are consumed and as more and more wealth is accumulated. However individuals' satisfaction levels are not easily measured or compared. Bundles of goods may be ranked in order of satisfaction (an ordinal measure) but satisfaction values (a cardinal measure) cannot be given to them.

Satisfaction does not increase directly in line with consumption or wealth. In theory at least, a rich person gains less in increased satisfaction from an additional increment of consumption or wealth than a poor person does. This is the well-known principle of **diminishing marginal utility**. And beyond a certain point, individuals may become satiated with consumption and also, perhaps, income, so that their aggregate utility level falls.

Diminishing marginal utility: the tendency for the increase in total utility associated with consumption of one additional unit of a good to progressively diminish as more of the good is consumed.

Utility: the satisfaction that comes from the consumption of goods and services, as well as from income and wealth.

But consumption – and hence demand – cannot increase indefinitely. Both are limited by available income. So individuals have to choose how to allocate their scarce income between alternative bundles of goods. The example below shows the theory of how this is done.

 Scarcity and choice

An *indifference curve* (Figure 6.1) plots points of *equal* satisfaction derived by a consumer from *alternative* combinations of two goods – here being pizza and cola. The analysis can be extended to multiple goods without a loss of rigour.

Note the shape of the indifference curve – it is convex to the origin. This means that if you start with lots of cola but not much pizza you are willing to give up several cans of cola so as to gain an additional slice of pizza *and* keep your satisfaction level the same. But if you start with lots of pizza and not much cola you are willing to give up pizza to get more cola. As you move along the indifference curve, the rate of exchange between pizza and cola

(Continued)

(Continued)

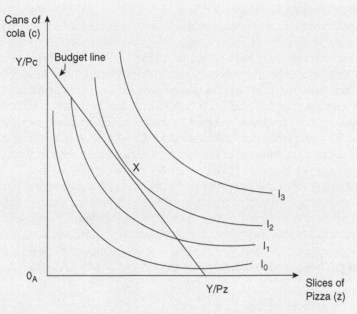

Figure 6.1 A consumer's allocation of income between alternative goods

to keep your satisfaction level constant changes. Additional cans of cola become more valuable to you when you have few of them – likewise for pizza slices. This rate of exchange is the *marginal rate of substitution* (the MRS, or dc/dz).

A single indifference curve relates to just one level of satisfaction. Plotting over the range of an individual's satisfaction levels maps utility against alternative bundles of goods (I_0 to I_3). The indifference curves may change their shapes, as the MRS changes with increased overall consumption, but they will never cross, since *different* bundles of goods cannot yield the *same* satisfaction level.

But how does the individual decide on the level and combination of goods to consume? Clearly this depends on income and the relative prices of the goods. Suppose you have an income of y. If you spend it all on pizza you can buy y/p_z slices, where p is the unit price of pizza. Likewise, if you spend all your income on cola, you can buy y/p_c cans, where p_c is the unit price of cola. The amounts of pizza and cola you can buy with any given amount of income depends on the ratio of their *relative* prices: that is $(y/p_c)/(y/p_z)$, shown by the slope of the budget line in Figure 6.1.

The rational consumer's expected utility will be maximized by choosing that bundle of goods that yields the greatest level of satisfaction attainable *given the budget constraint*. This is where the budget line is tangent to the

(Continued)

(Continued)

highest-attainable indifference curve (Point *X* in Figure 6.1). Here, the slope of the indifference curve is equal to the slope of the budget line ($dc/dz = (y/p_c)/(y/p_z)$). This says that, for an individual's utility to be maximized subject to income, the MRS of cola for pizza must be equal to the ratio of their relative prices.

Now think about exchange between rational individuals. Any pair of individuals has their own indifference curve map. How can they best allocate the scarce supplies of pizza and cola between them, in order to maximize their individual satisfaction levels, subject to their (usually different) income levels? Figure 6.2 shows total pizza/cola space for individuals A and B, together with their respective indifference curve maps. Any point inside the rectangle shows the distribution of pizza and cola between the two consumers.

Suppose the initial distribution of pizza and cola between A and B is at point Z – the intersection of two of their respective indifference curves. This distribution is inefficient because if A moves along their indifference curve to point Y, B can reach a higher indifference curve (*i.e.* become better off) *leaving A's utility unchanged*. At point Y, the MRS_{pc} for A is equal to the MRS_{pc} for B. It is now impossible to make B any better off without making A worse off.

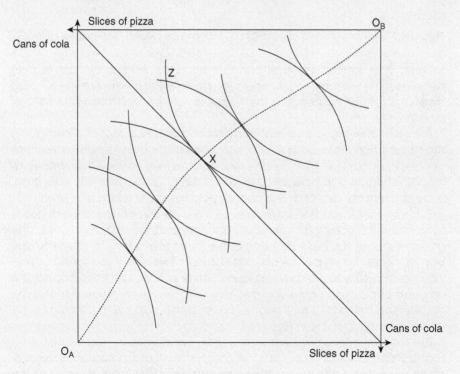

Figure 6.2 Two consumer equilibrium: the Edgworth box

(Continued)

(Continued)

Depending on the allocation of income between the two consumers, their optimal combinations of pizza and cola are given by the path of the points of tangency between their indifference curves. This path, shown by the dotted line in Figure 6.2, is the *contract curve* between the two individuals. Given *any* distribution of income between them, it will always be in their individual and joint interests to move to a point of exchange that is on the contract curve. Then each has attained the highest level of utility it is possible to reach, subject to their respective incomes, and the utility of one now cannot be further increased without reducing the utility of the other.

This position is *Pareto efficient* (see the section on Pareto efficiency below). In gauging efficiency it takes no account of the distribution of income among consumers. So long as the consumers are on their contract curve, it does not matter whether one is rich and consuming much, and the other poor and consuming little, or whether their wealth and income are approximately equal.

Utility: the individual as supplier

To this point we have considered the theory of the individual as consumer, but the analysis can be extended to the individual as supplier. Although this may cover the supply of various factors, including financial or intellectual capital, it typically relates to the supply of labour or work effort.

As before, scarcity and choice are important. Time is finite and limited, in both the short and the long term. Individuals must choose between work and leisure. The self-interested rational person has to balance the amount of effort required to gain a wage income against the loss of the enjoyment of leisure. Following the style of the analysis of consumption, the individual's willingness to supply labour to a particular job is a function of a number of factors, the most important of which are the wage, the wage offered by other jobs, and the price of leisure. The price of leisure is the wage foregone by choosing not to work. This is an example of *opportunity cost*.

Clearly, the supply of labour will normally be a rising function of the wage. But as the wage (= income) increases for any given supply of effort, at some point the income may become sufficient so that the individual prefers to take more leisure rather than still more income. In other words, the price of leisure has fallen below the cost of working. These wage-effort relationships are represented by a labour supply curve that becomes backward-bending.

This fundamental analysis of the individual in the labour market is necessarily simplistic. Many, indeed perhaps most, people in advanced market economies are not motivated solely by the immediate monetary reward from their work effort. Satisfaction, skills development and human capital building, job security, future income, and the influence of peer-group norms are all important. Moreover, in the capitalist firm as we know it, workers have little or no choice over the hours worked once they have entered into a contract of employment – but they may have rather more discretion over the effort they put in.

Fully fledged labour market analysis, and human resource development and management, are much more sophisticated than we can see in this simple model. Yet it does help us to relate the demand for goods and services to their supply – the crucial issue for most organizations.

Demand

The importance for business of the theory described above is that it underpins the concept of the demand function. Demand for a good (or service) is driven by its price, the prices of alternatives, and by income. Other variables can be added to capture the effects of influences such as advertising, innovation, and tastes and fashion.

A standard form of the demand function is:

$$Q_d = f(P_o, P_s, Y, Ad, ...)$$

where:

- Q_d is the quantity demanded
- P_o is the price of the good ('own price')
- P_s is the price of substitutes or complements
- Y is income
- Ad is advertising expenditure

The usual relationship between demand (Q_d) and own price (P_o) is a negative one – the higher the price, the lower the quantity demanded. This gives the familiar downward-sloping demand curve (Figure 6.3). However the relationship between demand and the other variables is usually positive – the higher the income, the higher the quantity demanded.

Economics, marketing and strategy are very interested in the sensitivity of demand to changes in these variables, measured by *the ratio of the proportional change in demand to the proportional change in each of the variables* on the right hand side of the expression for the demand function. This is the notion of **elasticity**.[2]

The **own price elasticity of demand** is given by $[-\Delta Q_d / Q_d]/[\Delta P_o / P_o]$ – that is, the proportional change in demand in relation to the proportional change in price. The negative sign indicates the *inverse* relationship between demand and own price. If the price of the good falls by 5 per cent and, as a direct result, demand increases by 10 per cent, the elasticity is –2. If the price falls by 10 per cent and demand increases also by 10 per cent, the elasticity is unitary (-1). It is convention to ignore the negative sign. Then an elasticity greater than 1 can be termed 'high', while an elasticity less than 1 is 'low'. The other main demand elasticities are **cross-price elasticity** (the change in demand for the good in relation to the change in the price of a substitute) and **income elasticity**.

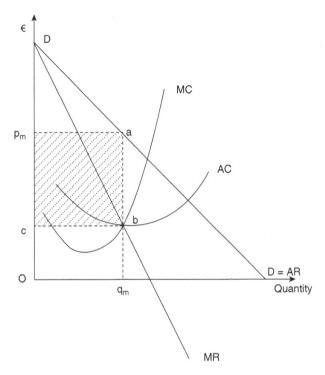

Figure 6.3 The firm as price maker

Elasticity: the sensitivity of the response of one economic variable to the change in another.

Own price elasticity of demand: the ratio of the proportionate change in the demand for a good to the proportionate change in its price.

Cross-price elasticity of demand: the ratio of the proportionate change in the demand for one good in response to a proportionate change in the price of another.

Income elasticity of demand: the ratio of the proportionate change in the quantity demanded of a good to the proportionate change in consumers' income.

Changes in the demand for a good can be the outcome of a change either in its own price or in one or more of the other variables on the right-hand side of the demand function. A change in own price results in demand changing through a movement *along* the demand curve (DD in Figure 6.3). But a change in demand on account of a change in one of the other variables is represented by a *shift* in the demand curve. For convenience in MBA Economics, the own-price demand curve is usually assumed to be linear. A consequence of this is that the own-price elasticity of demand *varies* over its length. As will be shown in the section below, this framework of demand analysis is crucial for understanding the behaviour of the firm's revenue.

The Organization

Organizations bring resources, or inputs, together to produce outputs. Normally we would expect the value of the final output to be greater than the value of the inputs – that is, organizations add value. Co-ordinating activity within the framework of an organization, which is the key function of management, is in general more efficient than if all the economic agents act in an individual and unco-ordinated manner. Value added per unit of output can be increased by raising the contribution from revenue, or by reducing costs, or by a combination of both of these.

Revenue

Conventionally in Economics, the firm's revenue will depend upon the market demand it faces, while its costs will be influenced by the price and amount of the inputs it uses and the technology and efficiency with which these are co-ordinated. The section on Demand showed the demand curve for the firm and for the market is typically inverse (downward-sloping) and can be described by an equation of the form:

$$P = a - bQ \qquad (1)$$

The firm's total revenue *(TR)* depends on the interaction between price *(P)* and the quantity sold *(Q)* as the firm's decision makers vary one or the other. So, multiplying equation (1) through by Q gives:

$$PQ = TR = aQ - bQ^2 \qquad (2)$$

This is an equation for a parabola: as Q increases *TR* at first increases rapidly, then once past the point of inflexion more slowly, until eventually it reaches a maximum before starting to decline (see Figure 6.4). A revenue-maximizing firm, uncon-strained by other considerations, will obviously choose q_r as its output. At this point a very small variation in the quantity sold will have no discernible effect on total revenue (i.e. *dTR/dQ = 0*). The relationship between a change in output (*dQ*) and the induced change in total revenue (*dTR*) is **marginal revenue**.

Marginal revenue: the change in total revenue associated with the sale of one additional unit of a good.

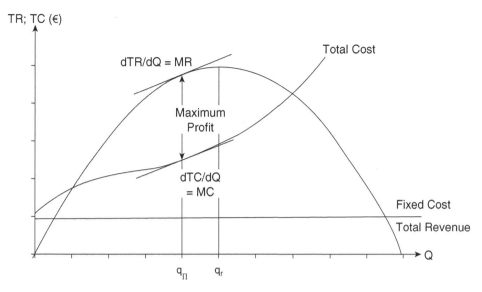

Figure 6.4 Revenue, costs and profits

From equation (2):

$$dTR/dQ = MR = a - 2Q = 0 \text{ (when TR is maximized)} \tag{3}$$

Note that the *slope* of the marginal revenue curve described in equation (3) is *twice* that of the demand curve in equation (1), while the intercept with the vertical axis *(a)* is the same (see Figure 6.3). Knowledge of the marginal revenue is crucial for identifying the price-output pair at which the firm's profit is maximized.

The production function

On the resource side, the efficient firm will achieve the least cost for any given level of output, or what amounts to the same thing – the maximum output for any given level of costs. By relating output, revenue and costs, the firm can then identify and attain the expected maximum profits.

The firm's costs will depend on the prices and quantities of the inputs or the factors of production that it uses. Early economic theory identified the factors of production as labour, capital, land, and enterprise. Enterprise, including risk-bearing, might be considered a special form of labour. Today most firms' principal inputs are labour, capital, materials, and energy. Since materials and energy are the results of productive activity by other firms, we can consider the general **production function** as the relationship between the quantity supplied *(Q_s)* and the two inputs of labour *(L)* and capital *(K)*:

$$Q_s = f(L,K) \tag{4}$$

> **Production function**: the technically determined relationship between a given set of inputs and the maximum output obtainable from it.

In the long run, when the quantities of both L and K can vary with output, the relation with output is unlikely to be strictly linear. With an expansion of output, either or both of the inputs may increase:

- less than in proportion (**increasing returns**)
- more than in proportion (**decreasing returns**), or
- directly in proportion (**constant returns**)

> **Increasing returns to scale**: the more than proportionate increase in output associated with a given increase in all inputs.
>
> **Decreasing returns to scale**: the less than proportionate increase in output associated with a given increase in all inputs.
>
> **Constant returns to scale**: the growth of output in direct proportion to increases in all inputs.

In the short run, theory assumes that the firm will be unable to vary its capital stock *(K)* and that labour will be the variable factor. The 'law' of (eventually) diminishing returns will be intensified. As more labour is applied to the fixed stock of capital, the increment of additional output (the **marginal product** – *MP*) will start to diminish beyond a certain point.

Given the wage rate *(w)*, the **marginal cost** *(MC)* is given by *w/MP*. Together with marginal revenue, marginal cost is crucial in the theory of the firm for the calculation and identification of the firm's profit-maximizing price and output.

> **Marginal cost**: the change in total cost associated with the production of one additional unit of a good.
>
> **Marginal product**: the change in total output associated with the input of one additional productive factor unit e.g. labour, capital.

As well as showing how factor inputs vary as output changes, the production function indicates the optimal choice of technique, that is, the least-cost combination of labour and capital for any given rate of output. The analysis parallels that for income-constrained consumer choice among alternative goods, considered on page 149.

Assuming a continuous array of alternative techniques, different combinations of labour and capital will yield a given rate of output. Figure 6.4 shows the relationship: the **isoquant** plots the locus of labour-capital pairs that will produce a given output. As with the **indifference curve** in consumer analysis the isoquant is convex to the origin, indicating that the **marginal rate of technical substitution** *(MRTS)* of labour for capital will vary as the combination of the two inputs changes.

Indifference curve: the locus of points showing alternative combinations of the consumption of two goods that yield the same level of utility to the consumer.

Isoquant: the locus of points showing alternative combinations of two inputs (usually labour and capital) that will yield the same rate of output.

Marginal rate of substitution: the rate at which a consumer is willing to trade units of one good for units of another while maintaining the same level of utility.

Marginal rate of technical substitution: the rate at which units of one factor of production can be substituted for units of another, leaving the overall rate of output unchanged.

How does the firm choose its most efficient technique – the labour-capital combination that is consistent with the least costs and maximum output? Output is constrained by the budget that is available. This in turn depends primarily on current and prospective revenues. The labour-capital combinations that are possible given the budget constraint will depend on the relative prices of the two factors.

Suppose that the total budget available for production is Y. Then if the price (= wage) of labour is w_1 and the price of capital (for which the interest rate is a proxy) is r_1, the budget line is determined by its intercept on each axis: Y/w_1 and Y/r_1 respectively (see Figure 6.5). The firm will combine labour and capital in the amounts and proportions shown by point A at which the budget line is tangent to the highest attainable isoquant. Here, the ratio of relative factor prices (r_1/w_1), or the slope of the budget line, is equal to the slope of the isoquant (dK/dL). The slope of the isoquant shows the MRTS of capital for labour. Note that at point A the firm employs relatively more of the services of capital than of labour – the chosen technique is *capital-intensive*.

Now suppose that labour (at wage w_2) becomes cheaper relative to capital (at interest rate r_2). The optimal combination of labour and capital is shown by point B. The technique has thus now become *labour-intensive*.

The idea of the smooth isoquant that is convex to the origin assumes a large array of alternative combinations of labour and capital that will produce a given output. In reality of course this is unlikely to be so. Techniques (production assembly lines, for example) typically have fixed ratios of capital to labour, allowing little or no variation as the relative prices of the two factors change over a wide range. The marginal rate of substitution of one factor for another is then zero, giving an

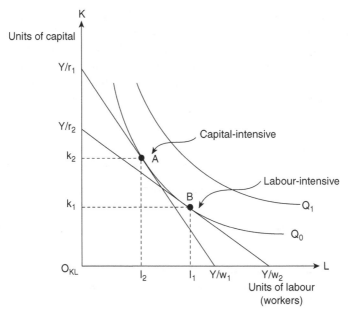

Figure 6.5 Choice of technique and relative factor prices

L-shaped isoquant. The technological alternatives are extreme: either an almost complete loss of mechanization, with production being carried out by many workers with few implements (labour-intensive production), or a shift to almost complete automation (capital-intensive production).

The introduction of new techniques as the outcome of invention and innovation (technical progress) allows a given output to be produced with *fewer* inputs of labour and capital, or allows *more* output to be produced with a given quantity of labour and capital. The effect is to move the relevant isoquant inwards towards the origin. Technical progress may change the shape of the isoquant by affecting the MRTS. This will cause the point of tangency with the budget line to change and so will affect the proportion in which the two factors are combined.

Isoquant analysis provides the final link between the factor, product and consumer markets, and hence gives the conditions for a general equilibrium: firms are producing at least cost the combination of goods for which they are best suited and which best meet the demands of consumers. As we shall see when we discuss Pareto efficiency, for this overall equilibrium to obtain requires a state of perfect competition.

Costs

Economics sees the costs of an organization as deriving directly from the production function. Any given rate of output (Q) needs a precise input of the factors of production of labour and capital. If the prices of the factors are known (wages for labour and the rate of interest for capital), then the total costs (*TC*) of production are also known. From this it is a short step to calculating the **average total cost** (*TC/Q*) and marginal cost ($\Delta TC/\Delta Q$).

Average total cost: total cost per unit of output.

The parallels between cost analysis in accounting, finance and economics are inevitably close and Chapter 5 in this book contains useful material relating to the costs in management accounting. However, Economics is distinctive in recognizing not only the costs that are directly attributable to specific production or other types of economic activity, but also the costs incurred by choosing one option at the expense of others, and the impact that production has on other members of society who are not involved in the processes of production or associated transactions and exchange.

The necessity of choosing between the production of alternative goods, given the assumption of scarcity in a fully employed economy, means that the benefit that would have come from an alternative activity is foregone. This is the notion of **opportunity cost**. Rational decision makers in organizations will select the most attractive potential opportunity from a given set of choices; that is, they will minimize the opportunity cost.

Opportunity cost: the benefit foregone by choosing one course of action rather than the next most highly valued alternative.

We are well aware that economic activity has effects that are both beneficial and detrimental and that these go far beyond those who are directly involved. Environmental degradation and human-made climate change are obvious examples here. Such effects impose costs on society, in both the present and the future. They are known as negative **externalities**, or spill-overs. Accurate economic cost accounting needs to include opportunity costs and externalities, together with the directly attributable costs.

Externalities (or spill-overs): the wider costs or benefits of a transaction between two or more parties that are not captured in the market price.

Following the conventional production function-based cost analysis in Economics, we can separate the short period from the long period. In the **short period** one or more factors of production are fixed in supply because of decisions made in the past. In the **long period** the supply of all factors can be varied.

> **Short period**: the period in which the input of one or more factors of production is fixed.
>
> **Long period**: the period in which the input of *all* factors of production can be varied.

Considering first the short run, the presence of fixed factors means that some parts of total costs are also fixed (**fixed costs**), while the remainder of the total costs will vary with output (**variable costs**). The concept of fixed costs includes **sunk costs**, which are the costs associated with assets which cannot be changed in use (an oil refinery, for example).

> **Fixed costs**: costs of production associated with inputs of productive factors that remain fixed as output is varied, on account of the technical conditions of production.
>
> **Variable costs**: costs of production associated with inputs than can be varied, proportionately or otherwise, as output is varied.
>
> **Sunk costs**: fixed costs associated with specific assets that have no alternative use.

Variable costs will normally increase with the rate of output, but as the production function analysis has shown, not necessarily in direct proportion. So variable costs – and hence total costs, since TC = FC + VC – will reflect the effects of increasing, constant and diminishing returns (Figure 6.4).

The important derivatives from total costs are average cost (TC/Q) and marginal cost ($\Delta TC/\Delta Q$), or the *change* in total cost with a unit change in output. The key outcome from the standard theory of the production function in the short period is that the average cost curve is U-shaped and is cut from below at its minimum point by the marginal cost curve (see Figure 6.3).

In the long period, when all the factors and their costs can be varied, the constraint imposed by fixed costs no longer applies. The owner-managers can now choose the firm's capacity that best suits their market expectations and their (usually profit-maximizing) objectives. From the theory of the production function it is unlikely that constant returns to factor inputs, and hence constant unit costs, will obtain over the whole range of feasible outputs. More likely, over the initial output span, which may be a substantial fraction of the whole, increasing returns will be achieved as the scale of operations is increased.

This is the well-known notion of **economies of scale**. Economies of scale are significant when the required output to achieve least long-run average costs is large in relation to the size of the market. Industries in which scale economies are usually regarded as significant include: bulk chemicals; financial services; motor vehicles; oil refining; pharmaceuticals; and steelmaking.

> **Economies of scale**: the less-than-proportionate rise in total cost as output is increased, causing costs per unit of output to decrease progressively.

The question now arises of whether dis-economies of scale – rising long-run average costs – are inevitable and unavoidable as the scale is continuously expanded. On this point, the jury is still out. At any given time, precipitous increases in scale through investment in new facilities or through mergers and acquisitions will incur higher unit costs as the existing management and other resources are stretched and unanticipated issues and events are met.

However in the longer term operations can be rationalized and technical, marketing, information and managerial systems will improve, and knowledge and experience will increase. Globalization has seen the development of innovative and strongly competitive enterprises of unprecedented scale and with worldwide reach. Therefore dis-economies of scale may not be inevitable. But to set against this complacency, there is an extensive array of examples of disastrous mergers that have destroyed shareholder value.

Pareto efficiency

Having now reviewed the characteristics of demand, supply and markets, the economist's idea of overall, or economic, efficiency can be explained. **Economic efficiency** takes account of both **technical efficiency**, which requires least-cost production, and **allocative efficiency**, which requires that scarce outputs from scarce resources are distributed efficiently among consumers. Achieving economic efficiency is often termed a **Pareto optimum**, after the Italian economist Vilfredo Pareto (1848–1923). The prime principle of such an optimum is that no agent, consumer or producer can be made better off without making another agent worse off.

> **Economic efficiency**: the allocation of (scarce) resources to their highest valued use and the production and distribution of goods and services at the lowest possible cost. Society's resources are allocated so that no change in the allocation can further improve anyone's well-being without making someone else worse off.
>
> *(Continued)*

(Continued)

Technical efficiency: maximization of output at least cost from any given set of inputs.

Allocative efficiency: the distribution of output and resources such that consumers' common marginal rate of substitution between goods is equal to the marginal rate of transformation of one good into another; therefore it is not possible to make one consumer better off without making another worse off, neither can the production of one good be increased without reducing the output of another.

Pareto optimum: the allocation of commodities and inputs is such that it is impossible to make one individual better off without making another worse off.

In these terms, economic efficiency is achieved through the operation of perfect competition. Perfect competition maximizes the aggregate of *consumer* and *producer surplus* (see page 166–7) by requiring price (P) to equal marginal cost (MC). $P = MC$ is one of the key rules in Economics. From the consumer's side, the price paid reflects the marginal utility of the good purchased. Rational consumers will equate marginal utility across all goods purchased, so as to maximize their overall utility. At the same time, the marginal rate of substitution between any two goods will be the same for all consumers, because otherwise the utility of one consumer could be improved by reallocation without diminishing the utility of another.

From the producer's side, the price obtained by the sale of the last unit of the good produced matches the marginal cost of production. Here the producer is earning a normal profit and must be producing at least the cost, otherwise competition would drive the firm out of the market.

A Pareto optimum provides a benchmark against which the welfare consequences of deviating from perfect competition can be assessed. This is particularly important in business economics in analyzing the impact of a monopoly and of market failure. But note that the Paretian system takes no account of equity. There are no value judgements about the appropriate distribution of income in society. Efficiency will be attained just as well with very unequal income distributions as with more equal ones. Neoclassical economics deals with this dilemma by imagining a social planner who has complete knowledge of society's overall welfare or utility function and who achieves equity by making use of re-distributive instruments such as lump-sum (income) taxation that leaves relative prices unchanged, and thereby avoids violating the Pareto principle. It is not hard to see the practical limitations of these assumptions.

An alternative theoretical approach to Pareto efficiency and economic welfare, and one which pre-dated it, was developed by the philosopher Jeremy Bentham (1748–1832), a mentor of J.S. Mill. Bentham took a utilitarian view of society, arguing for the greatest good for the greatest number. This means that moving to the point of maximum economic or social welfare involves both winners and losers; unlike the Pareto process, improving one person's welfare can be at the expense of another's. For this to be equitable and moral requires compensation for the losers from the winners. Such 'trade-offs' are now an important element in cost-benefit analysis.

Both of these notions of economic efficiency are static ones, in which the competitive process seeks and eventually attains an equilibrium. But in reality competition is a dynamic phenomenon in which risk-taking and innovation will destroy entrenched market positions and encourage new products and suppliers to rise to maturity. This process of **creative destruction**, closely aligned with the work of the Austrian-born economist Joseph Schumpeter (1883–1950), requires monopoly elements to be present in markets and cannot be reconciled with the notion of a stable equilibrium. It is also the concept of competition and efficiency that will be recognized by analyses in other parts of the MBA, in particular in Marketing and Strategic Management.

Creative destruction: the process of invading entrenched market positions through innovation and enterprise, associated with the work of Joseph Schumpeter.

Markets and Strategies

This part of the chapter brings together the organization's revenues and costs and relates them to its objectives. The objectives are affected by conditions in the market, which in turn will affect the shaping and pursuit of strategy.

The profit-maximizing firm

The starting point of conventional ('neoclassical') microeconomics is that firms will seek to maximize their expected short-run profits. Figure 6.3 shows the conventional revenue and costs representation for the profit-maximizing firm. The firm sets its output (q_m) at the level at which the last unit produced and sold will generate exactly the same additional (marginal) amount to total revenue as its production adds to total cost. Price (p_m) is then determined by the point on the demand curve corresponding to an output of q_m. Total profit is the area $p_m abc$. Together with the analysis of Figure 6.4, this gives the well-known (but often not well-understood) rule that the firm's expected profits are maximized when the marginal revenue is set equal to the marginal cost.

Assuming that organizations are interested solely in single-period **profit maximization** is, of course, a gross abstraction from reality – but still a helpful one at the initial stage of analysis. It focusses our attention on the marginal conditions (MR = MC) which is one of the most important concepts in Economics.

The analysis can be extended to include more realistic objectives than short-period profit maximization. Most organizations will take a longer view. Strategies will be shaped not only by the owners (including the shareholders in an incorporated business) but also by managers, employees, customers, and other stakeholders. Some part of short-period profits may be foregone now in order to stimulate future demand and to grow the business.

If managers are recompensed wholly or in part on the basis of sales value or volume they may aim to maximize sales, or sales growth rather than profits, at the expense of profits to shareholders. Moreover, since managers will have an immediate and detailed knowledge of the business that will not be available to shareholders and others with stakes in it, they may avoid maximizing anything, choosing instead to enjoy a steady income and a comfortable lifestyle, and subject only to keeping the shareholders satisfied – a situation that has been termed 'satisficing'. If the firm has a degree of monopoly power in its market that protects it from competition, this condition can be sustained for some time. As the economist John Hicks (1904–1989) commented, 'the best of all monopoly profits is a quiet life' (Hicks, 1935).

This standard economic model of the firm is modified by conditions in the product and factor markets in which it operates. For the purposes of this brief review, three product market stereotypes can be identified: perfect competition, monopoly and oligopoly.[3]

Perfect competition

Perfect competition is the starting point for the analysis of the impact of market form on firms' behaviour. It is a framework that is both very well known and very irritating to MBA students and economists alike because it is so far removed from conditions that are actually encountered in markets. But its value lies in the insights it gives into the concept and nature of economic welfare and the conditions under which welfare may be increased, if not maximized.

Perfect competition: a market form with many buyers and sellers who are completely informed and none of whom can influence price, which reflects the marginal cost of production.

In perfect competition firms have no coercive power in the market. Demand conditions are set by consumer preferences and costs are determined by the technology of the production function and relative factor prices. The firm is a pricetaker, accepting the same market conditions as its competitors and unable to influence them unilaterally. Information is complete and instantaneous and available to all market participants. There are no barriers to entry or exit.

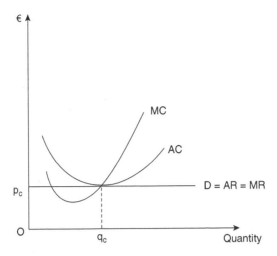

Figure 6.6 The firm as price taker

As Figure 6.6 shows, the main difference between the perfect competition model and the conventional analysis with which this discussion began is that because the firm is a price taker its demand or average revenue curve is horizontal. Competition among the existing firms in the market, together with the threat or reality of a new entry, drives the demand curve down to the point at which it is tangent to the AC curve. The geometric conditions mean that this is the least unit cost point and the price, at output q_c, is equal to it. They also mean that P = AR = MR = AC = MC.

Any higher price is unsustainable because the profits it would generate would instantaneously attract a new entry and drive the price back to the minimum cost point. In a similar fashion, any lower price would incur losses that would drive some firms out of the market, causing the price to rise. Remember that *economic costs*, which we are using here, include sufficient financial return, or **normal profit**, to keep the firm's assets in its particular industry. The return reflects the assets' opportunity cost. So in these terms the profits shown in Figure 6.3 are excess or supra-normal profits. The power of perfect competition is to eradicate them, to reduce the price and increase output to the benefit of consumers, and to set the price equal to the marginal cost (P = MC).

> **Normal profit**: the rate of profit just necessary to keep assets in their present use in a perfectly competitive market. Normal profit is treated as a cost to the firm.

This last point is crucial. The equality of price with marginal cost means that the price paid by the consumer of the last unit purchased *just equals* the resource cost incurred in producing it. If price is not equal to marginal cost, then either too much (P < MC) or too little (P > MC) is being produced in relation to the resources available to society.

The marginal cost pricing rule satisfies the condition for a general equilibrium in the factor, product and consumer markets (see the sections on the Organization and the Individual above). More importantly, in the real world of business it provides important guidelines for investment decisions, particularly in the public sector, for competition policy, and for the regulation of utilities and other enterprises that have public service obligations.

Monopoly

Monopoly is at the other end of the spectrum of competition. Strictly speaking it refers to a single monolithic enterprise that commands the whole of its market. But in practice the concept can be applied just as well to a firm that has a very strong market position and is insulated from new competition by entry barriers. Figure 6.3 shows the essential welfare elements of monopoly.

Monopoly: strictly speaking the market form characterized by the presence of a single seller, but more generally a market form with a dominant seller.

By comparison with the firm in perfect competition the price is higher, at p_m, and the output lower, at q_m – a clear indication of a welfare loss, all else equal. But the welfare analysis can be carried further. Since the figure can be related to a single monopoly enterprise, the revenue and cost conditions are those that will hold in the market as a whole. Under perfect competition, the price (= average revenue) would equal the marginal cost. Assuming that aggregate revenues and costs in the whole market are the same under perfect competition as they are under monopoly (that is, there are no economies of scale), it is clear that setting the price equal to the marginal costs benefits the consumer by giving a greater output at a lower price than under monopoly.

In the market as a whole under perfect competition, all consumers who choose to purchase pay p_c. The demand represented by the segment of the demand curve above this price reflects those consumers who are prepared to pay *more* than the price in the market. The money value of their demand is the **consumer surplus**. It is clear that more consumers are willing to pay above the prevailing market price under perfect competition than under monopoly.

Consumer surplus: the total value of the willingness of consumers to pay above the market price, represented diagrammatically by the area under the demand curve and above the price line.

> **Producer surplus**: the total value of revenue in excess of what is required to induce a firm to supply – diagrammatically, this is the area below the price line and above the supply curve.

The movement to monopoly reduces the consumer surplus in two ways. First, the greater part of the reduction is captured by the producer: the **producer surplus** is shown by the area $p_m abc$ in Figure 6.3. But importantly for considerations of welfare, because the market demand curve is negatively sloped part of the consumer surplus is lost altogether. Economists term this the **deadweight loss**.

> **Deadweight loss** (of monopoly): the loss in total (consumer *plus* producer) surplus arising because a monopolist produces less than the total surplus-maximizing output.

Oligopoly

The final market stereotype to be considered is **oligopoly** – a word coined by economists in a similar form to monopoly to describe the limited competition between the few producers or suppliers that are large in relation to the total market. Oligopoly is the competitive form that is closest to the reality of many markets in mature economies. Oligopolists have market power but are not completely protected from competition.

> **Oligopoly**: a market populated by a small number of competing firms, typically of a similar size, whose strategic actions are characterized by mutual recognition and interdependence.

In fact, they will recognize the presence in the market not only of each other but also of potential new competitors and they will take account of their actual and potential competitive actions. It is this *interdependence* among competitors that is the distinguishing feature of oligopoly. It contrasts sharply with firms' independence under monopoly and their lack of market influence under perfect competition. And, importantly, it introduces the notion of strategic behaviour, so building a strong link with business analysis and policy.

The basic theory assumes a small number of firms (usually two) of similar size producing similar products at a similar cost with identical knowledge of the market. A new entry to the market is completely blockaded, so the rivals will consider only each other's actions and make decisions simultaneously. Formal collusion to achieve a joint monopoly is prohibited.

In these circumstances, the rational self-interested profit-maximizing firm will make its output or price decision on the basis of the decision it believes its rival will make. Consider first that the decisions made are about output. Thus if Firm A believes that its rival Firm B will produce x_b units of output in a market in which the total demand at a given price is X, Firm A's residual demand is x_a (= $X - x_b$).

By varying the price assumption, Firm A can derive its residual demand curve, and from it, its residual marginal revenue curve. Like all profit-maximizing firms, Firm A's best response to its rival's anticipated decision is given by the output at which MR = MC, and from which it will have no incentive to move, so long as the market conditions remain unchanged.

By extension, Firm B's strategic approach will be the mirror image of this. Both firms can vary their expectations about the output decisions of the other and so develop a series of best responses to alternative outputs. It is clear that the market equilibrium will be at the price-quantity pair which brings both firms to their respective best response points simultaneously. Neither will have an incentive to move away.[4]

Reflecting the work of the Nobel prize-winning mathematician and economist John Nash (1928–), the general situation in which oligopolists will simultaneously attain best response positions is termed a **Nash equilibrium**. Because the specific decisions considered here are output-based rather than price-based, the position in this example is a **Nash-Cournot equilibrium**, after the initial work of the French economist Antoine Augustin Cournot (1801–1877).

Nash equilibrium: each firm chooses the strategy that maximizes its profit, given the strategies of the other firms in the market; there is no incentive for any firm to move away from this position.

Nash-Cournot equilibrium: a Nash equilibrium (q.v.) in which firms' choice of strategy is in terms of the quantities supplied.

Output-based decisions in oligopoly are most likely where firms cannot easily alter their rates of production, for example where capacity has already been built and fixed expenses are a significant part of the total costs. Given that individual firms' residual marginal revenue curves are downward-sloping, and assuming for convenience that the marginal costs are constant, in a Nash-Cournot equilibrium the market price will be higher, and the aggregate output lower, than under perfect competition. But because the firms have not achieved the joint monopoly position, prices will be lower and the output higher than under monopoly. Thus, in terms of economic welfare, a Nash-Cournot equilibrium rests somewhere between perfect competition and monopoly.

Suppose now that the oligopolists' decisions are based on price rather than output. This is likely to occur when firms can more readily adjust their outputs to meet conditions in the market, for example, if they are bidding for contracts. Analysis of price-based decision making follows the early work of another French mathematician and economist, Joseph Bertrand (1822–1903); the equilibrium in this case is a **Nash-Bertrand** one.

Nash-Bertrand equilibrium: a Nash equilibrium (*q.v.*) in which firms' choice of strategy is in terms of the prices set.

The outcome under a Nash-Bertrand equilibrium is very different from that under Nash-Cournot conditions. In Nash-Bertrand, each firm anticipates the price that its rival will set. Given that the products of the two firms are undifferentiated, customers will buy the cheapest one. The incentive will be for each firm to undercut the price of the other, all the way down to the point at which the price is equal to the marginal cost; that is, the outcome under a Nash-Bertrand oligopoly will be identical to that in perfect competition. The price will not fall below the marginal cost because below that point it will be in firms' best interests to shut down rather than continue to produce.

In reality, markets that have the characteristics of oligopolies show a diversity of competitive rivalry patterns. Firms tend to have strong mutual recognition and similar strategies where they are of a similar size, are large in relation to their market, have similar cost structures, produce similar products, face relatively stable demand, and interact frequently in the market.

Repeated interactions will enable firms to react to the actual decisions of their rivals and also to take steps to bring sanctions against behaviour they regard as unacceptable. If, for example, one firm cuts its price or increases its output in relation to the prevailing equilibrium, its rival may retaliate even more aggressively. The expectation of mutual damage may reinforce the implicit collaboration of the equilibrium. Thus, for a Nash equilibrium to be sustainable, the threat of retaliation must be credible.

The danger of releasing uncontrolled aggression by changing output or price decisions unilaterally can lead oligopolists to compete more subtly and rather more safely. Differentiating products in terms of quality, distribution channels or advertising and marketing can enable prices to vary without the risk of significant losses of sales volume. The provision of several products and services may be bundled together – broadband, television and telephone services, for example – and customers will be encouraged to enter into long-term supply contracts.

However, implicit collusion in oligopolistic markets does not endure indefinitely. Firms may make unilateral output or price changes, assuming their long period effects will not be immediately apparent to their competitors and so will not result in swift retaliation. Other firms may attribute variations in sales volume or realized prices to changes in the general market conditions rather than to the aggressive actions of competitors. Furthermore, a technical change can create new markets, enable new firms to enter existing ones, make business models redundant, and sweep away enterprises that were once dominant. The recorded music industry is a prime example here. The main revenue generator used to be compact discs, and before that audio tapes. It is now artists' concerts. And the influence of the music recording and publishing companies has been dramatically reduced by the internet.

Game theory

Oligopoly theory and the modelling of firms' interdependent and complex strategic behaviour have been formalized, made precise, and enhanced by the application of the Theory of Games. **Game theory** has its origins in the joint work of John von Neumann (1903–1957), a mathematician, and Oskar Morgenstern (1902–1977), an economist. Their (1944) book *Theory of Games and Economic Behavior* (reissued in 2004) laid the basis for a wide range of strategic decision making applications, not only for Economics but also in fields such as military strategy, politics, medicine and the law. Nowadays, some pit-stops in Formula One motor sport are scheduled using game theory.

> **Game theory**: a framework for analyzing strategic behaviour in the context of decision making.

In games players will have strategies, take actions, and anticipate rewards (pay-offs). Rational players will aim to maximize their payoffs, taking account of the actions of their rivals. Games can be co-operative or, as is most usually the case in oligopoly, non-co-operative. Exactly in line with oligopoly theory described above, a stable (Nash) equilibrium position is reached when each player simultaneously achieves their best response and there is a credible threat of retaliation if either party departs from this best position.

The example below gives two simple and related examples of a duopoly game in which decisions are taken simultaneously and each player has full knowledge of the other's strategies and actions, thereby illustrating the principles of game theory and its application in the strategic analysis of oligopoly.

 Game theory

SmartAir and FleeceAir are two passenger airlines intending to compete in the same market. Each has to decide on the level of service to be offered: full-service or low-cost 'no frills'. SmartAir makes the first move. Figure 6.7 illustrates the 'game tree', showing the pattern of the game and the anticipated payoffs.

(Continued)

(Continued)

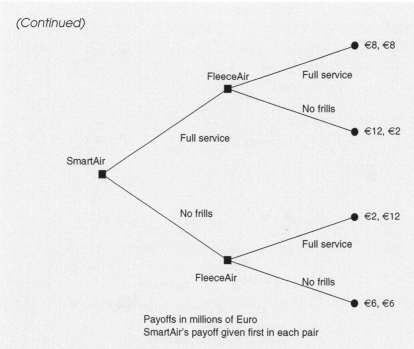

€8, €8

FleeceAir — Full service

No frills

€12, €2

Full service

SmartAir

No frills

€2, €12

Full service

FleeceAir — No frills

€6, €6

Payoffs in millions of Euro
SmartAir's payoff given first in each pair

Figure 6.7 Dominant strategy equilibrium (based on Morgan et al. 2006)

The game can be understood by starting with the *last* decision made and working back to the initial decision – a process of **backward induction**.

> **Backward induction**: the process of analyzing game-theoretic strategic decisions working from the final outcome.

FleeceAir has to decide on its actions if SmartAir chooses to offer full-service *or* no frills. If SmartAir decides on full-service, FleeceAir's best response is also to choose full-service. Each airline gets a payoff of €8 million. But if SmartAir chooses no frills, FleeceAir's best response is still to choose full-service – it gets a payoff of €12 million while SmartAir's payoff drops to €2 million. So FleeceAir's best strategy is *always* to choose full-service, whatever SmartAir decides to do. This is FleeceAir's *dominant* strategy – that it will always play.

Now consider SmartAir: the airline is *always* better off choosing full-service, *whatever* FleeceAir does. Choosing full-service earns SmartAir €8 million if FleeceAir also decides to offer full-service, or €12 million if its rival selects no frills. Both these payoffs are greater than those available to SmartAir if it chooses no frills. Thus, choosing full-service is also SmartAir's dominant strategy.

(Continued)

(Continued)

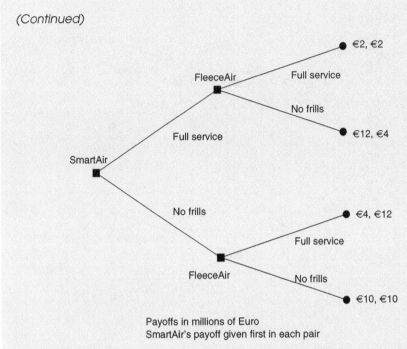

Payoffs in millions of Euro
SmartAir's payoff given first in each pair

Figure 6.8 One player dominant strategy (based on Morgan et al. 2006)

Both airlines have identical dominant strategies and the market will reach a Nash equilibrium from which there is no incentive to move.

But now take a look at the game tree represented in Figure 6.8. FleeceAir's best (dominant) strategy is to choose no frills if SmartAir decides on full-service (a €4 million payoff for FleeceAir) and to choose full-service if SmartAir selects no frills (a €12 million payoff for FleeceAir). But now SmartAir has no dominant strategy – what it should do for the best depends on what its rival chooses to do.

SmartAir, as the first mover, anticipates that, if it selects full-service, FleeceAir will choose no frills. The respective payoffs will then be €12 million and €4 million. This represents a Nash equilibrium with only one player having a dominant strategy.

But suppose SmartAir thinks that FleeceAir will offer full-service whatever happens; that is, that FleeceAir will continue to keep to its previous dominant strategy. SmartAir will then offer no frills, obtaining a much-reduced payoff of €4 million, but preventing FleeceAir from spoiling the market for them both by choosing full-service had SmartAir also chosen full-service. This is also an equilibrium, but it is not credible. If SmartAir did *actually* choose full-service, FleeceAir *at the point at which the decision was made* would select no frills, because that would give it the better payoff (€4 million as against €2 million).

This style of analysis can be extended easily to other aspects of oligopolistic markets. One of the most important here is the threat of entry. Both the incumbent firm and the potential entrant will form views of the price and output conditions that will prevail in the market after entry has occurred. The potential entrant has two options: to enter or not to enter. The incumbent will then decide how to respond once entry has, or has not, taken place.

Any stated or implied threat of retaliation on the part of the incumbent if entry does take place must be credible in order to be effective in deterring entry. Should such an entry occur, the incumbent in its own self-interest must then adapt to the presence of its new competitor. The usual outcome to a game of this sort is that the payoff associated with the incumbent firm's best response strategy will be lower than if it had maintained its monopoly position.

Incumbent firms can take pre-emptive action to deter entry by irreversibly changing the post-entry payoffs that are anticipated. The steps here will include a substantial increase in capacity; significant expenditures on research and development to lower costs or to improve the quality and the range of goods produced; registering patents to prevent or restrict competitors' production; and tying customers in by offering to match the terms of sale of new entrants. Some of these steps can be used to drive down the post-entry price below that of the potential entrant's marginal costs.

Other applications of game theory in oligopoly are associated with the absence of complete information. Where information is imperfect because rivals are unable or unwilling to communicate implicitly or explicitly with one another, an equilibrium position in the market may be unsustainable because of the temptation to take unilateral action to achieve individual advantage at the expense of other firms – in other words, to 'cheat'. Indeed formal cartels, where they are legal, and other informal market-sharing agreements are typically undermined eventually by the erosion of the best strategic response positions. The outcome is worse than if the rival firms had been able to collude. Games such as these are in the well-known form of the 'prisoners' dilemma'.

Where information is incomplete, players have to work on the basis of probabilities. But the quality of information can be improved when rivals engage repeatedly in the market. Each can then anticipate better the strategies and actions of the other and take steps to retaliate against unco-operative behaviour. The expectation of retaliation, of course, then serves to impose discipline.

Networks

The strategic interlinkages that are at the core of game theory are allied closely with the identification and analysis of networks. Networks in Economics are connections between 'players' who will interact in the processes of exchange and co-operation. These 'players' include individuals, products, processes, firms, industries, and innovations. Network analysis extends and qualifies the concept of the market mechanism. Whereas well-functioning markets are impersonal and inclusive, networks are personal and exclusive.

By the standard of the efficient market, therefore, networks introduce imperfections. Repeated interactions between players may increase the strength of the relationship between them and raise the barrier to new players joining the network. On the other hand, the prior existence of a network can assist the launch of a new product or the introduction of an innovation. In terms of economic welfare the first case represents a negative network externality, while the second shows a positive externality. Network analysis introduces new and interesting insights into the economics of business strategy, its welfare impacts, and the grounds for public policy interventions (see Pepall et al., 2007).

Missing markets

Neoclassical microeconomics, of the kind reviewed so far, has as its main objective the attainment of a general equilibrium in which scarce resources are fully and efficiently employed; the total surplus (consumer and producer) is maximized; and equity is achieved through redistributive lump-sum taxation. A necessary condition for this is that efficiency and equilibrium are achieved simultaneously in *all* markets. In reality, of course, this is like baying for the moon – it is simply unattainable in full or perhaps in any significant part.

Markets may be distorted by monopoly or **monopsony** power or may be missing altogether. When this is the case, attempts to achieve general or partial equilibria must involve public policy interventions in the market mechanism. The main instruments to deal with the distortions associated with monopoly are: competition policy; public ownership; privatization; regulation; and industrial policy.

Monopsony: a market form characterized by the presence of a single buyer.

This chapter so far has been a brief summary of conventional welfare economics. The emphasis has been on attaining an overall economic welfare equilibrium that is also an optimum for society as a whole. Rational self-interest and fully functioning markets in all parts of the global economy will bring this about. Any market imperfections need to be removed, corrected, or compensated for by government intervention.

While this approach informs all microeconomics courses in MBA and other business-related programmes, it is a long way removed from the reality of the markets and from the economic and strategic perspectives as seen by business. Market power and advantage are driven and sustained by market imperfections that arise from and encourage enterprise, innovation, and the pursuit of abnormal profits and returns. Equilibrium conditions are destroyed rather than built by the competitive process – Schumpeter's 'creative destruction'.

Disruption can therefore drive profitability, investment, and economic growth through innovation and enterprise. But what are the causes and impacts of the financial and economic cycles that are persistent characteristics of market-driven economies? This question has, of course, been given particular point by the global financial crisis that began in 2007.

The fundamental causes of economic cycles – involving movements in inventories, investment, and international trade – are well known and now also fairly well understood. But extreme financial bubbles challenge our assumptions about the prevalence of information transparency and rational behaviour in markets. Like the theory of finance itself, the economics of financial markets is built on the **efficient markets hypothesis** (EMH). On this basis, the value of marketable securities – equity, bonds, and other instruments – is determined by the present value of their expected future income streams. New information is immediately captured in the price so there is no scope for any individual or group of investors to gain an advantage.

Efficient markets hypothesis: with complete information, competitive markets, and rational behaviour on the part of market participants, the valuation of marketable assets will be determined by the present value of the expected future income stream, making it impossible for individual investors to gain an advantage.

Sequential movements in the price of a security (day-by-day or minute-by-minute), and hence its rate of return, will therefore be random and unpredictable – the **random walk theory**. Complete information and rational agents should be sufficient, therefore, to guard against 'irrational exuberance' and eventual disillusionment on the part of investors. Yet speculation can – and clearly does – drive up asset prices, both financial and real, beyond any rational level, leading inevitably to collapse. Much research has been, and will continue to be, directed towards this phenomenon. The explanations include: herd instinct behaviour involving less informed, less experienced investors; an appetite for risk based on access to credit at unsustainably low interest rates; and borrowing to finance continuing asset purchases in an attempt to sustain an upward price momentum. However, our understanding of financial markets is far from complete and the primacy of the efficient markets hypothesis is under critical review.

Random walk theory: in the presence of full information, the current rate of financial return on a stock or other traded security is independent of both past and future expected returns.

The Organization's External Environment

Until now this chapter has considered the basis provided by Economics for the strategic decisions that organizations must make about the generation and deployment of their resources. These decisions have to be taken in the context of the wider environment in which any profit or not-for-profit organization must operate and over which it may have little or no influence, but which must still be recognized, anticipated, and taken into account when forming and implementing strategic actions.

The overall environment of business is typically considered in terms of political, economic, social, and technological factors (PEST analysis, the shortened form of the PESTEL analysis discussed in Chapter 9 on Strategy). The final part of this chapter, therefore, looks briefly at those factors that can specifically influence the economic environment of business as well as their impact on the strategies of firms and other organizations.

Economic growth

The overall economic activity of a country or region is typically measured by its **gross domestic product** (GDP) – the output of all goods and services arising within the country or region in a given time period, usually a year. GDP can be measured either at current prices – which will include the effects of movements, usually upwards, in the general level of prices (price inflation) – or at constant prices – which will discount price level changes and represent the volume, rather than the value, of output.

> **Gross domestic product (GDP)**: the output of final goods and services produced within the spatial boundaries of a country or other jurisdiction in a given period of time, usually a year.

On the expenditure side, GDP is composed of household spending, fixed asset formation (capital investment), government spending on goods and services, and net exports (that is, exports *minus* imports). On the income side, the main components of GDP are income from employment and self-employment, the profits of companies together with the trading surpluses of public sector and other organizations, and rent from property.

An increasingly important criticism of the conventional GDP measurement and analysis is that it neglects the social and environmental costs and benefits of economic activity. Developments in social accounting are now addressing this, even to the extent of trying to measure 'happiness'.

In relation to expenditure, GDP is driven by:

- Household spending, which is influenced among other things by after-tax incomes, outstanding financial commitments (mortgages and other borrowings), interest rates, preferences for saving (deferred spending), unemployment, and expectations about the future (confidence)
- Investment, on which cost of finance, profits, public spending, the stage of the business cycle, and confidence will have significant effects
- Government spending on goods and services, which is sensitive to the overall size of the economy, the demographic structure, revealed voter preferences

about the size and activities of the state (public choice), taxation revenues, and the budget balance

- The volumes of exports and imports, which will reflect and be influenced by international competitiveness (in terms of price and/or quality), exchange rates, costs and productivity, and capacity availability

Fluctuations in economic activity arise because of cyclical movements and shocks. The economic cycle – which in mature market economies is typically around seven to ten years in length – is influenced mainly by variations in capital investment and in the level of international trade. Shocks come from unsustainable booms that end in recessions and these increasingly have their origins in global, rather than domestic, factors. Booms and recessions are closely associated with speculation and risk-taking in financial and other asset markets (real estate in particular), and with excessive monetary and fiscal expansion.

Economic models attempt to simulate and predict movements in the key components of GDP and its associated variables that include employment, prices, and interest rates. Experience so far shows that models are much better at forecasting trends over time than predicting cyclical turning points or the occurrence of shocks – which are unpredictable by their definition.

Individual sectors of the economy will be affected differently during each stage of the cycle. Sectors with high income elasticities in relation to GDP – such as leisure and tourism, high technology, financial services, real estate and commodities – will do well during upswings. Energy, pharmaceuticals, health care services, education and agriculture are examples of sectors that tend to be robust in recessions.

The trend of economic growth as measured by GDP per head of the total population of a country is influenced principally by the demographic structure, the degree of participation in the labour force, productivity, institutional factors, and the extent of engagement in the world economy (globalization). Countries in which the age distribution is being skewed towards the upper end (Japan, for example) will find it difficult to maintain their previous pace of growth. Labour force participation is affected primarily by cultural factors, in particular the involvement of women in the workforce, and by the length of time spent in full-time education.

Productivity – as measured by output per worker or output per hour worked – is a function of the investment in technology and human capital. Research and development, invention, and innovation contribute improved products and increased efficiency. Human capital is built through education, training, and experience. Together, improved technology and human capital interact to push productivity higher than would be the case for one of the factors alone – this is termed the **total factor productivity** effect.

Total factor productivity: the contribution to output growth that is associated with the interaction of labour and capital rather than with the amounts of their input. The concept is associated primarily with the work of Robert Solow.

Institutional factors are society's customs and practices. These are important for understanding why countries' long-term growth rates tend to be persistent and different from one another. In statistical terms, trend growth rates tend to be path-dependent making accelerated growth difficult to sustain.

In spite of the global financial crisis that started in 2007, the growth of world output and trade since 1980 has been remarkable by any standard. Globalization has enabled developing and emerging economies to engage with the world economic community and has also helped to sustain output growth, employment, and investment in the more mature economies.

Two principal developments associated with globalization have been the multilateral reductions in tariffs and the removal of non-tariff barriers to international trade co-ordinated by the World Trade Organization (WTO), and the de-regulation and liberalization of international financial markets. Other factors here include the growth of regional trading blocs, such as the European Union and the Association of South-East Asian Nations (ASEAN), and increased economic migration as regional labour markets have become more integrated. Among the emerging economies, the growth of natural resource-endowed countries such as Brazil, Russia, India and China (the so-called 'BRICs') has been particularly significant.

However, while the economic and social benefits of globalization have been generally recognized, concern is being expressed that the process has gone forward too quickly. International financial flows, reflecting the large imbalances between saving and borrowing among trading partners and affected by speculation and excessive risk-taking, have become volatile. This volatility has started to undermine the stability of the world economy. Following the increases in interest rates in the United States that began in 2005 and their subsequent impact on mortgage lenders and the housing market, worldwide money and credit markets became frozen.

Countries have begun to address trade deficits by re-erecting tariff and non-tariff barriers to imports, while at the same time in some cases giving assistance to domestic production and supply networks, employment, and exports. This shift to localization has gained added strength by a recognition of the damage to the environment that is associated with the international trade in commodities and manufactured goods.

While these concerns are legitimate and important, any threat to the continued integration of the world economy risks impairing economic growth by reducing the benefits coming from international specialization and comparative advantage.

Macroeconomic policies

The main macroeconomic instruments that are available to countries to support economic growth and to mitigate the impact of cycles and shocks are monetary and fiscal policies, and trade and exchange rate policies. **Monetary policy** has been dominant in advanced market economies since the inflation-driven financial crises of the mid-1970s and – through the International Monetary Fund (IMF) and the

World Bank – has been important also in influencing the development of some emerging economies.

> **Monetary policy**: the use of monetary instruments, typically interest rates, to influence medium-term price inflation and to contribute to macroeconomic stability.

In applying monetary policy an independent Central Bank targets price inflation in the medium term, typically two years ahead, by means of influencing market interest rates. This is done principally by the sale and re-purchase of government bonds ('repos') to set official interest rates, which in turn will influence rates in the financial markets as a whole.

Figure 6.9 outlines the transmission mechanism of monetary policy. Official rates influence market rates, asset prices (residential housing and equities in particular), expectations, and the exchange rate. This in turn affects demand, both from the domestic economy and from abroad, and impacts on domestic and import prices – and hence, on overall price inflation.

This approach to monetary policy was generally seen as successful until the onset of the financial and banking crisis in 2007. It required flexible financial, product, and labour markets in order to operate. Subsequently, the focus of policy has switched away from the risk of *rising* prices (inflation) to the risk of *falling* prices (deflation) and this has led to Central Banks using unconventional means ('quantitative easing') to boost and sustain financial liquidity.

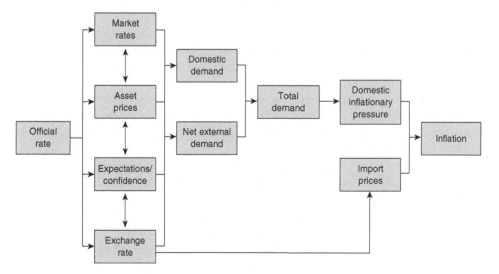

Figure 6.9 Transmission mechanism of monetary policy

In sharp contrast to monetary policy, fiscal policy (taxing and government spending) was the dominant form during the period that started with the reconstruction of the world economy after 1945 and continued until the rise of monetarism in the 1970s. It is intimately associated with the work of John Maynard Keynes (see page 145).

Fiscal policy works primarily on the demand side of the economy. A fiscal stimulus (government spending that is greater than taxation receipts) tends to boost final demand, output, employment and prices, while fiscal restraint (taxation greater than spending) tends to hold back inflation and economic growth in the short term.

> **Fiscal policy**: adjusting the balance between the revenue from taxation and other resources and public expenditure to influence key macroeconomic variables, in particular output, employment, investment, and prices.

However, fiscal policy only works with considerable lags and some uncertainty, and is also attenuated by international trade and investment, so it is not suitable for short-term management of the economy. Moreover, it fell out of favour with politicians, policy makers, and some economists in the 1970s when it appeared to be simultaneously associated with rising prices and rising unemployment ('stagflation'). But it has been generally acknowledged that a prudent fiscal policy, in which budgets are balanced over the economic cycle as a whole, is a key instrument in achieving stable and sustainable growth in the longer term.

The global financial crisis has obliged the governments of several major economies to increase their fiscal deficits sharply in an attempt to curb the fall in economic activity and support a revival in growth. Returning to an appropriate balance between revenue and expenditure will be a major challenge in the medium term.

Much less international consensus of agreement exists about appropriate **trade and exchange rate policies**. On the one hand, stable exchange rates and open markets – as in the 16-member Eurozone of the European Union – may be seen as curbing inflationary pressures, particularly from wages; encouraging productivity growth; and discouraging speculation in the currency markets. On the other hand, exchange rate flexibility can be argued to allow an adjustment to the changing macroeconomic and competitive conditions without unduly impacting on output growth and employment.

Trade imbalances (i.e. deficits *and* surpluses), which by definition are the counterpart of net inflows and outflows on the underlying capital account, can be justified on the grounds that they reflect and enable increased integration of the global economy and the transfer of funds between regions with, respectively, high and low preferences for aggregate saving. But against this, trade and investment imbalances can be associated with sharp fluctuations in the global economy if pre-emptory and unanticipated steps are taken to bring them more into balance.

Summary

This chapter has critically reviewed the framework of analysis of Economics as it relates to business and management in general and to the MBA in particular. It began with the crucial issue that gives Economics meaning and relevance – humankind's need to make choices given the scarcity of resources. The weight of current analysis is still resting on the assumption of rational behaviour through which individuals and economic organizations will seek to maximize their net benefit. Consumer theory gives insights into the fundamentals of demand while production theory explores the various relationships between capital, labour, and technology. These two key pillars of microeconomic theory support the construction and analysis of an organization's income and costs, whether in the private, public, or social domains.

A consideration of market form and competitive behaviour – specifically with respect to perfect competition, monopoly and oligopoly – not only contributes to the understanding, formulation, and implementation of effective business strategy, it also enables the economic welfare of the market mechanism to be assessed. Recent developments in game theory and network analysis are particularly important here. Identified deficiencies in the way in which markets operate help to suggest and explain interventions which are intended to correct or compensate for economic welfare detriments that may be associated with a lack (or distortion) of competition.

The final step is to set the organization within its broader national, regional and global context. Here an analysis of the composition and growth of the aggregate economy, as represented by GDP, becomes important. Understanding the purposes and impacts of macroeconomic monetary, fiscal, and trade and exchange policies is crucial at this point.

This whole review is against the background of shocks to the global economy and the resulting turbulence and uncertainty that are currently challenging the conventional economic analysis that is based upon the assumptions of rational behaviour and a self-balancing market mechanism. These challenges offer exciting opportunities for original research that has the potential to enrich economic theory and its contribution to the MBA programme, not only directly but also through its links to other subject areas, in particular accounting and finance, operations and human resource management, and above all, strategy.

From the standpoint of the business community in general, and the MBA in particular, Economics and its practitioners need to adopt a positive approach towards enterprise and innovation which recognizes the crucial role that business plays in driving economic activity and improving economic and social welfare. Overall – despite the effects of the business cycle and the associated financial turbulence, together with (justified) concerns about inequalities in global income and wealth – market-led production, distribution, and innovation have improved the human condition immeasurably over the past 300 years (see Beattie, 2009).

Above all, economic analysis must now provide business decision makers with:

- A coherent and robust defence against the over-reaction to the global financial crises of the first decade of the twenty-first century in the forms of protectionism and exclusive regionalism
- Techniques of analysis to sustain and improve the efficiency of production, distribution, and exchange
- Guidance on the design and application of public policy interventions to make sure that the first two goals are attained

If I offer that menu to my cold and sceptical MBA class, shall I be able to enjoy my lunch without ending up with indigestion?

Questions for reflection

1 Research and development, innovation and enterprise disrupt existing markets and their established patterns of competitive behaviour, giving scope for the creation of new sources of market power. Does this make the economist's notion of market equilibrium irrelevant for the analysis and understanding of business strategy and performance?
2 The proposed Harvard Business School 'MBA Oath' commits its alumni to embrace ethical principles in their professional activities and, like the medical Hippocratic oath on which it is modelled, 'to do no harm'. Conventional microeconomic theory relies on the principle of the pursuit of individual self-interest to achieve maximum economic welfare. Is this principle about to collapse?
3 You are thinking about investing in a proposed new chain of fast-food restaurants that will feature healthy eating and environmental awareness as its unique selling propositions. What insights from game theory can help you in making your decision whether or not to invest?
4 The competition authority is reviewing possible detriment to economic welfare associated with a supermarket operator's 40 per cent share of the relevant national market. This share is twice the size of its nearest rival's. What will be the likely initial depositions to the competition authority from:

a the supermarket operator
b its main rival
c a foreign-based retailer that is considering entering the national market
d an association of independent ('corner shop') shopkeepers
e a pensioners' association
f the competition authority's chief economist?

5 A significant body of evidence suggests that, more often than not, mergers destroy rather than enhance shareholder value. Can this evidence be reconciled with the economist's initial assumption that firms are short-period profit-maximizers?

Further reading

Books

Baye, M. (2010) *Managerial Economics and Business Strategy*. Maidenhead: McGraw-Hill.

Green, S. (2009) *Good Value: Money, Morality and an Uncertain World*. London: Allen Lane.

Keat, P.G. and Young, P.K.Y. (2009) *Managerial Economics: Economic Tools for Today's Decision Makers*. Upper Saddle River, NJ: Pearson Education.

von Neumann, J. and Morgenstern, O. (2004) *Theory of Games and Economic Behavior*. Princeton, NJ: Princeton University Press. 60th anniversary edition.

Journals

Arnold, M. and Parker, D. (2009) 'Stock market perceptions of the motives for mergers in cases reviewed by the UK competition authorities: an empirical analysis.' *Managerial and Decision Economics*, 30: 211–233.

Coase, R.H. (1937) 'The nature of the firm.' *Economica*, 4: 386–405.

Kay, J. (2009) 'The rationale of the market economy: a European perspective.' *Capitalism and Society*, 4 (3).

Phelps, E.S. (2009) 'Refounding capitalism.' *Capitalism and Society*, 4 (3).

Sachs, J.D. (2009) 'Rethinking macroeconomics.' *Capitalism and Society*, 4 (3).

Notes

1   Tony Cockerill is a Fellow of Magdalene College and a member of the Faculty of Economics, University of Cambridge. He is also Emeritus Professor of Applied Economics at Durham Business School. Study and research support provided by the Faculty of Economics and Magdalene College at Cambridge and by the Leverhulme Trust (Research Award EM 20239) is gratefully acknowledged. The chapter benefits from the insights and comments of Toke Aidt, Brian Deakin, Geoff Harcourt, John Pickering and Chander Velu, together with those of members of my Cambridge microeconomics classes of 2008–09 and 2009–10. The usual disclaimer applies.

2   Strictly, *point* as opposed to *arc* elasticity.

3   These conditions reflect different amounts of power on the seller's side. It is possible also for buyers to be able to exert power in the market: the market form where there is a single buyer facing a (large) number of sellers is a monopsony.

4   Standard intermediate microeconomics textbooks give the formal proof of this. See, for example, Morgan et al. (2006).

References

Beattie, A. (2009) *False Economy: A Surprising Economic History of the World*. London: Viking.

Coates, J.M., Gurnell, M. and Rustichini, A. (2009) 'Second-to-fourth digit ratio predicts success among high-frequency financial traders.' *Proceedings of the National Academy of Sciences of the United States of America*, 102 (2): 623–628.

Harcourt, G.C. (1995) 'What Adam Smith really said.' In *Capitalism, Socialism and Post-Keynesianism: Selected Essays of G.C. Harcourt*. Aldershot: Edward Elgar.

Hicks, J.R. (1935) 'Annual survey of economic theory: the theory of monopoly.' *Econometrica*, 3 (1): 1–20.

Morgan, W., Katz, M. and Rosen, H. (2006) *Microeconomics*. Maidenhead: McGraw-Hill Education.

Pepall, L., Richards, D. and Norman, G. (2007) *Industrial Organization: Contemporary Theory and Empirical Applications*. Oxford: Blackwell.

Smith, A. (1976) *The Theory of Moral Sentiments* (ed. D.D. Raphael and L.L. Macfie). Oxford: Clarendon.

Smith, A. (1977) *Wealth of Nations*. Chicago, IL: University of Chicago Press. p. 18.

Von Neumann, J. and Morgenstern, O. (2004) *Theory of Games and Economic Behaviour*. Princeton, NJ: Princeton University Press.

7 Operations Management

Key concepts

Bullwhip effect; Capacity; Concurrent engineering; Enterprise Resource Planning (ERP); Just in Time; Logistics; Materials Requirement Planning (MRP); Operations management; Operations strategy; Product and service development; Supply chain; Supply chain velocity

This chapter offers an introduction to the key principles and concepts of operations management. All organizations perform various operations in order to deliver something to their customers. This 'something' may be tangible, such as an iPod, or intangible, such as the applications that go on that iPod. The chapter will discuss the key approaches and techniques used to manage operations for the effective delivery of products and services to customers.

By the end of it the reader should be able to:

- Define operations management
- Understand the differences between products and services and the processes needed to deliver them

- Understand the philosophies for planning and controlling operations
- Understand the key principles of product and process design
- Understand quality and its definitions
- Critically evaluate the impact of the above on business performance

The chapter is structured as follows. The next section reviews some of the key historical developments in operations management. It then defines operations management by explaining the transformation process and the key associated activities within the context of a supply network. After this the chapter introduces the concept of operations strategy and links it with that of the development of an organization's strategy. The key philosophies of managing operations, focussing on the pull and push systems, are described. It then introduces the processes followed to design products and services and to define quality. In the final section there is a discussion of some of the critical views of operations management, arguing that the above philosophies often advocate a significant element of control. Indeed throughout the chapter several criticisms of the process philosophy of operations management are explained.

The Importance of Managing Operations

The practice of **operations management** has been around for as long as mankind. Humans have always had to develop and manage processes in order to reconcile their resources with environmental requirements or often with threats. This is a key premise of operations management and one that still holds true today. In fact operations management is something that occupies most of our personal and professional lives. For instance, when we travel through an airport we are going along a very carefully designed process that will take us through the carpark to the departure gate. Similarly, organizing a personal event, like a dinner party, will require a careful designing of various processes to ensure that we reconcile our resources – such as the food, the drinks, the cooker, and of course our house – with the needs of the environment i.e. our own and our friends' entertainment. Nevertheless, operations management is not only about *designing* processes, it is also about *ensuring* their efficient, safe (for those involved) and environmentally benign operation. When we run our event we have to plan and control its smooth operation, without delays, encompassing the supply of dinner courses and drinks, ensuring the safety of our guests, and disposing of rubbish appropriately. It is therefore fair to say that at different parts of our lives we become operations managers and thus responsible for reconciling resources with environmental needs. Operations management, and its principles, therefore, are, not limited to an organization's function. Almost all functions will have to organize their processes and resources to meet some environmental or market requirements. A marketing department will have to develop and manage a process to collect and analyze customer data, which will subsequently help inform that organization's marketing strategy. It is therefore important not to dismiss the management of operations as the responsibility of a function but to understand and implement its principles.

What is operations management?

From the above introduction we may conclude that operations management may involve several overlapping notions such as process management, value, and a reconciliation of resources with market requirements. When a product is manufactured, or when a passenger goes through an airport, a process is followed. Put simply, this process is trying to add value by transforming an input into an output. So, in the case of a manufactured product, value is being added when the raw material is transformed into an end product, or in the case of the airport, value is being added when passengers' states are 'transformed' as they move from the carpark to the departure gate.

In any transformation process, there are usually two types of resources as shown in Figure 7.1. The first is referred to as *transformed* and includes those resources that are being changed through the process. In manufacturing this would include raw materials whereas in services this would include customers and information. The second type of resources is referred to as the *transforming* and includes the equipment, staff and technology that make the transformation happen. For instance, in a restaurant, the building, tables, kitchen, and of course the staff are responsible for transforming its customers into fuller and happier individuals. In the rest of this chapter, this terminology will be used several times.

From the above we can conclude that operations management refers to the management of those activities that are responsible for converting inputs into outputs within an organization. The outputs are usually the products or services offered by the organization to the market.

It should also be noted though that these activities rarely operate in isolation. The output of one process may be the input to a different process and so on. In fact these processes could be positioned in different organizational settings with information and materials often changing hands across an operation. This network

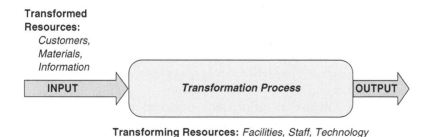

Figure 7.1   Transformation process

of operations is often referred to as a supply chain, and its management as supply chain management.

> **Operations management**: the management of the interconnected activities that convert inputs (raw materials, customers, and information) into outputs (products and services) to reconcile an organization's resources with its market requirements.

A Historical Development of Operations Management

In tandem with the practice of operations management, its scholarship can be traced to before the Middle Ages (Voss, 1995). However, it is since the advent of the steam engine and the concept of standardized parts (attributed to Eli Whitney) that operations (then, production) management started being widely perceived as an independent discipline. Later, Frederick Taylor's principles of scientific management (division of labour, standardized work, managerial hierarchy) and Henry Ford's use of the assembly line gave rise to the mass production paradigm (see Chapter 2 on Organizational Behaviour) while they further encouraged the development of industrial engineering as an academic discipline. During the Second World War, several management science techniques were developed aiming at controlling and allocating the resources needed to fight the war. As a consequence, after hostilities had ceased, the field of operations/production management was heavily influenced by a reductionist philosophy and was centred on a set of mathematical Operations Research techniques. In this paradigm, each aspect of operations management was considered as an independent problem and its solution was sought using numerical optimization techniques. Since the 1970s the mass production paradigm has gradually been replaced with the development of new production paradigms and techniques characterized by holism, such as total quality management (TQM) and just-in-time (JIT), and originating mainly from Japan. Although no single paradigm has yet dominated in the same way that mass production did, several approaches to managing operations have become popular. Such approaches include *lean production* (Womack et al., 1990), *mass customization* (Pine, 1999), and *agile manufacturing* (Kidd, 1994). In addition, as the USA and other advanced economies evolved into service economies, concepts of manufacturing management started to be used in the service sector to standardize work and increase efficiency. As a consequence, from the late 1950s and early 1960s scholars moved from researching industrial engineering and operations research to looking at production and eventually operations management.

Another development that influenced operations management was *process-based management* and the associated notion of Business Process Reengineering (BPR) (Hammer and Champy, 1993) which was very popular in the early 1990s (see Chapter 2 on Organizational Behaviour for further discussions of this idea).

In fact, initially, both lean production and BPR became very popular and 'threatened' to redefine operations management because they were considered as panaceas for reducing costs and increasing efficiency in a period characterized by economic recession and corporate downsizings: the former by intensifying and speeding up work and the latter by using information technology to consolidate work activities. But both required appropriate institutional frameworks of labour flexibility in order to succeed. Lean production demanded job rotation and the precise coordination of collective work (Lazonick, 1991), whereas BPR required legislation that would support cost-free 'hire-and-fire' (Hamel and Prahalad, 1994). Hence, despite initial enthusiasm and reported successes, as the world economy moved out of recession operations-based prescriptions for corporate success were displaced by strategic management techniques promising success in more optimistic times. The historical evidence suggests, quite logically, that operations management is more popular in times of economic recession (how to survive with less in existing markets), whereas strategic management prevails in times of growth (how to create new markets, or take advantage of growing markets).

Several of the techniques developed during the Second World War focussed on the effective distribution of machinery and supplies to troops or, as it is more widely known, 'logistics' (Van Creveld, 2004). Following the end of the war, increased deregulation, globalization, and advances in information technology encouraged firms to outsource their logistical operations to third parties. Outsourcing enabled several firms to reduce costs and focus on their core capabilities. As outsourcing brought increased efficiencies logistics gained more prominence, and consequently logistical operations from each firm were linked to the entire supply chain.

The above brief history of the discipline of operations management shows that much of its early development had its origins in the manufacturing of physical products. Indeed, some of the seminal research and subsequent knowledge that has been created has focussed on the efficiency of operating manufacturing plants. This was partly driven by the perceived importance of the manufacturing sector in economies around the world. The advent of services as an important pillar of the economy has significantly changed this perception. As a result, several of the concepts and principles developed in the early part of the discipline's life have now been adapted to services. As the next section will explain, however, there are some limits to this adaptation. Services include some unique attributes that limit the transfer of knowledge from manufacturing to service operations.

Differences between products and services

As explained in the previous section, early developments in the discipline of operations management have focussed on the manufacturing sector. However, operations also need to be managed across services. For instance, a bank will operate with very few or no physical products. However, most of us who have visited banks will have also experienced a process. We will have joined a queue and then spoken to a bank employee, who in turn will have dealt with our inquiry following a standard procedure (unless of course our inquiry was unique or we were wealthy enough to have the bank manager talking to us). Furthermore when we do visit a bank we expect this process to be efficient and to add some (abstract in this case) value. From the bank's perspective, they would like to utilize their resources efficiently to meet the market requirements. Managing the delivery of services, therefore, includes several of the operations notions discussed in the previous section (process management, value, and the reconciliation of resources with market requirements). There should therefore be some scope for transferring the knowledge and concepts developed for managing manufacturing operations to managing services. To do so, however, it is important to appreciate the differences between products and services and their implications. There are three fundamental differences here; intangibility, customer involvement, and the timing of production. These are discussed in more detail in the sections following.

Intangibility of Services

The most apparent difference between products and services is the intangibility of the latter. When we purchase a bicycle we have a physical product to demonstrate as evidence of our purchase. When we purchase a holiday however there are very few, if any, tangible elements that we are left with. This intangibility of services has several implications for the management of the processes that deliver it. The first is that it is difficult to define and measure quality. When defining and measuring the quality of a physical product, it is also relatively easy to define what quality means and how to measure it. For instance, a bicycle needs to be of a certain weight and height, it should include a certain number of gears, and so on. The same however cannot be said for the quality of a holiday. Although there may be some aspects of the holiday that can be easily defined and measured – such as the time it takes to arrive at our destination, the proximity to any monuments worth visiting and so on – there are several other aspects that may be a lot more difficult to define. These could include the hotel's ambience, the perceived quality of any activities, and of course the friendliness of the serving staff. All of these are difficult to define and even more difficult to measure.

A second implication of the intangibility of services is that it makes it difficult to understand the value added by the organization that is delivering this service. This difference is best illustrated with an example. When purchasing a watch it is relatively easy to understand how value has been added to the transformed resource. The metal was cut and bent by the watchmaker and carefully put together to create the watch we are purchasing from the shop. However, the same cannot be said for an insurance policy. An insurance policy is intangible and unless a claim is made no perceived value is added by the insurance company.

Customer involvement

The active involvement of the customer in the delivery of a service is a second significant difference between products and services. Customers are inevitably part of the service delivery. Several of the services a bank may offer will require an active input from the customer. For instance, withdrawing money from an ATM requires the customer to insert a card, key in a code, make a few selections, and so on. Any failure by the customer to successfully complete these tasks will lead to a service failure.

As with the intangibility of services discussed in the previous paragraph there are some implications to this difference. One is that the customer often needs to be trained to deal with the process where their involvement is required. Withdrawing money from the ATM will require them to know how to use the machine. Similarly, ordering food in a restaurant will require customers to understand and familiarize themselves with the ordering process, as some restaurants demand a greater customer input than others. Therefore, a service cannot be fully automated.

A second implication of customer involvement is the difficulty in managing quality. The perceived quality of the service will be affected by the customer's ability to deal with those parts of the service they are responsible for. Some will be keener to learn how to use new processes and technologies than others. Consequently the perceived quality of the service they receive will also depend on their ability and willingness to learn about the process.

Timing of production and consumption

The third fundamental difference between products and services is that of the timing of production and consumption. Services are produced and consumed instantaneously. A product can be produced, stored and sold at different moments in time. Furthermore, and if the product is of any value to another party, we can resell it. This is not easily done with a service. For example, a theme park experience has to be produced and delivered while the customer is present. After the experience is complete there is nothing left to resell.

These fundamental differences notwithstanding, several of the principles and knowledge developed for the management of manufacturing processes can be transferred to create efficient services. Yet it is important to appreciate that such a transfer of knowledge has limits and often new knowledge and best practice have to be generated for the effective management of services. It is not surprising then that more recently specialist academic journals (such as the *Journal of Service Operations Management*) have been created, aimed at specifically developing knowledge for service operations.

Key operations management components

So far in this chapter we have examined the context of operations management, its historical development, and some fundamental differences between products and

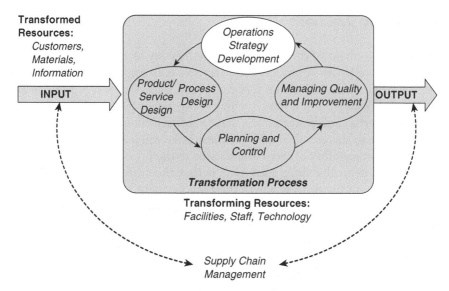

Figure 7.2 Operations management components

services. In this section we will explore the main components of operations management. These are the key activities that an operations manager will have to deal with at different moments in time. As shown in Figure 7.2, these components include the development of *operations strategy* (i.e. how operations and processes are integrated within the entire organization and how they contribute to that organization's strategic objectives); the *design* of the product or service that will be delivered and its production and/or delivery processes; the *planning and control* of the processes' execution so that the required performance in terms of efficiency, safety and environmental concerns is met; the *improvement of the processes* and the management of quality. Finally, any operation does not exist in a vacuum but is part of a larger chain of operations. Therefore the final component of operations is the management of the supply chain.

In the following sections we will discuss these in more detail.

The Development of Operations Strategy

Operations strategy deals with the total transformation of inputs to outputs and links corporate-level strategic management to operations management. It is concerned with how to meet current and future challenges by addressing questions about the development of the operational issues explained above. The key distinction between operations strategy and operations management is the level of analysis. Operations management deals with the daily challenges of meeting demand. Operations strategy deals with the pattern of decisions that determine an operation's long-term ability to meet its market needs. Examples of such decisions include new product development processes, policies on long-term capacity, the level of vertical integration, and the nature of process technology.

Operations strategy: the pattern of decisions that determine an operation's long-term ability to meet its market needs.

Similar to the evolution of thinking in operations management explained in the previous section, historically operations strategy was seen as the development of strategy for the manufacturing department. As a result older texts will refer to operations strategy as 'manufacturing strategy'. Although much of the research and ideas about this type of strategy were developed with the manufacturing function in mind, many concepts have subsequently been transferred to the service sector. This transfer of knowledge has taken into account the differences between products and services discussed in the previous section.

Operations strategy perspectives

Traditionally, operations strategy has been viewed as a reconciliation of the demands imposed by the market with the internal operations resources, developing strategic initiatives from both top-down and bottom-up (Slack and Lewis, 2007). Although there have been alternative views and paradigms as to what operations strategy is and how it is or should be formulated (Voss, 1995), this four-perspective view can be considered as the one that embraces most of the concepts related to operations strategy. The following sections explain these in more detail.

The market requirements perspective

As operations are relevant to businesses that need to meet market demands, operations strategy also needs to identify how it can support the organization in competing in the marketplace. Typically, the identification of market needs lies within the responsibilities of the marketing function. However, the market position that a business, and subsequently its operation, occupies, is a choice that will affect other areas within the firm. For instance, a computer provider would not be able to re-position itself as a provider of, say, camping equipment, simply because the marketing department identified a need. The marketing department would have to identify the needs within the context of operations' capabilities and relevant market needs. This gradual and iterative identification process should ensure that the marketing and operations functions are aligned and that these can support an organization's corporate strategy.

Identifying how a firm will compete in the marketplace requires a process exploring the market needs to take place. Often marketing departments will divide the market into smaller segments (Kotler et al., 2009). This market segmentation helps focus operations on delivering the right product or process to the right person at the right quantity, and of course at the right time (see Chapter 4 on Marketing). Although this sounds like a simple statement and one that most of us as consumers will understand, several operations strategies lack focus and attempt to be all things to all people.

A good example of the need for operational activity to be in alignment with the market segment in which the business is trying to function, is a restaurant that sits in the middle of a big tourist city. Being in such a location visitors to the city would typically expect a relatively basic restaurant with quick service and which offered some traditional dishes. The operations strategy of such a restaurant would therefore need to focus on speed and quality. Although diners may appreciate a very long menu with several mouth-watering choices, they could become suspicious of the freshness and authenticity of the food. Although this is a relatively easy concept to perceive, most of us will have had experience of restaurants in such locations where the operations fail to implement this simple formula. Often this is because they lose sight of the market segment they are trying to satisfy and try to please everyone.

The operations resource perspective

The second perspective starts from the premise that most of an organization's resources will lie with the operations function. An organization is there to sell something to the market. As discussed earlier, this something may be a physical product or service. As the operations function is ultimately responsible for delivering this product or service, its resources are critical for the perceived performance of the organization in the market.

In contrast to the previous perspective, the starting point for the operations resource perspective is understanding what the resources of the operations function are and what they are good at. Then the relevant decisions that will be taken will try to strengthen this aspect of the operation and exploit it in the market. The development of the operations strategy would then aim to identify the operation's capabilities.

An important distinction needs to be made between a capability and a process. A process usually relates to the steps taken to complete an operation. These are relatively easily codified and mapped so that most can follow what has to be done once they have received some training. Capabilities on the other hand will usually relate to the intangible resources that help differentiate one operation from another. Therefore according to this perspective operations strategy starts from the identification of these intangible resources, which may include supplier relationships, technology and process knowledge and experience, and new product and service development skills (Slack and Lewis, 2007). Chapter 9 on Strategy also discusses capabilities in terms of their contribution to competitive advantage.

The intangible resources need codified processes to be delivered. For instance, the development of new products requires formalized procedures and sign-off stages which will ensure that a new product or service is aligned with the organizational strategy and that it will meet the relevant criteria before it is introduced to the market. However, being creative and being able to read and understand the market to develop new products takes more than following a series of predetermined steps as is discussed later in the chapter.

The top-down perspective

The more traditional view of operations, or until recently *manufacturing*, strategy is that it is one of the functional strategies of an organization. In this context operations strategy is hierarchical and is seen as responsible for delivering the decisions taken at an organization's corporate level. This is a very familiar approach for organizations that are large and centralized.

For example, a university will often take decisions centrally about the nature of the student population, its research status, and the links with industry. It will then set and agree targets and the overall mission for individual departments. Finally, individual functions within each department will agree the priorities and organize their processes to meet the individual functional strategies, and consequently the business strategies, and ultimately the corporate strategy.

The bottom-up perspective

Although the top-down perspective is in principle one that many people working for businesses would associate with (i.e. 'we always do what the boss wants us to do'), in reality strategy is not formulated and implemented so linearly. Often senior management will ask for the views of individual functions before they develop a strategy. When this is the case, strategy also reflects the collective experience of the people working within the individual functions of an organization.

So, taking the previous university example further, the bottom-up perspective would argue that strategy is developed from the daily activities and collective experience of individual departments. This gradually builds consensus between the departments and the central university administration which in the long run will lead to the development of a high-level strategy, either tacitly or explicitly.

Performance Objectives

As discussed earlier an operation should focus on the needs of the market. Regardless of the perspective adopted, an operation is likely to try to focus its efforts to ensure it excels in at least one area. The key areas that an operation can focus on are often referred to as 'performance objectives', as follows.

Quality

This refers to an operation's ability to meet or exceed customer expectations. This of course is a general statement which technically could capture all of the objectives for an operation or indeed for an organization. At the same time, defining quality is a complex issue. This is because different people will have different views on quality.

The issue becomes even more complex when considering services. As was explained earlier, a key component of the service delivery is the customer – that is, the customer is part of the service. When this is the case the level of quality will also depend on their ability to follow the rules of the service that he or she is part of. So the resulting perceived quality will depend on the customer and it will also be assessed by them. Some of the key views and definitions of quality are discussed later in the chapter.

Flexibility

This second performance objective refers to an operation's ability to change according to different customer requirements. These changing requirements may be identified across several dimensions. The most important are volume and product. Volume flexibility refers to the ability of an operation to change the number of products it creates or the customer it serves. For instance, an operation may provide an organization with a competitive advantage when it can provide varying levels of volume for products and services. This is an easy concept to describe when thinking about volume flexibility in a manufacturing operation which usually translates into a higher inventory. That is, a manufacturing organization can provide different levels of volume when it has excess inventory. Although this goes against several 'lean' principles (Womack et al., 1990), if the market segment appreciates the increased flexibility, and subsequently is prepared to pay a premium for it, then excess inventory may provide a competitive advantage. The concept is less clear when dealing with services. In this case the inventory is perishable. For instance, a call centre that does not have enough operators on standby when there are high call volumes will not be able to recover any loss of business.

Product flexibility, on the other hand, refers to an operation's ability to change its products and services depending on customer needs and offer a wide variety of products. In a market where customers have more fine-grained requirements, providing higher variety products increases the possibility of satisfying market needs (Dowell, 2006). Product variety has traditionally been defined across two dimensions: fundamental and peripheral (MacDuffie and Sethuraman, 1996). Fundamental variety refers to inherently different models (e.g. a Honda Accord versus a Honda Civic). Peripheral variety refers to the options offered for the same core design (e.g. satellite navigation and electronic stability control on a Ford Focus). Being able to offer both at relatively short notice can provide an organization with a competitive advantage.

Speed

This performance objective refers to an operation's ability to do things quickly. This is usually measured as the sum of the time it takes to complete a process and the length of time it takes to deliver the output of that process. In the production of physical products this is relatively straightforward to measure and visualize as the two different times are usually distinct. However, this may not be the case in services.

Often the service is being 'produced' while it is being 'delivered' and 'consumed'. For instance, when calling a call centre the operation has to deal with the customer's enquiry and hopefully keep them happy. In terms of time the operation may be broken into some distinct stages, but from the point of view of the customer the time it takes from dialling the call centre until the problem is solved is the critical part.

Cost

The final objective is that of cost. Needless to say, this is the most important. A penny saved in any operation is a penny in profits. Even if the operation belongs to a non-profit organization a penny saved may be put towards a future project or service. As a result cost is often traded off against the other four perspectives. An operations strategy often focusses on reducing cost. However, the extent of the eventual trade-off depends on the focus of the operation. For instance, a company that focusses on the delivery of high quality service may increase its operating cost. As common sense would suggest, if such a situation is not valued by the customer then this additional cost should be treated with caution.

Product and Service Development

So far the chapter has explained two key components of operations management: operations strategy and planning and control. The third area the chapter will discuss is that of **product and service development**. As was depicted in Figure 7.2, product and process development (or *design* as it is often referred to) is one of the key components or tasks that an operations manager will have to deal with. Any organization will have to create something that a customer will want to buy. Private organizations will need to develop products and/or services that will sustain or improve their market positions, whereas public organizations have to create a service that the public will need and be prepared (or more often obliged through taxes) to pay for. For instance, schools offer education through a process that needs to be carefully designed to ensure that the chosen curriculum is delivered to pupils. In this section we explain some of the key processes involved in the development of new products and services.

Product and service development: the series of steps followed to develop new products and services, starting with the generation of ideas and ending with the product launch.

An important distinction that is often made is between the development of a product and the development of the process that will deliver the product or service. Although it is often considered a bad practice, product and processes can be designed independently. For instance, the designers at a car manufacturer can design a concept

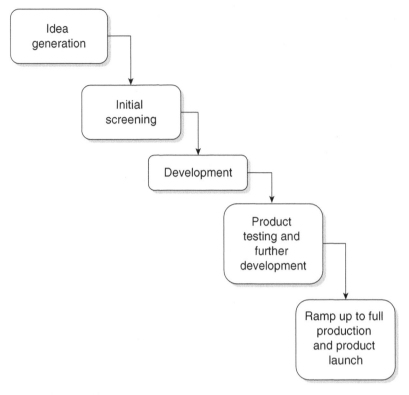

Figure 7.3   Product development stages

car following approval by marketing and other company divisions. This design can then be passed on to the process engineers who will develop the processes and procedures necessary to produce the car in the desired numbers. This distinction is more blurred in the development of new services. As was explained earlier in the chapter, the customer constitutes a key part of the service delivery while a service is produced and consumed simultaneously. It is therefore difficult to disengage the development of the service and the process that delivers it. For instance, the customer experience in a restaurant depends on the successful completion of several processes, e.g. waiting, being taken to the table, billing, and of course being served with food. Therefore, the development of the process is integrated with the development of the service.

The activities that are involved in the development of a product are linked closer in service development than they are in the development of physical products. The general sequence of activities that is usually followed to develop a product or a service is the one shown in Figure 7.3. While contextual factors – such as the type of industry, the size of an organization, and the type of the product developed – will affect the nature and labelling of these activities, the development process is likely to follow this sequence.

The following sections explain in more detail each of these stages.

Idea generation

The first stage is that of generating new ideas for the product or service to be developed. To do this organizations will look at both external and internal sources. External sources will include customers, suppliers, competitors, marketing companies, and government legislation. Internal sources will include the research and development department, the general staff, and often quality problems associated with existing products. Although these idea sources may be abundant, identifying those that are specific to an organization's context and extracting the ideas is a significant challenge. The nature of the challenge will vary across several dimensions such as the newness of the product and its familiarity with the existing processes (Danneels and Kleinschmidtb, 2001). Namely, it is relatively more difficult to conceive ideas for products and services which are entirely new to both the organization and the industry. However, it is products like these that often prove to be a significant success. A good example of this is Apple's iPod, which despite being new both to the firm and the market has proved a significant success and a market changer. There is therefore a need for the systematic collection of ideas.

Initial screening

If the previous process has been completed successfully several new ideas will have been collected. In this stage these ideas are evaluated to select the ones that are more likely to be successful. There are several structured models that exist in the literature and are often employed by organizations to evaluate and select the best ideas methodically. Such models are evaluating new product ideas against the criteria set by organizations. These may include, but are not limited to, the return on investment, the alignment with the organization's capabilities and strategy, feasibility, and risks.

Models to assist in the assessment of ideas vary from basic checklists to complicated mathematical models which can assess ideas against various complex criteria including the probability of success. Although these models may create an illusion of certainty (i.e. the selected ideas *will be successful*) they should be treated with some caution. This is because these are often based on assumptions which, if they do not materialize, may undermine the outcome of the process. In fact one of the key benefits of using such a structured approach in the assessment of ideas is to make these assumptions explicit.

The successful completion of this process will lead to the elimination of some of the ideas created during the idea generation stage. The ones that will remain will be fed into the next stage – development.

Development

At the start of this stage some ideas will have been eliminated whereas those that remain are likely to have been carefully evaluated. During this stage the ideas are developed further. The nature of this development is likely to depend on the nature of the product and industrial sector. For instance, in the pharmaceutical sector the development stage may take several years to complete (Tsinopoulos, 2007) as it could involve several disciplines across various sectors and adherence to detailed processes to comply with legislation imposed on the development process by various countries' governments. On the other hand, the development stage for mortgages will require relatively less time, although they too may have to adhere to strict legislation.

The output from this process will again depend on some contextual factors such as the industrial sector and the nature of the product. Nevertheless a concept or a prototype is usually expected. In the automotive industry, this stage will usually conclude with a prototype which can then be tested in the next section. In services, this prototype may be a focus group or a simulation of the service that will be delivered. Theme parks will often create detailed simulations of new rides before they progress to a full commissioning.

Product testing and further development

At the start of this stage the ideas put forward earlier will have been developed and depending on the nature of the product a prototype will have been created. During this stage the prototype will be tested to ensure the product's or service's adherence to the criteria created earlier. This stage is also likely to include the customer to ensure that the new product or service operates as has been expected by the (usually untrained) customer. At the end of this process further refinements may need to be made to 'iron out' any problems identified during the testing process and before full production is initiated.

Ramp up to full production and product launch

This is usually the final stage of the formal new product development process and involves the handing over of the product to production. In a service context this final stage relates to the delivery of the product to the final consumer. Often this stage is linked with the development of a marketing strategy and will trigger the initiation of various activities aimed at bringing the tested product or service to the final customer (Kotler et al., 2009).

New product development process criticisms

The presentation and discussion of the new product and service development stages discussed above are linear. That is, each process has to be completed before another one begins. This process has often been criticized, as it may lead to more time being spent and possibly reduced creativity. The aim of implementing such a systematic process is largely to eliminate uncertainty. Following a rigorous process of evaluation, development and the testing of ideas reduces the risk of undesired consequences and, hypothetically, increases the chances of market success. However, it is these uncertain attributes that are often associated with creative behaviour (Bonner et al., 2002; McCarthy et al., 2006). More specifically, it is often argued by innovation researchers that when we find ourselves in messier, less structured situations we are more likely to demonstrate creative behaviour. Therefore, when creating new product development processes it is important to ensure that enough flexibility is allowed in order to ensure that creativity is not compromised.

Process design

Often process design will follow the product or service design. Process design determines how a product will be produced or how a service will be delivered. In some cases the product and process design will take place concurrently. **Concurrent engineering**, or simultaneous product and process design, is a sought-after practice because it reduces the time to market as well as development costs (Pisano, 1997). It does so, first, by considering all the stages described above early on in the new product development process, and second, by concurrently conducting the design activities. Namely, what the stages described previously as distinct processes will now occur in parallel. The main benefit of this approach is that the development process is accelerated whilst considerations surrounding quality are dealt with early on.

Concurrent Engineering: a systematic approach to product development that considers all the development stages in parallel from the outset.

Types of processes

Processes can be categorized into different types according to the products and services that are produced or delivered by them. Manufacturing processes are distinguished into: *project* processes, that are suitable for the production or construction of one-of-a-kind products (ships, buildings, motorways, etc.); *jobbing* processes, that are very flexible processes for the production of low-volume customized products, such as those produced in machine shops and printing shops; *batch* processes, that have a medium-level flexibility for the production of items in batches, such as mechanical and electrical equipment; *line or mass* processes, that have low flexibility for the production of high volume products, such as cars; and *continuous* processes, that are for the production of products in fluid forms as in the chemical, pharmaceutical and food industries.

As for services, there are *professional services* processes, which are knowledge-based or advice-based services involving high customer contact and high customizations, met through consultants and lawyers; *service shops*, which are service processes of medium customization, met through banks and retail shops; and *mass services*, which involve limited customization and high volume of transactions, such as in call centres.

Process layout and flow

This concerns the ways in which workstations, or resources, are organized spatially. The objective is to achieve a smooth flow to the production of goods or the delivery of services without bottlenecks and delays while making efficient and balanced use of resources. Typically, there are four types of process layout:

- *Fixed-position* layout, where the good or service to be produced does not move, is suitable for project and professional services processes (e.g. ship construction, management consultancy)
- *Process or functional* layout, where similar resources are grouped, is more suitable for jobbing, batch and service shops processes (e.g. hospitals)
- *Cell* layout (the resources to meet all immediate processing needs are co-located – something between functional and product layout) is appropriate for batch processes and some service shop processes, as well as for some mass processes (e.g. computer components manufacturing, a sleep-study unit in a hospital)
- *Product* layout, where all the resources for the production of a particular product or the delivery of a specific service are put together (dedicated resources), is more suitable for line and continuous processes, as well as for mass services (e.g. vehicle assembly, a self-service restaurant)

Planning and Control

The third component of operations management is that of planning and control. This refers to the activities responsible for delivering the products and services to the customer. As was explained earlier, operations management aims to meet market need. This component is responsible for planning and controlling those tasks that produce the product or the service that the customer purchases. It includes the methods followed to organize the various activities and the systems that can help provide the relevant information. As explained in this section there are some differences in the philosophies used to manage these systems.

The main distinction – and the one this section will focus on – is that of push and pull systems. While there are some additional systems that are often advocated, these two have taken up a lot of operations managers' time in recent years and offer the foundation on which several control systems have been built.

Before presenting these two systems, the section briefly reviews two important components of planning and control: *capacity management* and *inventory management*.

Capacity management

Capacity is defined as the maximum level of value-added activity that an operation can undertake over a period of time. It is measured in different ways and over different levels. For example, it can be measured as the number of all types of vehicles a factory can produce in a year, or as the number of guests that a hotel can accommodate in a night, or the number of workers a production line needs in a shift, etc.

Capacity: the maximum level of value-added activity that an operation can undertake over a period of time.

Capacity planning and control is an important operations management activity because it affects costs, revenues, working capital, quality, speed of response, and the flexibility of the operation and the entire firm. There are three capacity management strategies used in operations:

- *Level capacity*, that attempts to keep output from an operation, or its capacity, constant, irrespective of demand
- *Chase capacity*, that attempts to adjust output and/or capacity to demand fluctuations by techniques such as overtime and idle time, varying the size of workforce, using part-time staff, and subcontracting
- *Influence demand*, that tries to match demand to the available capacity by appropriate pricing and other promotional techniques

Frequently, inside operations, capacity management is considered as a *queuing* problem and mathematical models have been devised to facilitate analysis and optimization. An example of such a model is illustrated in the next section.

Example of queuing models

There are a number of queuing models formulated to calculate performance metrics – such as waiting time and work-in-process – of an operation for different capacities, expressed in terms of the number of service stations. In general, queuing systems are characterized by four parameters and described in the form $A/B/m/b$:

- A: the statistical distribution of arrival times
- B: the statistical distribution of processing/service times
- m: the number of parallel servers
- b: the maximum number of items allowed in the system

The most frequent distributions used for A and B are the exponential distribution (M) and the general distribution (G). Then, $M/G/3/10$ denotes a queuing system in which items arrive exponentially; processing times are distributed according to the general distribution; there are three servers in the system; and the maximum number of items allowed in the system (in queues and in the servers) is 10 (usually the last parameter is omitted as it is assumed to be an open system).

For $M/M/m$ systems, the waiting time in the queue is given by

$$W_q = \frac{u^{\sqrt{2(m+1)-1}}}{m(1-u)} t_e$$

where:

- u is the utilization of the servers (processing rate/arrival rate multiplied by m), and
- t_e is the mean processing time

For $G/G/m$ systems, the same metric is given by

$$W_q = (\frac{c_a^2 + c_e^2}{2})(\frac{u^{\sqrt{2(m+1)-1}}}{m(1-u)})t_e$$

where,

- c_a is the coefficient of variation of arrival times (parameter of A), and
- c_e the coefficient of variation of processing times (parameter of B)

Using the above expressions we can calculate m, the number of servers (e.g. bank personnel) that are required to serve a particular customer arrival rate, with a customer waiting time not exceeding a specific value W_q, assuming that we know the statistics (mean and variation) for processing times.

Inventory management

Although, as we will see in the following sections, MRP systems (see below) have replaced the issue of inventory management with that of the smooth movement of materials, information, or customers through the operation, and pull systems claim to be inventory-free, in reality inventories do still exist and must be managed.

In fact, inventory management has been traditionally considered as the principal issue of concern for production management because it is the only way to balance production and demand. Its core activity has been the determination of order (to supplier) quantity and/or the production batch size so that neither excess inventory is produced nor shortages occur. Besides this, inventory management has to do with how stock is replaced. Two main review and re-order policies are common: *continuous review*, where inventory-related decisions are made when the inventory reaches a particular level, and *periodic review*, where the same decisions are made at particular time instances. These policies are often aligned with the planning philosophies as explained in the following two sections.

Determination of order quantity

One common approach for deciding how much to order when stock requires replenishment is by using the model of *Economic Order Quantity* (EOQ). EOQ is given by the formula

$$Q_o = EOQ = \sqrt{\frac{2C_oD}{C_h}}$$

where

- Q_o is the quantity to order
- C_o is the total cost of placing an order
- C_h is the cost of holding one unit of product for a period of time, and
- D is the assumed steady and perfectly predictable rate of demand per time period.

The EOQ model assumes instantaneous replenishment. If we assume that P is the rate of replenishment we have a value of Q_o (*Economic Batch Quantity* or EBQ), given by:

$$Q_o = EOQ = \sqrt{\frac{2C_oD}{C_h(1-\frac{D}{P})}}$$

Suppose that we have a demand of 80,000 product units per year; placing an order costs £50; and holding one unit of product in stock costs £1.5, then

$$Q_o = EOQ = \sqrt{\frac{2\times50\times80,000}{1.5}} = 2309 \text{ units}$$

If we assume that stock can be replenished at a rate of 10,000 units per month, then demand becomes 80,000/12 = 6,666.7 per month, and

$$Q_o = EOQ = \sqrt{\frac{2\times50\times6,666.7}{1.5\times(1-\frac{6,666.7}{10,000})}} = 1154.7 \text{ units}$$

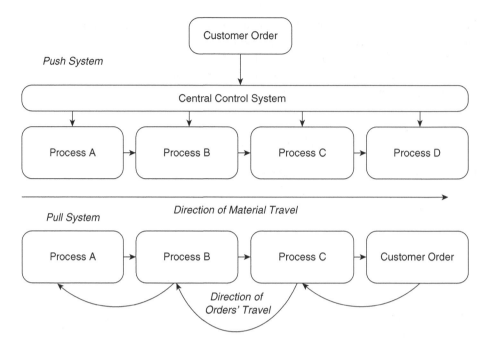

Figure 7.4 Push and pull systems

Inventory models, however, have been criticized as being oversimplifying and based on unrealistic assumptions. For instance, in the example above the demand is known and smooth. This is not always a realistic expectation as the demand for products may depend on several unpredictable and unknown factors. For this reason, in operations practice, stochastic or simulation models are often employed when more reliable estimates are required.

Push systems

This type of system is the more traditional one and also relatively easier to visualize. In push systems the trigger to start an operation lies with the preceding process. As shown in Figure 7.4 material is moved from left to right. Each process adds value to the material it receives from the preceding process and then delivers its outcome to the following process. Each process also starts as soon as it receives material from the preceding operation. Therefore material is being *pushed* from left to right. Often such systems are managed centrally by using electronic control systems that include information on each operation's needs. For instance, they may include information about the components that need to be manufactured, about how they will be assembled, about lead times, and about customer orders and forecasts.

One of the important benefits of these systems is the sense of control that they create. Hypothetically, the central control system is able to monitor the processes, respond quickly to changing needs, and quickly identify and address any problems. As a consequence of this several such systems have been developed, often referred to as MRP (**Materials Requirements Planning**) and ERP (**Enterprise Resource Planning**).

Materials Requirement Planning (MRP): a software-based planning and control system used to manage mainly manufacturing processes.

Enterprise Resource Planning (ERP): an extension of MRP to cover many aspects of the organization, including materials, assets, financial and human resources.

On the other hand, push systems have been accused of leading to increased inventories. As material is pushed through the system this often leads to the creation of stock which is not necessarily needed by the following process or indeed by the customer. Push systems are therefore appropriate for those situations where there is a variation in demand which can be relatively accurately forecasted.

An additional disadvantage of the push system is loss of control by the operator. As indicated earlier, the decision of when to start an operation lies with the central control system. This approach is (in general) trying to eliminate the uncertainty which is often associated with processes that are repeatedly conducted by humans. As a result its implementation may lead to a loss of morale.

Finally, push planning and control systems – such as ERP systems – have been heavily criticized for overstandardizing operational processes and taking control of the business, thereby reducing its strategic differentiation options (Davenport, 1998).

Pull systems

At the other end of the spectrum in pull systems the trigger to start the operation lies with the following operation. Referring back to Figure 7.4. Process A will not start unless Process B has requested an output of its process. Similarly B will not start unless C has made a request, and D will not start unless the customer has requested something. The main advantage of this pull or *Just in Time* system lies in the low use of inventories. As processes only produce what is needed when it is needed there is no (or very little) generation of additional unnecessary stock. This is one of the big advantages of this system and one that has convinced several manufacturing organizations to attempt the switch from push to pull systems.

Just in Time: a management philosophy that focusses on the reduction of waste through the effective implementation of a pull management system.

A second advantage of this type of system is the claim that it can lead to better quality. Operators of a process who know that the outcome of their work is going to be used in the next process immediately become more accountable. Consequently, the quality of their work increases and they make sure that their equipment is well maintained as any stoppage will have a direct impact on the remaining processes.

A third advantage of the pull system is the potential improvement in supplier relationships. The quick turnaround time needed to make these processes work requires careful and detailed coordination with the suppliers' processes. Often suppliers' systems have to be developed to ensure they can operate under the quick turnaround times required by pull systems. As a result of this requirement the implementation of pull systems encourages several organizations to work more closely with their suppliers than they would otherwise do. Lower inventories and quicker turnaround times also make processes more dependent on the suppliers' processes. Toyota – one of the pioneers of this system – has spent much of its energies in developing their suppliers over several years to ensure that they can respond to the demands of a pull system. As a result of this process Toyota has grown and is now one of the biggest automotive manufacturers in the world. The Toyota production system has also served as a benchmark for several organizations beyond the automotive industry.

As with push systems, pull systems have some disadvantages. The first relates to situations where long lead times are unavoidable. Processes that operate in just in time mode need to be quick to respond. Naturally, there are some processes that are both unavoidable and slow. For instance, heat treatment processes require a long time to complete (often days). Similarly, if some materials or subassemblies are sourced from a remote location, as is increasingly the trend, operating a pull system becomes more difficult. This is because some processes will take too long to complete and as a result there will be a need to retain some safety stock.

An additional disadvantage of using pull systems is that of rushed working. As a process only starts when its output is needed, every job will have to be completed as quickly as possible. Any problem will lead to delays and potentially customer dissatisfaction. Proponents of this approach, however, argue that such processes can be clearly identified and decoupling points can be built in aiming at linking such long processes with pull systems (Christopher and Towill, 2000).

Critical perspectives on pull systems, and more generally on the Toyota production system and lean production, argue that their apparent success is not the result of their internal mechanisms but it is rather the outcome of the institutional arrangements of collective capitalism in Japan where the core element is planned coordination at different levels (firms, departments, work teams) (Lazonick, 1991). In addition, there is evidence that the practice of pull systems in Toyota is characterized by a limited potential for creativity and innovation; narrow professional skills; worker isolation and harassment; dangerous conditions on the production line; accident cover-ups; excessive overtime; and a poor quality of life for workers (Mehri, 2006).

Choosing between the two systems

As can be seen from the brief introduction above to the pull and push systems, they both come with advantages and disadvantages. Furthermore, the two systems are likely to meet different customer needs as their response times are also likely to be different. Selecting between these is thus a decision that depends on the nature of the operation, and the type of market where it exists. Recently there has been an increasing trend for more operations to switch to pull systems. The promise of reduced costs through reduced inventories and improved quality has convinced several operations managers to make the necessary investment for the adoption of these systems.

Push and pull systems in services

Thus far the discussion of push and pull systems has focussed on the manufacturing sector where many of these techniques originated. Pull and push systems, however, also exist in services. For instance, consider some airlines' processes. Passengers are being pushed through the system. The check-in process starts as soon as the passenger arrives at the check-in desk. After this process is complete, the passenger moves on to passport control which will start processing as soon as that customer arrives. After this, the passenger will move on to the waiting area where they will join other passengers (stock) before they board the plane. As soon as there are enough passengers the gate will open and let everyone on the plane. All of this is controlled by a central system managed by the airport. This also controls other aspects of the airport including airport fees, shop transactions, luggage handling, and so on.

On the other hand, consider a fast food restaurant. Processes remain idle until a customer walks in. Only after the customer places an order does the food start being assembled. The food itself is being pulled through the operation. Every subsequent operation starts only after the operation that follows it has requested its output. In fact, fast food restaurants constitute some of the most visible pull systems.

As in manufacturing, the choice between pull and push systems in service operations depends on the nature of the service and the type of market where it exists. As shown in the previous examples, the traditional airline model is better suited for a centrally controlled push system whereas pull systems have effectively created an entirely new restaurant segment.

Quality Management and Improvement

The third key component of operations management is that of quality. This ensures that the products, processes, and planning mechanisms explained in the previous sections are adhered to. Quality management is an area that has drawn a lot of attention over the last few decades both on the practitioner and academic sides. The main reason for this is that quality is perceived as an important outcome of the operation and one that the whole organization is often judged on.

Over these decades several views on quality have been developed. These have led to different definitions of the term and in turn to different methodologies for its management. The following sections review some of the key ones and conclude with an introduction and discussion of quality management systems.

Quality as excellence

One of the popular meanings of quality is that of excellence. A quality service is an excellent service. For instance, flying business class or staying in a five-star hotel is associated with excellence. This is largely a customer-driven view of quality and one that is often implied by the marketing strategies of those organizations who want to convince their customers of the uniqueness of their organization's products. Despite this popular view of quality it is difficult to measure this and thus difficult to control.

Quality as fit for purpose

A second view of quality is that of fit for purpose. Each product or service is designed to fulfil a need and/or desire. A quality offering is thus what best fulfils this need or desire. This view of quality is more tangible and can be measured. More importantly, it can enable product and service designers to develop systems that can identify customers' needs and take steps to fulfil them. As a consequence of this several methods have been developed that aim to systematically translate customer requirements to design specifications. These include Quality Function Deployment, Taguchi methods, and Six Sigma. The first two were developed by Japanese automotive manufacturers aiming at *translating* customer need into design specifications (Slack et al., 2005). The third, Six Sigma, was developed by Motorola in the 1980s and has since become very popular. It is based on an infrastructure of people who are often referred to as 'Black Belt', 'Green Belt', etc., who use quality management and statistical methods to address minimizing process variability.

Quality as an error free process

A third view of quality is the one that stems from the premise that processes can be *right first time* and thus actions can be taken to ensure that they are error free. A quality offering is therefore one that is created with no errors. If it is a physical product this implies there are no faults in its components. If it is a service, error free implies that all the individual components making up the service will be delivered as expected by the customer. Several quality management techniques have originated from this premise. Most are based on a statistical analysis of data produced by the processes and aim at controlling the processes, i.e. identifying early on when a process is operating outside its pre-defined parameters and taking appropriate action to correct it.

Quality determined by perceptions and expectations

The final view of quality discussed in this chapter is one that encompasses those discussed above. According to this view, a quality offering is one that meets or exceeds a customer's expectations. This involves trying to identify the value a customer extracts from an offering and then assessing its quality according to the level of perceived value. A cheap flight, for instance, may be perceived as being excellent quality if it meets or exceeds a customer's expectations, which may consist of a complex combination of price, punctuality, safety, and cleanliness. Evaluating the quality of a flight may require a careful examination of the combination of these parameters.

Quality management systems

The above discussion indicates that there are several views and definitions of quality. These create a significant challenge for a manager who is responsible for managing the quality of an organization's products and services. This challenge becomes even more important when considering the supply chain. Namely, buyer companies will often have to select between various suppliers depending on the quality of their product and services. For complex operations the number of suppliers may be high which then makes the process even more complex. In response to this increasing complexity, during the 1970s several large (mainly automotive) manufacturers in the USA created individual quality standards that potential suppliers needed to adhere to if they wanted to supply them. These standards were evaluated regularly and included an examination of the processes in place to monitor and control quality.

These quality standards represented a big step towards the development of today's quality management systems, such as those offered by the international standards organization ISO. ISO realized early on that there was a significant similarity between various manufacturers' approaches and embarked on a mission to standardize the processes for managing quality. This then simplified the processes that individual suppliers had to go through in order to have their processes accredited or audited before they could supply certain consumers. Instead of having to adhere to quality standards set by individual customers they would have to meet the standards set by an internationally recognized organization.

Several quality management standards were created following the establishment of the organization. The ISO, a Swiss-based organization, now has over 610,000 members. Although this approach has its criticisms, with bureaucracy and a lack of personal freedom being the key ones (Martínez-Costa and Martínez-Lorente, 2003; Martínez-Costa et al., 2009), it has simplified the accreditation processes.

Supply chain management

Over the last two decades, globalization and free trade worldwide have augmented the importance of supply chain management. There is a plethora of definitions and approaches on what constitutes a **supply chain**, and what supply chain management is. However, we can still embrace the basic meaning of a supply chain by simply stating that this consists of all the stages involved, directly or indirectly, in fulfilling a customer request. In other words, a supply chain is made up of linked activities of production, transportation, warehousing, ordering, stocking in retailer outlets, purchasing, etc.

> **Supply chain**: a network or chain of all the activities involved in delivering a finished product to the end customer.

The management of a supply chain entails decisions at three categories or phases (Chopra and Meindl, 2001):

- *supply chain strategy or design*, where a company decides on how to structure the supply chain, i.e. how to interconnect activities, the location, and the capacities for production and warehousing facilities, the products to be manufactured and/ or stored at various locations, the modes of their transportation, information systems to be used, etc. Supply chains are designed according to strategic objectives which may be either *efficiency*, i.e. low cost, or *response/flexibility*, i.e. high level dependable service for the end customer.

The alignment of product and supply chain characteristics drives the strategy process.

> **Supply chain velocity**: the speed at which products move through the supply chain from the manufacturer to customer.

- *Supply chain planning*, where a company decides which markets to serve from which location; which activities will be subcontracted, when and where back-up stock will be held; the timing and size of marketing promotions, etc. Planning establishes the parameters for how a supply chain will function over a specified period.

- *Supply chain operation*, where a company allocates individual orders to inventory and production; decides which orders will be batched to a specific transportation mode; sets delivery schedules; places replenishment orders; etc. The notion of **logistics** that concerns the physical distribution of goods belongs to this category of decisions.

Logistics: a term in supply chain management that is broadly analogous to physical distribution management.

Both materials and information will flow in a supply chain. Goods will move from the suppliers of raw materials to the end customers. Information will flow in the opposite direction. Consequently, supply chain management as a business function will concern the coordination of the movement of goods through the supply chain from suppliers to manufacturers to distributors to retailers and end customers, and the transmission and sharing of information such as sales forecasts, sales data, promotion data, etc., among members of the chain.

The dynamics of a supply chain

Frequently, inaccurate or distorted information will travel through the chain like a bullwhip uncoiling. The **bullwhip effect** causes wrong quantities to be ordered throughout the chain. The causes of this phenomenon are: *individual members' demand forecasting* based on inventory levels and not on actual demand; *order batching*, i.e. order placement at specific time intervals as sums of units sold and not after each unit sold; *price fluctuations* that will cause companies and consumers to buy products before they need them; and *rationing and shortage gaming*, where the demand will exceed supply and producers will ration members of the supply chain.

Bullwhip effect: inaccurate or distorted information created in the supply chain moves from end customer to raw materials' producers.

The bullwhip effect can be counteracted by making end seller information available throughout the entire supply chain, by eliminating order batching (or batching in smaller quantities), by stabilizing prices, and by eliminating gaming in the supply chain.

Sourcing

Sourcing concerns the determination of the right number of suppliers, the type of relationship with them (short term or long term), and the number of suppliers for each part or product, so that the spread of risk in having a diverse supply base is balanced with the normally higher cost of buying smaller quantities from more than one supplier. However, the most important sourcing decision for a company is whether or not to buy a component or service, or to provide it by itself – in other words, which activities to *insource* and which to *outsource*? In this context, *vertical integration* is a measure of how much of the supply chain is owned or operated by the manufacturer. Independent of the degree of vertical integration, the role of information systems in the coordination of the supply chain is crucial. Technologies such as e-purchasing, e-distribution and RFID (Radio Frequency Identification Technology) have made possible the coordination of supply chains that can extend across different countries and different continents.

Supply chain management criticisms

Supply chain management is not free of criticisms. One point of such criticisms is that the field of supply chain and logistics management has been dominated by the idea that their constituting activities are designable; namely, supply chains can be constructed according to desired performances and operated by managers who will not question designs and not be influenced by the context within which they live and work (Aastrup and Halldórsson, 2008). In addition, the designability assumption may lead to a strong positivism in supply chain management (that is, considering the supply chain as a machine) that completely ignores, or is not interested in, what happens inside the 'black boxes' that constitute the nodes of the chain. Desired performances may be achieved by extreme and unethical work practices such as the exploitation of child labour, or severely damaging the environment (Klassen and Johnson, 2004; New, 2004a).

At the opposite end of the spectrum we can find approaches associated with a social construction perspective of supply chain and logistics management. These maintain that the notion of supply chain is actually a social construction with interpretation flexibility, with each interpretation serving specific interests and supporting specific power structures, usually those of large multinational corporations (New, 2004b). As New argues, there is a danger that specific social constructions may be legitimized on the basis of the acceptability of academic abstractions made to facilitate the study of specific issues. These abstractions are then adopted by specific parties with related interests and promoted as reality. Then, as frequently happens, they are used by academics and researchers to obtain new results, and so on.

A Critical Perspective on Operations

As discussed in the historical account given earlier, the departing points for modern operations management are the system of 'scientific management' put forward by

Taylor and the assembly line of Ford. Their principal ideology, which argues for the division of tasks and standardization, offered a logical and intuitive way to impose centralized control economically by removing the uncertainty that was inherent in human operations. Taylor's insistence in presenting his method as 'scientific' and independent of, and immune to, the interests of individuals and groups brought *technocracy* to the field. Although pure Taylorism no longer dominates the scholarship and practice of operations management, its underlying principles are still present. The mathematics-based approaches deducted from this ideology were sufficient for the analysis, design, and optimization of work activities in relatively simple organizational environments. More recently, however, the global sociopolitical environment has changed, service industries gradually have become the most typical economic form, and the adoption of information technologies has resulted in decentralization, debureaucratization, and employee participation. Consequently, the cost of centralized control has become ineffective and economically unsustainable.

Today, in many modern organizations, there is an increasing tendency towards distributing control to individuals and groups of individuals which will include customers and suppliers. Due to the uncertainty inherent in human behaviour, quantitative approaches to the analysis and design of operations are not sufficient to fully control and accurately predict the outcome of a complex transformation process. More abstract themes like organizational culture, identity, service management, leadership, and charisma are explicitly taken into account as they often have an impact on organizational processes. As a result, a turn towards a more conceptual and context-specific operations management has been noticed over the last few years. Nevertheless, the discipline of operations management is still characterized by an overly technocratic flavour and themes like those above exist only on its periphery. This is despite the realization that the design and control of more effective processes require the creation of more pleasant and creative working environments, where human-related issues are at the centre.

A final key criticism for modern operations, also related to its 'scientific' principles, is its relation to the natural environment. In fact, as is also evident in this chapter, environmental issues have only been marginally considered in the development of the practice and scholarship of operations management. The economic benefit of the firm has in general been the primary focus of attention, often above that of the natural environment. In fact, the impact of the environment is sometimes considered as a limiting factor in the maximization of economic performance. Nonetheless, manufacturing and service operations-related activities have a direct impact on the environment due to the utilization of energy and the generation of waste. Therefore, operations management needs to include the environmental policy as an explicit issue in the development of its strategy, design and planning, and control areas.

Summary

This chapter has introduced some of the key principles and concepts of operations management. It has discussed the key approaches and techniques used to manage operations for the effective delivery of products and services to the customer. Operations management and the management of processes in general take up a significant amount of a manager's time regardless of whether his/her title includes the term 'operations', making the issues discussed in this chapter a set of important concepts that can help improve an organization's performance. These should, however, be treated with caution. Often the effectiveness and creativity of humans – critical components of most systems – are positively related to the same uncertainty that the management of processes is trying to eliminate. Too strict an application of the management of processes can therefore lead to dull and repetitive processes that may discourage innovation. A lack of processes such as the ones introduced in this chapter can, on the other hand, lead to chaos. An effective operations manager is therefore someone who can balance process management and creative behaviour.

Questions for reflection

- What are the key operations strategy decisions and how can they affect an organization's ability to meets its customers' expectations?
- What are the limitations of new product development processes and how can these be addressed?
- What are the differences between push and pull systems and how should an organization decide which system to use?
- How can an organization reconcile the differing perceptions of quality to ensure it meets its customer's needs?

Further reading

Hayes, R.H. and Wheelwright, S.C. (1979) 'Link manufacturing process and product life cycles.' *Harvard Business Review*, 57 (1): 133–140.

Hayes, R.H., Pisano, G., Upton, D. and Wheelwright, S. (2005) *Operations, Strategy, and Technology: Pursuing the Competitive Edge.* Chichester: Wiley.

Hill, T. (2000) *Manufacturing Strategy: Text and Cases* (2nd edn). Basingstoke: Palgrave.

Machuca, J.A.D., González-Zamora, M.d.M. and Aguilar-Escobar, V.G. (2007) 'Service operations management research.' *Journal of Operations Management*, 25 (3): 585–603.

Schmenner, R.W. (1994) *Plant and Service Tours in Operations Management* (4th edn). New York: Macmillan.

Vollman, T.E., Berry, W.L. and Whybark, D.C. (1997) *Manufacturing Planning and Control Systems* (4th edn). New York: Irwin/McGraw-Hill.

References

Aastrup, J. and Halldórsson, Á. (2008) 'Epistemological role of case studies in logistics: a critical realist perspective.' *International Journal of Physical Distribution and Logistics Management*, 38 (10): 746–763.

Bonner, J.M., Ruekert, R.W. and Walker, O.C. Jr (2002) 'Upper management control of new product development projects and project performance.' *Journal of Product Innovation Management*, 19 (3): 233–245.

Chopra, S. and Meindl, P. (2001) *Supply Chain Management: Strategy, Planning and Operation.* Englewood Chiffs, NJ: Prentice-Hall.

Christopher, M. and Towill, D.R. (2000) 'Supply chain migration from lean and functional to agile and customised.' *Supply Chain Management: An International Journal*, 5 (4): 206–213.

Danneels, E. and Kleinschmidtb, E.J. (2001) 'Product innovativeness from the firm's perspective: its dimensions and their relation with project selection and performance.' *Journal of Product Innovation Management*, 18 (6): 357–373.

Davenport, T.H. (1998) 'Putting the enterprise into the enterprise system.' *Harvard Business Review*, 76 (4): 121–131.

Dowell, G. (2006) 'Product line strategies of new entrants in an established industry: evidence from the US bicycle industry.' *Strategic Management Journal*, 27 (10): 959–979.

Hamel, G. and Prahalad, C.K. (1994) *Competing for the Future: Breakthrough Strategies for Seizing Control of Your Industry and Creating the Markets of Tomorrow.* Boston, MA: Harvard Business School Press.

Hammer, M. and Champy, J. (1993) *Reengineering the Corporation: A Manifesto for a Business revolution.* New York: Harper Business.

Kidd, P.T. (1994) *Agile Manufacturing: Forging New Frontiers.* New York: Addison Wesley.

(Continued)

(Continued)

Klassen, R.D. and Johnson, P.F. (2004) 'The green supply chain.' *Understanding Supply Chains: Concepts, Critiques and Futures.* Westbrook: S. N. a. R. pp. 229–251.

Kotler, P., Keller, K.L., Brady, M., Goodman, M. and Hansen, T. (2009) *Marketing Management.* Englewood Cliffs, NJ: Prentice-Hall.

Lazonick, W. (1991) *Business Organization and the Myth of the Market Economy.* Cambridge: Cambridge University Press.

MacDuffie, J.P. and Sethuraman, K. (1996) 'Product variety and manufacturing performance: evidence from the international automotive assembly plant study.' *Management Science,* 42 (3): 350–369.

Martínez-Costa, M. and Martínez-Lorente, A.R. (2003) 'Effects of ISO 9000 certification on firms' performance: a vision from the market.' *Total Quality Management & Business Excellence,* 14 (10): 1179–1192.

Martínez-Costa, M., Choi, T.Y., Martínez, J.A. and Martínez-Lorente, A.R. (2009) 'ISO 9000/1994, ISO 9001/2000 and TQM: the performance debate revisited.' *Journal of Operations Management,* 27 (6): 495–511.

McCarthy, I.P., Tsinopoulos, C., Allen, P. and Rose-Anderssen, C. (2006) 'New product development as a complex adaptive system of decisions.' *Journal of Product Innovation Management,* 23 (5): 437–456.

Mehri, D. (2006) 'The darker side of lean: an insider's perspective on the realities of the Toyota production system.' *Academy of Management Perspectives,* 20 (2): 21–42.

New, S. (2004a) 'The ethical supply chain.' *Understanding Supply Chains: Concepts, Critiques and Futures.* N. S. and W. R: 253–280.

New, S. (2004b) 'Supply chains: construction and legitimation'. In S. New and R. Westbrook (eds), *Understanding Supply Chains: Concepts, Critiques and Futures.* Oxford: Oxford University Press. pp. 69–108.

Pine, B.J. (1999) *Mass Customization: The New Frontier in Business Competition.* Harvard: Harvard Business School Press.

Pisano, G. (1997) *The Development Factory Unlocking the Potential of Process Innovation.* Boston, MA: Harvard Business School Press.

Slack, N., Chambers, N. and Johnston, R. (2005) *Operations Management.* FT/New York: Prentice-Hall.

Slack, N. and Lewis, M. (2007) *Operations Strategy.* London: Financial Times/Prentice-Hall.

Tsinopoulos, C. (2007) 'Strategy formation in pharmaceutical drug discovery'. In M.H. Sherif and T.M. Khalil (eds), *Management of Technology: New Directions in Technology Management.* pp. 295–310.

Van Creveld, M. (2004) *Supplying War.* Cambridge: Cambridge University Press.

Voss, C.A. (1995) 'Alternative paradigms for manufacturing strategy.' *International Journal of Operations and Production Management,* 15 (4): 5–16.

Womack, J., Jones, P.T. and Roos, D. (1990) *The Machine that Changed the World.* New York: Rawson Associates.

8 Corporate Social Responsibility (CSR)

Key concepts

Business case; Business ethics; Ethical codes; Ethical consumerism; Social accounting; Socially responsible investment

By teaching social responsibility business schools can instil in each of their students the skills to change the world – and the intention to make a difference. (Ban Ki-moon, UN Secretary-General)

The opening quote by Ban Ki-moon provides an indication of how widely accepted and endorsed corporate social responsibility (CSR) has become. It seems the transition of CSR from the periphery of business and societal thought to the mainstream is complete. Globally, governments are endorsing CSR and acting to curb corporate 'irresponsibility' in the wake of the financial crisis, civil society institutions collectively demand greater accountability, consumers are increasingly making purchasing decisions based on ethical criteria, the socially responsible investment market is forecast to quintuple in 5 years, universities have doubled their CSR courses in less than 10 years, and CSR activities are apparent in virtually all nations, both developed and developing. For its part, the business community engages with CSR and reports on its progress more so than at any other time in the past and has even formed its own associations specializing in the topic.

Despite its widespread exposure, the concept remains contested. The fundamental question of whether business should have social responsibilities beyond making profits, as long as it is adhering to the law, doggedly remains (albeit less debated than it was). Further questions follow: what does CSR actually entail? If a company is to assume social responsibilities, to whom should the business be responsible? How can social responsibility be enacted? When can a firm be considered socially responsible? Many more questions exist and this has meant CSR remains a vague notion to many, open to numerous interpretations both in theory and practice.

The following chapter attends to these questions and in so doing helps provide a working knowledge of CSR. It also demonstrates that CSR, as a discipline, is maturing from being this vague notion to becoming a meaningful tool for business and social improvement. It begins by defining CSR and tracing the concept's development. Arguments for and against CSR are then presented, the relationship with business ethics addressed, and the issues in CSR management presented. Finally, environmental matters and the future of CSR are considered.

Defining CSR

Despite the popularity of the term, there is no agreed definition of what CSR actually means. To understand the reasons for this, firstly consider the constituents of the term 'CSR' itself. 'Corporate' indicates a specific form of business ownership (essentially defined in terms of legal status and ownership of assets), yet CSR is now widely applied to any for-profit (and sometimes not-for-profit) enterprise. 'Social' is an all-encompassing term that relates to human society and the myriad issues (e.g. poverty, hunger, equality, drug abuse) that affect it. Further, people often do not instinctively consider 'social' as including the environment – an important aspect of CSR. As for responsibility this can be variously defined as a 'duty' to society, as being 'accountable' to society, or being 'trusted' by society. CSR suffers from a vague terminology that is open to many interpretations.

In practice using the term 'CSR' remains popular, but often the 'social' will be dropped in favour of 'corporate responsibility', or the 'corporate' will be dispensed with to leave 'social responsibility'. In addition to this, many other related (or synonymous) terms have arisen including 'sustainability', 'corporate citizenship', 'corporate responsiveness', 'corporate social performance', and 'responsible business'.

Beyond the terminology definitions also often differ, as Table 8.1 demonstrates. This difficulty in defining CSR reflects the evolving nature of the concept and contributions from various constituents such as academics, governmental and non-governmental groups, and the business community.

Perhaps the most common thread that runs throughout the definitions of CSR is that it is usually considered as 'beginning where the law ends'. When a company

Table 8.1 A selection of CSR definitions

'The obligations of businessmen to pursue those policies, to make those decisions, or to follow those lines of action which are desirable in terms of the objectives and values of our society'. (*Bowen, 1953: 6*)

'... refers to the firm's consideration of, and response to, issues beyond the narrow economic, technical, and legal requirements of the firm'. (*Davis, 1973: 312*)

'... relates primarily to achieving outcomes from organizational decisions concerning specific issues or problems which (by some normative standard) have beneficial rather than adverse effects on pertinent corporate stakeholders'. (*Epstein, 1987: 104*)

'A commitment to improve community well-being through discretionary business practices and contributions of corporate resources'. (*Kotler and Lee, 2005: 3*)

'We (the U.K. Government) see corporate responsibility ... as the voluntary actions that business can take, over and above compliance with minimum legal requirements, to address both its own competitive interests and the interests of wider society'. (*HM Government Corporate Responsibility Report, 2009: 5*)

'A concept whereby companies integrate social and environmental concerns in their business operations and in their interaction with their stakeholders on a voluntary basis'. (*European Commission, 2010, see http://ec.europa.eu*)

'... integrating ethical, social and environmental considerations into every aspect of our business'. (*McDonalds Corporation, 2010, see www.aboutmcdonalds.com*)

goes beyond its legal requirements in an effort to make a positive contribution to society, it is engaging with CSR. There are those who would consider the act of making profits legally as being socially responsible because, for example, this creates employment and provides the incentives to develop products and services that will improve people's lives. This perspective will be considered later. However most would agree CSR truly starts when firms go 'above and beyond' in positively contributing to social improvement. For example, Marks and Spencer and Reckitt Benckiser actively seek to reduce their carbon emissions beyond any current legal requirement. Sainsbury's supermarkets voluntarily removed fish that the Marine Conversation Society considered were among the most threatened from its shelves, and Barclay's Bank staff facilitate skills sessions to help homeless people gain employment.

The History and Development of CSR

Those who have already written about the origins of CSR would tend to agree that Harold Bowen's (1953) book, *Social Responsibilities of the Businessman,* was the first thorough examination of the relationship between business and society. Archie Carroll (1999) gives him the enviable distinction of being the 'Father of Corporate Social Responsibility' and Carroll and Shabana (2010) proclaim that the book was at least a decade ahead of its time.

Figure 8.1 The development of CSR

This is not to say that no-one had considered the topic before this. Scholars and industrialists had been making notable contributions, mostly in the United States, since the early 1900s when modern corporations started to become fully developed and to grow in size to eventually dominate most of the USA's major industries (Hoffman, 2007). From this early period, Chester Barnard's (1938) *The Functions of the Executive* and Theodore Kreps' (1940) 'Measurement of the Social Performance of Business' stand out, as do the contributions of a number of industrialists. For example, George Perkins of US Steel noted, '... The larger the corporation becomes, the greater becomes its responsibilities to the entire community' (Petit, 1967, cited in Hoffman, 2007: 60). And in 1917 Henry Ford declared in an interview published in the *Detroit News* that his only aims in life were to enable 'a large number of people to buy and enjoy the use of a car' and to give 'a larger number of men employment and good wages'. 'And let me say right here', he continued, 'that I do not believe that we should make such an awful profit on our cars. A reasonable profit is right, but not too much' (Lewis, 1976: 100). Lewis notes that such statements were probably unprecedented in the business world of the time.

Taking Bowen's book as the starting point for serious attention to be paid to CSR, it is valuable to look briefly at how the concept has evolved since Bowen's early ideas to be able to properly understand its place in the world today. Bowen's position on CSR was that given the power and size of businesses, their decisions would have considerable social impact. Businesses had to be obligated to consider the social consequences of their decisions. Bowen's was a moral position and like many of the early examples of philanthropy influenced by religion (his book was commissioned by the Federal Council of the Churches of Christ in America). However it was this lack of a business rationale for the concept that meant it was not widely embraced by the business community. Although some corporations saw its value as a public relations strategy at a time of changing social values in the USA, it was not wholeheartedly advocated. Corporate executives felt that any resources given to social causes could only hurt the bottom line. Another problem was that Bowen's (and his contemporaries') ideas were vague in relation to the nature and extent of a corporation's social obligations. The main reason though why CSR showed very little theoretical and practical growth – although there was popular support – over the next 20 years was bitter arguments with the opponents of CSR. Theodore Levitt wrote about the dangers of social responsibility in the influential *Harvard Business Review* (Levitt, 1958), but the most renowned opposition came from the economist Milton Friedman (1962), who called CSR a 'fundamentally subversive doctrine'. The arguments against CSR will be considered later, but while it has progressed a great deal since then, this debate continues to linger on today.

During the 1950s and 1960s CSR stagnated in practice because its opponents argued it was incompatible with the economic objectives of business. For CSR to gain legitimacy, it was recognized that researchers needed to demonstrate it was not at odds with economic performance. During the 1970s conceptual advances were made in showing that CSR was, in fact, in the best long-term interests of shareholders. The underlying assumption was that if corporations did not support their local communities in aspects such as education, health, housing, crime prevention, and homelessness they would deteriorate. These businesses would then lose their critical support structure and customer base. It was in each firm's own interest to consider the social environment and hence this argument became known as 'enlightened self-interest'. The (at least theoretical) reconciliation of social and economic objectives rejuvenated the CSR journey. What was needed next was more empirical evidence that its social and economic goals were not at odds, as well as more practical guidance on how firms could engage with CSR.

The most well known (certainly one of the most cited) works dealing with what CSR should include was developed by Archie Carroll (1979; 1991) who integrated and built on previous studies. Carroll identified four categories of social responsibility: economic (produce goods and services that society wants and sell them at a profit); legal (the laws and regulations under which business is expected to operate); ethical (over and above these legal requirements); and philanthropic/discretionary (voluntary activities).

Carroll contended that the economic and legal responsibilities must be 'required', the ethical responsibilities 'expected', and the discretionary/philanthropic responsibilities 'desired'. It was the inclusion of economic responsibilities that was a major reason for the general acceptance of his model in the business community. Carroll represented these four categories as a pyramid, with economic responsibilities at the base, the implication being that if a business did not fulfil its economic responsibilities, the other levels of the pyramid would be moot. For executives, this meant that making profits was part of being socially responsible. However, Carroll later emphasized that, '… it may be understood that the essence of CSR and what it really refers to are the ethical and philanthropic obligations of the corporation towards society' (Carroll and Shabana, 2010: 90).

Carroll's work proved useful in categorizing what a business should attend to in order to be socially responsible, but who should the organization be responsible to? Being responsible to 'society' was too vague a notion to be utilized by managers. The major breakthrough came from R. Edward Freeman (1984) who built upon earlier work to produce the stakeholder theory of the firm. Grouping 'society' into stakeholders who have a legitimate interest in the corporation and to which the corporation has a responsibility, was clearly helpful for operationalizing CSR. Firms could assess the relative priorities of stakeholder claims and target their CSR practices accordingly. Figure 8.2 depicts how the stakeholder management model differs from the traditional management model. According to this model, all stakeholder needs have to be balanced. This includes the needs of the shareholders as well as those of, for example, the community. Therefore, like Carroll's model, the economic and social objectives must both be considered when enacting social responsibility.

The period from the late 1990s to the mid-2000s was particularly notable for research attempting to link CSR with corporate financial performance. This will be considered in more detail in the next section, but it is worth realizing here that the focus on financial gains from CSR activities has received some criticism and also contributed towards a public cynicism towards CSR, particularly in light of the global financial crisis. There is little doubt that while there were many companies genuinely interested in making a positive contribution to society, there were others who were using CSR as a strategic resource to improve their bottom line. It has been claimed that the primary motive here was economic rather than social improvement. In this manner, these practices emphasized what was in the best interests of the firm, which was not always what was in the best interests of society. For example, causes that would broadly appeal to a company's customer base were being enthusiastically supported while other causes with less popular consumer appeal were being avoided, thereby causing them to become marginalized.

Despite the cynicism and the financial crisis forcing companies to deal with stark economic realities, the interest in CSR has not waned. Indeed quite the reverse has happened – society has become more attuned to the behaviour of firms. There have been claims for more responsibility, not less. The difference now is that the focus is shifting to how CSR can lead to lasting social and economic improvements. The current trend in CSR is thus a shift away from the 'business case' towards the 'social and business case'.

The state of CSR teaching and academic research

A review of the history and development of CSR would not be complete without briefly addressing the academic community's role. Universities have been criticized

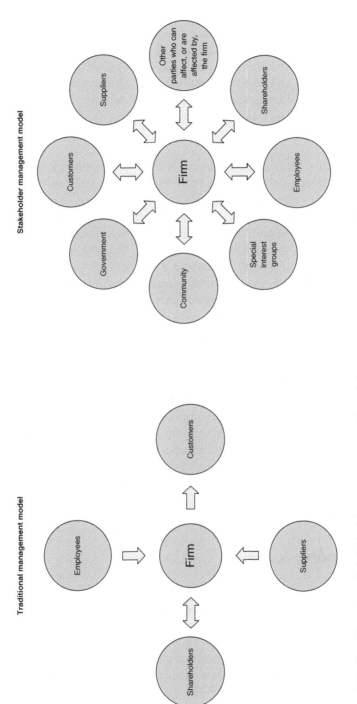

Figure 8.2 Traditional and stakeholder management models

for being slow to take up the CSR mantle. University CSR research, certainly up until a decade ago, was the domain of a few academics pursuing an individual interest. Although CSR outputs have much improved of late, this claim could still be made today when compared with the amount of research undertaken in other traditional business and management subjects. The Beyond Grey Pinstripes survey[1] focusses on the social and environmental aspects of MBA teaching and research. Of those schools participating in the 2009 survey (and who are therefore likely to consider themselves strong in this area), only 7 per cent of faculty had published scholarly articles in peer-reviewed business journals that addressed social, environmental or ethical issues.

Business school CSR teaching has found itself in the spotlight following the global financial crisis. Headlines such as 'Academies of the Apocalypse? Business Schools have, so far, escaped the wrath directed against the bankers – but should they bear some blame?'[2] began to appear in the popular press. Because many of those involved in these perceived irresponsible banking practices were business school graduates, the question began to be asked of what were they being taught? A business school education had been criticized for having a curriculum that was dominated by socially irresponsible and ethically dubious assumptions of certain core theories and concepts that had been predicated upon maximizing shareholder value: this would discourage CSR (Matten and Moon, 2004; Stewart, 2004). However, there is evidence that this is now being addressed. The Beyond Grey Pinstripes survey reported that in 2001 34 per cent of schools surveyed required their students to take a course dedicated to business and society issues. In 2009, the same survey revealed that figure had risen significantly to 69 per cent. Further, the main business school accreditation bodies (such as EQUIS, AMBA, and the AACSB)[3] have made their CSR requirements significantly more stringent. And initiatives such as the United Nations Principles of Responsible Management Education[4] have been implemented by nearly 300 academic institutions around the globe so far. The current drive is towards 'mainstream' CSR by interweaving it into all subjects – such as finance, marketing, accounting, and human resource management – rather than being left as a separate course.

The Arguments for CSR

The arguments for CSR can be grouped into economic, moral, and pragmatic. The first argues that a business should engage with CSR because it is in the firm's financial interests to do so. If the motive was purely economic Friedman, for instance, would argue that this is not CSR but simply profit maximization. However, if the motive is to produce some social good and at the same time benefit (or at least not harm) the bottom line, then there is an important need to pursue the business case in order to provide a long-term CSR engagement that is not heavily dependent on economic fluctuations.

The business case for CSR

Business case for CSR: Attempts to identify tangible business benefits gained from engaging with CSR.

Much of the research by academics, non-governmental organizations, and consultancies has tried to argue the **business case** for CSR by demonstrating a positive correlation with Corporate Financial Performance (CFP). However, the results have been mixed,[5] as was well encapsulated by Michael Barnett (2007) when he noted that after more than 30 years of research the link between CSR and financial performance had only become murkier. Coupling CSR with CFP is inherently difficult as there are many potential mediating variables and situational factors. For example, one of Cadbury's CSR programmes is to provide work placements for homeless candidates. Whether this will actually increase the company's profitability in the short term by increasing productivity is questionable given that there may be more skilled labour available. However, these profitability gains may come in the long term in other ways. Cadbury claims the campaign has increased team-working, morale, staff development, and motivation.[6] There are also other potential benefits such as an enhanced reputation that may attract and retain socially conscious customers. This example points to a limitation for some business case research that attempts to link CSR to CFP. The benefits of CSR may be less tangible than financial and CSR is multi-faceted, involving many different potential practices from sponsoring a local football team to providing funds for medical research. Focussing on the potential mediating variables of the CSR-CFP has demonstrated a more fruitful arena for research.

Reputation

Socially responsible investment: an investment strategy that considers both the financial return and social improvement.

Firms that engage with CSR can enhance their reputation with vital stakeholders such as customers, investors, employees and suppliers. Taking each group in turn, the firm that develops a positive CSR perception among customers may then benefit from this attraction of new customers as well as from the loyalty of existing ones. For example, when Kraft Foods re-launched its Kenco coffee brand with the Rainforest Alliance certified seal, its freeze-dried volume share grew by 7.2 per cent.[7] A socially responsible reputation can also attract investment. The **socially responsible investment** movement seeks to invest in companies not only for financial return, but also for social improvement. At the end of 2007 global responsible investment assets under management (AUM) were estimated at $5 trillion (US). This is predicted to rise to $26.5 trillion by 2015, which will be 15–20 per cent of the total global AUM.[8] Employees may also be attracted towards, and retained within, socially responsible firms. In the fight for high calibre talent, employers are increasingly finding their socially responsible credentials being examined.

Perhaps the strongest evidence within the reputation perspective is that the major influence on the business is not so much carefully cultivating a positive reputation, but avoiding a negative one. Examples of positive outcomes from CSR practices have already been presented for Kraft Foods and Cadbury. An example of a negative outcome can be seen when Kraft was in talks to merge with Cadbury: it promised to keep the Somerdale factory in the UK open but less than one month after the deal was signed in January 2010, Kraft announced this would close with the loss of around 400 jobs. The announcement was criticized by the UK government, condemned in the press, and it destroyed the trust of more than 5,000 workers remaining in the UK and Ireland. Cadbury, a 186-year old firm with a prominent history of advancing employee welfare, found its brand damaged in an instant. Nike similarly found itself caught up in a vociferous campaign against its perceived exploitation of workers in developing countries who produced its goods in the mid-1990s. Although the company has since initiated actions to address this issue (in 2010, *Fortune* magazine ranked Nike at 24 out of 346 firms for social responsibility) the company still seems to find the perception hard to shake off.[9] And Nestlé has been the subject of the longest consumer boycott in history because of its infant milk powder marketing practices in poor countries.

'Good management'

Firms that embrace a stakeholder perspective of CSR must necessarily engage with their stakeholders. This is simply 'good management' which should mean firms better understand their stakeholders and vice-versa. The result is, for example, better customer solutions, more efficient supply chains, and a greater understanding of the community in which the firm operates.

People management and development

IBM Spain has worked with the Semilla Association which helps school leavers who have left without basic qualifications and disadvantaged children to find a job. When assessing the value of the programme to IBM the company states, 'The volunteers have reported a real enjoyment of being involved in the program and feel that it has helped to develop their own skills … IBM also feels that it has helped with staff retention, as it has given employees another reason to stay with the company as they feel they are making a valuable contribution and making a real difference'.[10] This example demonstrates a commonly cited reason for an engagement with CSR – people management and development. Improvements in motivation, job satisfaction, morale, teamworking, and skills have all been documented by firms as positive outcomes of their CSR activities.

Cost reductions

In order to reduce the environmental impact of its Uncle Ben's brand jars, Mars created new moulds which altered the design and reduced the height, enabling a 6 per cent weight reduction to be achieved, and produced an overall saving of 450 tonnes of glass per year. Ford introduced a strategy to reduce the environmental impact of its Dagenham, UK plant which, the company claims, resulted in more than €4 million in savings.[11] By giving to the community, a company may find it is eligible for tax breaks. These examples demonstrate that savings can be achieved through certain CSR practices.

Recognizing that both CSR and business performance are multi-faceted, SustainAbility (2001) conducted one of the few studies that broke down both CSR and business performance into different dimensions (see Table 8.2). SustainAbility compiled their study by reviewing the existing literature, sustainability reports, case studies and examples, and then by drawing insights from SustainAbility's consulting work with major corporations in the field.

Table 8.2 The 'business case' for CSR: dimensions of CSR versus dimensions of business performance (adapted from SustainAbility, 2001)

Dimensions of corporate social responsibility	Dimensions of Business Performance (strong evidence)			
	Strong positive impact	Moderate positive impact	Weak positive impact	Negative/no impact
Ethics, values and principles (The degree to which a company screens its actions according to a set of tangible values and principles)	Brand value and reputation; Risk profile	Human and intellectual capital	Shareholder value; operational efficiency; customer attraction; licence to operate	
Accountability and transparency		Operational efficiency		
Triple bottom line commitment (environmental, social and economic)		Shareholder value; human and intellectual capital; risk profile	Access to capital	
Environmental process focus (minimizes any adverse environmental Impacts)	Shareholder value; operational efficiency; access to capital; risk profile	Customer attraction		

(Continued)

Table 8.2   (Continued)

Dimensions of corporate social responsibility	Dimensions of Business Performance (strong evidence)			
	Strong positive impact	Moderate positive impact	Weak positive impact	Negative/no impact
Environmental product focus (embedded environmental principles throughout a product's life cycle)	Innovation	Operational efficiency	Operational efficiency	
Socio-economic development (uses resources to support the social and economic development of communities)	Brand value and reputation	Human and intellectual capital	Risk profile; customer attraction; shareholder value	Operational efficiency
Human rights (contributes to the protection of human rights)				Operational efficiency; innovation
Working conditions (fosters a high-quality work environment and work-life balance for its employees)	Revenue; operational efficiency; human and intellectual capital	Shareholder value	Customer attraction	
Engaging non-business partners (engagement with external stakeholders to increase mutual understanding and co-operation)		Revenue	Human and intellectual capital	

It must be accepted here that situational characteristics are important. What may be successful for one firm may not be so for another. Whether or not a firm deals with brands, the industry it is in, its size and location, as well as many other factors will influence any possible business benefits. Limitations to the assumptions of the business case have also been expressed. For example, although there is a growing evidence base to support positive business outcomes from certain CSR activities, it has been suggested that this only holds up to a certain point. Once socially responsible behaviour becomes a norm, it will no longer be a source of competitive advantage. Another limitation falls on small and medium enterprises (SME). Most CSR research focusses on large companies and the few studies that have been conducted on SMEs seem to suggest that these businesses do not work in an environment that supports the benefits outlined by the broader business case.

Moral and pragmatic arguments

The moral arguments generally begin with the power and influence of business in society. When nations and corporations are ranked by gross national income and total sales respectively, 47 of the first 100 on the list are corporations (Ball et al., 2010). The world's two largest corporations on the (2009) *Fortune* Global 500 list are petroleum refining companies, with revenues getting close to $500 billion each. Wal-Mart directly employs over two million people, with many more millions reliant on its operations. With this comes an enormous influence on the lives of people, communities, and the environment. The moral argument goes that with this influence must come responsibility. A similar argument runs that these corporations inevitably cause social problems (such as pollution) and therefore also have a responsibility to solve them. Further, these corporations could not exist without, for example, employees, suppliers, customers, and the community infrastructure around them and therefore must have a responsibility to them beyond using them for their own ends.

More pragmatic arguments, as well as the 'enlightened self-interest' one previously presented, note that it is in the best interests of businesses to assume their social responsibilities because if they do not do so governments will act – and possibly in an unpleasant and unrealistic manner. For instance, in response to the financial crisis, then UK Prime Minister Gordon Brown called for an end to the 'age of irresponsibility' by the introduction of tighter global financial regulation. There has also already been widespread governmental action on issues such as packaging, waste, health and safety standards, product warranties, and credit practices. Finally, it is argued that the business world should act in a socially responsible manner because the public strongly supports this.

The Arguments Against CSR

Milton Friedman's admonition of CSR gained widespread attention when his piece, 'The Social Responsibility of Business is to Increase Profits', was published in the *New York Times Magazine* in 1970. He countered CSR on a number of fronts. Firstly, the workings of the free market system would hold business accountable: for example, protecting the environment is a generally accepted social norm. If a firm was exposed as polluting the environment, customers would choose not to deal with that firm and so it is in the business's own interests not to do so. Secondly, managers who spend money or resources on social objectives at the expense of corporate profits are spending someone else's money. Friedman provided the example of a manager who may decide to hire 'hardcore' unemployed instead of better qualified available workers to contribute to the social objective of reducing poverty. If this action were to cause reduced returns to stockholders, the manager is obviously spending their money. If the actions raise the price to customers, he is then spending the customers' money. Similarly if the actions lower the wages of some employees, he is spending their money. Thirdly, if the workings of the free-market system do not make firms more accountable, it is the role of government to address social issues. Businesses pay taxes to help provide for this. Fourthly, if managers are charged with social responsibilities, what expertise do they have? They are presumably experts in running a company, but not in social issues such as alleviating poverty or drug abuse. Fifthly, including social objectives will muddy decision making and divert business from its core objective of making money. It is worth drawing on Friedman's arguments at length because they are still well-known today and have been developed by other authors. However, it must also be acknowledged that these were formulated decades ago in the USA and in a far different business context. For example, globalization has considerably widened the scope of business operations and so it is much harder for governments to effectively regulate business activities.

There are further arguments against CSR. As previously indicated, if business is to choose to support social objectives, it is likely to choose those causes which have a broad appeal and neglect those that don't. It is also possible for very powerful businesses to become social engineers and use their considerable resources to promote their own socio-political world view. Media Transparency[12] has claimed the Walton Family Foundation (funded by Wal-Mart) devotes a significant portion of its holdings to boosting conservative political candidates and a conservative social agenda centred on the privatization of public education. They imply this is being done so as to influence what is being taught in US schools and meet their own conservative views.

Business Ethics

Business ethics: a field of study that deals with what is morally right, wrong, fair, or just in business situations.

Often CSR issues will be presented in such a manner that businesses are viewed as reified entities that act and are therefore responsible. For example, the chemical plant down the road is polluting the river. A sportswear brand employs child labour. A moment's reflection would reveal that it was the employees (predominantly managers) who actually made such a decision. CSR necessarily involves employees, either individually or as groups, in grappling with ethical dilemmas. Further, the stakeholder perspective of CSR involves a balancing act between (often competing) interests. For example, shareholders may want higher profits, employees' safer working conditions, customers more environmentally friendly production. This is where **business ethics** comes into play. This field of study deals with what is morally right, wrong, fair, or just in business situations. It also deals with dilemmas that are outside of the legal framework. For example, meeting the legal requirements for product safety is not an ethical issue but whether the firm needs to exceed these minimum levels because they believe it is in their customers best interests is. Some issues can be considered to be more about business ethics than social responsibility. For example, surfing the internet on company time may be viewed as more of an ethical issue rather than as a firm's

Table 8.3   Where individual action enters into CSR (Maclagan and Campbell, 2010)

Where individual action enters into CSR

1   Where individuals articulate their personal values in policy formulation, decision making and in the resolution of moral dilemmas in the CSR context.
2   At the interpersonal level, where individuals are involved in dialogue, value-conflicts and negotiations regarding CSR formulation and implementation.
3   Where individuals are strongly opposed to what they see as wrongdoing by the organization or by their colleagues.
4   Where individuals are acting in relation to institutionalized corporate systems for CSR, such as codes of ethics.
5   Where at the 'organization-environment' interface individuals engage in interaction with the company's stakeholders (e.g. a purchasing agent who chooses one supplier over another because of their commitment to human rights).

Table 8.4   Influences on ethical decision making in the workplace

Individual factors

- Cultural values
- Religious values
- Personal integrity

Situational factors

- System of rewards
- Obedience to authority
- Bureaucracy
- Organizational culture

responsibilities to society. Maclagan and Campbell (2010) help identify where individual action (and the need for moral deliberation) explicitly enters into the CSR realm (see Table 8.3).

Traditionally dealing with ethical matters in business has been dealt with by drawing on ethical theories, for example, utilitarian (an action is morally right if it results in the greatest good for the largest number of people), rights (basic entitlements that should be respected in every action), or justice (fair treatment of individuals). Ethical dilemmas can then be analyzed according to these theories to allow decision makers to view the issue from a variety of perspectives.

Also important here is recognizing those individual and situational factors that may be influencing ethical decision making (see Table 8.4). In practice, managers may not have the time or expertise to consider ethical theories (although they may draw on them intuitively), individual and situational factors when deliberating over a moral dilemma. To help managers and other employees in this regard, these principles and factors can often help to generate codes of ethics, the ethical components of mission statements, and ethical tests to help resolve ethical dilemmas at work which will be considered in the next section – managing CSR.

Managing CSR

Identifying and engaging with stakeholder groups

It has previously been mentioned that for a firm to be 'responsible to society' this is considered too broad a notion to be actionable. A major step forward here was the development of the stakeholder theory of the firm by R. Edward Freeman in 1984. This theory helped define those persons a business should be responsible to. Traditionally this was to owners or shareholders. The stakeholder perspective broadened this to include all stakeholders who were defined as '… any group or individual who can affect, or is affected by, the achievement of the organization's objectives' (Freeman, 1984: 46). A firm now needed to consider its customers, suppliers, the community, the government, special interest groups and many others in its decision making. Often the interests of these groups would be varied and conflicted. To manage this Freeman (1984) initially drew a distinction between primary and secondary stakeholders. Primary stakeholders are those whom the company cannot survive without (e.g. customers, employees, shareholders, the government, community) and secondary stakeholders are those who influence the company or are affected by it, but who are not essential to its survival (e.g. the media, special interest groups). For managers, they are more accountable to primary stakeholders, but they cannot ignore secondary stakeholders who could wield significant power in certain situations such as boycotts or critical media coverage. The following considers some of the issues involved when dealing with various stakeholders:

Shareholders

The importance and legitimacy of shareholders in CSR has long been debated. Shareholders are often concerned with rising profits and good dividends. For managers, this tends to mean a focus on short-term growth, possibly at the expense of their responsibility to other stakeholders. However, the rise in socially responsible investors is changing the perception that shareholders are motivated solely by financial self-interest.

Consumers

> **Ethical consumerism**: intentionally purchasing (or avoiding) a product or service because of personal moral beliefs and values.

Price and quality remain key factors in consumer decision making, but socially responsible criteria have dramatically increased in importance. One study revealed that 60 per cent of UK consumers were prepared to boycott stores or products because they were concerned about their ethical standards and three-quarters of British consumers would choose a product on the basis of green or ethical issues.

Similarly over 75 per cent of Americans would boycott stores selling goods produced in sweatshops (Hertz, 2001). However, there are some notes of caution to be found here. Research consistently demonstrates that the percentage of consumers who actually convert their intention of avoiding a product or company because of perceived low ethical standards into practice is considerably less. Also, for consumers and firms alike, the range of issues to embrace (and to avoid) can be overwhelming. For example, the list of consumer boycotts advocated by *Ethical Consumer* magazine includes multinational corporations such as Wal-Mart, Proctor and Gamble, and Kimberly-Clark, as well as entire countries such as China, Japan, and Canada. The reasons for these boycotts are also varied – for example, Adidas, for using Kangaroo skin to make some types of football boots, and the British Heart Foundation, for animal testing.[13] These issues aside, consumers are a powerful force for changing firm behaviour. So much so, that Noreena Hertz debated in a speech at Cambridge the issue of whether it was better to 'shop than vote?'. Her thesis was based upon, including other factors, the speed at which consumers could force firms to become more socially responsible: this was contrasted with the inability of governments to do the same. Hertz (2001: 190) declared, 'While governments dithered about the health value of GM foods, supermarkets faced with consumer unrest pulled the products off their shelves overnight. While nations spoke about ethical foreign policy, it was corporations who actually pulled out of Burma rather than risk censure by their customers. When stories broke over the world of children sewing footballs for Reebok and Nike for a pittance, what did governments do about it? Nothing, whereas corporations stepped in with innovative plans for dealing with the child labour problem'.

The government

It is generally agreed that the role of governments remains important in CSR. Although CSR really begins 'where the law ends' because of its voluntary emphasis, it is government who must set the minimum requirements for socially responsible behaviour and establish 'a level playing field'. How much state involvement exists differs around the world. For example, in the USA the state has traditionally played a smaller role than in mainland Europe, with firms in the former having more discretion involving CSR practices and the latter being more so obliged through legislation. Leaving social improvement entirely to the state has a number of problems. Firstly, governments can be effective within their own borders but have far less authority (if any) across borders. In an age of globalization governments also find policing the multinationals problematic. If tough business laws are passed regarding employee welfare, the environment, or any other social issue, then firms can easily move to a country with less strict legal parameters. Secondly, the state is generally very reliant on business for economic growth and thus reluctant to pass any legislation that may inhibit this. For these reasons governments have been described as rather weak and dependent stakeholders. Despite this, their role cannot be underestimated. If an issue causes widespread public concern, governments can and do act. However, for the most part it appears that their role has primarily turned away from attempting to force CSR via legislation towards helping businesses to voluntarily enact their social responsibilities.

Employees

The employer-employee contract sets out the basic legal requirements of the two parties, but it is the less formal psychological contract that is the focus of CSR. These 'unwritten rules' include the beliefs, perceptions, expectations, and obligations that make up the agreement between individuals and the organizations that employ them (Thorne et al., 2008). For instance, employees are likely to expect that their wages and benefits will be fair, their working conditions will be comfortable, and their safety will not be compromised. When the psychological contract is perceived as being met or exceeded, employees will then view the company as socially responsible and may reward it with behaviours such as loyalty, commitment, and creativity. A simple illustration of the potential social and business benefits of employee engagement is provided by Centrica. This company recognized that back problems were a particular concern for its 9,000 British Gas engineers. By introducing back care workshops, the firm not only improved the health of their engineers, it also reduced absence by 43 per cent.[14]

The community

The community surrounding a business provides it with a critical support structure. In turn, the community relies on that business to provide employment and thereby support many indirect benefits such as the housing market, the revenue for shops and services, and attracting further investment. Issues that will concern the community can vary in place and time. A search of the social issues that affect New York returns neighbourhood regeneration, gangs, transport, immigration, and schools, whereas the issues that concern Lilongwe, Malawi, are poverty, HIV/AIDS, education and skills development, and an awareness of social heritage. Equally there are differences within countries. In the UK, the City of London is likely to have different pressing social issues from those of Manchester. A further problem comes in defining 'community'. Other stakeholders such as shareholders, employees, and customers are clearly demarcated. Community on the other hand is more difficult to determine. A community will normally refer to people within a certain proximity to the firm, however, there may be some living next to the firm who will have very little involvement, or interest, in its activities. And how far away from the firm can someone live and still be considered a part of the community?

These two issues direct firms when engaging with their community in terms of CSR. Firstly, they must decide who the 'community' is. Secondly, they must determine the social issues that are most urgent in that place and target their CSR activities appropriately. In doing so, the community can then respond by providing the company with legitimacy and support.

A further issue is that in many cases a community will have arisen that is almost entirely dependent on a single firm. This has happened in industries such as mining, shipbuilding, steel and car plants. Here firms have faced the dilemma of whether to pull out when economic conditions have deteriorated and hence decimate entire communities. In some cases this appears to have been unavoidable, but in others there have been claims that a company had pulled out when it was still profitable and found it could be more profitable elsewhere. In doing so, companies have been accused of exploiting communities, moving to wherever provides the most lucrative business conditions, and then moving on as soon as another community becomes more favourable.

Prioritizing stakeholder issues

The preceding section has demonstrated that stakeholders can often have competing interests and complex relationships. Analyzing stakeholders via the legitimacy, power and urgency framework helps decision makers understand how to balance these claims. Legitimacy refers to the perceived validity of a stakeholder's claim on the company. Employees, shareholders, and customers are likely to have high validity in comparison to a special interest group. Power refers to the capacity of the group to influence the business. Here, depending on the issue, special interest groups may wield significant power and customers relatively little. Urgency demands whether or not the group's claim on the business requires immediate attention. The power, legitimacy, and urgency that stakeholders possess can help managers judge the relative importance of various stakeholders' interests (Mitchell et al., 1997).

Mission and values statements

Statements of corporate aims now frequently include a social dimension. For example, *Coca-Cola*'s mission statement is 'To refresh the world ... To inspire moments of optimism and happiness ... To create value and make a difference'. Alternatively firms may produce a separate 'values' statement that focusses on their social beliefs. Although very common in the business world – and indeed Buchholtz and Carroll (2009) include a stakeholder-inclusive values statement as one of their three strategic steps to successful stakeholder management – others would argue there is little evidence to suggest these have a significant impact on employee behaviour (Bart, 1997). Enron's motto was 'Respect, Integrity, Communication and Excellence', yet the company gained the dubious distinction of being a symbol of corporate fraud and corruption. However, the 'credo' of Johnson and Johnson has often been cited as a powerful influence on employee behaviour. This statement of values, crafted by Robert Johnson in 1943, spells out how the company expects its employees to behave and expressly states they must 'put the needs and well-being of the people we serve first'.[15] In 1982 the company was thrust into the spotlight when its Tylenol capsules were laced with potassium cyanide, leading to the deaths of seven people. When deciding how to react, the employees turned to the credo to decide what was required of them. Although the company could have reliquished responsibility and blamed what happened on the isolated actions of a mentally unstable individual it did not do so, and rather decided to 'put the needs and well-being of the people we serve first'. The firm's prompt action, such as recalling around 30 million bottles of Tylenol and subsequently working on tamper-proof packaging before the drug was reintroduced, led to the incident being regarded as a model for corporate responsibility.

Codes of ethical conduct

BAA's Code of Ethics Policy: every employee of BAA should:

- Treat everyone with dignity and respect listening carefully to our stakeholders
- Treat the company's assets and equipment as you would your own
- Operate within the letter and the spirit of law, exercising power and influence responsibly
- Respect the laws and customs in countries in which we operate. (*See www. baa.com*)

These codes help employees decide on their actions by showing what is expected of them when ethical dilemmas arise. There has been much research looking particularly at the content and effectiveness of **ethical codes** in recent years fuelled by their increased use by companies. Estimates in the UK are that around two-thirds of large firms have some form of ethical code, whilst in the USA they appear in almost all large firms (Crane and Matten, 2007). Crane and Matten claim that this is perhaps less about what a code says, and more about how it is developed, implemented, and followed up. The effectiveness of these codes seems to be enhanced by acts such as thoroughly communicating them, encouraging participation and buy-ins, and disciplining breaches. Ironically, critics have claimed ethical codes are covert mechanisms to control employee beliefs and behaviours and are therefore intrinsically 'unethical'.

Employee induction and training

For many firms this has become an important method of communicating the firm's commitment to social responsibility. When IKEA opened its Belfast store it recruited staff based on values that fitted with those of the firm (such as simplicity, humility, thrift, and responsibility) rather than previous retail experience. These values were then further reinforced during the induction and mandatory values workshops once people were employed.[16] In regard to CSR training, due to this being relatively new to the university curriculum and corporate training offerings, few managers who are now in senior positions have had any form of formal CSR education. The result has been a growing demand for this type of activity and a number of training and consultancy firms have built capacity in this area.

Social accounting

> **Social accounting**: the process of auditing and reporting an organization's social, ethical, and environmental progress.

The field of **social accounting** attempts to do for the social sphere what financial accounting does for the financial arena i.e. auditing and reporting on progress. Both focus on informing external stakeholders, but the latter deals with financial issues and is a legal obligation, whereas the former deals with social, ethical and environmental issues and is (in most countries, although this is changing) voluntary. There are, as yet, no universally accepted guidelines on issues such as what should be included in a social report, how performance should be assessed, or how a report should be communicated. That said, a number of frameworks have emerged. Some are methodologies developed by companies such as Shell, the Body Shop and Traidcraft, and then emulated by others. Some have been provided by non-profit groups like AccountAbility's AA1000 series or Social Accountability International's SA8000. One of the most successful has been that of the Global Reporting Initiative which claims to be the world's most widely used sustainability reporting framework, being used by around 1,500 organizations in over 50 countries.[17] At a national level many governments now publish environmental reporting guidelines, including the UK, France, the Netherlands, and Sweden. Also worthy of note is the United Nations Global Compact which provides ten socially responsible principles and encourages reporting on the implementation of these.[18] Because of the absence of a generally recognized framework, the CSR reports that companies provide tend to vary significantly in their depth and quality. This has in turn led to criticisms of some companies' reports as being self-serving and ill-defined with claims poorly evidenced.

However, the KPMG International Survey of Corporate Responsibility Reporting (2008) provides reasons for optimism.[19] Firstly, 79 per cent of the largest 250 companies worldwide provide separate CSR reports, up from 52 per cent in 2005. Secondly, the survey also notes improvements in the quality and efficacy of reporting. Wim Bartels, Global Head at KPMG Sustainability Services, writes in the foreword to the survey, 'But would these reports pass the "green-wash" test? For the first time in the 15 years we have been doing this survey, we think they just might. Nearly all of the Global 250 companies that report also publish a corporate responsibility strategy with defined objectives. Our findings show that management systems are maturing, and that reporting is likely [to be] the result of a systematic approach to corporate responsibility that includes a strategy, management system, stakeholder engagement, reporting, and assurance' (p. 2).

Environmental Issues

Environmental issues cover:

- Climate change
- Energy
- Water
- Biodiversity
- Waste
- Deforestation
- Food
- Chemicals and toxins
- Air pollution

The natural environment is worthy of special note for two reasons – firstly, because damage to the natural environment causes social problems that are shared globally, and secondly, because it has become a topic in its own right, emerging from beneath the umbrella of CSR. Often firms will consider and report on their environmental responsibilities separately to their social responsibilities. The natural environment differs from other CSR issues because the subject generally relies on physical, rather than social, scientists to assess the impacts of business activity and provide solutions. Although environmental factors have been considered in industries such as agriculture for many years, with the environmentalist movement becoming particularly apparent in the 1960s, the topic has noticeably gained more attention within CSR in a short space of time. The reason for this has been the growing weight of evidence demonstrating the significant impact business has had on the environment, such as climate change, pollution, biodiversity, deforestation and the like. However this is also because despite a raft of environmental legislation, in an age of globalization, governments have been unable to act effectively. For example, in tackling climate change the Kyoto protocol and its successor the Copenhagen Accord were subject to a good deal of criticism. For many it has been argued that it will only be efforts by business in voluntarily curbing their own environmental impact and coming up with new innovations that will make any lasting difference. For the business world some of the strongest evidence of a business case has been demonstrated by environmental responsibility.

The Future of CSR

The global financial crisis has been a turning point for CSR. Critics had argued that when a severe economic downturn appeared companies would concentrate on their basic survival and the 'luxury' of social responsibility would be discarded. On the surface, there is evidence that this has indeed happened. At the end of 2008, a poll of charity chief executives by the Charities Aid Foundation found 88 per cent expected their income to drop significantly. When Lehman Brothers collapsed around 2,000 volunteers and £2 million were lost to deprived communities in central London. Charities had become reliant on banking's largesse, but now it was difficult to justify giving money and resources away while simultaneously announcing thousands of job losses. However, if one delves beneath the surface, this 'old style' CSR with its emphasis on philanthropy was never going to be sustainable. Companies can only give when they have something to give and charities had become reliant on, at best, a very uncertain form of aid.

The result has been that CSR has not gone away as the critics suggested it might. Calls for more responsibility have come from governments and a concerned public alike, who have had a wake-up call on the influence seemingly remote business decisions have had on their everyday lives. Even the critics have softened. *The Economist* magazine, well known for being deeply sceptical about the concept, produced a CSR supplement in 2008 called 'Just Good Business'.[20] Citing Michael Porter of the Harvard Business School, the introduction neatly highlights the problems of CSR's past: 'despite a surge of interest in CSR, in most cases it remains too unfocused, too shotgun, too many supporting someone's pet project with no real connection to the business'. It concludes that, '... done badly, it [CSR] is often just a figleaf and can be positively harmful. Done well, though, it is not some separate activity that companies do on the side, a corner of corporate life reserved for virtue; it is just good business' (p. 4). Confirming the continued popular support for CSR, *The Economist's* intelligence unit produced a survey showing that only 4 per cent of respondents thought CSR was 'a waste of time and money'.

Businesses with poorly reasoned, non-strategic, window dressing CSR practices which provoked cynicism in the past have derived little benefit from their CSR activities and quickly dispensed with them. Those companies who had a deeper understanding of CSR did not abandon their actions when times got tough – some have even increased their commitment. For example, in 2009 Mars announced that its entire cocoa supply would be produced in a sustainable manner by 2020. Marks & Spencer announced its Plan A CSR initiative in 2007, forecast to cost £200 million, in highly uncertain times. The reason for their behaviour is simple. As well as being able to positively contribute to the society without which companies cannot exist, it is 'just good business'. Mars is worried about their cocoa supply which has dropped in recent years, and two years after introducing Plan A Marks & Spencer has saved more than they invested in energy and waste savings as well as cultivating a 'green' reputation.

The future lies in replacing the perception of CSR as marginal activities that do little to alter corporate behaviour or make any lasting contribution to society. Executives now talk of CSR being a business mainstay and the firm's 'standard operating procedure', essential for both business and social improvement. CSR is learning from the past and what is now emerging is a leaner, more efficacious concept.

Questions for reflection

1 What were the major steps in the development of CSR?
2 What are the arguments for and against CSR?
3 How can CSR potentially improve business performance?
4 What is the relationship between business ethics and CSR?
5 What tools are available to manage CSR?

Further reading

Books

Blowfield, M. and Murray, A. (2008) *Corporate Responsibility: A Critical Introduction.* Oxford: Oxford University Press.
Buchholtz, A. and Carroll, A. (2009) *Business and Society* (7th edn). South-Western/ Cengage Learning.
Crane, A., Williams, A., Matten, D., Moon, J. and Siegel, D. (eds) (2008) *The Oxford Handbook of Corporate Social Responsibility.* Oxford: Oxford University Press.
Filho, W. and Idowu, S. (eds) (2009) *Professionals' Practices of CSR.* Frankfurt: Lang.
Harvard Business Review on Corporate Responsibility (2003) Boston, MA: Harvard Business School Press.
Kotler, P. and Lee, N. (2005) *Corporate Social Responsibility: Doing the Most Good for Your Company and Your Cause.* Hoboken, NJ: Wiley.
Thorne, D., Ferrell, O. and Ferrell, L. (2008) *Business and Society: A Strategic Approach to Social Responsibility.* New York: Houghton-Mifflin.

Websites

- Business in the Community: www.bitc.org.uk
  Organization consisting of major companies involved in CSR. Highlights best practices, research, case studies, etc.

- BRASS – Centre for Business Relationships, Accountability, Sustainability and Society at Cardiff University: www.brass.cf.ac.uk
  Research centre with useful research findings and links.

- CSR Europe: www.csreurope.org
  European-wide organization dedicated to promoting CSR, featuring free download-able CSR magazine, CSR jobs page, and a large database of reports, case studies, articles, etc.

- SustainAbility: www.sustainability.com
  Thinktank whose website includes many of their research reports in full text.

Notes

1 See http://www.beyondgreypinstripes.org
2 *Guardian* newspaper, UK, 7 April 2009
3 EQUIS (European Quality Improvement System); AMBA (Association of MBAs); AACSB (Association to Advance Collegiate Schools of Business)
4 See http://www.unprme.org/
5 See, for example, Orlitzky, M. et al. (2003)
6 See http://www.bitc.org.uk/resources/case_studies/cadburybaoh.html
7 See http://www.bitc.org.uk/resources/case_studies/afe2295_sc_kraft.html
8 Robeco and Booz & Company see http://www.robeco.com/eng/images/Whitepaper_Booz&co%20SRI_final_tcm143-113658.pdf
9 For example, the Australian Broadcasting Company and Sky News have both run recent high-profile pieces regarding the conditions of workers in Indonesia who supply Nike
10 See http://www.bitc.org.uk/resources/case_studies/ibm_spain_online.html
11 See Business in the Community www.bitc.org.uk
12 See mediatransparancy.org
13 See www.ethicalconsumer.org
14 See http://www.bitc.org.uk/resources/case_studies/centricabritish_gas.html
15 See http://www.jnj.com/connect/about-jnj/jnj-credo
16 See http://www.ikea.com/ms/en_US/jobs/join_us/ikea_values/index.html and http://www.bitc.org.uk/resources/case_studies/ikea_diversity.html
17 See http://www.globalreporting.org
18 See http://www.unglobalcompact.org
19 See http://www.kpmg.eu/docs/Corp_responsibility_Survey_2008.pdf
20 'Just Good Business', *The Economist*, 17 January 2008

References

Ball, D., Geringer, J., Minor, M. and McNett, J. (2010) *International Business: The Challenges of Global Competition* (12th edn). New York: McGraw-Hill.
Barnard, C. (1938) *The Functions of the Executive*. Cambridge, MA: Harvard University Press.
Barnett, M. (2007) 'Stakeholder influence capacity and the variability of financial returns to corporate social responsibility.' *Academy of Management Review*, 32: 794–816.
Bart, C. (1997) 'Sex, lies, and mission statements.' *Business Horizons*, 40 (6): 9–18.
Bisoux, T. (2008) Uniting Nations, Uniting Business, BizEd, July/August: 16.
Bowen, H. (1953) *Social Responsibilities of the Businessman*. New York: Harper.

(Continued)

(Continued)

Buchholtz, A. and Carroll, A.B. (2009) *Business and Society* (7th edn). South-Western/ Cengage Learning.

Carroll, A.B. (1979) 'A three-dimensional conceptual model of corporate social performance.' *Academy of Management Review*, 4: 497–505.

Carroll, A.B. (1991) 'The pyramid of corporate social responsibility: toward the moral management of organizational stakeholders.' *Business Horizons*, July–August: 39–48.

Carroll, A.B. (1999) 'Corporate social responsibility: evolution of a definitional construct.' *Business and Society*, 38: 268–295.

Carroll, A.B. and Shabana, K. (2010) 'The business case for Corporate Social Responsibility: a review of concepts, research and practice.' *International Journal of Management Reviews*, 12 (1): 85–105.

Crane, A. and Matten, D. (2007) *Business Ethics: Managing Corporate Citizenship and Sustainability in the Age of Globalization* (2nd edn). Oxford: Oxford University Press.

Davis, K. (1973) 'The case for and against business assumption of social responsibilities.' *Academy of Management Journal*, 16: 312–322.

Epstein, E. (1987) 'The corporate social policy process: beyond business ethics, corporate social responsibility, and corporate social responsiveness.' *California Management Review*, 29: 99–114.

Freeman, R.E. (1984) *Strategic Management: A Stakeholder Approach*. Boston, MA: Pitman.

Friedman, M. (1962) *Capitalism and Freedom*. Chicago: University of Chicago Press.

Friedman, M. (1970) 'The social responsibility of business is to increase its profits.' *The New York Times Magazine*, 13 September.

Hertz, N. (2001) 'Better to shop than vote?' *Business Ethics: A European Review*, 10 (3): 190–193.

HM Government Corporate Responsibility Report (2009) available at http://www.berr.gov.uk/files/file50312.pdf (*accessed 15/03/2010*).

Hoffman, R. (2007) 'Corporate social responsibility in the 1920s: an institutional perspective.' *Journal of Management History*, 13 (1): 55–73.

Kotler, P. and Lee, N. (2005) *Corporate Social Responsibility: Doing the Most Good for Your Company and Your Cause*. Hoboken, NJ: Wiley.

Kreps, T. (1940) 'Measurement of the social performance of business.' In *An Investigation of the Concentration of Economic Power for the Temporary National Economic Committee*. Washington, DC: US Government Printing Office.

Levitt, T. (1958) 'The dangers of social responsibility.' *Harvard Business Review*, 36: 41–50.

Lewis, D. (1976) *The Public Image of Henry Ford: An American Folk Hero and His Company*. Detroit: Wayne State University Press.

Maclagan, P. and Campbell, T. (2010) 'Corporate responsibility, individual action, and the curriculum', unpublished manuscript.

Matten, D. and Moon, J. (2004) 'Corporate Social Responsibility education in Europe.' *Journal of Business Ethics*, 54: 323–337.

Mitchell, R., Agle, B. and Wood, D. (1997) 'Toward a theory of stakeholder identification and salience: defining the principle of who and what really counts.' *Academy of Management Review*, 22 (4): 853–886.

(Continued)

(Continued)

Orlitzky, M., Schmidt, F.L. and Rynes, S.L. (2003) 'Corporate social and financial performance: a metaanalysis.' *Organization Studies*, 24: 403–411.

Stewart, C. (2004) 'A question of ethics: How to teach them?' *The New York Times*, 21 March.

SustainAbility (2001) 'Buried treasure: uncovering the business case for corporate sustainability.' Available at www.sustainability.co.uk.

Thorne, D., Ferrell, O.C. and Ferrell, L. (2008) *Business and Society: A Strategic Approach to Social Responsibility* (3rd edn). New York: Houghton Mifflin.

9 Strategy

Chapter overview

Key concepts

Ashridge portfolio display; BCG matrix; Complexity perspective; Experience curve; Five forces framework; Game theory; GE matrix; Generic strategies; Knowledge-based perspective; Mission; PESTEL; Porter's diamond; Positioning approach; Power perspective; Practice perspective; Product-growth matrix; Resource-based view; Scenario planning; Strategic group analysis; Strategy clock; SWOT matrix; Value chain analysis; Vision

---

Strategy (or strategic management) is widely considered to be the capstone course of an MBA programme. It is often taught after core functional areas such as accounting and finance, marketing and human resource management because knowledge of these subjects is considered essential to the understanding of strategy. Indeed, strategy is similar to organizational behaviour in that, while there is a growing body of work in strategy itself, the field also makes use of knowledge from other subjects. For example, research from organizational behaviour is employed to understand the processes of strategy making, implementation and change. Strategy is also closely linked to marketing and international business. Indeed, it should also be noted that many functional areas have now added a strategic dimension to what they do and so we now have strategic marketing, strategic HRM, and so on (see the relevant chapters elsewhere in this book).

While there is a long history of strategy in the context of military activity and war (indeed the Greek word *stratēgia* has its origins in *stratēgos*, meaning a general, *stratos*, an army, and *agein*, to lead), compared with other subjects on the MBA strategy has developed a body of academic knowledge in relatively recent times. The embryonic discipline was given shape by writers such as Chandler (1962), Ansoff (1965) and Andrews (1971) in the 1960s and 1970s, while the industrial economist Michael Porter's seminal text on *Competitive Strategy* was published in 1980. Some writers are now of the opinion that strategy in the twenty-first century has reached a crossroads and needs to radically shift its direction away from these early beginnings.

This chapter will first look at the more traditional approaches to strategy which have come from a broadly industrial economics base and will then examine some contrasting views which include work in the area of complexity and the 'strategy-as-practice' perspective – the latter arguably being sympathetic to some of the critiques outlined in Chapter 1.

What is Strategy?

The traditional or 'classical' view, as Whittington (2001) has defined it, is that strategy is about the long-term future direction of the organization. It is to do with the scope of a firm's activities and the basis for its competitive advantage. In other words it is about which products or services a firm should offer to certain markets given its particular configuration of skills and competencies and the prevailing threats and opportunities it perceives. Strategy is thus seen to be about the survival and success of the firm and relates to the more consequential and important strategic decisions (as opposed to operational ones, see Chapter 2) that generally bring in senior management. Hambrick and Frederickson (2001) provide a useful overview of the major areas of strategy. They distinguish five key elements, all of which must align and support each other. These are the *arenas* in which a firm will be active (in terms of products, markets, geographic areas, core technologies and value-creation strategies); the *vehicles* to enable the firm to achieve its aims (for example, by internal development, joint ventures, licensing, franchising, or acquisitions); the *differentiators* (the basis on which the firm will compete, for example image, customization, price, styling or product reliability); and the *staging* (the speed and sequence of moves necessary to realize the strategy). Overlaying all these the fifth element, *economic logic*, is about how the firm will get its returns (for example, by having the lowest costs through scale advantages or attracting premium prices through an unmatchable service, and so on).

We can distinguish different levels of strategy; firm-level strategy relates to the overarching vision and mission of the organization, while strategy at the level of individual business units is more about how to compete in particular markets. Strategy also comes about in different ways. The traditional view tends to see strategy as more planned and deliberate, decided in advance to achieve particular outcomes. Yet strategies can also emerge over time, the result of various decisions and actions which happen to coalesce though this would not have been planned at the outset. More recent writing has tended to give weight to this aspect of strategy, stressing the fluidity and on-going nature of the process and the frequent lack of direction and managerial control. Between the two positions it is recognized that some strategies are a mixture of deliberate and emergent, with firms deciding on a broad direction and then various aspects of strategy emerging over time. Finally, some strategies are simply imposed with firms having to respond to pressures in the environment either from competitors, customers, government or other sources – and perhaps therefore these should not be graced with the name 'strategies' at all.

Traditional views

The classical approach of the **positioning** school has traditionally dominated work in this area. Its foundations lie in the work of authors such as Porter (1980, 1985), Ansoff (1965) and Andrews (1971) and this perspective sees strategy as being about finding a fit between the firm and its environment, understanding the company's internal *s*trengths and *w*eaknesses in the context of the perceived external *o*pportunities and *t*hreats. This is encapsulated by the **SWOT matrix**, which while often used can be criticized for its tendency to produce long lists of internal and external factors without much discrimination or dynamism.

Positioning approach: a perspective that suggests strategy is concerned with matching a firm's internal strengths to its external environment in order to achieve a sustainable basis for competitive advantage.

SWOT matrix: a framework for identifying an organization's internal strengths and weaknesses in relation to its environmental opportunities and threats.

The job of strategists therefore is to ensure a fit between the firm and its environment by developing an understanding of the current situation and a strategy to achieve a future desired situation. In theory, this is given focus by an overarching **vision** (sometimes referred to as the 'strategic intent') which defines an aspirational future state for the firm. The vision of Komatsu, the multinational construction and mining company, was famously given expression in the pithy 'encircle Caterpillar' rallying cry, used to focus attention on the need to beat their bigger rival in Caterpillar's home market in the USA. The vision of Avon, the direct seller of beauty products, is somewhat lengthier:

> To be the company that best understands and satisfies the product, service and self-fulfilment needs of woman globally. Our five values are Trust, Respect, Belief, Humility and Integrity. We believe that everything we do, everything we say, and everything we produce as a company are infused with these values. (Source: http://www.avon.uk.com/PRSuite/whoWeAreMain.page, accessed 20 August 2010)

Corporate Mission

The Mitsubishi Electric Group will continually improve its technologies and services by applying creativity to all aspects of its business. By doing so, we enhance the quality of life in our society. To this end, all members of the Group will pursue the following Seven Guiding Principles.

Seven Guiding Principles

1 Trust
   Establish relationships with all stakeholders based on strong mutual trust and respect.
2 Quality
   Provide the best products and services with unsurpassed quality.
3 Technology
   Pioneer new markets by promoting research and development, and fostering technological innovation.
4 Citizenship
   As a global player, contribute to the development of communities and society as a whole.
5 Ethics
   Honor high ethical standards in all endeavors.
6 Environment
   Respect nature, and strive to protect and improve the global environment.
7 Growth
   Assure fair earnings to build a foundation for future growth.

Figure 9.1 Mitsubishi Electric Group Mission Statement (source http://global. mitsubishielectric.com/company/crop/mission/index.html, accessed 20 August 2010)

Vision: describes the desired long-term future aspirations of an organization, sometimes referred to as its 'strategic intent'.

The **mission** statement refers to the key purpose and direction of a firm though in practice the concepts of vision and mission are sometimes used interchangeably. An example of a mission statement taken from Mitsubishi Electric group is given in Figure 9.1.

Mission: describes the fundamental purpose or objectives of an organization and how it will achieve its vision.

Once a firm has an overall understanding of its main purpose (not necessarily a foregone conclusion – critics point here to the frequent lack of clarity and agreement about such fundamental issues), key activities in the process of strategic

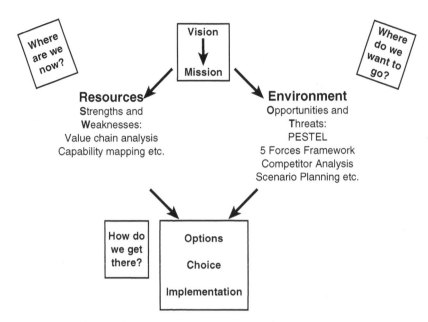

Figure 9.2   Traditional view of the elements of strategy

management will include the *analysis* of internal resources/capabilities and external conditions to arrive at some options, the *choice* (decision) of a preferred option, and its *implementation*.

Generally speaking, the main emphasis is on techniques and frameworks for analysis, as the sub-title of Porter's (1980) book *Competitive Strategy – Techniques for Analysing Industries and Competitors* – makes clear. These techniques can be roughly divided into two areas – those that analyze the environmental opportunities and threats and those that explore the firm's internal strengths and weaknesses. The overall framework can be depicted diagrammatically (see Figure 9.2). Some of the best known techniques are now discussed.

Analyzing the competitive (external) environment

Taking the external perspective first, the **PESTEL** framework is a way of identifying key environmental influences and refers to the following factors: Political (such as taxation policies and government stability), Economic (such as inflation, business cycles and disposable income), Sociocultural (demographics and lifestyle changes), Technological (new discoveries and inventions, rates of obsolescence), Environmental (ecological concerns, energy consumption and 'green' issues) and Legal (for example competition and employment laws). It may be useful to further distinguish Local, National and Global levels for each of these factors, an analysis sometimes referred to as LoNGPESTEL. A central concern is how far particular factors might affect an organization and when their impact might be felt (is it an immediate issue or a longer-term problem?). The difficulty is that until particular strategies have been chosen (and implemented) it is not certain how such elements might actually affect the firm. Care also needs to be taken about applying the analysis to large, complex organizations such as Disney which operate in a variety of markets with different products and brands.

Taking a more detailed look at the competitive environment, one of the best known ways of analysing this is Porter's **Five Forces framework**, which identifies the five factors that are believed to shape competition for a particular strategic business unit in a firm (see Figure 9.3). The Porterian view is that it is the structure of the industry which gives rise to competitive possibilities (and closes others off) and is therefore a major determinant of firm performance. The framework suggests that *rivalry* amongst existing competitors will be affected by factors such as their relative size, industry growth rates, high fixed costs and barriers to exit; the bargaining power of *buyers* is increased when they are concentrated, can change suppliers easily, and there is a threat of backward integration (i.e. the buyer acquires the supplier); *supplier* power is increased when they are concentrated, switching from one supplier to another is difficult, and there is a threat of forward integration (i.e. suppliers can compete with buyers). The threat of *entry* depends on how far things like access to distribution channels, significant capital requirements, economies of scale, customer loyalty, experience, legislation, or anticipated retaliation by existing providers can offer a serious barrier to firms wanting to enter the market, while the threat of *substitute* products and services depends on how easy it is to substitute and the relative cost and performance implications of doing so. The dynamic interplay of these five forces is also influenced by stakeholders and the wider regulative (and societal) framework.

Five Forces framework: an approach developed by Michael Porter to identify the forces that shape competition in a business sector.

Once again, if not used with caution such a framework can lend itself to the generation of long lists of undifferentiated factors. The challenges are to identify the relevant industry (there may be more than one), the factors that really matter and when they might have an impact, how forces may combine or change and how competitors might be affected, as well as what might be done to influence these factors. This links to Competitor Analysis which is concerned with profiling current and potential competitors in order to identify their strengths/weaknesses, the strategies that they might adopt, and how they might react to your own strategic moves.

The framework has received some strong criticism, and it has been suggested (Coyne and Subramanian, 2000) that the increasing proliferation of a variety of 'co-dependent' systems such as cooperative ventures, alliances and networks (see the discussion in Chapter 2 about networks and organizational structure) and higher

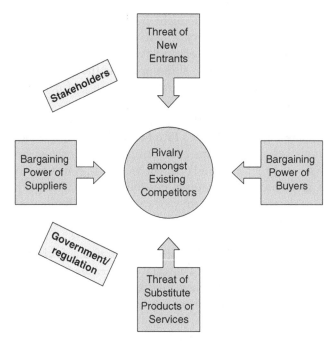

Figure 9.3 The Five Forces Framework (adapted from Porter, M.E. (2008))

levels of uncertainty means that the environment is now so markedly different that this framework is no longer relevant to current business situations. Some would also view cooperation as just as important as competition, maintaining that the 'complementors' (Brandenburger and Nalebuff, 1998) – namely products or services that directly complement another firm's offering thus making it more attractive (for example digital cameras and colour printers, anti-virus software and computer programs) – are important enough to constitute a 'sixth force'. This point about cooperation is picked up again below.

Analyzing how your overall offering compares with those of competitors is a key requirement for understanding your competitive position. Porter also developed earlier work on **Strategic Group Analysis** (SGA) to identify the configuration of organizations competing within an industry. Strategic groups are firms in an industry that share a similar business model or compete on similar bases. Groups are identified by using a number of the characteristics which form the basis of competition, such as a range of products or services, the geographical spread, and the number of market segments covered. As an example some analysts suggest that, in the car industry, Toyota and Nissan share a similar strategic group (Nohria and Garcia-Pont, 1991), and it is easy to see that the hand-built specialist cars of the Morgan car company would occupy a separate one. However the allocation of companies to particular groups is not as easy as it sounds, because the possibility of using a variety of dimensions in different combinations means that there are different ways to construct strategic groups. Some have therefore argued that these groups only exist in theory rather than in reality. In addition, since firms operate within different market segments, there is some confusion about demarcations based on strategies and demarcations based on products. While SGA should be about the former, in practice sometimes these are muddled. Discussions about the basis for competition compared with others in the market may be a useful focus for internal debate, but such discussions should also be mindful of customer needs. As Johnson et al. (2008) point out SGA is about 'producers' and this should be coupled with an understanding of consumer needs, for example through the 'value proposition' and market segmentation (see Chapter 4 on Marketing).

Strategic Group Analysis: an attempt to group together firms which are operating with similar business models or competing on similar bases.

While looking at the competitive environment we will briefly mention **game theory** which, while not necessarily in the mainstream of orthodox thinking, has been influential in shaping our understanding about business behaviour. A branch of applied mathematics, game theory simulations range from the simple to the very complex, but in essence they try and model what one competitor believes another will do in a particular situation. Hence they also try and predict outcomes where one person's choices will depend on those of others. Often such situations mean that one individual does better at another's expense and where one person's loss exactly balances out another's win this is termed a zero sum game (total losses minus total wins = 0). Thus in the field of strategy, game theory has been used to try to understand and predict the moves and countermoves of other competitive players. However it is also utilized in many other business areas, particularly economics (see Chapter 6), and can be seen as part of a developing organizational economics approach.

Game theory: a way of modelling behaviour in situations where the outcomes of strategic choices are dependent on the choices made by other players.

Moving beyond the individual firm to the nation, it has been suggested that global forces will impact on the potential competitiveness of different countries and also on particular industries within these countries. In his (1990) book *The Competitive Advantage of Nations*, Michael Porter draws on empirical evidence to put forward a way of evaluating the factors that may give a national advantage in what has become known as **Porter's Diamond** (see Figure 9.4).

In this framework, *factor conditions* refer to factors of production and include human resources (e.g. skilled labour), natural resources, capital, infrastructure, and

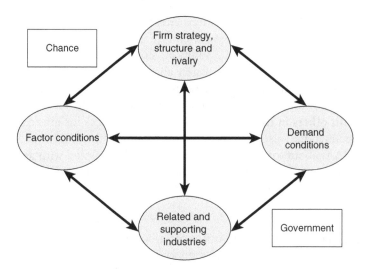

Figure 9.4   Porter's Diamond: Factors shaping national advantage (adapted with permission of Free Press, a division of Simon & Schuster, Inc., from *The Competitive Advantage of Nations* by Michael E. Porter. Copyright © 1990, 1998 by Michael E. Porter. All rights reserved)

knowledge. While there is a clear link with standard economic theory Porter argues that important factors can be created rather than inherited and the absence of natural advantages may lead countries to be creative about developing their own ways round this. For example, the high price of land in Japan means that storage space is scarce and expensive, making just-in-time inventory systems a sensible strategy as well as a potential source of competitive advantage. *Demand conditions* refer to home customers' expectations which shape the way the industry develops. Sophisticated and demanding customers mean that firms are driven to develop high quality products in order to cater for their existing customer base, giving them an edge over competitors globally. Staying with Japan, it is argued that Japanese consumers' interest in high-tech electrical and electronic equipment has been a spur to the innovative and technologically sophisticated gadgetry of companies like Sony and has also contributed to their global domination in these industries. In terms of *related and supporting industries* it is suggested that a strong group of related and supporting industries complement each other and help to build a nexus of connected and mutually beneficial organizations. Examples here would include the Italian leather goods industry, Silicon Valley in California, and the automobile industry in Detroit. *Firm strategy, structure and rivalry* refers to the way firms set goals and are organized and managed, and the belief that strong domestic competition will generate the pressure to innovate and improve. Alongside these, *government* can influence the other elements, for example by influencing the supply of key factors, demand conditions in the domestic market, and shaping the competitive environment. Since not everything is under managerial control *chance* events may also play their part. Once again, it is important to understand the way these factors interact so that the dynamism of these interrelationships is not neglected. Some have argued that the Diamond model is rooted in the past (Jeremy, 2006), showing how industrial clusters have emerged over time.

Porter's diamond: a framework put forward by Michael Porter for understanding the factors that give national competitive advantage.

If the situation is complex and the environment turbulent and unpredictable **scenario planning** might be used. This is where a number of alternative scenarios are worked through in some detail. Each is based on different but internally consistent sets of assumptions and propositions which give rise to contrasting visions of the future. So, for example, an oil producer might develop scenarios for a future in which significant new oil fields are discovered, or where reserves run out quicker than expected, or where there are major developments in alternative fuel sources. Indeed Shell has been a leader in utilizing sophisticated scenario-planning techniques – something of a necessity when oil exploration is a capital intensive business with long lead times and uncertain outcomes.

Scenario planning: the development of a series of contrasting views about the future, each based on a set of internally consistent assumptions, used to facilitate strategic planning.

Analyzing internal resources and capabilities

Having examined the external environment, we now turn to take a look at the other half of the SWOT matrix: the organizational factors that contribute towards achieving competitive advantage. Once again Porter (1985) has provided a widely used framework. His **value chain analysis** is a way of delineating the internal elements of the firm that contribute towards 'margin' (that is, profit); see Figure 9.5. These are broadly divided into Primary and Support activities. Primary activities are those directly concerned with the processes of making and delivering a product or service to the customer. These comprise *inbound logistics* (receiving, storing and distributing the inputs required to create the product or service); *operations* (concerned with the transformation of inputs into outputs); *outbound logistics* (order processing and distribution); *marketing and sales* (advertising and selling); and *service* (installation, training and repair). As the name suggests, the Support activities support the Primary activities and include *procurement* (acquiring the inputs); *technology development* (for example product design or process developments); *human resource management* (all the aspects associated with recruitment, training, development and rewarding employees); and *firm infrastructure* (organizational systems such as finance, accounting, quality control and general management).

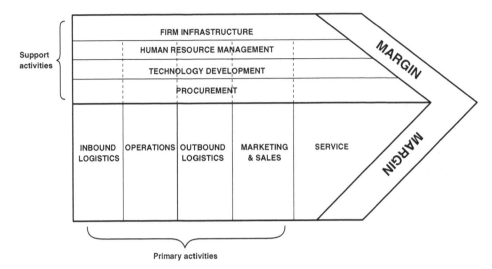

Figure 9.5   Porter's Value Chain (reprinted/adapted with permission of Free Press, a division of Simon & Schuster Inc., from *Competitive Advantage: Creating and Sustaining Superior Performance* by Michael E. Porter. Copyright © 1985, 1998 by Michael E. Porter. All rights reserved)

> **Value chain analysis**: identifies the value-adding activities within a firm and along supply chains and distribution networks that add value to the final product or service.

The framework can be used to identify the cost and value of different activities. However, the dotted lines indicate that the support activities can be linked with the primary activities (except for the firm infrastructure which overarches the entire value chain) and indeed it is the way that different activities are linked together that may be an important source of competitive advantage. For example, Wal-Mart's in- and outbound logistics and distribution capabilities are the core technology of its operation and span many areas of the value chain, allowing the company to maintain low inventory levels, while excellent information systems permit speedy replenishment of store items. In many ways Wal-Mart can be thought of as essentially a distributor rather than a retailer. But value chain analysis goes beyond any one organization. The links between organizations have become increasingly important (for example with supply chain management) and thus it is argued that the links between the organization (or a specific business unit), its customers, and its suppliers should be seen in their entirety. Again, Wal-Mart's and other firms' use of RFID (Radio Frequency Identification) allows the organization to coordinate supplies, monitor inventory, and speedily respond to (or indeed anticipate) fluctuations in customer demand.

In some ways value chain analysis itself links together the earlier work discussed in this section, which was primarily concerned with understanding the external competitive environment, with more recent work which stresses the need to understand the particular organizational capabilities which set it apart from the competition. While the former has often been labelled an 'outside-in' perspective – looking at the organization from the outside – the latter is more of an 'inside-out' view – looking at the internal resources and capabilities that give the firm an edge within a particular competitive environment.

This latter view, often called the **resource-based view** (RBV), has generated a prolific amount of work in the last 15 to 20 years or so. Building on Penrose (1959, 2009) and given conceptual impetus by Wernerfelt's (1984) paper 'A resource-based view of the firm', but subsequently developed by a host of other authors, the emphasis is on understanding the particular configuration of assets and resources that contribute to competitive advantage. This perspective suggests that firms competing in the same industry may have very different resources available to them. From this vantage point, it is not the products and services themselves that form the basis of competition but the way that internal resources are utilized that allows the creation of these products and services in the first place. Thus firms compete on competences or capabilities not products or services.

> **Resource-based view**: a perspective that suggests the basis for competitive advantage is the bundle of strategically valuable resources and capabilities available to the firm.

Before we proceed any further, it should be noted that the terminology used by different authors is not always the same. In particular, the terms *competence* and *capability* are not always precisely defined and have been used somewhat interchangeably. Prahalad and Hamel, in a much cited early article, discuss the core competence of the firm arguing that in fact a firm is a portfolio of competencies and asserting that:

> Core competencies are the collective learning in the organization, especially how to coordinate diverse production skills and integrate multiple streams of technologies …
> If core competence is about harmonizing streams of technology, it is also about the organization of work and the delivery of value. (1990: 82)

They cite the example of Sony's skills in miniaturization and Philip's optical-media expertise as being evidence of firms that have developed specific competencies. They also contrast the rise of NEC through the 1980s with GTE's demise during the same period, suggesting that NEC's success has been based on the company's ability to understand and develop three interrelated streams of technology. Similarly, Canon's core competence in optics, imaging and microprocessor controls has allowed it to enter markets as diverse as copiers, laser printers, cameras and image scanners.

Recent writing tends to prefer the term 'strategic capability', defined below, and we will use this from now on. However, whether we talk of competences or capabilities the focus of this perspective is on the need to understand the particular resources of the firm, to recognize that these are organization-wide rather than belonging to particular departments or functions (that is, they are spread across the value chain and perhaps link to others outside the firm – compare the thinking of business process reengineering in Chapter 2) and that managers need to work out how these resources can be transformed into capabilities that will deliver value to the customer.

So the basic building blocks of capabilities are resources or assets. These fall into two types: tangible and intangible. Tangible assets are those that are more readily identifiable and also embodied in the firm's physical resources, labour force and finance. Intangible resources are not so easy to distinguish – they include things like reputation, knowhow and information – but can be extremely important sources of differentiation and competitive advantage. Jay Barney (1991: 101) comprehensively divides resources into three areas: physical capital resources (technology, plant and equipment, geographic location and access to raw materials); human capital resources (training, experience, judgement, intelligence, relationships and insights of individual managers and workers in a firm); and organizational capital resources (a firm's formal reporting structure, formal and informal planning, controlling and coordinating systems, and the informal relations among groups in a firm and between a firm and those in its environment). It can be acknowledged that, from this view, '... the balance sheet is a poor shadow of a firm's distinctive competences' (Teece et al., 1997: 717).

The literature commonly distinguishes between basic 'threshold' resources which meet the customer's minimum expectations and therefore allow the firm to stay in business and those that are in some way strategic, providing the basis for competitive advantage. But what makes a resource strategic? Barney (1991) suggests four criteria. Resources must be:

- *Valuable* – resources need to be something that contributes to the firm's effectiveness, for example by exploiting environmental opportunities and/or neutralizing threats
- *Rare* – the resources need to be ones that are not readily found elsewhere amongst competitors so, for example, a firm might be on an 'approved supplier' list which gives it preferred access to customers
- *Imperfectly imitable* – in other words these valuable and rare resources must be ones that competitors cannot readily acquire themselves: this may be the result of a set of *unique historical conditions* that have given rise to the resource; *causal ambiguity* (where the link between these resources and competitive advantage is not easily understood even by the firm itself); and *social complexity*, for example where the resource emerges as a result of complex interpersonal relationships amongst managers that are not easily controlled or managed
- *Non-substitutable* – the resources need to be such that they cannot be readily substituted by another firm using a different resource

But having valuable, rare, imperfectly imitable, and non-substitutable resources is only a first step. The challenge is to identify them and then nurture, combine and deploy them in ways that will create an advantage. It may even be the case that, recognizing a gap, managers will seek to craft new resources, either by building or

buying in particular knowledge or expertise, or by forming collaborative relationships with other parties. From this perspective it even makes sense to join forces
with competitors on occasions – if they have a specific set of resources or expertise
that will be complementary (Hamel et al., 1989). This gives a rather different
rationale for strategic alliances, mergers and acquisitions than the more traditional
view which often sees these as a quick way of simply buying market share. The
resource-based view emphasizes the need to understand the underlying synergies
that will create capabilities (and hence profits) for the future.

In this vein, the discussion has moved on to examine these capabilities in more
detail, in particular the dynamic interplay between them which forms the basis of a
firm's ability to compete. The 'dynamic capabilities framework' has been put forward
by Teece and colleagues (Teece et al., 1997; see also Teece, 2007). This perspective
recognizes that while some resources are 'sticky' – that is, in the short run firms are
stuck with what they have (Teece et al., 1997: 514) – in the long run managers need
to renew competences and reconfigure assets and skills to continue to be competitive.
So firms need to manage the dynamics between existing resources and the on-going
creation of new ones. Three classes of factor help determine a firm's dynamic capabilities: *processes*, *positions* and *paths* (Teece et al., 1997: 518). Processes are the
managerial and organizational routines and practices which permit coordination and
integration, learning and reconfiguration/transformation. Positions refers to the firm's
difficult-to-trade assets, including particularly its knowledge, reputation and relationships as well as its financial assets and market position. Finally, paths recognizes the
path-dependent nature of many of these aspects in that processes and positions are
often a result of complex historical factors that have shaped the present situation and
may constrain future action. As with earlier work, it is recognized that the capabilities
that result from this interplay between processes, positions and paths are only likely
to bring a competitive advantage if the capability is not easily replicated or imitated.
It should also be said that some other work has acknowledged that the management
of resources will be shaped by the dynamic environmental contexts in which firms
operate (Sirmon et al., 2007), providing a bridge back to the positioning school.

This view makes much of the role of knowledge, know-how and learning, and
links to discussions in Chapter 2. Indeed Mintzberg et al. (2009: 231) depict this
perspective as a hybrid which brings together the positioning approach (Teece and
colleagues also repeatedly stress the need to ensure a fit with the environment) and
work on organizational learning.

In critiquing this view the dynamic capabilities framework is held as especially
relevant to multinational enterprises in high technology, globalized environments
(Teece, 2007), which begs the question of how relevant it is to the bulk of small and
medium-size enterprises (SMEs) that make up the larger part of most economies.
This last point about the focus being primarily on large firms is a key criticism that
has been levied at much of the traditional view, and it should be borne in mind that
the relevance of many of these models to SMEs and to so-called 'third sector' organizations (charities, voluntary and not-for-profit organizations) is often questionable.

There are even more wide-ranging and trenchant criticisms of where exactly such
mainstream work in strategy has finally led us. Johnson and his colleagues have put

the answer very frankly. According to them, such thinking has brought us to '... a cul-de-sac of high abstraction, broad categories and lifeless concepts' (Johnson et al., 2003). For example, while the categorizations may be increasingly fine-grained, it is still difficult to discriminate between those resources that can be controlled by managers and those that cannot. Furthermore, even if identified, there is a dearth of pragmatic advice on what managers can do in practice. As Teece himself acknowledges:

> One should note that the identification of the microfoundations of dynamic capabilities must be necessarily incomplete, inchoate, and somewhat opaque and/or their implementation must be rather difficult. Otherwise sustainable competitive advantage would erode with the effective communication and application of dynamic capability concepts. (2007: 1321)

In other words it is very hard to be precise about where capabilities come from and if we were able to pin this down they would no longer form the basis of competitive advantage.

These musings have led to the beginnings of alternative ways of thinking about strategy, most notably embodied in the 'strategy-as-practice' perspective which we will examine later. Before we do so we first need to see where all this analysis – of both external and internal factors – has taken us. Examining the two halves of the SWOT matrix gives rise to some alternatives which then need to be implemented. We shall begin by looking at the array of strategic choices open to managers.

Strategic choices

Choices operate at two levels. There are decisions to be made at the level of individual business units about how they compete and, for larger companies, at the corporate level when decisions need to be taken about which business units to support. We shall first examine the business unit level.

Choices at the strategic business unit level

Choices at the business unit level will crucially depend on there being a clear and agreed understanding about which units in the organization are the strategic business units (SBUs); this is an assumption that cannot always be taken for granted.

Porter (1985) suggests that there are essentially three ways of competing, either by having lower costs than competitors or by differentiating oneself from them, and then by applying either of these to a broad or narrow scope called 'focus'. This is the basis of his **generic strategies**, shown in Figure 9.6. The lower cost strategy is about trying to have the lowest costs in the industry and this can be aimed at a wide segment of the market (cost leadership) or a narrow one (cost focus). Ways of achieving lower costs would include efficiency savings, through the **experience curve** (see below), and – where possible – through economies of scale. Similarly differentiation is about developing distinctive products or services, through higher quality, better performance, or unique features that are of value to customers. Again differentiation can be focussed on a broad or narrow market segment. According to Porter, the worst thing is to be 'stuck in the middle' having no clear strategy or pursuing a strategy unsuccessfully. However

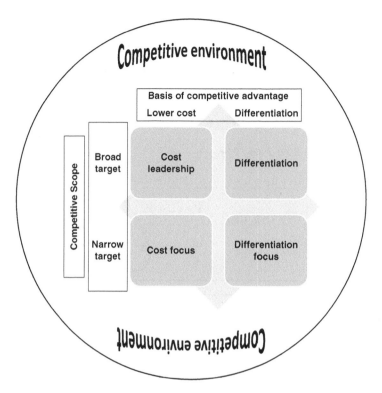

Figure 9.6 Generic strategies (reprinted/adapted with permission of Free Press, a division of Simon & Schuster Inc., from *Competitive Advantage: Creating and Sustaining Superior Performance* by Michael E. Porter. Copyright © 1985, 1998 by Michael E. Porter. All rights reserved)

there are problems with the definitions here. For example, some have confused cost leadership with having low prices. The competitive environment is also not static and the choice of strategy has to be sensitive to any retaliatory manoeuvres by competitors or changes to their strategy. Figure 9.6 adds the competitive environment to the framework to reinforce the point that choices are not fixed and will need to reflect the dynamics of the competitive landscape. Finally the assumptions of the framework have been criticized, with many commentators arguing that companies such as Sainsbury's supermarket chain and Caterpillar have long pursued a strategy that combines low cost and differentiation – based on high quality in both cases.

The experience curve: concerns the relationship between the costs of production and cumulative production quantity, suggesting that as cumulative experience increases the unit costs will decrease.

Generic strategies: Porter's competitive strategies based on cost, differentiation and focus.

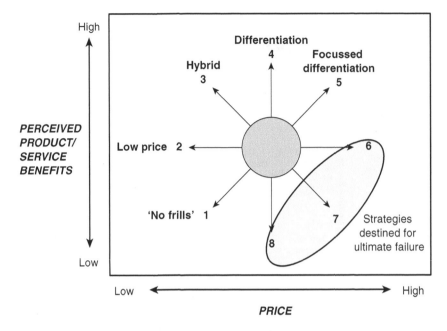

Figure 9.7 The strategy clock (from *The Essence of Competitive Strategy* by David Faulkner and Cliff Bowman, and *Exploring Corporate Strategy: Text and Cases* by Gerry Johnson and Keran Scholes, both printed by Prentice Hall. Reprinted with permission)

In answer to some of these criticisms, and building on earlier work by Cliff Bowman (Faulkner and Bowman, 1995), Johnson and his colleagues (2008) have put forward the **strategy clock**, which tries to encompass a range of strategy options at the business level (see Figure 9.7).

> **The strategy clock**: a depiction of a range of competitive strategies based on price and perceived product/service benefits.

Positions 1 and 2 on the clock are about a 'no frills' offering or a low price. This is appropriate when the customer is primarily concerned with price, although the perceived product or service benefits must still meet their minimum requirements. These strategies are likely to be segment specific.

The hybrid strategy (Position 3) is about offering differentiation *and* a low price. This depends on having a low cost base that allows enough margin to be realized to enable the reinvestment that will create and sustain the bases of differentiation.

Positions 4 and 5 are also strategies of differentiation. Both are about having added value as perceived by the customer. Position 4 is a broad differentiation strategy which aims to offer better products or services than competitors at the same or a higher price. Position 5 is about offering premium price products, usually to a specific market segment.

Position 6 is about increasing prices but offering a standard product. In the short-term margins may increase but there is a strong risk of losing market share to competitors. Position 7 is about increasing prices but offering a lower value product which is really only realistic in monopolistic situations. The final strategy at Position 8 is about offering a reduction in benefits but maintaining the price which is also likely to lead to a loss of market share. These last three positions (6, 7 and 8) are ultimately unsustainable and are likely to lead to failure in the long run.

Choices at the corporate level

At the corporate level decisions need to be made about which strategic business units should be supported and which should be divested. Portfolio analysis is used for this purpose and work in this area demonstrates that it is not only academics who have contributed to the field; strategy has maintained strong links with consultancies such as McKinsey and the Boston Consulting Group (BCG). In terms of evaluating a range of business units, the BCG Growth-Share Matrix – a tool for portfolio planning – proved to be particularly attractive in the 1970s when trends for diversification meant that firms had to decide on which areas of their portfolio to invest in, develop and promote (the consequent implications for areas such as accounting and finance, research and development, and marketing are clear). The Growth-Share Matrix uses the current market share and potential growth rates share to differentiate between businesses as depicted in Figure 9.8. 'Star' businesses have a high market share of a growing market; 'cash cows' have a high market share of a mature market; 'problem children' (sometimes referred to as 'question marks') have a low market share of a growing market; and 'dogs' have a low market share in a static (or declining) market. The framework is built on the premise of the product life cycle (which postulates that products go through stages of birth, growth, maturity and decline) which dictates that all businesses will become cash cows or dogs eventually, and the experience curve which, as noted above, suggests that experience leads to a lowering of costs. Aside from 'dogs' which are thought to be evidence of a failing business that will soak up resources which could be better used elsewhere, the trick is to have a balanced portfolio in order to facilitate cash flow as low growth businesses can provide surplus cash that can be invested in high growth areas.

However critics view the matrix as being far too reductionist and simplistic (Mintzberg et al., 2009: 100), suggesting that market and market share growth rates cannot always be measured with precision, that the labels are value-laden and may be self-fulfilling (give a 'dog' a bad name ...), and that there may be important complementarities and synergies between businesses that are hidden by such a framework.

The **GE Matrix** (Market Attractiveness-Business Strength matrix), originally developed for General Electric (GE) by McKinsey, offers a slightly more developed way of evaluating a portfolio of businesses. The proposition is that long-term profitability is based on the attractiveness of the relevant market (attractiveness is defined by multiple factors such as market size and growth rate, barriers to entry, industry profitability, and competitive structure) and the position of the business in comparison with its competitors (looking at factors like market share, brand equity, distribution channels, manufacturing capability, and company image). While somewhat more sophisticated

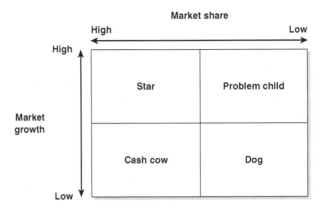

Figure 9.8   The BCG Growth Share Matrix (adapted from Product Portfolio Matrix © 1970, The Boston Consulting Group)

in that we have now moved from having two dimensions to including a number of elements, the matrix still suffers from similar labelling and definitional problems.

In passing it should be mentioned that GE spawned another framework, the PIMS (Profit Impact of Market Strategy) analysis, which attempted to isolate the strategy variables associated with performance (particularly ROI – return on investment). PIMS developed an extensive database of several thousand businesses (which is still being added to) and found that factors such as a strong market share, company image, lower costs, and quality products appeared to be associated with a strong performance. However, as commentators have noted, the database has been skewed towards large and established companies; these associations (correlations) are not causal explanations (for example, does a high market share lead to high profits or is it the other way round); and there is little available to help managers actually achieve these advantageous positions.

The make-up of a portfolio will differ in terms of its diversity. Some portfolios will comprise SBUs that offer very different products or services while others will be more homogeneous. The term 'related diversification' refers to strategies that may include the development of new products or markets but where the firm still operates within its current repertoire of capabilities. 'Unrelated diversification' means developing a heterogeneous range of products or services that will take the firm outside of its current capabilities. This kind of organization is often called a conglomerate and these enjoyed particular popularity in the 1960s when interest rates were relatively low. However they stretch the expertise of the parent company and may also limit the possibilities for synergies between businesses, though they do spread risk.

Overall, the management of a business portfolio poses two related questions. The first is how far the portfolio can allow the firm to exploit its distinctive current or aspirant strategic capabilities – in fact this should inform decisions about which businesses to support and which to divest. The second is how far the parent company can add value to the whole operation. On the one hand, the corporate 'headquarters' could simply be a drain on resources and creativity, with the SBUs needing to fund costly infrastructural overheads while being tied down by bureaucracy and the company as a whole losing focus and direction. On the other hand, the parent company could be a source of investment, and may facilitate economies of scale, serve to realize and manage synergies between different SBUs, and avoid duplication and waste by offering specialist and cross-business services.

This second question is about 'corporate parenting' and here the work done at Ashridge Strategic Management Centre by Goold, Campbell and others is particularly relevant (see, for example, Goold et al., 1993a and b). The original work identified three different ways in which the corporate headquarters of large, diversified organizations could seek to manage their portfolios and add value to them: the *strategic planning*, *financial control* and *strategic control* styles. The strategic planning style is where the parent company is actively involved in decision making to establish a long-term strategy but the performance targets are set flexibly. Both the financial control and strategic control styles emphasize devolved responsibility and tight financial control, however while the former sets demanding financial targets how to achieve them is largely left to the business units or profit centres. The strategic control style is more active in the on-going review, challenge and monitoring of business level strategies.

Developing this further, the **Ashridge Portfolio Display** considers two dimensions – 'feel' (the degree to which the corporate parent understands the factors critical to the success of the SBU) and 'benefit' (the match between what the SBU needs and what the parent can provide) – in order to identify four ways in which the parent might benefit the SBU. *Heartland* businesses are those the parent understands and can add value to and should therefore form the core of the parent's strategy. *Ballast* businesses are well understood but need little assistance from the parent, so these should probably be either left alone or divested. *Value trap* businesses can seem to provide good opportunities for adding value but the parent will not have the necessary feel or understanding so may in fact do more harm than good. Finally, *alien* businesses will have no place in the portfolio because they will need help but the parent company will not have the requisite skills or understanding to add value. In all, the parent's own corporate strategy needs to drive the choice of businesses and the role the corporate parent should adopt (Collis et al., 2007).

Ashridge Portfolio Display: a framework for identifying the potential for a corporate parent to add value to strategic business units.

So how are judgements to be made about which strategic choice is best? Clearly there are many complex factors to take into account. We have already mentioned the need to establish how far the choice capitalizes on the firm's capabilities. But the strategy must also be able to take advantage of opportunities and be feasible. In other words, the strategy must be congruent with the firm's position and be able to be realized. In part this means that environmental threats, including those from hostile competitors, will not prevent the strategy from going ahead. But there are also issues of costs and resources. Here strategy draws on other disciplines so that financial indicators can be used to assess financial costs, returns and risks, marketing research can identify those options that may meet market demands, human resources can evaluate how far there are appropriate resources and skills to implement the strategy, and so on. Finally, there are important questions about how far stakeholders will support the choice and whether internal factors such as the organizational culture and ability to change will help or hinder. The material covered in Chapter 2 on organizational behaviour is particularly relevant here. Overall options need to be assessed in terms of their suitability, acceptability and feasibility – that is, how far they fit with the current circumstances, how acceptable the outcomes are to stakeholders, and how realistic they are given the firm's strengths.

Realizing strategic choices

How can strategic choices be realized? In broad terms most options are about trying to develop products and markets. In this respect Igor Ansoff's (1957) work identified a range of ways whereby organizations could develop their business. In effect, the choice is about offering either new or existing products in new or existing markets, as depicted in the now familiar **Product-Growth Matrix** (see Figure 9.9). Each quadrant encompasses a different strategy with an associated level of risk.

Market penetration is where existing products are offered to existing markets. Growth can be achieved if existing customers use more of your products, you can persuade non-users to use your product, or you can attract the customers of competitors – all of which potentially increases your market share. This strategy may also be used to consolidate an existing position. The key point is that the company does not depart from its current product-market strategy. Overall this is a fairly low risk option.

Market development is where existing products (or those with relatively minor adaptations) are offered to new markets. Ansoff gives the example of an airline

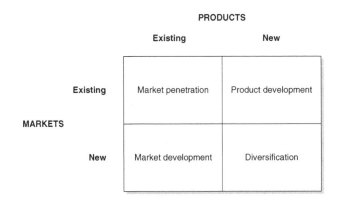

Figure 9.9 Product-Market Growth Matrix (based on Ansoff, 1957)

adapting passenger transporters to carry air cargo. Another example would be Lucozade, which was originally marketed for convalescents and sick children, but is now being marketed as a sports drink and targeted at the health and fitness market.

Product development is where new products are targeted at existing markets. For example Interflora, one of the best known flower delivery companies, now sells a range of other gifts to customers that can be delivered in the same way.

Diversification is where new products are targeted at new markets. So, for example, Marks and Spencer's flower delivery service was a new venture for one of the UK's best known retailers, originally mainly known for its clothing, and part of a wide-ranging portfolio of on-line businesses which includes wine and white goods as well as clothing. Indeed the company has operated a policy of diversification, moving into food retailing as well as home products and financial services. Diversification is generally regarded as the most risky strategic option as this means moving away from what is familiar and may require new facilities, skills, knowledge, and capabilities. The challenge for a parent company is to manage the variety inherent in a diversified range of offerings and to ensure that potential synergies are exploited to add value which will offset the costs associated with managing them.

Product-growth Matrix: a framework for understanding the ways a firm can develop its business through market penetration, market development, product development and diversification.

But how might the strategies of market penetration, market development, product development, and diversification be realized in practice? Essentially there are three ways: by internal development, by mergers and acquisitions, and by strategic alliances/joint ventures.

Internal development is where the firm uses its own resources, for example to develop a new product or launch a new marketing campaign. This might mean increasing research and development or marketing spend, or buying in new capabilities to move into new areas which will allow the firm to diversify.

Mergers and acquisitions are where the firm merges with or acquires another company in order to create new product streams or get into new markets. In globalized industries this is a significant way of gaining a presence outside the home market and an important strand of international business. It is often perceived as a high risk way of achieving growth since it is relatively permanent (and therefore costly to undo) and needs considerable effort to effect. Indeed much of the research on the success of mergers and acquisitions suggests that the financial rewards are often not realized and points to the importance of human factors, particularly the challenge of bringing together different organizational (and often national) cultures (see Chapter 2 on Organizational Behaviour).

Strategic alliances are relatively less permanent ways of building relationships with other organizations and include a wide range of activities. These cover licensing agreements, joint ventures, franchising, subcontracting, and various ad hoc arrangements with others. As we have seen, the focus on capabilities means that even competitor organizations can be considered as potential partners, as well as other organizations such as external research and development (R&D) agencies, universities or government departments. The discussion of network organizations in Chapter 2 is relevant here.

International strategies

An obvious way of developing the business is to consider becoming more international by operating in different geographical markets. This touches on the expansive field of international business and while there is not space enough here to look at this in detail the salient areas are touched on below.

We have already introduced Porter's Diamond which offers an explanation of how home-based factors provide a competitive edge to particular industries at an international level. But what drives a firm to operate internationally? Essentially, there are four groups of factors. These comprise *government policies* (either inhibiting growth domestically and so driving a firm to develop elsewhere, or attracting a firm because of favourable policies such as tax advantages or various forms of economic support); *market factors* (having an international customer base); *cost drivers* (including economies of scale, having access to technology or labour); and *competitive factors* (the existence of globalized competitors or having activities in a number of countries that require a more coordinated and global strategy).

Companies operating in international markets have two key and seemingly contradictory decisions: how to get sufficient economies of scale to reduce costs (most easily achieved through standardization and a universal offering) and how far to be responsive to local requirements (which may require differentiation). There are therefore different ways of being 'international'. A company can either follow a *global standardization* strategy by emphasizing the cost reduction and minimizing local differentiation, a *localization* strategy which focusses on catering to local tastes and demands (meaning cost reduction is not so easy), or an *international* strategy which means offering a universal product but without reducing the cost structure. Clearly an international strategy works best where companies can offer a product that serves universal needs but the competition is not intense. As Jones and Hill (2009) point out, for many years Xerox found itself in this fortunate position. The usual method of development is to centre some production or R&D functions at home while establishing manufacturing and marketing activities in other countries or regions. However many writers now argue that a *transnational* strategy, which tries to combine both low cost and differentiation while fostering the flow of skills between subsidiaries, is increasingly necessary in competitive globalized industries (Jones and Hill, 2009).

Finally, how do firms enter new international markets? There are a number of ways. One of the simplest is simply to *export* goods, another is to offer *licences* to other companies to manufacture products elsewhere, while a third way is to offer *franchises* which are a development of the licence agreement whereby another company not only produces the product but also incorporates other agreed aspects such as working methods. McDonalds is one of the best know organizations that operates this way. Similar to other methods of development the list also includes *joint ventures* and wholly-owned *subsidiaries*/foreign direct investment.

Overall, whether a company operates on a truly international basis or whether it operates in a mainly domestic market, it will do so in an increasingly globalized world. As Thomas Friedman (2005) eloquently describes, developments in technology, changes in work patterns, vastly increased communication and information availability, and global supply chains have all led to an environment in which our products, services and customers are connected by complex relationships that span the globe. Thus many firms will have to consider an international dimension within their strategic plans.

Managing strategic change

Even when a course of action has been decided (i.e. a choice has been made and ways of achieving it recognized) a key issue remains of how to manage its implementation. As noted in Chapter 2, it is one thing to decide on a strategy but something else to put it into effect. As mentioned earlier, this is really about managing organizational change. It is therefore recommended that you have a look at the sections on Organizational Culture and Managing Change and Decision Making and Power in Chapter 2.

The McKinsey 7S Model is often used to depict those internal elements which need to be considered to manage a company in an holistic way. The hard elements are the Strategy (long-term plans); the Structure of the organization (the way the firm is organized); and the Systems (processes and routines). The soft elements are the Skills (capabilities); Staff (number and types of personnel); and Style (the corporate culture and managerial approach). These elements shape and are shaped by the Shared Values of the firm. This model alerts us to the fact that strategy needs to connect to these different areas and in turn be influenced by them. While the model seems straightforward these factors are complex and herein lies the challenge of trying to effect strategic change.

But making strategy happen is not just about internal factors. The degree to which the various stakeholders will go along with what has been proposed is a critical question and companies are often advised to carry out a stakeholder analysis to ascertain who will support the strategy and who will need persuading. Stakeholders can encompass a wide range of interests including, for example, shareholders, customers, suppliers, and competitors, as well as employees.

Finally, there is the link between strategy and performance. Assessing the overall performance of the firm is not straightforward since there are many possible measures. Models such as the Balanced Score Card will attempt to show how different perspectives – financial and customer, internal business processes, and the learning and growth of the firm – can be combined to give a more comprehensive picture of a firm's performance. However the challenge here is both to identify meaningful indicators of performance and also to disentangle complex cause-effect relationships.

Critiques of Traditional Approaches and Some Alternative Perspectives

There are some significant criticisms that can be levied at the approaches outlined above. We firstly summarize some of these, before looking at some alternative ways of understanding the realm of strategic management.

Critiques

Emphasis on large corporates
While traditional strategic management appears to be manifested in frameworks and theories that are assumed to be universally prescriptive in nature, much of the work seems rooted in 'big business'. Small and medium-sized enterprises, public sector and third sector organizations (which together actually make up the bulk of most economies) seem relatively neglected, so much so that separate literatures have grown up to try and remedy this because it is recognized that there are important differences between these organizations and large corporates. Yet in the main, the mainstream strategic management literature – apart from the odd case study or two in some textbooks – tends to assume its central tenets are central for all kinds of organizations.

Emphasis on planned, deliberate policy
Traditional views tend to see strategy as an intended, deliberate, activity that is the product of rational thought, analysis, and careful calculation. But the danger of having deliberate plans is that they can quickly cease to be appropriate in a fast-changing world, acting as a straitjacket rather than facilitating success. In these circumstances more emergent, or incremental approaches (see Chapter 2) characterized by good learning and flexibility may be better (see the next point).

Formulation, then implementation
Traditional views give the impression that strategy is decided and then actioned, and indeed the organization of the material above has been chosen to reflect this. This is problematic for two reasons. Firstly it may not be true. Incremental approaches show how formulation and implementation are woven together. Strategy may follow an iterative rather than a linear process, with strategic decisions being reformulated as the implementation progresses. The other reason is that this division between strategy formulation and execution separates out the deciding from the doing. Akin to Taylor's distinction between mental and manual labour (Chapter 2) this appears to exclude those who are closest to what is really going on from strategy making.

Emphasis on the Top Management Team (TMT)
Linked to the above, there seems to be an assumption that strategy is the province of those at the top of the organization. They are the architects of the plan. But this

neglects the important role that others may have not only in formulation but also in translating and shaping strategy as it is realized.

Basis in logic and rationality

While we do not want to suggest that strategists are illogical and irrational (though of course it is a possibility!), traditional views tend to give the impression that strategy is underpinned by infallible logic and reasoned choice. This neglects the bounded rationality (Chapter 2) within which most managers have to operate because situations are usually too complex to fully understand all the possibilities and permutations of different choices. It also neglects the role that interpretation plays in strategy. For example, the firm's environment is not 'given' but needs to be understood and made sense of, which leaves room for a variety of translations and (re)constructions. Traditional approaches to strategy tend to underplay the individual and socially constructed nature of our world and the complex human processes inherent in strategic processes.

Calculation rather than creativity

The emphasis in traditional perspectives has tended towards rational analysis, often grounded in calculation. Comprehensive information gathering, working logically through models and the detailed analysis of numerical (especially financial) data are the hallmarks of this approach. However this neglects the creative, serendipitous, and intuitive side of human behaviour which may have an important part to play in what goes on in organizations. An alternative view would see strategy as a craft rather than a science.

The fallacy of control

Traditional views seem to hold the implicit assumption that managers need to be in control; that their job is to understand the environment, the firm's capabilities and its overall position in the competitive arena, and then act to set a future course and steer the organization towards it. But how much control do managers actually have? Only very large firms can exert some control over the environment and most firms struggle to manage change, implying that controlling even the internal factors is not straightforward. Indeed in an organizational ecology perspective the firm doesn't so much choose a strategy, but is itself 'chosen' by a process akin to evolutionary selection. In this view, survival depends on occupying a suitable competitive niche – if a firm finds one it thrives, if it does not, it dies.

So is strategy primarily about proactivity and decisiveness, or simply about reacting as quickly as possible while maintaining the illusion that everything is under control; is strategy as much about managing perceptions as managing the firm?

A lack of attention to ethical and moral concerns

To some degree the overriding concerns of competitive behaviour, with its emphasis on beating the competition, being market leaders, winning competitive battles and so on appears to pay little attention to underlying ethical and moral considerations. While corporate social responsibility and ecological issues now feature prominently on corporate agendas a cynical view would see this as simply capitalizing on customer concerns rather than representing a sincerely held moral position. The underlying message of strategy seems to be nasty, brutish and short term, so that corporate scandals such as the Enron accounting irregularities, or controversial activities such as Royal Dutch/Shell's operations in Nigeria, or indeed the global collapse of the banking sector in 2009 are inevitable and not one-off aberrations. It could be argued that the strategy field pays too little attention to such malignant features of the economic system.

The neglect of power

A view of strategy epitomized by objective calculation overseen and sanctioned by the top of the managerial hierarchy seriously neglects the subtle and far-reaching effects of power in shaping strategic processes. The influence of powerful groups can shape the interpretation of a firm's position and strategic possibilities. Since power is not fixed but may move between a variety of changing coalitions the prevailing view of the firm's current and future strategy is never definitive but open to reinterpretation and revision. This is developed below.

An a-contextual view

As we have noted elsewhere in this book, so much of management theory comes from the West. This is no less true of strategy, where so many prominent researchers and consultants come from North American and European cultural traditions. There is therefore an inherent cultural bias. No wonder then that the rise of Japan and the so-called Asian tigers (Hong Kong, Singapore, Taiwan and South Korea) and the emerging economies of Indonesia, Thailand and Malaysia have given Western commentators such pause for thought. For many it seemed that there were some crucial differences in Asian business. These include the expectation that all employees, even those at the lower levels of the hierarchy, will be involved in and committed to developing the company's future, a strong work ethic, open communication, a willingness to take a more holistic view of the issues taking into account 'soft' as well as 'hard' data and personal experience, and an approach which emphasizes learning and adapting in response to changing circumstances (see the sections on national cultures and Japanization in Chapter 2). Of course a highly skilled workforce and tight control over socialization and production processes are also key features, but even so the point is that different cultural traditions will influence strategic thinking (Nonaka and Zhu, 2011) – something that traditional views of strategy tend to underplay or ignore.

Diachronic and synchronistic modes of thinking

This last point is more subtle. It can be argued that orthodox strategic management tends to offer a view of the world that is grounded in linear, sequentially ordered processes, and where particular causal relationships lead to specific outcomes. I am calling this diachronic thinking, and this can be contrasted with views which see the world as less clearly defined, where multiple, on-going and fluid connections (of people, organizations, events and so on) give rise to patterns that form and re-form under conditions of flux and uncertainty. Such 'patterns' are open to various concurrent interpretations as people make sense of and respond to what they perceive. I call this second view 'synchronistic' to refer to the dynamic, complex array of parallel activities that influence strategic processes and which sees 'outcomes' as being causally ambiguous. The first view seeks to 'get a fix' on the world (or the environment, or the firm's position in that environment) while the second is sceptical of this, considering that any such 'fix' is inevitably transitory, a momentary island of stability in an ocean of transience and impermanence. The diachronic mode emphasizes order and control, the synchronistic mode emphasizes the continual re-ordering which occurs through the temporary alignment of people and events.

Fixed categorizations versus dynamic classifications

The final criticism leads on from the last point. Orthodox approaches to strategy are littered with frameworks and models which box different elements in order to categorize them. The ubiquitous SWOT matrix is but one example. This seems typical of Western thought in its eagerness to separate and divide, to create distinctions and dualisms. This emphasis on 'either/or', while highlighting contrasts, has two dangers. It may oversimplify in its attempt to fit all phenomena into a box, ignoring similarities and over-emphasizing differences and, perhaps more worryingly, it suggests a stability in strategic positions, product characteristics, market opportunities, or whatever, that may be misplaced. Other cultural traditions, and philosophical positions (for example, see the section on postmodernism in Chapter 1), mistrust rigid either/or demarcations, instead preferring to acknowledge the indeterminate nature of much of life and being comfortable with looser, more dynamic associations of factors.

These criticisms prepare the ground for alternative perspectives. To begin with, it can be seen that even the basic definition of strategy as a long-term *plan* means that other ways of conceiving strategy are neglected. As Mintzberg and his colleagues (2009) argue, it can also mean a *pattern* – that is, a stream of consistent behaviour over time (the difference is the plan is a deliberate or intended strategy and the pattern is strategy that is actually realized). Strategy can be a *position* – as the firm seeks to find a niche in which it can best leverage its particular capabilities (compare the positioning approach, above) – but it can also be a *perspective*; that is the '... organization's fundamental way of doing things' (Mintzberg et al., 2009: 13). Finally strategy can be a *ploy* – a way of outwitting the competition.

Alternative perspectives

There are a number of perspectives that might be considered to vary from traditional approaches. We will deal with four here with some offering a greater contrast than others. The **knowledge-based view** could be considered an extension and development of the resource-based approach; the **complexity view** stresses the complex and non-linear relationship between strategy and action; the **power perspective** takes us further away by emphasizing the political nature of strategy; and the **practice perspective** centres on the processes involved in creating strategy, particularly focussing on human activity.

The knowledge-based perspective

As suggested above in some ways this builds on the resource-based view in that one of the key assets or resources available to the firm is its knowledge base. A distinction is made between explicit and tacit knowledge. Explicit knowledge is formalized, known, and can be more readily communicated and shared. It can also be codified, that is put into a form that can be disseminated. A manual, a textbook, and an expert system are all examples of codified knowledge. Tacit knowledge is uncodified. It is based on personal beliefs, hunches, and intuitions which are internalized and often subconscious so that people do not always fully recognize what they know or how they do things.

The use of technological systems that try to capture knowledge in the organization is increasingly prevalent and the whole area of information management has become commonplace, with specialist occupational roles growing up to carry out this function. The challenge is to transform tacit knowledge into explicit knowledge and then capture and bring together both individual and organizational knowledge (Kogut and Zander, 1992; Nonaka and Takeuchi, 1995) to create new knowledge. This links to the idea of the learning organization and knowledge management (see the discussion on learning and knowledge in Chapter 2).

Thus knowledge can contribute to a firm's dynamic capabilities. But this depends on the degree to which knowledge is transferable, capable of being aggregated (that is, brought together with existing knowledge), and able to be appropriated by the firm. In this view, the role of the firm is to coordinate and integrate the specialist knowledge of its members (Grant, 1996). However knowledge can be also gained from external sources. The importance of external ties (Eisenhardt and Santos, 2006) is important as these boundary-spanning collaborations (for example with scientific communities or other research agencies) can contribute to the development of information-rich networks that can provide a spur to innovation and the acquisition of new knowledge. It can also be a rationale for mergers and acquisitions to bring knowledge resources within the firm.

The knowledge-based perspective: a view that stresses the role of knowledge and learning in creating organizational capabilities and competitive advantage.

Yet there are fundamental questions unanswered by this approach. The conceptualization and measurement of knowledge are not agreed and the way in which knowledge is socially constructed tends to be underplayed. Furthermore, the link between knowledge and firm performance is unclear. Research on this crucial relationship is relatively sparse and those studies that do exist use a variety of performance outcomes (for example, survival, growth and market segment dominance and profit, see Eisenhardt and Santos, 2006: 149).

In summary, it can be argued that this perspective is really an extension of the resource-based view. While it has some potential, the assumption that knowledge is *the* key resource can be questioned and fundamental issues concerning the definition, measurement and, importantly, the ownership of knowledge pose significant problems and raise serious questions.

The complexity perspective

As noted in Chapter 2, drawing on complexity science, writers in the field of Organization Studies have depicted the organization as a complex system and have therefore questioned the degree to which managers can actually control what goes on. The implications for strategic management are profound for if there is little possibility of control the notion of planning a long-term strategy is thrown into question. The basic tenets are that since organizations comprise a large number of elements that interact dynamically and non-linearly within the environment this means that small changes can be amplified and so produce large effects which are not always possible to anticipate (Maguire et al., 2006). Fluctuations are an endemic part of the process and while this does not mean a state of permanent disorder it does mean that there is temporary disorganization or 'order arising from (seeming) chaos'. For managers, while it may be possible to anticipate some changes and learn over time about how they are wrought this view poses problems for traditional perspectives where the accent is on mapping out a defined course of action and implementing it.

The complexity perspective: a view that emphasizes the non-linear nature of much of organizational action and the unpredictable and interconnected human activity from which strategic processes may emerge.

Ralph Stacey is one writer who has used these ideas as a basis for work in the field of strategic management (Stacey, 2007). At the heart of his perspective is an emphasis on the dynamic patterns of interactions and interconnections within and between evolving populations of organizations and groups of individuals. In looking at strategy Stacey is wary of the view that sees it as a linear process of choice and action – cause and effect – instead emphasizing circular or mutual causality. So, for example, a manufacturer doesn't simply make what the customer wants, customer demands are shaped by what is already offered. Thus customer demand influences what is offered but is itself influenced by the offering. Stacey is particularly interested in the interaction between people created by 'iterated processes of communication and power relating' (2007: 410). Strategy evolves through these 'complex responsive processes' as the everyday local interactions between people form patterns or themes that organize the experience of being together (Stacey, 2007: 358). Managers can have intentions about what to do, they can identify leverage points, design structures and choose people to carry out tasks and so on, but these actions and decisions arise from the interactions executives have both with each other and with other people, and managers cannot design the responses that will occur. Strategy emerges from these on-going, complex, iterative interactions.

Overall, while in the long term there is usually quite a lot of stability in the system, in the short term there is much flux and transformation which can produce unexpected, even counterintuitive, results. While some elements can be managed (Maguire et al., 2006) the overall implication is that attempts to exert tight controls over the strategic direction of a firm are likely to be thwarted and may betray a failure to understand how complex systems really work.

The power perspective

As noted above traditional views of strategy emphasize a rational calculative approach to strategy formation which is primarily in the hands of senior management. Traditional views thus see strategy as being a politically neutral tool to achieve effective organizational performance (Levy et al., 2003). But Clegg et al. (2011) see strategy as fundamentally a political process, and Mintzberg and his colleagues (Mintzberg et al., 2009) identify power as a key ingredient in understanding what goes on. At the macro level firms can use power illegitimately to gain dominance in the marketplace through cartels and other clandestine moves to undermine competition. But going inside the organization, while orthodox views acknowledge the importance of stakeholders, they neglect the more subtle ways in which strategy may be shaped by political behaviour amongst elites and also the way in which those lower down in the organization may influence the way strategy is enacted. Critical management perspectives (see Chapter 1) give prominence to the role that power and politics play in the creation of strategies within the firm and in fashioning relationships between the firm and external parties. In particular a **power perspective** focusses on understanding and revealing 'the taken-for-granted assumptions and ideologies embedded in the discourse and practice of strategy' (Levy et al., 2003: 105).

Thus the processes by which strategy is negotiated and made manifest are of great interest as this can reveal the often covert practices by which particular actions emerge and are legitimated. Critical theorists (see Chapter 1) would be concerned with how ruling elites construct the strategic agenda, while poststructuralist interpretations would give account to the way power ebbs and flows between individuals or loosely formed and transient coalitions of interests. The power perspective, rather than seeing strategy as the quasi-scientific pursuit of competitive advantage, instead underlines the way in which different groups gain hegemonic dominance over strategic action.

The power perspective: a view that highlights the importance of power and political behaviour in shaping the creation and interpretation of strategic actions and events.

The 'practice' perspective

This more recent perspective began with an interest in the strategic practices that occur at the micro level of organizations. The quote above from Johnson and his colleagues (2003) about the cul-de-sac of current thinking in strategic management was the call to arms for a new branch of scholarship in the field which has gathered pace in the 2000s. The 'strategy as practice' approach or simply the **'practice perspective'** is still emerging and is therefore not as yet a fully developed and coherent body of work. Nonetheless its central arguments offer other ways of conceptualizing strategy, and seek to pose fundamental questions for more orthodox perspectives. One definition of 'strategy as practice' is given in a book of the same name where it states that it is 'a concern with what people do in relation to strategy and how this is influenced by and influences their organizational and institutional context' (Johnson et al., 2007: 7). While not the most enlightening of definitions perhaps most writers in the field emphasize their interest in 'strategizing', a word that is preferred because the verb form underlines the action-based nature of what is of interest.

The practice approach is a reaction to the lack of attention to the human side of strategy which is seen to mark out orthodox perspectives. Traditional approaches appear wedded to notions of strategy as being embedded in formal structures and systems (for example, plans and planning) where strategic choices are developed through abstract models and frameworks, almost devoid of human agency. Indeed even the resource-based and dynamic capabilities perspectives, which acknowledge the crucial role of human assets in creating superior performance, do not shed light on how this is realized through human action.

In contrast, the practice perspective sees strategies and strategizing as human activity, recognizing and giving weight to the messy interpersonal relations and political processes (Johnson et al., 2007: 5) that characterize these processes. In this way of thinking, strategy is not something a firm has, but what people in the firm do.

The practice perspective: a view that focusses on what people do when they engage in strategizing behaviour and the ways in which this shapes and is shaped by organizational and institutional factors.

As noted, the initial focus of this perspective has tended to be on the micro activities, the day-to-day routines and practices that people engage with in relation to strategy, as well as events such as strategy away-days and board meetings (see Hodgkinson et al., 2006). The broad intention is to understand strategy better by getting closer to what strategic actors in the organization actually do, engaging with practitioners rather than theorizing at a distance. For example, Jarzabkowski and Wilson (2002) explored the detailed activities of university committees in shaping strategic change and Maitlis and Lawrence (2003) looked at a (failed) attempt to introduce strategic practices in an orchestra.

However, it has been acknowledged that while this perspective opens up a potentially rich seam of research, there is a danger that paying too much attention to micro activities may lead to strategic irrelevance and a focus on decontextualized minutiae (Johnson et al., 2007: 26) – which does not take us very far forward. Thus writers in the field have argued that the practice perspective must take into account the societal and organizational context in which strategizing occurs. Whittington thus delineates three themes for research: society, practices (praxis) and actors. Taking each of these in turn, the practice perspective draws on social theory (referencing authors such as Foucault and Bourdieu; see Chapter 1) to understand the '...shared understandings, cultural rules, languages and procedures (..) that guide and enable human activity' (Whittington, 2006: 614). In this respect, it owes much to postmodern strands of thinking (see Chapter 1, and also Cummings [2002] which is an attempt to write a strategy text which is sympathetic to post-modern ideas). Secondly, as noted above, the perspective emphasizes the actual activity (or praxis) that strategy practitioners engage in, including the formal and informal meetings and routines, consulting interventions and more mundane conversations (indeed, there is a strong interest in the language and discourses used in strategy) that take place both at the top and lower down in organizations. Finally, 'strategy as practice' is concerned with the strategists themselves, all those involved in strategy development and implementation both inside and outside the organization, with the latter including consultants, management 'gurus' and so on. While this delineation is helpful, Whittington underlines the fact that they should not be seen in isolation. It is the interrelationship between these three themes – the linking together of macro and micro phenomena – that is of crucial importance. As an overview Jarzabkowski and Spee's (2009) review of existing research endeavours to show just what has been attempted in different areas of the field.

The strategy-as-practice agenda seems very broad and can appear to encompass everyone and everything. So what has been achieved so far? As indicated, the field is new and those looking for a well-defined set of seminal 'results' will be disappointed. Indeed it is perhaps misguided to look for generic, law-like 'findings' in this way. What is emerging is a series of rich and detailed studies which are beginning to show the subtleties of strategic processes in specific contexts, alerting us to the way in which social, organizational, and human practices interact to shape strategy. But while this may be interesting and revealing, the question of what this means for firm performance is uncertain, appearing to suggest that the practice perspective is not engaging with mainstream strategy concerns. This lack of attention to outcomes is recognized (Jarzabkowski and Spee, 2009: 87) but with the caution that we need to understand whose outcomes are being investigated (for example individual, group, 'organizational' or institutional) and how such performance criteria are constructed. Clearly this is 'work-in-progress' and time will show to what extent this perspective can offer a coherent alternative to mainstream theory.

Summary

This chapter began by looking at a range of material associated with traditional, orthodox ideas in the field of strategic management. It has covered work by academics and consultants keen to understand the role of the firm in its competitive environment, to make sense of the threats and opportunities that may exist, and to develop strategies to counter or take advantage of them. It has also provided an overview of some of the many tools and techniques for analysis and some of the strategic actions that a firm can pursue. While current thinking may suggest that a firm's dynamic capabilities lie at the root of competitive advantage and provide a rationale for strategic manoeuvres such as joint ventures or mergers and acquisitions, it is still not entirely clear how such capabilities can be created and leveraged. While work to understand this better continues, other writers have grown dissatisfied with these preoccupations. In particular, alternative views suggest that we need a deeper appreciation of how strategizing takes place in organizational settings and what organizational actors do when they engage in these practices.

Questions for reflection

1 What tools exist for analyzing a firm's competitive environment and what are their strengths and limitations?
2 What are dynamic capabilities and how can a firm develop these?
3 What part may knowledge play in developing a competitive advantage?
4 How can power and political behaviour shape strategy?
5 How far do alternative views of strategy add to our understanding of strategic processes and outcomes?

Further reading

Clegg, S., Carter, C., Kornberger, M. and Schweitzer, J. (2011) *Strategy: Theory and Practice*. London: Sage.

International Journal of Management Reviews (2009) 11 (1). Special Issue on the Frontiers of Strategic Management Research.

Mintzberg, H., Ahlstrand, B. and Lampel, J. (2008) *Strategy Safari: A Guided Tour through the Wilds of Strategic Management*. London: Prentice-Hall.

Whittington, R. (2001) *What is Strategy and Does it Matter?* (2nd edn). London: Thomson.

Websites

Strategy-as-practice website: http://www.sap-in.org
www.strategytube.net

References

Andrews, K.R. (1971) *The Concept of Corporate Strategy*. Holmewood, IL: Irwin.

Ansoff, H.I. (1957) 'Strategies for diversification.' *Harvard Business Review*, 35 (5): 113–124.

Ansoff, H.I. (1965) *Corporate Strategy*. New York: McGraw-Hill.

Barney, J. (1991) 'Firm resources and sustained competitive advantage.' *Journal of Management*, 17 (1): 99–120.

Brandenburger, A.M. and Nalebuff, B.J. (1998) *Co-opetition*. New York: Currency.

Chandler, A.R. (1962) *Strategy and Structure: Chapters in the History of the Industrial Enterprise*. Cambridge, MA: Harvard University Press.

Clegg, S., Carter, C., Kornberger, M. and Schweitzer, J. (2011) *Strategy: Theory and Practice*. London: Sage.

Collis, D., Young, D. and Goold, M. (2007) 'The size, structure, and performance of corporate headquarters.' *Strategic Management Journal*, 28: 383–405.

Coyne, K.P. and Subramaniam, S. (2000) 'Bringing discipline to strategy.' *The McKinsey Quarterly* (Anthology on Strategy), June: 61–70.

Cummings, S. (2002) *ReCreating Strategy*. London: Sage.

Eisenhardt, K.M. and Santos, F.M. (2006) 'Knowledge-based view: a new theory of strategy?' in A. Pettigrew, H. Thomas and R. Whittington (eds), *Handbook of Strategy and Management*. London: Sage. pp. 139–164.

Faulkner, D. and Bowman, C. (1995) *The Essence of Competitive Strategy*. London: Prentice-Hall.

Friedman, T. (2005) *The World is Flat*. London: Penguin.

Goold, M., Campbell, A. and Luchs, K. (1993a) 'Strategies and styles revisited: "strategic planning and financial control".' *Long Range Planning*, 26 (5): 49–60.

Goold, M., Campbell, A. and Luchs, K. (1993b) 'Strategies and styles revisited: "strategic control" – is it tenable?'. *Long Range Planning*, 26 (6): 54–61.

Grant, R.M. (1996) 'Toward a knowledge-based theory of the firm.' *Strategic Management Journal*, 17 (Winter Special): 109–122.

(Continued)

(Continued)

Hambrick, D.C. and Fredrickson, J.W. (2001) 'Are you sure you have a strategy?' *Academy of Management Executive*, 15 (4): 48–59.

Hamel, G., Doz, Y.L. and Prahalad, C.K. (1989) 'Collaborate with your competitors and win.' *Harvard Business Review* (January-February): 133–139.

Henderson, B.D. (1979) *Henderson on Corporate Strategy.* Cambridge, MA: Abt Books.

Hodgkinson, G., Whittington, R., Johnson, G. and Schwarz, M. (2006) 'The role of strategy workshops in strategy development processes: formality, communication, co-ordination and inclusion.' *Long Range Planning*, 39 (5): 479–496.

Jarzabkowski, P. and Spee, A.P. (2009) 'Strategy-as-practice: a review and future directions for the field.' *International Journal of Management Reviews*, 11 (1): 69–95.

Jarzabkowski, P. and Wilson, D.C. (2002) 'Top teams and strategy in a UK university.' *Journal of Management Studies*, 39: 355–387.

Jeremy, D.J. (2006) 'Business history and strategy.' In A. Pettigrew, H. Thomas and R. Whittington (eds), *Handbook of Strategy and Management.* London: Sage. pp. 436–460.

Johnson, G., Melin, L. and Whittington, R. (2003) 'Micro strategy and strategizing: towards an activity-based view.' *Journal of Management Studies*, 40 (1): 3–22.

Johnson, G., Langley, A., Melin, L. and Whittington, R. (2007) *Strategy as Practice: Research Directions and Resources.* Cambridge, MA: Cambridge University Press.

Johnson, G., Scholes, K. and Whittington, R. (2008) *Exploring Corporate Strategy.* London: Prentice-Hall.

Jones, G.R. and Hill, C.W.L. (2009) *Strategic Management Essentials.* Canada: South-Western Cengage Learning.

Kogut, B. and Zander, U. (1992) 'Knowledge of the firm, combinative capabilities and the replication of technology.' *Organizational Science*, 3 (3): 383–397.

Levy, D.L., Alvesson, M. and Willmott, H. (eds) (2003) 'Critical approaches to strategic management' in *Studying Management Critically.* London: Sage. pp. 92–110.

Maguire, S., McKelvey, B., Mirabeau, L. and Öztas, N. (2006) 'Complexity science and organization studies.' In S. Clegg, C. Hardy, T.B. Lawrence and W.R. Nord (eds), *The Sage Handbook of Organization Studies.* London: Sage.

Maitlis, S. and Lawrence, T.B. (2003) 'Orchestral manoeuvres in the dark: understanding failure in organizational strategizing.' *Journal of Management Studies*, 40 (1): 109–140.

Mintzberg, H., Ahlstrand, B. and Lampel, J. (2009) *Strategy Safari: Your Complete Guided Tour through the Wilds of Strategic Management* (2nd edn). London: Prentice-Hall.

Nohria, N. and Garcia-Pont, C. (1991) 'Global strategic linkages and industry structure.' *Strategic Management Journal*, 12: 105–124 .

Nonaka, I. and Takeuchi, H. (1995) *The Knowledge-Creating Company.* New York: Oxford University Press.

Nonaka, I. and Zhu, Z. (2011) *Pragmatic Strategy: Eastern Wisdom, Global Success.* Cambridge: Cambridge University Press.

Penrose, E. (1959) *The Theory of the Growth of the Firm.* London: Wiley.

Penrose, E. (2009) *The Theory of the Growth of the Firm* (with an introduction by C. Pitelis). Oxford: Oxford University Press.

(Continued)

(Continued)

Porter, M.E. (1980) *Competitive Strategy: Techniques for Analysing Industries and Competitors.* New York: Free.

Porter, M.E. (1985) *Competitive Advantage: Creating and Sustaining Superior Performance.* New York: Free.

Porter, M.E. (1990) *The Competitive Advantage of Nations.* New York: Free.

Porter, M.E. (2008) 'The Five Competitive Forces that Shape Strategy', *Harvard Business Review*, 86(1): 78–93.

Prahalad, C.K. and Hamel, G. (1990) 'The core competence of the corporation.' *Harvard Business Review*, 68 (3), May-June: 79–91.

Sirmon, D.G., Hitt, M.A. and Ireland, D.R. (2007) 'Managing firm resources in dynamic environments to create value: looking inside the black box.' *Academy of Management Review*, 32 (1): 273–292.

Stacey, R. (2007) *Strategic Management and Organizational Dynamics: The Challenge of Complexity.* Essex: Pearson.

Teece, D.J. (2007) 'Explicating dynamic capabilities: the nature and microfoundations of (sustainable) enterprise performance.' *Strategic Management Journal*, 28: 1319–1350.

Teece, D.J., Pisano, G. and Shuen, A. (1997) 'Dynamic capabilities and strategic management.' *Strategic Management Journal*, 18 (7): 509–533.

Wernerfelt, B. (1984) 'The resource-based view of the firm.' *Strategic Management Journal*, 5 (2): 171–180.

Whittington, R. (2001) *What is Strategy and Does it Matter?* (2nd edn). London: Thomson.

Whittington, R. (2006) 'Completing the practice turn in strategy research.' *Organization Studies*, 27 (5): 613–634.

10 Research Approaches

Chapter overview

Key concepts

Concepts; Construct; Deductive approach; Epistemology; Generalization; Inductive approach; Methodology; Methods; Ontology; Paradigm; Reliability; Theory; Validity

Most MBA programmes will require students to undertake some original research. While you may have had to do this to analyze a case study or to write an essay at various times during the course, the most comprehensive requirement for research comes when, as in many programmes, you have to produce a final project or dissertation. This often constitutes a significant part of the whole MBA, sometimes up to one third of the total marks or credits.

Even if you do not have to carry out a project of this kind, understanding the way in which research contributes to the development of knowledge and how to evaluate the research of others is an important skill for both MBA students and managers alike. This chapter will look at how to design a research project, different methodological approaches, particular methods of data collection, and hints and tips for writing a dissertation.

In terms of critical approaches to research it should be noted from the outset that the field of business and management has been dominated by a relatively narrow methodological stance. However, this has attracted much criticism and debate and since the 1980s there has been increasing interest in a much wider variety of research orientations and methods. More will be said about this in the section on methodologies below.

What is a Dissertation?

Before we get into the details of how to conduct research we need a brief discussion of terminology. Some MBA programmes require a dissertation, others a project, others a business report. There are some differences between these and it will be important for you to read carefully through the guidelines to see exactly what your programme requires you to do.

A dissertation is usually understood as a piece of work which focusses on the detailed examination of a business or management issue or problem. Carrying out a dissertation requires reviewing existing knowledge to identify what is already known; formulating some research questions to address the issue or problem which is of interest; collecting and analyzing data to answer the questions; and arriving at some findings which then allow conclusions to be drawn for theory and practice.

However, sometimes a project will mean something more like a business report. If the business report requires you to carry out some original research it will cover some of the same territory. The key differences will come in the emphasis and format. While it will still need to be rigorous and thorough, with careful attention being paid to what data (evidence) are gathered and the strengths and limitations of the material collected and used (just as in a dissertation), the theoretical underpinning may not be given such prominence, and the language and style of the document may be more direct. Overall, the emphasis is likely to require more about the implications of the work and recommendations for practice and the document will be presented in a style that is suitable for a business audience.

It should also be mentioned that many programmes permit students to undertake what is sometimes called a 'library-based' piece of work. Essentially this means that students are not expected to carry out 'primary research' (fieldwork) but can use secondary sources gleaned from prior studies, existing information, and research by others. This kind of exercise will usually require students to draw together a range of material in the context of a particular business or management issue. It will necessitate synthesis, critique and some analysis, but not the collection of primary data.

This chapter is primarily written for those students who are doing a dissertation which embodies some kind of fieldwork; that is, the collecting of some primary data through the use of research. However, in this chapter the terms 'dissertation' and 'project' will be used interchangeably and the information presented here will be very relevant to all types of MBA assessment that have a research element.

The purpose of a dissertation

Why have a dissertation as part of the MBA, what does it hope to achieve? There are a number of ways in which the dissertation adds to the programme and helps to develop key, transferable skills:

- It allows a student to investigate a specific issue or area of current business or management which is of particular (personal) interest or importance in greater depth than is possible during the rest of the programme
- It is about the *application* of knowledge to practice, so it takes learning from the classroom and applies it directly to real issues in specific organizational and business contexts
- It therefore facilitates an understanding of the relevance of theory to practice
- It often brings together different areas of the programme and so helps to integrate knowledge from across the MBA
- It allows the student to develop analytical and research skills
- It develops skills in self-organization and motivation as the dissertation requires students to manage their time and activities within a strict deadline

Overall, the development of in-depth knowledge and new skills (and potentially networks) may contribute to long-term career advancement. Depending on the nature of the topic chosen it may also help students to change careers, for example moving from a specialist functional area to a more strategic position in general management. Of course, it may also give students the knowledge, skills, and perhaps confidence, to develop their own business.

What it is not

A dissertation is not a PhD. Most obviously, it is not of the same scope or size as a PhD. Whereas a PhD usually takes a minimum of three years (full time), and often much longer, the MBA student will usually only have around three months (and around six months or so for a part-time student) so the research must be designed accordingly. A PhD can be in the order of 100,000 words while an MBA dissertation is more likely to be somewhere in the region of 15,000 words, though some are longer and some shorter. Another crucial difference is that the criteria for a PhD will often include the need to make 'an original contribution to knowledge' and to produce something 'of publishable worth'. In other words there are expectations that PhDs should make a significant contribution to what we know and that the research is of a quality that would be deemed fit for publication in a journal or some other means of dissemination which scholars in the field would recognize as being reputable. While some MBA students do produce excellent work and even publish their findings, this is not usually an expectation here or a requirement to pass.

But neither is the MBA simply another assignment, more-or-less the same as other assessed pieces of work but a bit longer. Nor is it simply a collection of individual assignments put together and called a dissertation. It needs to be an integrated, coherent piece of work, with a strong focus and argument running through it. There are different elements, and these will be discussed below, but these must be woven together so that they read as a whole to present a clear, lucid narrative.

Finally what your dissertation is not is a perfect piece of research. There is probably no such thing in that, with hindsight, most research could be done differently and probably better. You will need to pay careful attention to the advice below to produce the most robust and persuasive document that you can, but even then it will not be perfect. Understanding the strengths and the limitations of this kind of work is an essential skill which will stand you in good stead both in this activity and in business and management practice more generally.

How is it likely to be assessed?

Knowing how your dissertation is assessed gives you important information about what you need to do. What are your tutors looking for? Again, while you need to attend carefully to what your actual programme requires, here are some typical assessment criteria:

- The aims and objectives are clear, appropriate and feasible
- The dissertation makes use of, and critically evaluates, relevant literature and theoretical frameworks
- Suitable methodological approaches and methods are utilized and their strengths, limitations and ethical implications are understood and addressed appropriately
- Appropriate data are collected and competently analyzed
- The results and conclusions are substantiated (that is, they clearly emerge from and are linked back to the data)
- There are some recommendations, usually for both theory and practice
- The structure, organization and presentation of the dissertation are clear and appropriate
- The argument is coherent and lucid
- The work doesn't simply reproduce what is already known but adds to this in some way, perhaps by examining existing knowledge in a new context (for example, a different industry sector, or a specific company or country)
- The work is correctly referenced and is the student's own efforts!

How to fail

Undertaking a dissertation often appears to be daunting exercise and it is easy to get overawed by the prospect of having to produce a substantial piece of work, seemingly on your own. The process may seem unstructured compared to the rest of the MBA since, even though there may be a supporting Research Methods module and recourse to a dissertation supervisor (usually an academic member of staff who will provide guidance during the dissertation phase), much of the work will be done by the student on their own and motivation, project management, and time management are up to them. Here's some of the ways to increase the chances of failure – please make sure they don't apply to you!

- Forget about the dissertation until just before the hand-in date, thinking you can do it all in two weeks rather than the three months you have been allocated
- Don't seek advice from your supervisor or whoever else is delegated to support you
- Read forever but don't write anything
- Use displacement activities like tidying your desk, googling, photocopying journal articles and so on, rather than getting down to anything serious
- Choose a topic you aren't much interested in to begin with – you will be sure to positively loathe it by the end

Like any mountain the dissertation is not to be tackled in one big bound, but by using a series of much smaller and more manageable steps. This chapter will take you through them. Above all you will need to plan carefully and schedule activities so you have a clear timescale for their completion. Do not make the unfortunately all too common mistake of spending ages on the literature chapter or data collection and leaving too little time for the analysis and development of findings. The findings will need to be related to your research aims and objectives and the existing literature and this is really your chance to present your contribution to the field. This is also where many of the marks will be collected so make sure you have enough time to concentrate on this part and really think about what your findings are telling you.

Elements of a Dissertation

While each dissertation is different and there is no single blueprint for how to write and organize material, most dissertations will contain the following sections:

Abstract
Acknowledgements
Table of contents
List of figures
List of tables
Introduction
Chapter 1: Aims or objectives of the study
Chapter 2: Discussion of relevant literature
Chapter 3: The research setting
Chapter 4: Research design: methodology and methods
Chapter 5: Findings

Chapter 6: Discussion
Chapter 7: Recommendations and conclusions
References/bibliography
Appendix A
Appendix B and so on ...

Some of the above is self-explanatory but other sections need some clarification. So, the *Abstract* is a brief summation of the whole work. It is sometimes called an Executive Summary. You will usually be given a word count for this (generally around 300 words) and it should contain information showing what you did, how you did it, and what you found out. In other words, it tells the reader what the focus of the research is and why it is of interest/importance; gives the research questions or hypotheses; provides details of the research setting; outlines the methods used; gives a summary of the main findings pointing out how they add to/confirm/modify existing knowledge; and briefly states the implications for theory and practice. The Abstract is written last, after the rest of the dissertation – when you know what you have done and what you have found out.

Having an *Acknowledgements* section is optional. If you do want to acknowledge those who helped you especially during the dissertation (for example, family or close friends, as well as the companies and individuals who supported your research by sponsoring you or allowing you access for data collection), then a few lines or a short paragraph should suffice.

The *Discussion of relevant literature* is sometimes called a Literature Review. This is really a misnomer and may give the impression that what is called for is a comprehensive description of everything that other people have written on the topic of your research. Actually the focus of this chapter should be your own research topic, covering what is already known about it and where the gaps are that you hope to fill. So you need to refer to the work of others in order to discuss your own area of interest. In doing this you will also need to define key concepts, identify the major studies that have been carried out, review what is known, and highlight the gaps in our understanding. You should try not to merely describe what others have done but also evaluate it. What is required is a critical synthesis of the field of enquiry; a drawing together of relevant work and an evaluation of its merits and limitations. A key word here is 'relevance'. There is sometimes a temptation to try and bring in huge amounts of material which will superficially appear to indicate wide reading, but if its relevance is questionable it will not strengthen the argument, or persuade the reader (and marker), that your work has merit. It is often desirable to develop a conceptual framework which depicts the key areas to be investigated and the links between them. This can help to shape the research design and provide a structure for the data analysis and findings. We will say more about all this below.

As the name implies, the *Research setting* section provides information about where the fieldwork was carried out, for example the geographical location, industry sector, specific companies studied, the informants who contributed information, and so on. This can be a chapter in its own right, though it can also form part of the

Methodology chapter. The *Methodology* chapter discusses the research design in terms of the methodological approaches and methods employed (see below), providing a rationale for the choice of approach and an analysis of the strengths and limitations of the data collection methods utilized. It should also review any ethical implications of the research. It has to summarize the kind of data that were collected and explain how these were analyzed (sometimes data analysis is discussed in a separate Data Analysis chapter).

The *Findings* chapter presents the results of data analysis while the *Discussion* chapter reviews what the findings actually mean, relating these back to the literature chapter to explore the links between existing knowledge and this new evidence. The *Recommendations* chapter puts forward recommendations for theory and practice, highlighting the main findings and their relevance for existing theory and understanding, and also reviewing their implications for practitioners. Finally, the *Conclusions* chapter needs to review the aims and key findings, indicate the limitations of the study, highlight what has been learned from the exercise, suggest how it might have been improved, and identify areas for future research.

Figure 10.1 gives a diagrammatic overview of the key elements of the dissertation. It will be noted that the discussion tends to move from the general to the specific and back to the general again. This means starting with a discussion of the chosen topic in the context of what is generally known about the area, covering the key concepts, issues and debates, and then identifying where the gaps are and showing how the proposed research question(s) will explore these. It is rather like a funnel, beginning with the general domain and narrowing down to the particular focus of your dissertation. How this specific topic is to be studied (in what setting and with what investigative approaches) and what has been found out are then addressed. After this the dissertation needs to move again to a more general understanding of how these findings fit with previous knowledge, and the wider repercussions for academics and practitioners.

We now turn to look at these areas in greater detail.

Choosing a Topic

It goes without saying that the choice of topic is crucial for the rest of the dissertation. You should think strategically about what you want to do for a number of reasons. Firstly, you are going to spend the next months immersed in the subject so you certainly need to choose something you are interested in knowing more about and, hopefully, one that contributes to your understanding of a significant business or organizational issue or problem. More than this, you should be aware that dissertations can be used to develop or change your career. So, for example, if you work in the accounting field you might choose a topic that allows you to gain knowledge and understanding of wider financial issues in preparation for a more senior role in financial management in due course. Or, if you occupy a technical role in your firm, you might use the dissertation to focus on an area of general management and so develop your non-specialist knowledge and understanding. While for part-time

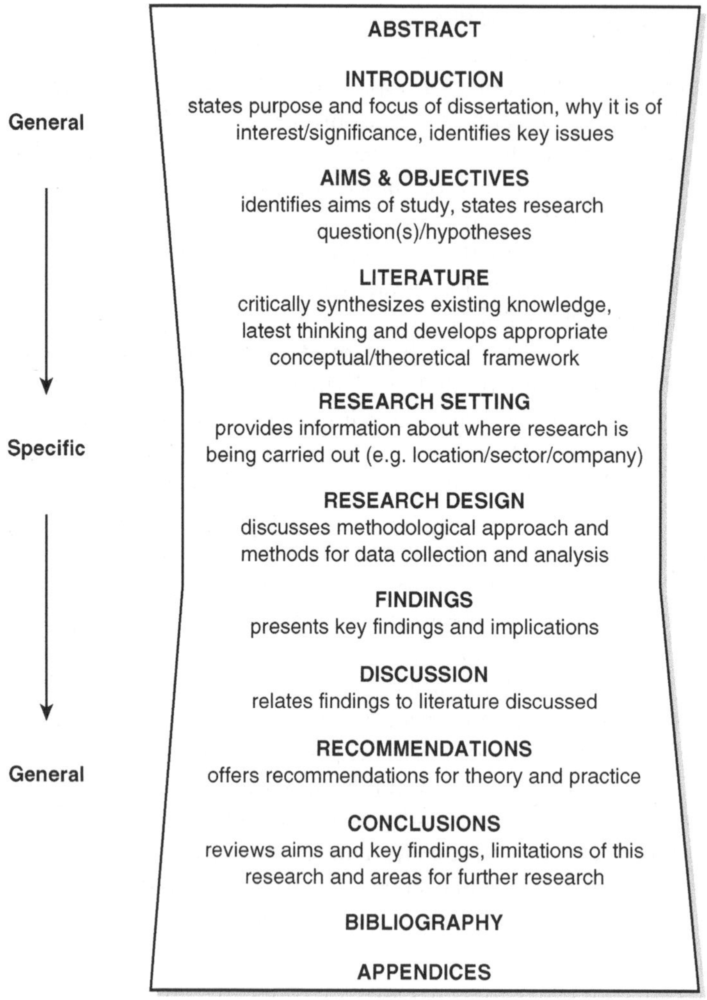

```
                              ABSTRACT

                            INTRODUCTION
  General          states purpose and focus of dissertation, why it is of
                       interest/significance, identifies key issues

                          AIMS & OBJECTIVES
                     identifies aims of study, states research
                            question(s)/hypotheses

                              LITERATURE
                   critically synthesizes existing knowledge,
                    latest thinking and develops appropriate
                      conceptual/theoretical  framework

                          RESEARCH SETTING
                   provides information about where research is
  Specific          being carried out (e.g. location/sector/company)

                          RESEARCH DESIGN
                    discusses methodological approach and
                    methods for data collection and analysis

                               FINDINGS
                    presents key findings and implications

                             DISCUSSION
                    relates findings to literature discussed

                          RECOMMENDATIONS
  General            offers recommendations for theory and practice

                            CONCLUSIONS
                  reviews aims and key findings, limitations of this
                      research and areas for further research

                            BIBLIOGRAPHY

                             APPENDICES
```

Figure 10.1   Elements of the dissertation

students already in employment this may not be an immediate priority, the need to make sound career choices and get some relevant experience is particularly urgent for the full-time student. Indeed it is not inconceivable that an impressive dissertation performance might lead to a job offer from the host organization. Finally, as mentioned above, a well-chosen topic may contribute enough expertise and confidence to make the leap into self-employment.

There are a number of ways for coming up with a subject for research. One way is to start with your programme of study and identify those subjects that you have found most rewarding and enjoyable and which you would like to know more about. Often students are fairly clear about what they like and dislike (for example you may have been fascinated by marketing but struggled with HRM, or vice versa). The next step is to work through the specific areas covered in your chosen subjects to see if there are particular topics or issues that especially appeal (for example, you might want to explore relationship marketing, customer relationship management or services marketing in marketing). While a dissertation is meant to bring together a number of different elements from across the MBA it is likely that you will focus on one core 'discipline' (say marketing), but utilize knowledge and research from other areas of the curriculum (for example organizational behaviour or strategy). An alternative way of identifying a dissertation topic is to start with business practice rather than the academic programme and focus on the problems and challenges you have experienced at work or topical issues that you would like to know more about. This is particularly beneficial for part-time students in current employment as you can use the dissertation to carry out a piece of work that is currently on your desk, or one that you have been unable to get round to because of a lack of time and space to do it. You will then have to relate your chosen aspect of business practice to some relevant academic topics or areas of knowledge. This may require some thought. Often you will find many academic areas that could be used to illuminate the problem and you will need to make a choice. The analogy with reading glasses may be helpful here. Think of the MBA as providing you with a number of pairs of spectacles. Each topic you have studied is like a pair of glasses in that it gives you a different view; some aspects are brought into focus or take on a different angle. You will probably need to look at your chosen issue through the lens of a range of academic 'spectacles' and decide which are likely to give the most revealing or insightful views or perspectives. This will shape your choice of reading for the literature chapter, but as your understanding develops through your reading this may also refine the choice of topic. So the topic may undergo some revision and refinement as you progress – like much of the dissertation, it is an iterative process. The choice of the research question(s) or hypothesis (hypotheses) emanates from this consideration of the topic, because you will also be identifying what it is you want to know and gradually formulating this into problem statements and research questions.

Some topics are popular, in that much has already been written about them and many studies already undertaken. This should not necessarily put you off; there will be much that you can learn from others' work to get you started. However, while there is not quite the same requirement for 'originality' as in a PhD, there is little point in adding yet another study to an already large pile, so do try and look for a different aspect, or angle, to pursue. On the other hand, if you find a topic that appears to have been neglected it might be that there is little existing work for you to go on but there is then the potential to add something new. But do be careful here – it might be that you are simply not framing the topic in the right way and in fact it can be related to more recognizable areas. So perhaps there doesn't appear to be much written about a particular problem with a new initiative, say a suggestion scheme, at work, but there is much written about organizational change, motivation, empowerment, innovation and reward strategies that might be brought to bear on the matter.

However, beyond thinking of a future career and being of interest, the choice of topic needs to meet the following criteria. It must be:

- Of appropriate significance/importance in the area of business and management
- Feasible (researchable)
- Manageable in the time available
- Symmetrical

We now look at each of these in greater detail.

Significance

The topic needs to be one that is of sufficient import to warrant a detailed examination. Something that is trivial or banal will not give you much to write about and the findings are likely to be of little importance to you or anyone else. Often this is to do with the depth of analysis, in that insignificant issues tackled superficially are not likely to produce much, whereas a deeper exploration of the same issue may yield rich insights. To take one example, a study of the setting-up and running of a single strategy 'away-day' in a firm is unlikely to prove very revealing if this merely described and documented. However, if the research is about the contribution of such 'away-days' to strategic practice and the study examines the phenomenon in depth, perhaps from the viewpoints of various stakeholders, as well as the roles, rituals and symbolic behaviour that characterize such activities, then there is a real possibility of making a contribution within the 'practice perspective' in strategic management (see Chapter 9).

Is the research feasible?

The feasibility of the research is something that should be taken into account in the formation of the topic and the design of the study itself. This has a number of aspects. First and foremost you need to consider the *size and scope* of the topic. Your supervisor will be able to advise you here but you need to bear in mind that your choice of research methods will influence this. For example, if you set out to do 100 interviews you will certainly struggle – 15–20 would be more realistic, depending on their length, depth, and the geographical location of interviewees. However 100 emailed questionnaires are quite possible. But of course you will have to decide if you can really get the data you need through questionnaires, so expediency is not the only important criterion. In addition to size and scope you will need to consider whether you are going to be able to collect data that are sufficient and relevant for your purposes. For instance, how easy will it be to obtain primary data about sensitive or undercover matters such as fraudulent behaviour in financial reporting, or government intervention in high profile takeovers, or power play on boards of directors? So *access* to relevant data is also a key consideration and there are two aspects to this. Firstly, some topics are inherently more challenging to get data on (for example, fraud and corruption, politics at work), and secondly, you may find it problematic to access the specific organizations or people you want to talk to. Not every organization will open its doors to researchers and not every manager has the time or inclination to get involved. This is where you may have to utilize your own networks and contacts to get you started.

Finally you should review your own *skill* set. If the type and amount of data you collect will require sophisticated quantitative analysis and this is not your strong point, you will need to assess how far you will be able to develop your capabilities in order to carry out what is required.

Is it manageable in the time available?

There are two aspects to this important matter of time. Firstly there is the question of whether you have enough time to do what is required. This is partly determined by the size and scope of course, but the *timing* of the fieldwork is also key here. It may be difficult to set up interviews with managers in firms during festivals such as Eid or Christmas or in vacation months. It will be necessary to take the local context into account, so don't expect many European academics to take part in a focus group in August (they will be on holiday, or writing, or at conferences), or many account- ants to respond to your questionnaire at the end of the tax year when they are pressurized to finalize the accounts.

Symmetry

A symmetrical research project is one that is set up in such a way that, almost what- ever the findings, you still have something to write about. This is usually a matter of how you frame the main research question. As an illustration, a dissertation which states that it will explore the link between the colour of iPhones and consumer purchase decisions, and then finds there is no link, is likely to be a very short dis- sertation. Far better to set up the research to examine the factors influencing pur- chase decisions. Similarly, if you want to examine strategic management in the Saudi Arabian banking sector it is probably not a good idea to phrase it like this: 'This dis- sertation will examine the formal strategic planning techniques used in developing strategy in the Saudi Arabian banking sector'. The reason for not doing so is that if you find Saudi Arabian banks do not use any formal strategic planning techniques you will be stuck. It is usually better to use a form of wording that allows for a number of different possibilities to emerge from the research, for example: 'This dissertation will examine the processes by which strategy is formulated in the Saudi Arabian banking sector'. If you want to you could add ' ... with particular emphasis on the role of formal strategic planning techniques'. This re-phrasing should at least allow you to write about aspects of the process other than formal planning tech- niques, should you find they are not used a great deal or that other techniques are more important.

Research Aims and Objectives

As the choice of topic firms up you will need to begin to specify the aims and objectives of the research. The aims are about the broad purpose of the dissertation while the objectives set out how these aims will be achieved. You will probably have one or two, even perhaps three (but usually no more than this), main aims. You may have more objectives, perhaps around four or five, consistent with these aims. There is no hard and fast rule about these numbers, but do bear in mind that too many aims suggest the scope may be too broad and too many objectives suggest the aims are too unfocussed.

So the *aim* of this chapter is to help students undertake their dissertations. The *objectives* are to outline how to choose a topic, carry out a literature 'review', select appropriate methods, and so on. Remember that at the end of the dissertation you will have to evaluate how far you have achieved your objectives, though it may be that your aims were not met in full for various reasons, including a lack of data or a change in your understanding of what could/should be achieved as the research progressed.

The Literature Chapter

This is one of the most important chapters in the thesis. In many ways it is the foundation upon which the rest of the dissertation stands and, generally speaking, the better your command of the existing field of knowledge, you more you can identify the gaps and what could be done to fill them. In order to write this chapter you will need to undertake a *literature search*, keep a *record* of what you have found, and write a *critical analysis and synthesis* of what is known about your area of study. You may then develop a *conceptual framework* to summarize what is known. Such a framework should also help in designing the research and organizing the findings. We now examine these in turn.

Literature search

As noted above, more has been written about some topics than others and your first job is to ascertain just what exactly is known. To do this you will have to undertake a literature search, utilizing secondary sources such as books and journals, magazines, newspapers, and the internet. If at first you find little on your chosen subject it may be that you have chosen a neglected topic (see above), but it is more likely that you are not using the right keywords. However, often the problem is not one of too little information but too much. You will usually have an idea of the relevant overarching academic disciplines (for example, marketing or economics) and so be able to search books, journals and bibliographic databases in those areas. You can then search within these domains using keywords to highlight the topics you are concerned with. Once again the funnel analogy is apt because you will begin your literature search fairly broadly and then narrow down to examine your particular specialist area. The section on Information Searching in Chapter 11 in this book will provide more help here. The literature you focus on should reflect a clear strategy in which you have carefully considered the different aspects of the topic and made a conscious decision about which of these are most salient for your research. You will need to articulate your search strategy in the dissertation and link this to the final design of your research.

It is particularly crucial to recognize that not all information will be of equal quality so you will have to exercise your critical faculties when evaluating what you are reading. For example, some journals are considered to be of a higher quality than others (usually meaning they are very selective about what they publish) but there is no universal agreement about which journals are at the top for each subject and those that tend to be contenders for the top place in most business and management subjects are overwhelmingly North American in origin which means a potential cultural basis will be at play. Nonetheless, 'peer-reviewed' journals are those that employ a fairly strict selection policy (where anonymized papers are reviewed anonymously by other subject experts who will give advice to the journal editor about rejection or improvements), and this system, although far from perfect, means that most papers in these journals are carefully scrutinized by a number of academics before they are published. Whatever the source, you will need to carefully assess the rigour of any fieldwork and the robustness of the argument in order to assess their merit.

Keeping records

It is vital that you keep a record of the literature sources you use. There is nothing more infuriating than to be in the throes of getting your finished dissertation ready for binding and to then discover that a reference is missing and you can no longer remember where you obtained it. Perhaps the best way of organizing this part of the process is to use a professional software tool such as EndNote which records and catalogues references for you and then can be used to produce your bibliography. The section on Referencing in Chapter 11 of this book explains how to reference correctly.

Critical analysis and synthesis

The opening chapter of this book provided information about what *critical analysis* is. In terms of the literature chapter this means you should ask yourself questions as you read material in order to scrutinize and interrogate it. For example, if the paper presents data you should question how the data were collected, whether the data are adequate/appropriate, and how far they entitle the author to make the claims asserted in the findings and conclusions. You should also think about the assertions and assumptions the author makes and whether these are justifiable. You will need to consider the strengths and limitations of the evidence and arguments and recognize the possibilities for partiality or bias. For example, it is highly unlikely that the findings will pertain to the entire global population so there may be issues of gender, race or culture to consider, or the research may have been undertaken in particular companies or sectors and therefore could present problems when extrapolating findings to other areas of business or management.

Overall you will need to analyze the literature and not merely describe it. Description is about saying what was done and what was found out, while analysis means evaluating the evidential basis for arguments and questioning the author's assumptions. In turn you must be careful not to make unwarranted assumptions and assertions in your own written work as your dissertation will be subjected to the same kind of scrutiny by your tutors.

You will certainly need to think about how to organize the material you want to use. What is needed here is a *synthesis* of the main issues and debates in a chosen field. This means bringing the work together in some way. It is sometimes helpful to identify the main themes in an area, or the key schools of thought or perspectives. These can then be compared, contrasted, and evaluated. What is not required is a detailed listing of all the relevant authors and their work one after the other with little argument or discussion linking them together. If you find you are writing along the lines of Bloggs (2009) said 'x', Singh (2007) said 'y' and Connors (2001) said 'z' you may be slipping into this format, which is not only tedious but also doesn't progress the debate. In addition it is only too easy to lose sight of the fact that you are meant to be focussing on your own research topic. Try and keep your own research agenda to the forefront of your mind when writing the literature chapter by ensuring that you keep referring to it when discussing others' work.

Conceptual frameworks, theory and constructs

While it is not obligatory, it is often useful to be able to develop a conceptual framework (sometimes called a theoretical framework) which can be used to guide the design of the fieldwork and organize the findings. We therefore need to understand what concepts are and the role of theory.

A **concept** is a mental idea of something. It is an abstract, generic representation that encapsulates the common characteristics of specific instances, ideas or occurrences. So, for example, the concept 'cat' signifies a family of animals that includes lions, tigers and leopards, as well as domestic pets like my cat Sox, who is sitting here watching me type. Similarly, 'personality' is a concept. When we talk of someone's personality we are referring to the set of relatively stable characteristics, behaviour patterns or traits that characterize a particular individual (see Chapter 2). The term 'personality' is therefore used as a shorthand word to denote these aspects of human nature.

> **Concepts**: generic mental abstractions that seek to encapsulate the common characteristics of specific ideas or occurrences.

Concepts are the building blocks of models and theories and you must identify the key concepts you will need to use, define them carefully, and show how these might be expected to relate to one another. This is the basis for your framework – an analytical tool which depicts the theories and concepts that will be used to guide your data collection and interpretation and postulates how they link to/influence each other.

An example of a conceptual framework is given in Figure 10.2. It shows the concepts thought to be important in achieving success when carrying out strategic decisions. The figure depicts two ways of managing the implementation of these decisions, either by having relevant experience which means managers are more familiar with what has to be done and can plan accordingly (by taking actions such as assessing the objectives, specifying the tasks, and providing the necessary resources which can help to ensure acceptability), or by having a receptive context which allows the implementation to be kept on the agenda (prioritization) and appropriate organizational structures to be put in place (see Chapter 2). The concepts here are familiarity, assessability, specificity, resourcing and acceptability, receptivity, prioritization, and structural facilitation. They are organized into two approaches, one labelled Experience and the other Readiness. The arrows show the relationship with each other (in this case what factors come before others) and with the final concept, that of achievement.

In this research the concepts were also defined in such a way as to make them measurable. For example, specificity was defined as 'the extent to which what had to be done was determined beforehand' and measured on a five-point scale from

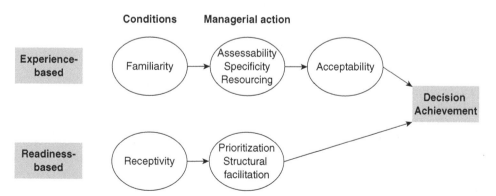

Figure 10.2 A conceptual framework for implementing strategic decisions (based on Miller et al., 2004)

5 (high) to 1 (low). Specificity therefore became a **construct** used in the research. A construct is a concept that is measurable in some way. So it is believed that intelligence (IQ) can be measured and there are various tests that try to do this. In this way IQ becomes a measurable concept – a construct.

Construct: a concept, aspects of which are measurable.

The organization of concepts in Figure 10.2 offers a theory of decision achievement. But what is **theory**? A theory is a suggested explanation of something, an integrated set of beliefs about how and/or why something works in the way that it does. In this case the theory is about what factors will enhance the chances that strategic decisions will be implemented successfully. We have theories about all kinds of areas in business and management; for example, about what factors contribute to competitive advantage, or what motivates people to work harder. Theories are used to explain what we see and, possibly, to predict what we might see.

Theory: an integrated set of beliefs or assumptions put forward to understand and explain a phenomenon.

Different methodological approaches treat the role of theory in different ways. More will be said about this in the next section but, put simply, some research will begin with an existing theory and seek to test some aspect of it through the collection and analysis of data (generally called **deductive** research) while other research begins with observations, data collection and analysis, generating theory as an outcome of the study (**inductive** research).

Deductive approach: draws from existing theory to generate hypotheses or research questions that are then tested to confirm, reject or modify that theory.

Hence the former starts with theory, collects data and produces findings, while the latter starts with the data to produce findings and theory. In practice, however, much research contains both deduction and induction in that theorizing guides some data collection but reflecting on the data leads to a refinement of the theory which in turn leads to further data collection and so on. The process is often iterative, and usually much messier than all this suggests.

Inductive approach: draws conclusions from observations to generate theory.

Thus the way the conceptual framework is constructed and used will depend on which methodological approach you will be taking. So with a more positivistic approach, where you are interested in identifying and understanding cause and effect relationships, a conceptual framework depicts the concepts that will be used in the research and postulates the relationships between them. Figure 10.2 is an example of this.

An interpretivist approach contrasts with this in that the emphasis is more on understanding what the concepts mean, particularly for those human actors under study. So rather than the researcher attempting to define the key concepts and ask the respondents questions about them, an interpretivist approach tries to find out how those being studied actually view the issues under examination, what they experience, and how they construct meaning about their experiences. The researcher may then use this knowledge to identify and create concepts. The former is more of a deductive approach while the latter is more inductive.

This discussion begins to highlight some of the issues involved in research design. We now turn to look at this in more detail, to understand just how these different methodologies and methods can shape a dissertation.

Designing and Carrying Out the Research: Methodologies and Methods

Once you have decided on the topic, there remain a number of choices to be made about the design of your research. You should have some idea of the kind of data you need to answer your research questions but which **methods** of data collection should you use – for example, questionnaires or interviews? Since this may be shaped in part by your thoughts about **methodology** we will discuss this before we move on to methods.

Methods: ways of collecting and organizing data.

Methodology: a set of principles or practices embodied in a particular approach to research.

Methodological approaches

The methodology is the broad approach taken in the study; the particular set of principles or practices that will serve to orientate the research. Importantly, different methodologies embody differing views about some of the central philosophical issues which shape our understanding of the world around us. These are issues of ontology and epistemology and some understanding of these terms is crucial if we are to make informed judgements about how to design and carry out a dissertation or project.

Firstly, **ontology**. Ontology is about how we conceive the world; it is concerned with the nature of 'being' – in other words, the fundamental nature of reality and our own existence. It is possible to take different ontological positions on this important point. An *objectivist* position sees the world as something that is a concrete, objectively observable reality which exists independent of our being aware of it. Understood from this perspective, organizations exist as tangible, ontological realities; they can be studied objectively and they have rules, regulations and purposes that constrain and often outlive the people who work within them. A contrasting ontological position to that of objectivism is *constructionism*. A constructionist position sees the world as something that is socially constructed, constantly created and recreated through our own perceptions, and only given meaning through our subjective interpretation of it. In this view organizational members are active in the construction of their own reality. But our understanding of the world is shaped through our on-going interactions with others so this process of construction is a social process – hence, 'social constructionism'. The objectivist view of organizations amounts to reification to the constructionist, who sees organizations as social phenomena continually in the process of self-formation, where meaning is not given but is continually being shaped and interpreted by organizational members.

Ontology: concerned with the nature of being and existence.

It should be mentioned that some writers use the term 'social constructivism'. Constructivism is about the process of cognitive construction and is usually associated with Vygotsky's (1978) work. It refers to the way an individual creates meaning and knowledge. Individuals do this in a social context (hence *social* constructivism) but it is essentially a psychological process. In contrast, social constructionism emphasizes the sociological rather than the psychological aspects and owes much to Berger and Luckmann's (1996) book *The Social Construction of Reality*.

Our ontological position – in other words the way we 'see' reality – is inextricably linked to the ways we believe we can obtain knowledge about it. This is to do with **epistemology**, the study of knowledge in terms of its nature, sources and limitations. Epistemology poses questions about where knowledge comes from, what constitutes 'valid' knowledge, and how we can justify our knowledge beliefs. How do we know what we know and how can we persuade others that our knowledge is valid? In the dissertation this is about how you can justify your findings and the claims you make for the robustness of your knowledge.

Epistemology: concerned with the nature of knowledge and knowing.

As with ontology, it is possible to take different epistemological stances. For example, positivism and interpretivism, mentioned above, have different epistemological positions. A positivist approach is very like the approach taken in the natural sciences. It is believed that knowledge about the world can be gained through observation and testing, and the emphasis is on looking for regularities in order to try and establish causal relationships. The ultimate aim is to identify patterns in individual observations in order to develop generalizations about the phenomena under study. Positivistic research tends to use **deductive approaches**, using theory to generate research questions or hypotheses that can be tested during the empirical work (empirical research tends to rely on observations, experience or experiments). Positivistic research tends to be objectivist, seeing the world as something that is amenable to systematic and objective observation, measurement and testing. The researcher stands outside the research and tries to make sense of what he or she is seeing. Historically the positivistic orientation has tended to dominate research in business and management.

In many ways interpretivism is seen as being in direct contrast to positivism. There are a number of distinct philosophical and sociological intellectual traditions within broadly defined interpretivist approaches – for example phenomenology, hermeneutics and symbolic interactionism – and while there are sharp distinctions between them, there are also some recurrent features. Interpretivists believe that the methods of the natural sciences are highly questionable when applied to human beings. Attempts to observe human behaviour objectively are unlikely to offer a meaningful understanding of it. Mere observation will tell you little about what the behaviour signifies, or about how the individual being observed has made sense of their situation and has therefore responded to it. To begin to make sense of human action it is necessary to comprehend it from the vantage point of the human actor. Furthermore, an interpretative perspective suggests that it is a fallacy to presume the researcher is objective. Such dispassionate scrutiny is not possible. The researcher stands inside the research, is part of it, and any interpretation is influenced by their own subjective perception as they make sense of what they are observing. This is even more so when the researcher actively 'intervenes' in the research setting, for example by conducting interviews, asking questions, and so on.

In addition to positivism and interpretivism there has been increasing interest in a third philosophical tradition, that of *critical realism*. Realism is akin to positivism in that both share the view that reality is external to the individual and is amenable to study by appropriate methods and techniques. However *critical* realism, a view most commonly associated with Bhaskar (1989, 2008), argues that the human world is fundamentally different from the natural world in that human actors are self-reflexive. That is, they can reflect on their situations and consciously act to change them; they are active in creating the social structures in which they operate. In Bhaskar's view, the role of scientists is therefore to try and understand the 'generative mechanisms' which give rise to particular patterns and regularities. Rather than seeing science as being a way of directly observing reality (as in positivism), in critical realism the scientist's conceptualization is simply a way of knowing that reality, but the

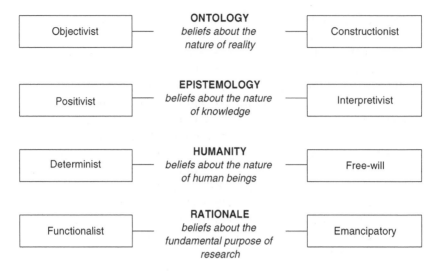

Figure 10.3   Factors potentially influencing methodological choices

identification and understanding of generative mechanisms allow for the possibility of change (Bryman and Bell, 2007: 18). Critical realism therefore takes an ontological stance that is neither straightforwardly objectivist nor constructionist. Human agency produces the social world but researchers cannot observe this directly, they can only attempt to distinguish the generative mechanisms and observe their effects.

Figure 10.3 summarizes some of the key factors that influence methodological choices and shows the broad dimensions of debate for each factor. As we have seen, ontological positions range from more objectivist to more constructionist orientations (accepting that this is not always a clear-cut distinction and it is possible to find positions mid-way: see Cunliffe, 2011). Issues of epistemology range from more positivistic approaches to more interpretivist ones, noting that it is possible to combine different approaches within research projects.

There are then two other factors to do with beliefs about human nature (humanity) and the fundamental purpose (rationale) of the research. The first of these refers to the degree to which it is believed that human action is pre-determined. This is a philosophical question. A deterministic perspective takes the view that there is no such thing as free will; that human action is completely conditioned by external condition and internal stimuli leaving no room for choice. A contrasting view suggests that humans do have free will and are therefore capable of considered decisions, choices and actions (Burrell and Morgan, 1993). While these are extreme positions, theories of business and management will often contain implicit assumptions about these issues. For example, it is argued that contingency approaches to organizational design are deterministic in nature as they give the impression that once the size, technology, environment and strategy are known, the structure of the organization is given, leaving little room for managerial choice (see Chapter 2 on Organizational Behaviour).

The final factor concerns the essential rationale for the research. This comes down to the researcher's own reasons for undertaking the work and, ultimately, his or her own set of values. At one end of this dimension the research is functionalist in nature. That is, the researcher's overall objectives are to understand and eventually improve current business practice. At the other end of the dimension the aim is to understand and change practice. While at first sight these may seem similar (improvements usually mean change) the difference goes deeper than this. A functionalist orientation takes the view that, while some aspects may not be perfect, the value system and structures underpinning business and management practices are fundamentally appropriate so that any change can be brought about within current parameters. An emancipatory orientation starts with the premise that existing arrangements are fundamentally flawed because the values underlying business and management practices are not shared, nor do they benefit everyone equally. This perspective highlights the inequities that exist between different groups in society and the negative consequences of businesses such as the unsustainable use of natural resources. Research taking a more emancipatory stance seeks to radically alter the status quo, arguing that change within existing parameters will not go far enough. This surfaces the political dimension to research which, while not often discussed, is always a latent concern. Doing research requires the researcher to consciously and critically consider his or her own value system, the real motive for undertaking the work, and to recognize the wider political implications of what they are doing. This relates to the discussion of critical approaches in Chapter 1 and is elaborated in the next section.

Traditional and more critical research paradigms

It can be argued that combinations of particular ontological and epistemological positions give rise to different **paradigms**. In the sciences, a paradigm is a relatively coherent set of practices and beliefs about how research should be done. So a paradigm encapsulates beliefs about the nature of reality and the most appropriate ways of exploring it. Different scholars have identified different paradigms (for example, see Burrell and Morgan, 1993) and there is a debate about the degree to which paradigms are absolutely distinct and incommensurable (that is inconsistent and therefore not able to be combined). Notwithstanding this debate, as we argued in Chapter 1, business and management research has been dominated by the functionalist paradigm. This paradigm tends to reflect an objectivist ontology and a positivist epistemology and is geared towards the improvement of business and management practice. Functionalist research views the world as an objective reality that can be observed in order to find regularities and patterns which the researcher can attempt to explain.

> **Paradigm**: a set of beliefs and assumptions about the world and the practices by which it can be understood.

However interpretivist approaches have become more widespread in recent years. For example, Tony Watson's book *In Search of Management* (2001) is a good example of an attempt to understand managers and management from the managers' own perspective but there is a wide range of other qualitative approaches. Postmodernist views (discussed in Chapter 1) tend to be sympathetic to the constructionist position. Postmodernism emphasizes that individuals create the reality they perceive and this 'reality' is subjectively experienced. This means that interpretations are fluid, malleable, and subject to change. So such things as organizational rules or processes are representations or symbols and are not fixed, stable entities but are subject to (re)definition, flux, and potential transformation. Critical realism has some resonance with postmodernism in this regard. However, it should be recognized that this subject is complex and the field has grown more diverse in the last few decades with an increasing variety of methodological approaches being utilized, particularly in qualitative research (Cunliffe, 2011). For the MBA researcher it is important at least to think about the rationale for undertaking the research and to then consider how ontological and epistemological factors might shape what is done in practice. This leads us to now look at different methods for collecting data, concentrating on those most widely used by students in business and management.

Methods

There are two broad groups of methods at the disposal of the social scientist: quantitative and qualitative. While quantitative methods are assumed to be usually associated with positivistic approaches and qualitative methods with interpretivist ones, in reality this is too simplistic. Researchers in more positivistic traditions will need to be sensitive to matters of interpretation (both by themselves and their informants), while researchers coming from an interpretivist perspective may sometimes want to quantify their findings.

Decisions about which methods to choose depend on what you want to know and the kind of data you need to answer your research questions. There are trade-offs between different methods which you will have to consider carefully. For example, an on-line survey might enable you to reach a larger number of people but you will only be able to ask a limited number of questions which will need to be fairly clear and straightforward. On the other hand, interviews are time-consuming but you can prompt and probe and your informants can use their own words to a much greater extent. The trade-off here is about breadth and depth. Case studies are often used if you are attempting to get an in-depth understanding of something, perhaps an investigation of leadership styles in a particular firm. You can use multiple case studies to compare and contrast but not too many because to achieve a rich and detailed understanding of each case will also take time.

Many research topics are complex and multi-faceted and you will also need to make judgements about the appropriateness of different methods. For example, would a questionnaire such as a climate survey be able to provide good quality data to explore people's understanding and perception of their own corporate culture, or would participant observation be a better way of investigating the potential subtleties of this topic? You will need to understand the range of different methods and make an informed choice which you will then have to justify in your dissertation. It should be said from the outset that all methods have strengths and limitations and therefore using a combination of methods (sometimes referred to as triangulation) may off-set the weaknesses of using any one approach alone.

We begin first by examining the quantitative methods most commonly used by students: *surveys* and *structured interviews*.

Surveys

Once you have decided what it is you want to find out from your research it is all too tempting to write down a few questions and rush out a questionnaire. This is unwise. Surveys, whether they are mailed or web-based or given out personally to respondents, need careful planning, preparation, and piloting.

Clearly you need to construct your survey so you can obtain relevant data that will answer your research objectives. Your literature review should assist in the development of survey questions and you will need to explain how the questions link back to the issues and gaps you identified in the literature chapter. Whether you use a pre-existing survey put together by other researchers or develop your own to fill the gaps in existing knowledge remember that the questions need to be clear and unambiguous. So try and avoid 'leading' questions (these invite the respondent to give a particular answer) and decide on which mix of 'open' questions (which allow the respondent to develop an answer in their own words) and 'closed' or pre-coded questions (where the respondent ticks a box to indicate which pre-given response they favour) is appropriate. Sometimes closed questions are scaled, for example from 'strongly agree' to 'strongly disagree', and may be followed by an open question which asks why the respondent answered in a particular way, or requests that they give an example. Think in advance about what information you need and how you will analyze the data so that you can organize data analysis.

Some survey research is positivistic and deductive in nature, so it is about testing a theory or hypothesis and establishing/exploring causal relationships. Your conceptual framework (see above) will indicate the important factors to be examined in terms of what is to be explained (termed 'the dependent variable') and what factors are presumed to explain this (the independent variables). In Figure 10.2 the dependent variable is decision achievement, while familiarity, assessability, specificity, resourcing, acceptability, receptivity, structural facilitation and prioritization are the independent variables put forward to explain achievement.

But surveys can also be utilized within a more interpretivist approach. In this case it would be usual to include more open-ended questions in order to collect personal interpretations and impressions that will allow you to explore how respondents understand a particular phenomenon. This kind of research is more inductive in nature and new theories may be generated as a result. Sometimes this will be the first stage in a research project in which theories will then be tested in the next phase of the research.

However if you are using surveys it is essential to pilot them first in order to ensure that the questions are clear and unambiguous, that the ordering is sensible, and that you are getting the information you need. Do try to make the questionnaire as short as you realistically can. You can safely make the assumption that most of your potential respondents have lots of other things to do and will not have the time or inclination to complete a lengthy questionnaire. While there are no hard and fast rules, two or three pages is probably sufficient before a respondent's willingness to participate begins to wane. Indeed access to respondents and non-responses are particular problems. You may improve your response rates by using personal networks, stressing the significance of your research, contacting people in advance and following up non-respondents, offering to send a brief summary of your results, and proffering incentives. You will probably have to modify the final instrument as a result of the pilot, perhaps by changing the wording, or adding or removing questions and so on. You should briefly discuss the pilot study and any modifications made in the Research Design section of the dissertation.

Structured interviews

Interviews can be structured, semi-structured, or open. Structured interviews tend to have pre-coded questions that are usually asked in the same order. The survey instrument is akin to a script for the interviewer. Semi-structured interviews usually contain a list of broad areas or issues that the researcher wishes to cover and may have a mix of open and closed questions. Open questions open up relevant topics for discussion. The respondent – or more accurately the 'informant', since the interviewee is not simply responding to a pre-set schedule of questions – will have some latitude to range more widely around the issue answering in their own words. The interviewer can probe or prompt to explore particular aspects, or change the direction of the discussion. Closed questions can be used to refine the answer (for example, by asking about the importance or priority of different aspects, how far the informant agrees with particular views, and so on). We will say more about interviews below.

There are many different ways to analyze quantitative data but the purpose of data analysis is usually to ascertain if there are regularities and patterns that can be identified and explained. Sometimes highly numerical data will require the use of statistical packages such as SPSS. Make sure you explain the process of data analysis and don't just present your findings without explaining how they have been arrived at.

We now turn to examine the most frequently used qualitative methods: *observation*, *focus groups*, and *unstructured interviews*. It should be mentioned at the outset that qualitative research emphasizes the interwoven nature of data collection and data analysis. Thus some data are collected and made sense of as the research continues and this will shape the collection of more data and so on.

Observation

As with interviews, observational methods range from more structured to less structured approaches. While all observation requires the researcher to watch, listen, interpret and record what they observe, structured approaches are relatively more prescriptive about what the central focus of the study is. In contrast, unstructured approaches take a much broader view of what constitutes 'relevant' data. The obvious drawback with the first approach is that the focus may turn out to be prematurely defined, too narrow, or simply wrong, while the drawback with the second is that everything becomes 'data' and therefore deciding what is relevant and what is not becomes challenging.

There are many broad research traditions that use observational techniques. Ethnography – which is much used in anthropological research – has a long established pedigree in the social sciences and refers to the study of people in their natural settings. There have been many studies based upon observing people in the workplace as they go about their normal routines and practices. The researcher aims to immerse themselves in the organization, seeking to see the world from the vantage point of organizational participants and understand the embedded nature of interactions and behaviour in this context. There are tensions here of course. How far should the researcher remain detached from the research setting and even if some objectivity is desirable how far is this possible? Indeed the researcher may be a participant in the research, for example if they are carrying out work in their own organizations, where it becomes *participant* observation. If the researcher is part of the research in terms of being actively involved in helping to reflect on problems or issues and find solutions then this becomes 'action research', and while there are many variants of this it amounts to the researcher being directly engaged with the process of generating explanations for phenomena. Consultants or other specialists often act as action researchers when they work with organizations.

Of course recording information is critical and sometimes those involved in the research will be asked to keep records or diaries or to record critical incidents to supplement the researcher's own observations. Often the researcher's interpretations will be fed back to those involved to provide some means of checking the veracity of the accounts, though this is not unproblematic, for it is generally accepted that there are likely to be many versions of events and no single 'truth'. How to analyze observational data is also a vexed question. Some researchers will attempt to generalize from the data to generate theories about what has been observed, perhaps moving on to other research settings in order to compare, contrast, and test findings. This is broadly the approach of 'grounded theory' which seeks to identify regularities in the data – be they behaviours, ideas, conversations or whatever – and by a process of categorization and classification seeks to build theory which can be tested in other contexts. However, some feel that this imposes an order and structure which may distort or reduce the 'richness' of the data. In this case the alternative is to utilize rich narrative accounts, often using the actors' own words as far as possible so as to minimize unwarranted or erroneous interpretations imposed by the researcher.

There is much discussion and much less prescription about how to analyze qualitative data. While analysis is likely to involve some concept-building, categorization and comparison, as we have seen there is a debate about how far this should go and it is probably the case that most researchers have to develop their own ways of organizing their data to some extent. There are software packages such as NVivo which can help with this process but, as might be expected, some researchers feel these may impose artificial structures on inherently messy and unstructured accounts. Notwithstanding all this, you will have to organize your data in some way to present a clear account for the reader (even if you stress the incoherence of the reality you observed!).

Focus groups

It sometimes makes sense to discuss topics with a group of people rather than in one-to-one settings. This means you can get more opinions and debate and collate a number of views at the same time. The size and composition of the group need to be thought about, as more than 10 or 12 may be difficult to control and big status differentials within the group may mean that lower-level employees are reluctant to speak out. You will need to identify the topics of discussion and plan the event, briefing people about what to expect beforehand and informing them about issues of anonymity if necessary. You will also need to have some way of recording what goes on. Allow about an hour for a focus group but be prepared either way if conversation is stilted or if you can't get a word in edgeways!

Interviews

We have already discussed different types of interviews above. Interviews in qualitative research are more likely to be less structured so there will be greater use of open questions and the emphasis will be on allowing the informants to use their own words. Of course it will still be important to outline the areas for discussion clearly and to perhaps consider the order questions will come in to help the flow of conversation. However, be prepared to be flexible and to listen carefully to what is being said and how it is said; try to be sensitive to non-verbal clues such as body language which may assist in your interpretation. As with all interviews it is necessary to have somewhere quiet and private where the interviewee feels comfortable. It will be important to have some way of recording the interview, either by note taking or by taping the interview (with consent), as it will be vital to capture the language and tone of what is being said. Be aware that transcribing interviews is a time-consuming process. Depending on your typing speed it will take around three times as long to type them as it will take to play them back. Make yourself some notes afterward on how things went and about any aspects of the language, context or behaviour that appeared significant given the nature of the discussion.

These, then, are the more commonly used methods. Of course we should not forget the collection and examination of secondary data in the form of archival information, company documents and reports, historical detail and so on which are usually needed whichever method you are using and which can provide important supplementary information.

Validity, reliability and generalization

Validity, **reliability**, and **generalization** are important ideas in research. These are not straightforward terms and their meaning and significance can vary depending on which methodological approach is taken. Broadly stated, issues of validity are concerned with whether the research 'measures' what it is supposed to measure – about how 'truthful' the results are. Hence a ruler is a valid measure of length while reliability is about the consistency of the measure: therefore a ruler also measures length in a consistent and replicable way. Yet reliability does not imply validity – even when an instrument gives the same result each time, it may not be measuring what it purports to measure. Thus we have the vexed debates about the meaningfulness of IQ tests, personality indicators and the like, which may have some reliability but may still lack validity. Generalizability is about how far results can be extrapolated to new situations.

Validity: how far the research 'measures' what it intends to measure.

Reliability: how far the research and findings are reproducible and consistent.

Generalizability: how far the findings are representative and can be extrapolated to other settings.

Qualitative researchers sometimes find these terms troublesome. In qualitative research the emphasis on understanding the unique reflections, interpretations and behaviours of individuals means these issues will take on a different significance. Each situation and setting is unique and therefore results are unlikely to be reproducible or generalizable in the same way. Instead of 'reliability' it could be argued that credibility or dependability is perhaps more appropriate. As far as validity is concerned the idea that there is one agreed version of 'the truth' is also problematic.

At the end of the day, as with much research, your dissertation will be an exercise in persuasion and you will need to persuade your reader that you have taken all possible care in your design and methods, minimizing any obvious bias or distortion to arrive at a plausible set of findings. No research is perfect so do not claim too much. Recognize and acknowledge the limitations and discuss how, with hindsight, you could have improved what you did. The MBA dissertation is about learning the craft of research, so show that you have reflected carefully on what you have learned.

Ethical issues

Ethics in research is of paramount importance. In general terms this means behaving with honesty and integrity in everything you do. This includes being open with participants about what you are doing, ensuring confidentiality where this is agreed, not falsifying or distorting data, or misrepresenting individuals taking part in your research. You will need to behave responsibly and professionally and operate on the basis of trust and informed consent, taking steps to ensure the anonymity of participants and sensitive company data unless disclosure is explicitly agreed. Do bear in mind your responsibility to all stakeholders, including your institution, your supervisor, and any participating organizations and individuals, as well as the wider research community, all of which means you should behave professionally and adhere to the tenets of good academic practice (for example, by not plagiarizing others' work). You will also need to recognize that there may be different perspectives on ethical issues in different cultures, so make sure that you understand the implications of these. Many institutions now require all researchers, including MBA students, to sign some kind of code of conduct in advance.

Findings, Recommendations and Conclusions

Your analysis of the data will give rise to some findings. The presentation of research results is often two-staged. The first is where you summarize the data collected and distinguish the main findings from each of the methods employed. The second stage is where you examine the overall results from the research and discuss the main themes and issues you have uncovered. This latter stage will require you to review these overall findings in the context of your research questions and the body of knowledge discussed in your literature chapter. In essence you will need to show how your results add to, confirm or modify existing work in the area, always bearing in mind the need to consider the limitations of the methods utilized (so make sure any claims can be substantiated). As indicated in Figure 10.1 the first of these is presented in the Findings chapter, the second in the Discussion chapter.

You will also need to consider the implications of your findings for other scholars and practitioners. This is usually part of a separate recommendations chapter and is where you consider how your work could be developed by other researchers and what your results mean for practitioners. Depending on the nature of your research, these recommendations for practice may be extensive and detailed. For organizational employees and sponsors this is likely to be the most informative and constructive part of the dissertation so you should spend time spelling out what your results actually mean for those engaged in business and management practices and other stakeholders.

The conclusions section again may be organized within a separate chapter. Here you will revisit the aims and objectives, discuss the degree to which these have been met, review the results and their limitations, identify any areas for future work, and show what you have learned from the exercise.

Writing Up

While the sections in this chapter have been written to follow the usual sequence of research activities, it should be recognized that, in reality, research is not carried out in a nice, neat series of logical steps, with each one following on when another is finished. It is messy and iterative. While on the whole you will be making progress sometimes it will feel like you are getting nowhere – or even going backwards! Take heart, most research is exactly like this. As James Watson, one of the scientists involved in discovering DNA, remarked in the preface to his controversial book on the project: '… science seldom proceeds in the straightforward logical manner imagined by outsiders. Instead, its steps forward (and sometimes backward) are often very human events in which personalities and cultural traditions play major roles' (Stent, 1980: 3). Having said this, you will want to write up your dissertation or project in a logical sequence in order to allow the reader to follow it (though of course you may want to explain how your thinking changed over time). As Robert Merton remarked in his review of the same book 'As far back as the early days of modern science, Francis Bacon was complaining that "never any knowledge was delivered in the same order it was invented"' (Stent, 1980: 213). However, do be sure to write linking sections to lead from one chapter to another; don't leave the reader to have to stumble through the dissertation trying to make sense of how one bit connects to another.

Finally, do recognize that there may well be times when you don't quite know where you are going. This is normal! The quotation below by the Cambridge mathematician Andrew Wiles who was writing about his breakthrough work on Fermat's Last Theorem (a mathematical problem having its roots in ancient Greece but formatted by Pierre de Fermat in 1637) sums up the process very well.

> One enters the first room of the mansion and it's dark. Completely dark. One stumbles around bumping into the furniture but gradually you learn where each piece of furniture is. Finally, after six months or so, you find the light switch, you turn it on, and suddenly it's all illuminated. You can see exactly where you were. Then you move into the next room and spend another six months in the dark. So each of these breakthroughs, while sometimes they're momentary, sometimes over a period of a day or two, they are the culmination of and couldn't exist without, the many months of stumbling around in the dark that precede them. (Andrew Wiles, quoted in Singh, 2002: 258)

So don't procrastinate, get on with it, accept that you will have to write a number of drafts and reorganize sections before it is acceptable and push ahead. Don't on any account leave all the writing-up until the end. Keep writing and refining and you will have something you can be proud of. And do remember to allow enough time for the final editing, proof-reading, checking of references, and so on. Aim to finish a good two or three weeks before the hand-in date to allow for all this and if you also need to have your dissertation bound allow for this too.

Finally, good luck! Enjoy this rare opportunity to have some dedicated time to get to grips with something that truly interests you in the messy, often chaotic and hard to fathom world of business and management.

Questions for reflection

1 What are you really interested in knowing more about in the area of business and management?
2 What kind of research can be feasibly carried out to explore your area(s) of interest?
3 Which research approaches will be most appropriate and do you have the research skills required?
4 What is the potential contribution of your study for practitioners, scholars and other stakeholders?

Further reading

Gill, J. and Johnson, P. (2010) *Research Methods for Managers*. London: Sage.
Golafshani, N. (2003) 'Understanding reliability and validity in qualitative research.' *The Qualitative Report*, 8 (4): 597–607.
Sonali, K.S. and Corley, K.G. (2006) 'Building better theory by bridging the quantitative – qualitative divide.' *Journal of Management Studies*, 43 (8): 1821–1835.
Wilson, J. (2010) *Essentials of Business Research: A Guide To Doing Your Research Project*.
    London: Sage.

References

Berger, P.L. and Luckmann, T. (1966) *The Social Construction of Reality: A Treatise in the Sociology of Knowledge*. New York: Anchor.
Bhaskar, R. (1989) *Reclaiming Reality: A Critical Introduction to Contemporary Philosophy*. London: Verso.
Bhaskar, R. (2008) *A Realist Theory of Science*. Oxford: Routledge.
Bryman, A. and Bell, E. (2007) *Business Research Methods*. Oxford: Oxford University Press.
Burrell, G. and Morgan, G. (1993) *Sociological Paradigms and Organizational Analysis*. Hants: Ashgate Publishing Ltd.
Cunliffe, A.L. (2011) 'Crafting qualitative research: Morgan and Smircich 30 years on.' *Organizational Research Methods* (forthcoming).
Miller, S., Wilson, D. and Hickson, C. (2004) Beyond planning: strategies for successfully implementing strategic decisions, *Long Range Planning*, 37 (3): 201–218.
Singh, S. (2002) *Fermat's Last Theorem*. London: HarperCollins.
Stent, G.S. (ed.) (1980) *The Double Helix – a Personal Account of the Discovery of the Structure of DNA*. New York: Norton.
Vygotsky, L.S. (1978) *Mind in Society: The Development of Higher Psychological Processes*. Harvard: Harvard College.
Watson, T.J. (2001) *In Search of Management*. London: Thomson Learning.

11 Study Skills

Key concepts

Plagiarism; Spider diagrams; Virtual learning environments (VLEs)

You will be introduced to various learning and teaching approaches on the MBA. These may include lectures, seminars, tutorials, study groups, and on-line learning. Whichever methods are employed, you will need a variety of skills in order to study and successfully complete your programme. These include information searching and being able to critically analyze the material you read, note-taking, referencing, writing assignments, taking examinations, making presentations, working in groups, and making use of e-learning resources. These are concerned with undertaking the academic requirements of the MBA, however there is another pivotal skill that you will find essential, that of time management. This chapter will help you accomplish the degree and make the most of your studies. However, before we deal with these skills in detail we will say a brief word about what is expected of you, as an independent learner, and how this relates to some of the themes and issues outlined in the opening chapter of this book

Learning Independently: Being reflective and reflexive

As a Master's student you will be expected to work on your own and take an active part in planning and managing your own learning. Naturally your tutors are there to provide guidance, and you will be supported in your learning both by them and by other students, but you will also be expected to take the initiative in scheduling your work outside the formal teaching periods and to take responsibility for your own education and development as you progress through the MBA. Independent learning means taking charge of your own learning so that your education can continue long after the MBA has ended. The MBA is then seen as a step on the journey of 'life-long learning' rather than merely an end in itself. Thus you will need to be self-directed: resourceful in seeking out information and knowledge and taking advantage of opportunities for professional and personal development.

But being independent has further connotations. It also means having your own opinions rather than merely reproducing those of others, being free to have your own views and express them. This links to the discussion of critical approaches in Chapter 1 where it was remarked that the MBA student will be expected to examine the underlying assumptions of the ideas and theories introduced in the programme and be critically evaluative of what he or she reads or is taught. So this is about having independence of judgement and requires you to have a questioning mind, to actively look for any flaws in arguments, to carefully scrutinize the underlying logic of assertions, and to weigh up the evidence for yourself in order to assess the merits of different points of view and arrive at your own conclusions.

As mentioned in Chapter 1, this is associated with ideas of self-reflection and reflexivity. In terms of self-reflection, the independent learner should think about how their own personality, life experiences, belief systems, attitudes and culture may influence their receptiveness to certain ideas or approaches. MBA students come to the MBA with an existing set of views, experiences and ways of seeing the world. Opening ourselves up to learning may require us to confront our own prejudices and taken-for-granted beliefs.

As Chapter 1 identified, the MBA encourages the 'reflective practitioner'; one who can critically reconstruct their own experience and thereby learn from it. This also relates to the notion of reflexivity, which is about how our ability to be mentally aware of ourselves and our behaviour turns back to affect our thinking and action. A reflexive individual is capable of considering themselves in relation to their own situation, and of also considering the situation in relation to themselves, recognizing there is a dynamic interplay between the two, each affecting the other. Thus the reflexive MBA student strives to be cognitively aware of the way they create the learning they experience. Put simply, learning shapes us and we shape our own learning.

However we must remember that learning and teaching are related. Chapter 1 covered some of the views debated in Critical Management Studies (CMS). One of the areas given prominence in CMS is power, in terms of the manifestation and effects of power in organizations and institutions. Educational institutions are no different to other organizations in this respect so it follows we should also consider power relations in the classroom between the teacher and the taught. A critical perspective would therefore be interested in those learning and teaching approaches that have moved away from the traditional 'expert' teacher and inexperienced learner model, recognizing that the 'student' is an active participant in the learning environment they co-create in the classroom and not merely a passive recipient of knowledge. This is especially the case with MBA students who will bring highly relevant real-world experience of their own to the class and may in fact have more expertise and up-to-date knowledge in their own specialist areas than the tutor. Critical pedagogies forcefully underline the independence of the learner and urge a consideration of the wider social context (in the classroom and beyond) in which learning is generated.

Thus independent learning on the MBA is self-directed by self-aware individuals who are also aware of the social context of learning. Let us now turn to the practical details of how to make the most of this MBA journey.

Getting Started

Whether you are studying full-time, part-time, or through a distance learning programme, you will need to plan your regime of study. This means setting aside time for reviewing your notes, reading around the topics, carrying out your assignments, revising for examinations, and so on. You will probably already know how you work best, but whether you are an early bird who prefers to study in the mornings or a night owl who can cope with late night sessions it is essential to allocate dedicated time for studying. You will also need to organize somewhere quiet to do so where you can carve out some uninterrupted time for the MBA, away from the distractions of friends and family life and other work.

How much of this you will need will very much depend on how readily you can make sense of the material and tasks, how quickly you learn, and how much you have to do. Bear in mind that a full-time course is equivalent to around 35–40 hours of work a week, some of which will be scheduled learning and the rest private study. A rough rule of thumb is to allow two to three hours of study for every one hour of teaching. You may well find you have peaks of activity and some quieter spells in between. Many MBA programmes will start with some intense study of the core functional areas of management and this period may feel rather pressured, especially if you are returning to study after some absence and need a while to get back into the studying habit. This foundation part is often followed by optional modules when the pressure often feels less intense. The third and final element of the MBA is usually a dissertation or project and this is where things can feel a little unstructured because often formal teaching stops and you will need to institute your own pattern of work. This is where self-discipline and good time management are essential to keep up the momentum and arrive at a successful conclusion.

Overall it is as well to remember that the MBA is more like a marathon than a sprint. There will be many different assessments (or hurdles – to keep the sporting analogy) to be completed and you will need to keep up with the work and keep going. This is especially challenging for part-time students who are also holding down a demanding job, particularly if you want to ensure that you still see your partner occasionally and that your children remember your name! But while you may sometimes feel disheartened that time constraints do not permit numerous essay re-drafts and extra polishing, the MBA is not always about achieving perfection. Of course you will want to do the best you can, but this may have to be the best you can manage in the time available. Try and think of getting the MBA as the beginning of learning, not the end. Learning is a process, not a final state, and the MBA will give you a grounding in many areas that you can continue to explore once the programme has finished. We turn now to look more closely at the skills you will require.

Information Searching

Reading around the subjects and obtaining information to help with assignments is a central activity on any degree. This section covers sources of information and how to begin searching.

Sources

These days there are so many sources that the problem is not usually having too little information but rather too much. It is likely that your tutor will recommend specific textbooks to get you started but you will be expected to go beyond these, and 'reading around' the topic will usually mean a better understanding and hence better marks in assessments. There will usually be many other books besides the course text to choose from and also increasing numbers of e-books available on-line. Your library will be able to advise you about which ones they subscribe to in the areas of business and management.

Once you have gained a basic understanding through the textbooks, academic journals will offer more in-depth knowledge and your lecturer will highlight those that are of particular relevance to their subject. There is often useful material in trade journals and the like as well and these should not be discounted, however articles from 'peer-reviewed' academic journals will have been through a fairly rigorous process of scrutiny by other academics before they are accepted. While this is not a guarantee of 'quality' (or interest!), it does mean that the articles that do get in such journals have been pretty carefully looked at by other – hopefully knowledgeable – academics. This gives some confidence that the research has been reasonably well founded and the arguments add up, so you should try and make wide use of articles in good quality journals in your own reading and writing.

There are various useful databases for the business and management student. Some offer collections of journals and abstracts, others provide company information, and there is also a range of dictionaries and reference works. Some of these services are free while others must be paid for. Your library will be able to tell you about what they subscribe to but some illustrative examples of useful resources are given below:

Journals and abstracts

- ABI Inform Global (journals and abstracts)
- Business Source Premier (journals and abstracts)
- Econlit (journals and books in economics)
- Emerald (journal and abstracts)

Dictionaries

- Dictionary of Business and Management
- Dictionary of Human Resource Management

Company and general business information

- Biz/ed (search engines and gateways to business and management sources on the internet)
- FAME (Financial Analysis Made Easy – detailed company information on UK and Irish companies)
- Global Market Information Database (GMID – international market research database)
- ICAEW (international company database)
- Mintel (market reports on European, US and UK specific consumer markets)
- ProQuest (wide range of research and information sources, including newspapers and dissertations)
- Source OECD (publishes research in education policy, international development, energy policy, transport, and urban and regional development)
- World Bank website

In addition you should try and keep up-to-date with current and business affairs through newspapers and magazines. Some of these have useful websites too, for example:

- *The Financial Times*
- *The Economist*
- *The Wall Street Journal*
- *The Guardian*

Of course there are also many other websites for specific companies and institutions. But while there is a host of internet sources and search engines it is only too easy to get lost or to spend hours of precious time getting distracted. While sources like Google and Google Scholar have their uses, just using these kinds of sources is not good practice and will probably mean you are overlooking seminal material in the journals. Here a word should be said about the ubiquitous Wikipedia. While it cannot be denied that this is a much used resource, it is hard to judge the quality of much of the material since it is not peer-reviewed in the traditional sense and many of the entries may contain errors or be written by non-experts. Your lecturer is unlikely to view it positively so it is best not to cite this source in your essays.

It is also worth mentioning the website Intute (http://www.vts.intute.ac.uk/) which offers a Virtual Training Suite comprising a series of free internet tutorials to help you develop research skills for university courses, including some specifically developed for business, management and economics students.

Searching

If you want to search for what has been written on a particular subject or topic there are a number of ways to proceed. You can browse through books in the library; you can use commercial abstracting or indexing services such as ABI Inform Global and do a keyword search; you can do a keyword search using a database of business and management journals such as Business Source Premier; or you can go directly to the likely journals and search within them.

If you search using keywords you will have to choose these carefully. Most searches start at a fairly general level to see what is available and then progressively narrow the scope as you understand the subject area and can be more precise about the particular aspects you are interested in. When searching you need to be careful about American/English spellings such as 'organization' and 'organization'. Some databases will permit the use of a wildcard symbol, usually * ? or $ to cover all eventualities (e.g. organi?ation will find 'organization' and 'organization'). Wildcards can also be used to truncate words (for instance environ* would find environment, environmental, environmentalism and so on).

You will have to decide on the scope of your search. You might want recent material only (say the last five years) or only material written in English, so you will need to specify this in your search. Boolean operators allow you to stipulate your requirements more precisely, for example by using AND to combine keywords that represent different concepts in a single search (e.g. business AND ethics), or OR to cover words that are similar in meaning (e.g. manufacturing OR production). Using NOT excludes those areas that are of no interest (e.g. motivation NOT Maslow), though care is needed here because such a search might well exclude general articles on motivation which will include Maslow's work amongst others'. Try 'The Boolean Machine' on kathyschrock.net/rbs3k/boolean/ to see the effect of using AND, OR, and NOT. It is best to check with your chosen database to see how it is set up and therefore find out how best to use it.

It is often wise to keep track of your searches. This would be mainly because you may want to re-trace your steps and remind yourself how you found particular sources of information. But if you are carrying out a search as part of a research project or dissertation the keywords you choose and the sources you select to track them will be part of your research strategy. This strategy will be shaped by your research design and, depending on what your search uncovers, this may in turn finesse your research focus. So your search strategy should be discussed as part of the project or dissertation (see Chapter 10 on Research Approaches).

Try to locate the articles that are really central to your area of research and use their reference lists or bibliographies to signpost other work that may be of interest. This 'snowballing' approach should help you map out the main studies, themes and ideas in the area. It is best to start with recent literature, especially if you can find a good article which summarizes the field to date. For example, The *International Journal of Management Reviews* is a good place to start for summaries of management subjects.

Reading and Taking Notes

At the start of the MBA you may find it takes quite a while to read academic articles. These can often be fairly lengthy, sometimes dense, and the language and style will not necessarily be familiar, especially if you are reading articles written in English and this is not your first language. Don't despair – you will get faster and learn shortcuts to reduce your reading time as you progress.

Some tips to help you get going:

- Don't feel you have to read every word – unless the paper is absolutely central to your interest or seminal in the field
- If the paper has an abstract or introduction which provides a summary read this first and then judge whether or not you need to read the paper in more detail
- Learn to skim read – read the beginning and the end to find out what the authors intended to do and what their conclusions were
- If you are good with numbers, or prefer pictures or diagrams, these might give a quick idea of what the key points are: conversely, if you struggle with numbers don't feel you have to check out every table or set of figures. With peer-reviewed articles you can usually assume several scholars have done this already (which is not to say they are fool-proof but you only have so much time ... !)
- If you find you don't understand some of the paper do read on rather than keep re-reading sections in the hope that they will eventually make sense: often you will find that the rest of a paper will help to clarify the earlier part
- If you really don't understand the paper, leave it and read something else. Unless it is absolutely central to your study, or your tutor has explicitly asked you to read it, there is usually a choice of material to look at, so choose something which you find more accessible. This is not to say you shouldn't try to get to grips with difficult material – this is sometimes necessary and can be rewarding – but if it is really impenetrable try other sources. If you are part of a study group it might be a good idea to ask if anyone else has made sense of it

Remember that reading is not simply about absorbing knowledge; as noted above it is also about critically analyzing what has been written, so you should mentally question the author's statements, assumptions, evidence, and conclusions. If the paper is an empirical one (i.e. there is some fieldwork) you should check the methodology to evaluate whether the findings are robust and how far the conclusions can be justified. See Chapter 10 on Research Approaches for more on this, but here is a checklist of the kinds of questions you should be asking:

- Who else has written about this topic?
- How do this author's views fit with other work in the area?
- What are the assumptions that have been made and can they be questioned?
- Are the methodology and methods appropriate and robust (for empirical work)?
- Is the author/their institution credible?
- Has anyone sponsored/funded the study and could there be bias here?
- What are the limitations of the study and have they been acknowledged?
- What about cultural bias – how does this limit the applicability of the article to other cultures and contexts?

Taking notes

It will be important to keep some kind of record of what you have read, usually in the form of notes. You will be able to use these to prepare for essays, for exam revision, and for general understanding. Note-taking is also an important skill to be employed when you are listening to lectures and seminars or even sitting in meetings. In this regard it is a generic skill for use in business and management practice and not just in academia. The novice may have a tendency to take too many notes at first and will end up with 'notes' that can be almost as long as the full article – which rather defeats the purpose. So try and train yourself to take notes once you have read a substantial part of what you are reading (say a journal article, or a chapter in a book) because then you are more likely to identify the major themes. If you have voice recognition software this can greatly speed up the process of recording notes.

Taking notes during lectures is vitally important. Estimates vary but you probably retain under a third of what you hear, perhaps no more than 15–20%. So sitting passively during lectures is likely to mean your attention soon wanders, whereas note-taking means you are actively engaged in the learning process. Since note-taking often requires you to paraphrase ideas in your own words (or pictures, see below) you are more likely to remember what is being said. Some students record lectures but this is very time-consuming process (remember that transcribing takes around three times as long as the recording, depending on your typing speed) and you should always ask the lecturer's permission before you do this.

Note-taking comes in a number of forms and you will need to find a method that is right for you and fit for purpose. You might consider the following:

- Summaries – brief synopses of the whole article (useful when you want a brief overview).
- Bullet points – lists of the key ideas in the article (useful if you want a more detailed reminder of the key points).
- **Spider diagrams or mind maps** – diagrammatic representations or pictures (useful if you want a summary of the key points and the links between them). There are different ways of doing this but it is usual to start by writing the main idea or theme (say of the lecture) in the middle of the page and then writing subsidiary ideas or sub-themes around the main theme, linking them to the central theme and to each other by lines to depict relationships. Sometimes the length of the line can indicate 'nearness' to the central idea (shorter lines will indicate a sub-theme which is closely related, longer lines will indicate sub-themes which are more tangential); sometimes the thickness of the line can indicate this (thicker lines can indicate a strong, or near connection, thinner or dotted lines a less closely related idea); or sometimes colour can be used to group points. The advantage of mind maps is that they show a more holistic view of the subject and the relationships between different aspects. (See Figure 11.1 for an example on the subject of 'Note-taking'.)

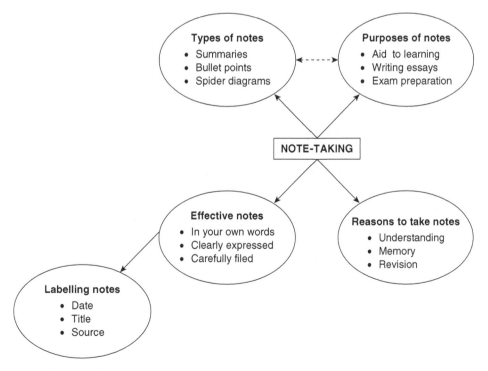

Figure 11.1 Spider diagram or mind map

> **Spider diagrams (or mind maps)**: a way of depicting ideas or points and showing the relationships between them.

Nowadays, there are software packages that provide templates for mind maps and also packages that provide assistance with the whole area of note-taking. For example, Inspiration helps to manage, sort and prioritize information, but there are many others such as AllMyNotes Organizer and Evernote and offerings are changing all the time.

However you take notes do remember to write the topic; the date you compiled them; and full details of information sources or lectures on them so you know what they are about. Leave space on the page so you can add additional information afterwards if necessary. If they are lecture notes do try and review them as soon as you can. It is amazing just how much other information you will be able to remember immediately afterwards and you can use this to clarify, amplify, contextualize, and amend your notes. It is also amazing just how quickly this very helpful supplementary information evaporates once you have sat through another few lectures or done something else. Finally, do file your notes somewhere safe using a method that ensures their easy retrieval later on.

Referencing

You will need to reference the ideas you have read about when you write your own assignments. Correct referencing is an essential skill for all students and incorrectly referenced coursework is likely to attract lower marks. Failing to use any references may be taken to mean you haven't done any reading and so don't understand the domain or that you have plagiarized the work of others. **Plagiarism** is using the work of others without proper acknowledgement and therefore passing it off as your own. It is a form of academic cheating and is usually penalized very severely so it is best to avoid this at all costs.

These are the circumstances when you should provide a reference:

- When you have used someone else's ideas, opinions, models or theories
- When you have referred to a specific fact or piece of information
- When you have quoted another author word for word (verbatim)

> **Plagiarism**: using the work of others without acknowledgement.

There are many different styles of referencing so you will need to check which style your institution requires you to adopt. Many institutions favour what is usually called the Harvard system and this is therefore explained in some detail. In this system you give the author's surname/family name and the date of their publication in the body of your essay and provide fuller details in an alphabetical list of references, often called a bibliography, at the end. The following makes this clearer.

In the essay

If you are citing this book in your essay you would give my surname in brackets plus the date: (Miller, 2011). This is the same for other sources such as journal articles. If there are two authors you must cite the second author as well (e.g. Khan and Jones, 2011), but for more than two give the name of the first author and then use 'et al.' (e.g. for Khan, Jones and Wong you would write Khan et al., 2011). If the article has no author, use Anon.

At the end of the essay

At the end of your work, in the alphabetical list of references, you would write: Miller, S. (2011) *The Essential MBA*. London: Sage. If you are referencing a journal article you would need to give the volume and, if provided, an issue number, plus the page range of the article (e.g. 30 (2): 11–19). If there is more than one author you will need to give them all in the list of references, rather than 'et al.'. Examples of how to reference books, journals and internet sources in the bibliography are given below.

Direct quotations

If you want to provide a *direct quotation* from your source in the essay you will need to enclose the quotation in quotation marks (' '). Within these quotation marks you must use exactly the same words as the original author and everything else must be identical, including punctuation, spelling, capitalization, italics or whatever. If you want to leave out some of the author's words you can use a series of dots (...) to indicate an omission but take care not to distort the meaning. If you feel the author has used an inappropriate or out of date word, or has misspelled something you can use the word [sic] in square brackets to denote that this is really what they said. When using a verbatim quotation you will need to add the page number to the name and date, e.g. (Miller, 2011: 12).

Secondary referencing

Sometimes you may want to cite someone's work which you have read in another source but not the original. This is called secondary referencing. So, for example, say you want to reference Blumberg et al.'s work which you have read about in a book by Wilson. In this case you should reference both the original author and your source (giving the page number). So in the essay you would write (Blumberg et al., 2005, cited in Wilson, 2010: 105). Most institutions will only require you to give the primary source (what you actually read) rather than the secondary reference in the bibliography. Obviously it is usually better, where possible, to use original sources if you want to directly access the author's own ideas.

Citing multiple articles with the same author

If an author has written more than one article you must put the articles in date order with the earliest first. If they have written more than one article in the same year use lower case letters 'a', 'b', 'c', and so on, to distinguish them (for example, Collins, 2010a; 2010b).

Here is a summary of how to reference different sources in the final reference list.

Books

Author's surname/family name and initials, (date), *title*, edition (unless a first edition), place of publication, publisher. For example:

> Gill, J. and Johnson, P. (2010) *Research Methods for Managers* (4th edn). London: Sage.

Chapters in edited books

The author of the chapter's surname/family name and initials, (date of the book), title of chapter, the word 'In' followed by the name of the editor(s) of the book, followed by the word 'ed(s)', *title of the book*, edition (unless a first edition), place of publication, publisher, page range for the chapter in the book. For example:

> Jeremy, D.J. (2006) 'Business history and strategy'. In A. Pettigrew, H. Thomas and R. Whittington (eds), *Handbook of Strategy and Management*. London: Sage. pp. 436–460.

Internet sources

Author's surname/family name or organization, (date of publication), title of article, web address, [date you accessed the article]. For example:

> Dinsmore, G. (2010) 'Fiat boss urges workers to accept sacrifices', *Financial Times* (online), http://www.ft.com/home/uk [accessed 9 July 2010].

Journal articles

Author's surname/family name and initials, (date), title of the paper, *name of the journal*, volume, issue, page range of the article. For example:

> Miller, S.J., Hickson, D.J. and Wilson, D.C. (2008) 'From strategy to action: involvement and influence in top level decisions'. *Long Range Planning*, 41 (6): 606–628.

Finally, you can make use of a system such as *Turnitin*, which is an on-line plagiarism checker used by students and teachers to check work for academic integrity. You upload your essay to the site and it will compare this with a huge range of material, including journals, books, other students' work and a vast amount of internet sources.

Once it has done this it will annotate your work, showing what percentage of this can be found in other sources and where these sources are. This then allows you to ensure that you are referencing appropriately and, if you do have a high percentage of material from elsewhere, where you might need to make more use of your own words.

Writing Skills

You will no doubt be asked to write a variety of assignments such as reports, case study analyses, short essays, and longer papers of various kinds. You may also be required to carry out a more substantial piece of work such as a project or dissertation. Projects and dissertations are discussed in detail in Chapter 10 on Research Approaches. This section deals primarily with reports and essays. We shall look firstly at reports.

The report

Reports are usually concise, focussed analyses or presentations of material on a specific issue, problem or topic that is addressed to a specific audience. They are often used to convey information in a clear, succinct and crisp manner, sometimes through the use of bullet points or numbered items, but you will still be expected to provide a robust argument, based on evidence, and any recommendations and conclusions should be substantiated.

You may be given a template for the report's format, but reports in general will usually have a brief introduction which will set out what it is about, a middle section which will provide the information/data/issues/analyses in numbered or subtitled paragraphs, and a final section which will give recommendations and conclusions. All of this must be prefaced by an Executive Summary which is a short (one or two paragraphs) précis of the whole document.

You should say at the beginning who the work is intended for, keeping in mind your audience's needs and expectations as you write the report. It is a good idea to have a title page, in which the title sets out what the report is about, says who the report is for, and gives both the date and the author. This can be followed by Acknowledgements (if it is necessary to thank individuals, for example participating managers, or companies who provided information), a Table of Contents, the Executive Summary, the Introduction/Main Body of the Report/Conclusions and Recommendations, References and Appendices (if used).

The essay

Essays are generally more discursive than reports in that they usually require some kind of discussion or debate. They are therefore often lengthier and will provide an in-depth examination of a topic or issue. They are also less likely to use lots of bullet points and more likely to be a deliberation of a question, issue or topic.

While each assignment will need you to customize your approach there are usually some elements which are common to most essays:

- The *introduction* sets the scene for what follows. It briefly outlines the topic, highlights the main themes/ideas to be covered, and describes the structure of the essay
- The *middle* section usually defines the key concepts and issues, discusses their meaning and relationship to each other, debates different views, and evaluates the strengths and weaknesses of different arguments. This is the heart of the essay where the writer addresses the essay question or topic in detail, synthesizes different bodies of work, considers the merits of different arguments, and forms their own opinion based on the evidence presented in the essay
- The *final* section provides recommendations (if required) based on the evidence and arguments presented in the body of the essay, offers a summary of the overall discussion (mentioning any limitations in the evidence or analysis), and presents the author's conclusions

Tips to enhance your writing skills

- Do your homework. Read your lecture notes, relevant chapters from the textbooks and journal articles, and do your own searching for relevant material. The better your understanding of the area as a whole, the more you will see how the topic of the report or essay fits in with broad debates in the field
- Highlight the key themes, ideas, concepts, and issues that you want to cover as you read around the subject
- Make sure you are aware of the key academic work in the area. If you write an essay without reference to any relevant theories or academic ideas you are probably on the wrong track. While you may not be required to reference extensively in reports (check the assignment brief carefully for guidance here) you will still be expected to show you have read and understood relevant work and have used it to compile your report
- Keep notes of your reading, remembering to keep track of your sources so you can reference them properly in the narrative and the bibliography. Be careful not to plagiarize work by other people
- Start writing as soon as you can, even if it's just rough notes. You can amend and polish later but having something written down will give you confidence that you can write 5000 words, or whatever, on the topic
- Make a one-page plan (this is a rough guide, a bit more or less might be needed depending on the word limit for the essay), outlining what you will cover in the order you will cover it, and include brief notes to remind yourself of important aspects you want to address

- Particularly in essays, remember that you will be expected to provide a critical synthesis of the work of others. This means that you should not simply describe what different authors say but compare and contrast different perspectives and offer some criticism of various views. If you find yourself starting every sentence with 'Jones says this' and 'Singh says that', stop and re-think your style. Not only is this a boring way to write (and to read) you are also dealing with each author separately. Try instead to discuss the concepts and ideas that are relevant to your topic, bringing in different authors to show how they have contributed to the debates. Remember also that you will be expected to have your own opinions too, but these should be backed up by evidence and careful argument
- As you begin writing, make sure you focus on the topic of the report or essay. Refer back to the essay question or report brief during your writing and demonstrate how what you are saying relates to this
- In terms of style it is usual to write in the third person, however if the question asks you to draw on your own experience it is usually more natural to use 'I'
- Be wary of making assertions, especially without evidence. Topics within business and management are often complex and hotly debated; there is rarely a simple and straightforward answer to complex business problems, so be careful with your choice of words. For example, 'it can be argued that ...' (giving evidence for the argument), or 'the research suggests that ...' are phrases that are often used to denote the conditional nature of 'facts' and arguments in these areas
- Ensure you give yourself plenty of time, allowing for re-drafts and revisions. Be prepared to edit your work to make it more coherent and to make it fit the word limit if you have been given one. Check the handing-in date and time and plan to finish well in advance of this to allow for last minute delays
- Proof-read your work very carefully and use the spell/grammar check software on your computer to assist you. It is all too easy to fail to 'see' errors once you have read the same passage a few times
- Pay attention to your presentation. A well-presented piece of work which conforms to the institution's requirements (for example, you may be asked to use double-spacing or to provide a contents page or use a specific referencing style) makes a favourable impression at the outset; a badly presented piece of work detracts from the content
- Finally, a piece of written work is about communication and persuasion. It is about communicating something to your reader and persuading them with your reasoning. So keep your reader in mind as you write and ask yourself questions such as: does this make sense, how does this relate to the question, and what evidence is there to support this statement?

Getting and using feedback

Your essay or report will usually be returned to you with a mark or grade, and some written feedback. View this feedback constructively and use it to improve the next piece of work.

Some typical comments can include:

- *The essay loses focus at times* – this is about the emphasis you have given to the topic. You may have got side-tracked or missed the point of what the essay was meant to be about. It may also be about how you organized the content. Say what the structure is going to be in advance in the introduction. Try and keep the main topic of the essay or report at the forefront of your mind when writing and relate specific ideas/discussions back to the topic. Use headings and sub-headings to signpost the main issues and themes
- *Argument unclear* – this could be to do with your understanding and/or your writing style. Make sure you have done enough preparation so that you under-stand the subject. Try and use simple, clear language and indicate the stages of your discussion with relevant headings
- *Not enough use of relevant theoretical or academic material* – this is obvious but make sure you actually *use* references and don't just cite authors
- *Little demonstration of understanding* – this may be because you aren't using rel-evant material in your answer. Even if you have read up on the subject, if you don't use the ideas, concepts or theories in your answer the tutor will not be able to give you credit for this

Taking Examinations

While it is probably fair to say that few people actually enjoy examinations it is possible, with good preparation and study skills, to organize yourself so that they present less of a threat to your blood pressure levels! As with other forms of assess-ment, preparation is critical for success. This section will cover how to revise for examinations and how to answer exam questions.

Preparation and revision

To begin with you will need to ascertain the format of the examination. The first consideration is will it be open or closed book? In other words, will you be allowed to bring in relevant materials (books, papers, or your own notes as in open book exams) or will these be prohibited? With quantitative subjects will you be provided with a formula sheet or a calculator? Next, what is the format of the exam? For instance, multiple choice examinations will provide you with a range of answers from which you must select the right one(s), but sometimes there will be penalties for incorrect choices – do check this. Sometimes exams will be based around a case study, often given out in advance, but with unseen examination questions. With this you will need to read the case study thoroughly in advance, then do any analyses that you think will be helpful using pertinent theories or frameworks. You will need to make yourself notes on what is going on in the case, what explanations can be given for what is happening, and what recommendations could be offered. Company case studies are often used in strategic management and so your preparation may include working out financial ratios, or applying relevant strategy frameworks to analyze the company's present position and make recommendations for the future. You could also do some research on the industry sector or other competitors. Some examinations will allow you to take your annotated case into the exam in which case you can write notes in the margins, underline or highlight sections and include some keywords or other memory aides. Practise answering your own questions on the case study or work with other students to think through the likely examination questions and discuss how you would tackle them.

The format of the examination is critical here because multiple choice exams are often designed to test your knowledge over a range of subject matter so you will have to revise more widely. Case studies will usually require you to apply particular knowledge or frameworks, and essay-type questions will want you to discuss something in depth so you will need a detailed understanding usually of fewer areas.

If the examination is going to centre on some areas of the course but not everything you will often need to select material for more intensive revision. It will still be essential that you have an overview of the whole course since this will provide the necessary context for the areas you intend to concentrate on, may let you make an attempt at answering other questions if you are unlucky and your chosen areas are not on the paper, and may also let you 'question spot' more accurately, helping to ensure you don't answer the wrong question by mistake.

Selecting is always risky because there is a chance your selected areas will not come up. However there are some ways of minimizing the risk. First identify the main topics you covered. What were the key emphases in class and the recommended reading? Did the tutor give any hints about what the key areas were? Look at past exam papers to see which topics have come up and the kind of questions asked. Then think about the topics you are most interested in, what you found easy to understand and what did not make sense. Unless it is absolutely central to the subject and/or is very likely to appear on the exam paper, forget those topics that you totally failed to get to grips with. If you didn't understand them in class, if further reading and study or discussing with other students still didn't illuminate them for you, then you are probably unlikely to master them now with the added pressure of looming exams. However, if these are central you had better buckle down to studying hard and get some help from fellow students or lecturers to give you the best chance of making sense of them at last. Decide how many topics you need to look at in depth – this will depend on the number of potential topics which could be covered and how many questions you have to answer and, most crucially, whether the exam paper is likely to weave together different areas of the course within any one question (again check the format of exam questions in advance). However many you choose to revise always try and have a 'reserve' topic which you can use if all else fails. As mentioned before, it is always best to have at least a working knowledge of the whole course to avoid getting completely caught out.

The aim of revision is to help your understanding and – if a closed book exam – your memory. You will need to develop a method that will help you recall essential information to write a convincing answer. In essence the process is one of synthesis and reduction, bringing together the relevant ideas and concepts and reducing them down to something that is memorable – which can be easily recalled and brought to bear on the question. Start with your lecture material, the notes that you made during reading and any other relevant sources. If you did not keep up with your studies during the programme you will have to do much more work now of course – read around the subject and do more research to get a thorough and in-depth comprehension. As you read, think of the issues raised, the points of controversy and debate, the research questions that have been addressed and those that are waiting to be resolved. Try to think of the likely questions that could be asked and work out your responses. Then go back to previous exam papers and give yourself a mock examination, under timed conditions, to give yourself some practice.

As you remind yourself of the central points and read around further, make new notes to act as an aide-memoire. Whether you use bullet points or a spider diagram (see above), you are aiming to refine and condense these notes until you can fit them onto a small piece of paper (a small index card is good for this). This should contain just enough – a few keywords perhaps – to prompt your recall. This is what you will look at just before the examination as the final preparation before you enter the examination hall.

Remember that while exam questions may use different wording, they are often asking you to consider the pros and cons of something or to evaluate the strengths and weaknesses of a particular framework, practice or point of view. So questions starting with 'Discuss', 'Evaluate', 'Critically analyze', 'Consider' , 'Review' or somesuch wording are really asking for broadly similar things. You will need to discuss the advantages and disadvantages, the arguments for and against, and to look at supporting and contradictory evidence to come to some conclusions. If you are being asked to analyse something (for example, a problem or situation) this means looking at it in detail, part by part, dissecting it to understand the causes (and probably offer some solutions). Remember to use any relevant tools and techniques you have been introduced to on the course. Remember too that Masters' students ought to critically analyze course material, carefully examining the assumptions, potential biases and contradictions in the evidence and offering a critique of the research or findings. You will usually be expected to offer your own opinion in the conclusions and this should be a balanced judgement based on the evidence you have presented.

The question may well ask for illustrations, either from your own experience or from cases and examples used in class. Much MBA assessment is about applying theory to practice so you might be asked about the relevance of academic work for the practising manager, or to use theory to answer questions about business problems or practices. If the exam question does not ask for practical examples do not spend too much time citing your own experience or case study material at length, a brief example should suffice.

Finally, a few obvious points. Do check the examination's start and end times to make sure you arrive on time (and on the right day!). Do try and get a good night's sleep beforehand; late night cramming may work for some people but there is every danger you will arrive tense, exhausted and in poor shape physically, unable to give of your best.

During the examination

- Don't panic! Breathe deeply and try and stay calm!
- Read the instructions carefully first. Make sure you know how many questions you have to answer in what amount of time, and whether there are any compulsory sections
- Read ALL the questions before starting. Don't just start on the first one that you think you can answer; there may be others that you can answer better further down the page
- Allocate time for each question and/or part of the examination and stick to it. Remember that answering two questions out of three brilliantly but leaving insufficient time for the third is unlikely to lead to a successful outcome. Two good answers will almost never fully compensate for a poor third one. This also applies to a multi-part question; look at the allocation of marks between parts (if these are given, if not you can generally assume they are equally weighted) and devote a proportionate amount of time to each
- Do a 'brain dump' for your chosen questions. Quickly get down everything you can think of in rough. This will give you the confidence that you at least have something to say, ease the strain on your memory, and prompt more ideas as you write. You can add to this as you remember things
- Identify the academic material, theories, concepts, ideas, frameworks and so on that you can use to answer the question. As with assignments, if you find you are not using any material covered in the course you are probably on the wrong track
- Mention key people who have contributed to the field you are writing about. It is not normally expected that you will produce full references and a bibliography (at least not for closed book exams) but you will gain marks for knowing key writers and researchers in the area
- Plan your answer. Do a quick 'essay plan' to help you think through your reasoning and construct a logical order for your answer. Remember that, like assignment essays, examination answers should have a clear logic and structure
- Do answer the question set and not one of your own choosing! It's very easy to see when a student has not revised a topic and so has tried to answer a question with irrelevant material
- Think about what the question is actually asking. Identify the keywords and provide a definition if necessary
- Try and be creative in your answer (without going wildly off-track). If there is other relevant material from the same course, apart from the obvious information you are using, mention this too and show how it relates to the question

- Use double spacing and leave gaps to add more material later if necessary
- If you can't remember something don't dwell on it – simply leave a space and come back to it later on in the exam
- Try and write legibly and use good English, spelling and grammar
- Do leave 5–10 minutes before the end of the examination to read through what you have written. It is amazing how often you will pick up on careless errors and mistakes at this point. This is particularly important for numerical examinations
- If you are running out of time, try and get something down – even if you have to resort to using bullet points

After the examination

- Forget about it!
- Move on and don't dwell on your performance

The most usual reasons for failure are not doing enough work, not answering the question set, not reading the exam instructions (and thus not answering the right number of questions for example) and poor time management. Don't let any of these happen to you. In addition, a very small proportion of students do find examinations intolerably stressful. If you are in this minority you should talk to your university (most institutions will have a student welfare officer of some kind) and perhaps your doctor to see what help may be available.

Time Management

A course in business and management requires you to be good at self-management, that is, at disciplining yourself to get down to work and manage your time effectively. These skills are indispensable in the workplace as well as for the MBA. As mentioned earlier, it is best to set up a routine for studying, organizing regular times of the day or week when you can make space for your MBA. This is very likely to encroach on your evenings and weekends, especially if you are studying while holding down a job and, as we said before, how much time you need will depend on the demands of the programme you are studying and how quickly you learn. It will also depend on how the programme is taught. A block taught programme might not leave much time in the week when there are intensive blocks of teaching, but there will be space either side of these dates. A part-time course which runs over a number of evenings during the week may mean that weekends are your best time.

Once you have decided when you will study, you will need to make a plan of what you will do and when, bearing in mind important dates in the MBA calendar such as assignment deadlines and exam dates. Of course you will also need to allow time for family and social life; there are likely to be some sacrifices for the MBA, but 'all work and no play' is not the recipe for a quality experience or for motivated study. The following points will help you make best use of the time you have:

- Decide where you are going to study. Do you have a quiet location at home, an office or unused bedroom, or would you find it easier to work in the university library? Will you have access to what you need in your chosen location, for example writing space, an internet connection, a printer?
- Make use of a diary and write in the deadlines for assessments (assignments, presentations, examinations and so on). Work out how long you will need to prepare for each and allocate that space in the diary now. While this allocation may have to be refined in light of your experience it is at least a start and will make you think about how you are going to fit everything in. Also note any important family or work events or festivals such as Eid or Christmas in the diary, so you can plan your studying around these
- Work out how many hours you will need for private study each week and decide how you will allocate these, for example a few hours every night and/or some more sustained studying at weekends, and note these in the diary
- Look at the schedule of teaching for the MBA and judge which areas of the course might be more demanding for you. Think about whether you need to allocate extra time in the study schedule for these. As an example, if your background is in operations and you haven't formally studied anything to do with 'people management' you might want to assign a little extra time when it comes to the HRM module (hopefully this will be compensated for by the Operations Management module needing less time)
- Decide what proportion of your study time you will need for the different elements of study, for instance writing up and reviewing your lecture notes; reading core textbooks; finding and reading journal articles; searching for more material; practising the skills and techniques taught in class; preparing case studies; organizing presentations; meeting with your study groups; preparing for your next classes
- Identify your most productive and less productive times of the day and then tackle difficult or challenging jobs when you are at your most alert and productive. Do more simple or routine jobs when your energy levels are not so high
- Before you begin studying make sure you have everything you need to hand such as textbooks, lecture notes, passwords for e-journals and other library and internet resources
- Set yourselves objectives for your study periods so you know what you want to achieve, then check if you did achieve it and feel a glow of self-congratulation when you have done so. This self-motivation is important; give yourself mini-targets and rewards during long sessions (e.g. a cup of coffee after you have read an article, or written your essay outline, or done the on-line tutorial or whatever)
- You may find it hard to concentrate at first. Get used to identifying your favourite distractions and exert your self-control to ignore them. Diversionary tactics

to avoid studying include aimless web surfing, reading irrelevant material, making photocopies of articles but not reading them, compiling numerous 'to do' lists, reorganizing your desk and socializing with friends to complain about your lack of time … but you will undoubtedly discover new ones for yourself!

- Try and train others not to interrupt you while you are studying and don't interrupt yourself by looking at emails, texting others and so on. Shorten unavoidable interruptions such as meetings and other commitments
- You will need to make on-going decisions about what is urgent and what is important. The two do not always coincide. Try and ensure you deal with what is important and don't spend all your time doing jobs that you like but are actually of low priority. Be aware that low priority tasks may not always demand perfection
- Part-time students in work might consider how they can delegate aspects of their full-time jobs. Sometimes a discussion with an employer or subordinates can reveal better ways of working
- You will have to learn to say 'no' to new commitments. You should be aiming to reduce your existing commitments during the MBA to leave time and energy for your studies
- With really big tasks, such as a major project or dissertation, try not to be overwhelmed by the seeming enormity of what you must tackle. Firstly break it down into bite-sized pieces to make it more manageable. Then design a project planning schedule (you could use a Gantt chart or critical path analysis if you want to get technical) which shows the start and end dates of the job and lists all the separate activities in a logical order in between, with each one time-defined within the boundaries of the project as a whole. This will help keep you on track
- In the first few weeks of your course you may find it revealing to check on what you have actually achieved during your study periods. What did you do, how long did it take, how much time did you actually spend on your chosen activities, and how much time was spent doing other things (wasting time?)? This is likely to be informative and you can then decide on how to improve your work rates in the future

Overall, the principles of time management are pretty easy to impart; what is needed is the resolve to follow them. As urged previously, make every effort to keep to deadlines. Once you start getting behind it will be very hard to keep up with new work while dealing with outstanding tasks and you may find yourself feeling increasingly overwhelmed rather than energized by your learning experiences.

Making Presentations

Presentation skills are indispensable for managers as well as MBA students. The art of being able to impart information in an articulate, concise, structured way, and in a manner that captures and retains the attention of an audience, is crucial in all kinds of circumstances, for example in job interviews, team briefings, presentations to senior management, and MBA assessments.

A presentation is about communication. For the MBA you need to think about the brief you have been given, who your audience is and what they expect to hear, and what you need to impart in the time available.

What is the brief?

Think carefully about what you have been asked to do and make sure you stick to the brief. If the presentation is about demonstrating a knowledge of certain theories or frameworks, be sure to use them. If you have to conduct some research (say, looking at a particular company or industry) make sure you have done your home-work before planning the presentation. If the brief includes a particular approach or style or audience (for example, a 20-minute report using a PowerPoint format to a board of directors) make certain you adhere to this. You may also have to prepare your presentation as part of a group, so make sure you read the section on group work below.

Who is the audience?

All communication should bear in mind the intended audience and aim to meet their expectations and requirements. So if the audience is primarily your lecturer you will need to demonstrate relevant knowledge and understanding, while if it is intended for managers you will need to ensure it is not too full of jargon and is relevant to practice – and so on.

How long have you got?

It is critical that you stick to the time scale you have been given. There is often the temptation to have far too much in a presentation because of the fear of running out of things to say, but it is usually the opposite problem that arises. Many inexperienced presenters will find themselves in the awkward position of being only part way through their talk but nearly out of time. This is often the case with PowerPoint talks, the most ubiquitous form of presentation. Many students will prepare far too many slides and then find they have to race through the final ones as the clock is ticking and time is running out. There is no hard and fast rule here but around 15–20 slides is probably enough for a 20-minute presentation because hopefully you are going to explain the slides and not simply read them out. If the ideas are complex you may need fewer than this. The key to successful timing is rehearsal.

Planning the presentation

Think about the topic you are making the presentation on and write down the key points you need to get across. Work out how much you need to say about each of the points and make yourself some notes to help you remember what you want to communicate. Put the points in a logical sequence. The usual structure of a presentation is as follows:

- Introduction – in this you will introduce yourself (and the members of the group if appropriate), the topic, and say how the presentation will be organized
- Body of the talk – this is when you deal with the main ideas and themes
- Ending – this provides a summary of what has been said and gives some recommendations and conclusions
- Thanks – these go to the audience for listening
- Questions – if the audience has some

Think about the methods you will be using for your presentation. You may choose to use a flipchart to indicate any key points or draw pictures – you can do this during the presentation which may be more spontaneous but perhaps look messy (and is your writing legible, especially at a distance?), or you could prepare flipchart sheets in advance. PowerPoint is the most usual tool for presentations but if you do use this be sure not to try and cram too much on each slide. Four or five key points is usually sufficient and besides highlighting the key ideas for the audience these can act as a memory aid for you. Don't just read the slides, instead aim to talk around them and to add supplementary or contextual information to what is on the slide. Try and find interesting and varied ways of presenting material; use pictures or diagrams, tables or graphs, video inserts or photographs. Humour can sometimes help the flow but beware of using gimmicks which might not work on the day. You may also want to produce handouts for the audience.

If this is a group presentation decide who is doing what – who will introduce the group, who will present (all of you or just a few?), who will chair the question and answer session, who will thank the audience for attending. If you want to look professional small details such as the dress code for members of the group are also important.

Rehearsing

Familiarize yourself with the room you will be presenting in. Find out where the light switches are and check where the computer or laptop will be, or how you can connect up your own laptop. Make sure you can work any audio visual aids you will be using such as a DVD player. If you have a PowerPoint presentation check that it runs on this system and any video links, etc. work correctly. Check out the space and seating arrangements and see if you will be able to move things around to suit your own requirements. If you are using flipcharts check the lines of sight in the room to make sure you place the stand where your audience can see it. Ascertain also where it is best to stand so you don't obscure the screen if you are showing a DVD or using PowerPoint.

It is not a good idea to write your presentation in longhand and read it out word for word. This sounds stilted and is not likely to enthral your audience. You will come across better if you have a few bullet points and then talk around them. This will sound more natural but, paradoxically, the more you rehearse this the more natural it will probably sound because you will gain in self-assurance and hence be more fluent. You are aiming to be confident enough to talk on your topic, not to memorize every word. In addition to your presentation, think of the kinds of questions you are likely to be asked and plan the answers to these as well.

Run through the whole presentation in front of an audience (friends, relatives or whoever you can persuade to sit through it). If you can, video it too. Note how long it takes, where you stumble or have difficulties explaining things. Try and be aware of your body language, dispense with unnecessary fidgeting or annoying mannerisms and try to maintain eye contact with your audience. Finally, remember to talk to them. This means facing them and not the screen!

Review your performance critically and repeat it. Most presenters, even those of many years' experience, will get nervous when presenting to an audience. The only way to improve this is to keep doing it.

Performing the presentation

Your rehearsals should have given you some confidence but you are bound to be apprehensive. Some deep breathing exercises may help. Allow plenty of time to get to the venue and to set up. During the presentation try and maintain a steady pace – we have the tendency to speed up when we are nervous so try not to gabble. Think about your body language and try and be responsive to the audience. You may even enjoy it! Afterwards think about what went well and what you will do to improve next time.

Working in Groups

Much of the learning and teaching on the MBA is likely to take place in groups. This mirrors the workplace where so much activity is carried out with others, for example in working parties or project teams and so on. Since MBA participants are usually experienced managers this is an excellent opportunity to get to know other members of the programme better, learn from their experience and expertise, and develop your own skills in team building. For students on distance learning programmes the virtual team is a vital way of building learning communities and also a means of support when participants have few other opportunities to interact.

You will probably experience different types of group work on the MBA. The most important point to make here is that whoever you are assigned to work with you will need to get on with them for the purposes of the task in hand. They may not necessarily be your chosen associates away from the programme but this is not relevant – working together requires a level of maturity, sensitivity and self-awareness, as well as a willingness to work through difficulties and differences of opinion.

Firstly read the section on groups and teams in this book (see Chapter 2) to get some idea of how groups work and the various problems to watch out for. If you are familiar with Belbin's team roles, or the Myers Briggs Indicator or some other personality tools these may help you to see the different characteristics of people in the group and appreciate and work with diversity. In international groups an appreciation of cultural differences is crucial in order to avoid misunderstanding; again read Chapter 2 to get some idea of how cultures may differ.

Here are some things to think about to get the best out of your group work:

- Decide on how you are going to communicate and circulate everyone's contact details (email address, mobile phone number and so on)
- Whether or not a group leader has been appointed make sure that you agree on roles, responsibilities and how you will work early on, where possible taking account of each individual's particular abilities, expertise and preferences. You may want to appoint a chair, someone to take notes at meetings and someone to act as time-keeper, or rotate these roles. Remember the forming, storming, norming, performing stages mentioned in Chapter 2 on Organizational Behaviour and make sure the development of your group proceeds effectively
- At an early meeting, brainstorm what the task is about and how best to approach it. Try to utilize the group's creativity and expertise to maximize the chances of a good outcome
- Draw up a schedule of activities and allocate individuals to take the lead on these (for example, information searching, reading around the subject, writing drafts of materials, preparing slides if there is to be a presentation)
- Agree on the milestones for a project as well as a schedule of meetings at critical stages to share ideas and progress the work, aiming for completion well in advance of the deadline. For students on distance learning programmes these may have to take the form of conference calls or on-line discussion forums. If the team is geographically dispersed try and arrange for at least one meeting early on where you can be on-line at the same time and 'socialize' as this will help to promote better working relationships. Even if much of your activity has then to be asynchronous because of different work schedules or time zones, try and timetable a couple of sessions where you can all be on-line together to check progress
- Have an agenda in advance of meetings, take notes during these and then circulate the information afterwards to ensure you have a record and everyone knows what they are meant to do

- Try and encourage everyone to take a full part. Be aware that some cultures and individuals may seem more reticent but this does not mean they are not engaging with the group. The chair should ensure that everyone is encouraged to speak and that stronger personalities do not dominate the meetings. Rotating the chair means that others will have an opportunity to get leadership experience
- Deal with problems expeditiously. If there is an element of the task you are uncertain about, seek clarification at an early stage. If there is conflict between group members try and sort it out before it becomes a problem (remember that debate is healthy but personal conflict is damaging). If one member is not attending deal with this politely but firmly. It may be appropriate to inform the tutor but do remember it is up to you to make the group function and not the tutor. Inevitably wavering commitments and differential contributions will occur on the MBA just as they do in the workplace

Virtual Learning Environments (VLEs)

Virtual learning environments, e-learning, and blended learning are all ways of using computer technology to support or provide learning resources. There are many VLEs such as Blackboard and WebCt and many MBA programmes will have extensive material available on on-line sites that will complement the taught sessions. These are often password protected and available through a portal to registered students. Make sure you find out what is available and make use of this additional resource. Sometimes tutors will also communicate with students through these sites and important information about teaching sessions or assignments will be posted there. In addition, discussion boards or chatrooms may be useful ways of conversing with other students. You will therefore need to log in regularly to keep updated. Even if a VLE is not used extensively in your institution, it is likely that some forms of blended learning – a mixture of traditional teaching plus e-learning – will be in operation.

Virtual Learning Environment: a platform that brings together on-line or electronic learning resources.

For distance learning students this may be a central way of getting hold of your material and also of making contact with other learners, so you will need to quickly find your way round these sites and get used to setting aside regular times to work through e-learning material.

Summary

This chapter has covered all the key areas that you will need to develop skills in to successfully complete your MBA. Many of these are not only useful for the MBA; they are also essential for other aspects of life including the workplace. Some such as note-taking will require practice; others such as time management will require will power; all will need the determination and resolve that are themselves essential qualities for the MBA.

Questions for reflection

1 How can I develop myself as an independent learner?
2 What practical arrangements do I need to make for my studying (such as organizing work and other commitments, planning a schedule for studying, finding somewhere to study)?
3 How can I make the most of learning with others through group work on the MBA?

Further reading

Burns, T. and Sinfield, S. (2008) *Essential Study Skills* (2nd edn). London: Sage.
Cameron, S. (2005) *The MBA Handbook: Skills For Mastering Management* (5th edn). Essex: Pearson.

Index